Byron, Hunt, and the Politics of Literary Engagement

I0593004

In the second decade of the nineteenth century, the British press began a campaign of critical abuse against Leigh Hunt, caricaturing the radical journalist as an upstart "Cockney" author whose literary talents were as disreputable as his politics. Lord Byron, on the other hand, was revered as a peer and a poetical genius who, the conservative press argued, would never befriend and collaborate with a writer like Hunt. Yet Byron did just that.

Byron, Hunt, and the Politics of Literary Engagement is the first full-length study of the friendship and literary relationship of two of the most important second-generation Romantic authors. Challenging long-held critical attitudes, this study shows that Byron and Hunt engaged in a creative and meaningful dialogue at each major stage in their careers, from their earliest published volumes of juvenile poetry and verse satire to their most celebrated contributions to Romantic literature: *The Story of Rimini* and *Don Juan*. Drawing upon newly recovered letters and unpublished manuscript material, this book illuminates the surprisingly durable and artistically significant friendship of Lord Byron and Leigh Hunt.

Michael Steier holds a Ph.D. from the University of Delaware. He has published articles on Byron, Hunt, and their circles in *Studies in Romanticism*, *The Byron Journal*, and *The Hazlitt Review*.

Routledge Studies in Romanticism

For more information about this series, please visit: https://www.routledge.com

Byron, Hunt, and the Politics of Literary Engagement

Michael Steier

Routledge
Taylor & Francis Group

NEW YORK AND LONDON

First published 2020
by Routledge
52 Vanderbilt Avenue, New York, NY 10017

and by Routledge
2 Park Square, Milton Park, Abingdon, Oxon, OX14 4RN

*Routledge is an imprint of the Taylor & Francis Group, an
informa business*

First issued in paperback 2021

Library of Congress Cataloging-in-Publication Data
A catalog record for this title has been requested

ISBN: 978-0-367-32135-2 (hbk)
ISBN: 978-1-03-209111-2 (pbk)
ISBN: 978-0-429-31688-3 (ebk)

Typeset in Sabon
by codeMantra

For my parents

Contents

List of Figures

Acknowledgments

This work owes intellectual debts to several individuals. Charles E. Robinson introduced me to the subjects explored in this book, and his scholarship and teaching inspired the undertaking and have guided the approach. Donald H. Reiman taught me the methods of textual scholarship, which have significantly influenced aspects of this study. Kevin Kerrane guided me to the British libraries and cultural institutions that were consulted during the research phase. Peter W. Graham supported my research in its earliest stages with opportunities to share ideas at International Byron Society Conferences. Timothy Webb has been a kind correspondent, answering my inquiries and providing vital information on the Byron-Hunt friendship. I thank the editor of *The Byron Journal* for allowing me to reproduce sections from a previously published article in Chapter 3. I am especially grateful to the editorial staff at Routledge and the two readers who provided advice and direction for this project.

I am also grateful to the following libraries and institutions for granting me access to their holdings: the British Library; the John Murray Archive at the National Library of Scotland; the National Art Library at the Victoria & Albert Museum; the University of Iowa Libraries; the Ward M. Canaday Center at the University of Toledo; the Rauner Library at Dartmouth College; the Houghton Library at Harvard University; the Kislak Center at the University of Pennsylvania; the Beinecke Rare Book & Manuscript Library at Yale University; the Bryn Mawr College Library Special Collections; the Pforzheimer Collection at the New York Public Library; the Berg Collection at the New York Public Library; and the Drew University Library Special Collections.

This book could not have been completed without the intellectual guidance and sure-handed editing of Kathleen Mallon. My debts to her are many.

Abbreviations

A	*The Autobiography of Leigh Hunt.* 3 vols. (London: Smith, Elder, & Co., 1850).
BEM	*Blackwood's Edinburgh Magazine.*
BLJ	*Byron's Letters and Journals*, ed. Leslie A. Marchand, 12 vols. (Cambridge, MA: Harvard University Press, 1973–82).
CLH	*The Correspondence of Leigh Hunt*, ed. Thornton Hunt, 2 vols. (London: Smith, Elder, & Co., 1862).
CMP	*Lord Byron: The Complete Miscellaneous Prose*, ed. Andrew Nicholson (Oxford: Oxford University Press, 1991).
CPW	*Lord Byron: The Complete Poetical Works*, ed. Jerome J. McGann, 7 vols. (Oxford: Oxford University Press, 1980–93).
E	*The Examiner.*
LBSC	Hunt, Leigh. *Lord Byron and Some of His Contemporaries* (London: Henry Colburn, 1828).
LHLL	*Leigh Hunt: A Life in Letters*, ed. Eleanor M. Gates (Essex, CT: Falls River Publications, 1998).
LHOL	*Leigh Hunt Online: The Letters.* The University of Iowa Libraries.
LJM	*The Letters of John Murray to Lord Byron*, ed. Andrew Nicholson (Liverpool: Liverpool University Press, 2007).
RR	*The Romantics Reviewed: Contemporary Reviews of British Romantic Writers.* Part A, *The Lake Poets.* Part B, *Byron and Regency Society Poets.* Part C, *Shelley, Keats, and London Radical Writers*, ed. Donald H. Reiman, 9 vols. (New York: Garland Publishing, 1972).
SWLH	*The Selected Writings of Leigh Hunt*, eds. Robert Morrison and Michael Eberle-Sinatra, 6 vols. (London: Pickering & Chatto, 2003).

Note on the Texts

All references to Byron's poetry are taken from *CPW* unless otherwise indicated. All references to Hunt's poetry and miscellaneous writings are taken from *SWLH* unless otherwise indicated. Primary materials have been transcribed with the kind permission of the National Library of Scotland and the British Library Board.

References to *The Examiner* (*E*) are cited by issue, date, and page number. References to *Blackwood's Edinburgh Magazine* (*BEM*) include the volume, date, and page number.

The Leigh Hunt letters in the Luther A. Brewer Collection at the University of Iowa (*LHOL*) can be accessed at *Leigh Hunt Online*: http://digital.lib.uiowa.edu/leighhunt

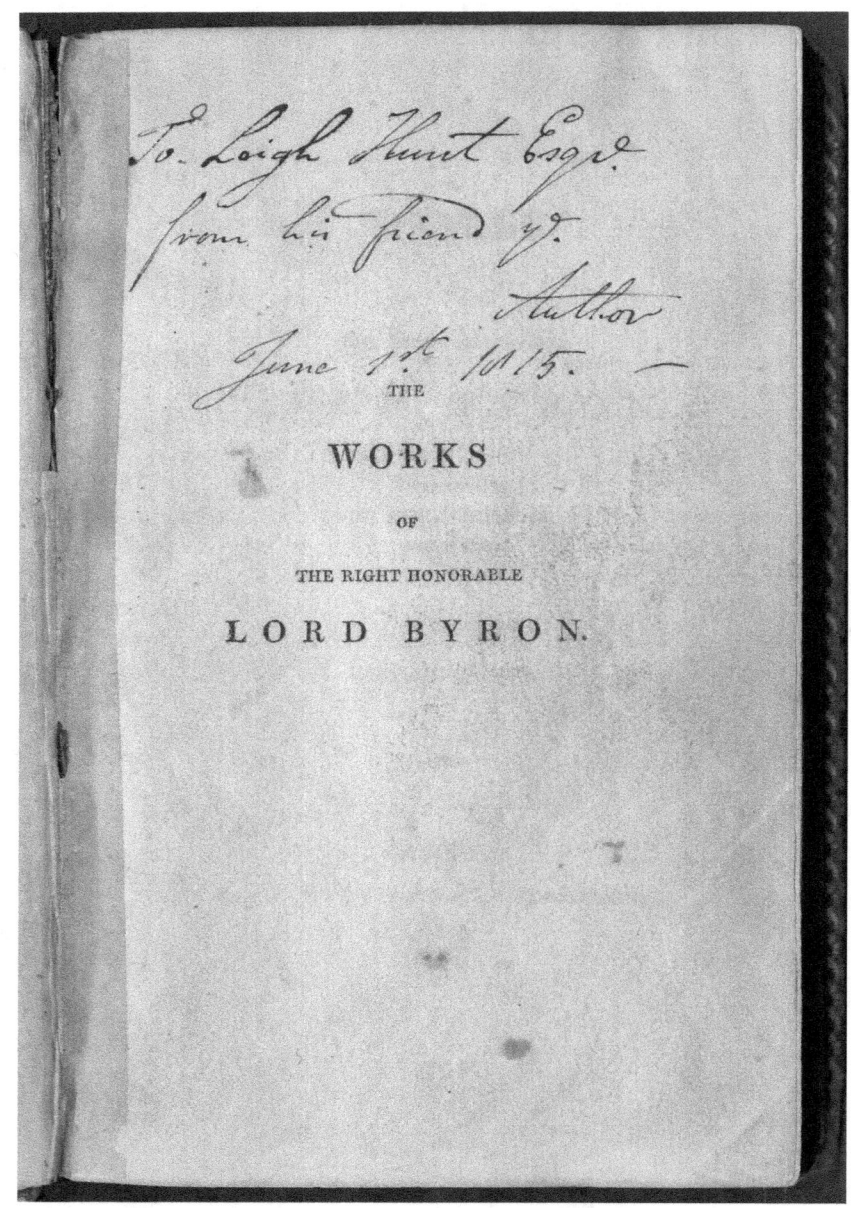

Figure I.1 Leigh Hunt's copy of *The Works of the Right Honorable Lord Byron* (1815). Courtesy of Dartmouth College Library.

Introduction

The Wren and the Eagle

On 20 May 1813, Lord Byron entered Leigh Hunt's prison cell at Horse-monger Lane Gaol in London's Southwark district, initiating a creatively meaningful but complex ten-year friendship and literary relationship. Percy Bysshe Shelley, who would later enter the circles of both writers, was acutely aware of the complexities of the Byron-Hunt friendship, describing the relationship as that between the wren and the eagle of ancient fable, in which the opportunistic wren reached new and otherwise unattainable heights upon the wings of the powerful eagle.[1] The Byron-Hunt friendship, to be sure, was one of intensity and duration, and its strength would have come as no surprise to mutual acquaintances like Shelley. Byron and Hunt both had liberal views in politics and were outspoken critics of the Regency. Both had been prodigies who published volumes of poetry before the age of twenty. Both had a passion for the stage and had frequented London's theaters. Both had produced lively verse satires on their poetical contemporaries. Both had a deep interest in Italian literature. Above all, both had, by the time they met, become famous—Byron for his highly marketable poetry and "scandalous celebrity," and Hunt for his libelous prose and political imprisonment.[2] For Byron, Hunt was from the beginning an "extraordinary character" and a "man worth knowing" (*BLJ* 3:228), and for Hunt, Byron was a "friend, whose burst of feeling [was] always worth listening to."[3] The primary aim of this book is to broaden our understanding of the Byron-Hunt friendship by attending to such statements and looking closely at the creative engagements that engendered them.

Byron's meeting with Hunt at Horsemonger Lane Gaol is now well known to scholars and students of second-generation British Romanticism. Over the past three decades, critical interest in Hunt has been steadily guided by several significant publications: major biographies from Ann Blainey, Nicholas Roe, and Anthony Holden;[4] a valuable collection of essays devoted to Hunt's artistic achievements and a reception history of his major works;[5] and a newly edited edition of Hunt's poetry and prose.[6] Jeffrey N. Cox's *Poetry and Politics in the Cockney School*, meanwhile, set the critical agenda for approaching Hunt's writing with a fresh and contextually informed understanding. For Cox,

Hunt's famed prison cell, with walls "papered" with "a trellis of roses" (*A* 2:148), was a symbolic center of Regency radicalism, a site where a diverse group of poets, artists, and intellectuals formed an intimate circle around Hunt, whose *Examiner* had been shaping public opinion since the political weekly first appeared in 1808.[7] In *Poetry and Politics,* Cox rightly places Byron within Hunt's circle of friends while hinting at the ensuing complexities.[8] Byron, notwithstanding his involvement with various clubs and societies, as well as his reputed role as a member of the "Satanic school" of poetry, treated poetical coteries, circles, and schools with suspicion or disregard, and Hunt's "Cockney School" was no exception.[9] We recall that Byron began and ended his career as a satirist with *English Bards and Scotch Reviewers* and *Don Juan,* respectively, by attacking the "Lake School" poets, whose narrowly conceived "fusion / Of one another's minds" (*CPW* 5:4, lines 35–6) fundamentally opposed his cosmopolitan imagination. Accordingly, Byron is not typically studied as a coterie poet, or as a committed member of any poetical group, and recent studies that have engaged in various ways with Cox's critical agenda by highlighting other Romantic coteries, kinships, and literary families have not included Byron within their interpretative framework.[10]

The complex personal and literary relations of Byron and Hunt, nevertheless, offer a particularly rich opportunity to extend Cox's insights while engaging with related work in the field by textual scholars, literary historians, and critics of Romantic celebrity and print culture. The present study is indebted to new advances in these areas as well as to a tradition of historicist scholarship dedicated to contextualizing the lives and writings of Byron and Hunt. The critical record shows that the Byron-Hunt relationship, in general, has not been favorably received despite its duration and intensity. Byron scholars, in particular, have been understandably suspicious of Hunt, who issued a sensational, anger-driven memoir of Byron (*Lord Byron and Some of His Contemporaries*) five years after the friendship came to a bitter and unexpected end in Italy in 1823.[11] Yet the recent recovery of long-neglected primary materials has revealed the relationship in a new and more critically suggestive light. Timothy Webb has led these recovery efforts while studying the Byron-Hunt relationship closely at different stages of its development. Analyzing the materials that shaped Hunt's autobiographical writings, for instance, Webb has illuminated the late portraits of Byron that Hunt created for a Victorian readership.[12] More recently, Webb has provided detailed accounts of the Byron-Hunt friendship during and after Hunt's years of imprisonment, publishing the surviving correspondence Hunt exchanged with the poet during a creatively significant period from 1813 to 1816.[13]

The majority of the known letters that Byron sent to Hunt, of course, have been available in Leslie A. Marchand's standard edition of Byron's correspondence, but with the recovery of Hunt's letters, we can now read these documents more meaningfully as part of an on-going dialogue. The launch of the Leigh Hunt Online Letters project at the University of Iowa, meanwhile, has made Luther A. Brewer's extensive collection of Hunt's letters available in holograph for the first time. In addition, Eleanor M. Gates has printed letters from the last phase of the Byron-Hunt friendship in her judicious *Leigh Hunt: A Life in Letters*, and there are several more unpublished letters dating from this later period in the John Murray Archive at the National Library of Scotland. As a whole, the correspondence shows an unquestionable degree of intimacy and helps establish a solid foundation for the importance of the friendship in the lives of both writers. It is through these letters, moreover, that we see crucial episodes and events in the Byron-Hunt story illuminated. The letters, however, tell only part of the story. While attention to the correspondence will be integral to this study, the book aims to supplement the existing scholarship by focusing on the creative engagements between Byron and Hunt as they unfolded in the private and public spaces of nineteenth-century British Romantic culture. Although there has been some critical interest in Byron's reading of Hunt's *Story of Rimini* and their collaboration on *The Liberal*, their literary engagements have not yet received the sustained attention that has been given to their other important literary friendships with figures such as Shelley, Thomas Moore, and John Keats.[14] There is no doubt that Byron and Hunt occupied unique and meaningful positions in each other's lives, and it is the premise of this book that the two friends also engaged each other as *authors* as they developed, refined, and marketed their poetry and politics over the course of the first three decades of the nineteenth century.[15]

Hunt's friendship with Byron was controversial in its own time, and an analysis of its public reception also highlights significant aspects of the politics that shaped Romantic authorship. Hunt's attempt to establish himself as a poet before the public through expressions of friendship with Byron led to inevitable embarrassments about class and social standing. Such embarrassments, however, were the consequence of diverse factors: the cultural politics of the Romantic reviews and literary magazines and, more generally, the class politics that permeated all aspects of Regency society. Yet Hunt made no attempt to appease his critics or join his contemporaries in accepting established conventions of authorship. His libel on the Prince Regent in 1812 made him an obvious target for conservative commentators throughout the 1810s and 1820s, and even into the 1830s. And his personal attack on William Gifford, Tory satirist and editor of the powerful *Quarterly Review*, in *The Feast of the Poets* did not improve Hunt's relationship with the Tory reviewers. Byron, on the other hand, proudly declared his allegiance to Gifford in *English Bards and Scotch Reviewers*, and the elder satirist became Byron's long-time editor under the publisher John Murray. Hunt, meanwhile, had also attacked Walter Scott and many other high-profile contemporaries in *The Feast of the Poets*, the satire that "made almost every living poet and poetaster [his] enemy" (*A* 2:84). Byron had attacked Scott in *English Bards and Scotch Reviewers* as well but suppressed his youthful satire as soon as he became acquainted with several of the individuals he had targeted in that poem. Hunt also took additional, calculated actions to maintain a principled independence from the polite circles of Regency society. He "declined" (*A* 2:108) a formal invitation to Holland House, whereas Byron embraced this popular site of Regency political culture during his years of fame in London. Byron, in other words, took the necessary steps to make his poetry and his personality palatable to a diverse cross section of readers, reviewers, and publishers, while Hunt pursued a more openly transgressive and, at times, ill-advised course.

Hunt's most provocative public act came in 1816 when he formally dedicated *The Story of Rimini* to Byron but deliberately left out the poet's title, addressing his friend: "My Dear Byron" (*SWLH* 5:165). John Wilson Croker of the *Quarterly Review* provided the first and most damning notice of Hunt's transgression: "we never, in so few lines, saw so many clear marks of the vulgar impatience of a low man, conscious and ashamed of his wretched vanity, and labouring, with coarse flippancy, to scramble over the bounds of birth and education, and fidget himself into the *stout-heartedness* of being familiar with a LORD" (*RR* C2:756). With the publication of *Rimini*, Hunt learned the hard lesson he must have anticipated: the politics of literary engagement presented an impenetrable barrier to authorial recognition. Croker's facile categorization of the Byron-Hunt relationship as a seemingly irreconcilable binary based on class and education helped establish the critical discourse for treating Byron and Hunt as discordant personalities—whereby critics could ignore Hunt's claims to authorship and even deny his right to friendship.

Opportunistic and exceedingly clever periodicals like *Blackwood's Edinburgh Magazine* would find entertainment value and marketable drama in Croker's politicized assessment of the Byron-Hunt relationship.[16] In the very first number of his infamous "Cockney School" series, John Gibson Lockhart recast Croker's characterization of Hunt, introducing the "Cockney" caricature that would turn the Byron-Hunt friendship into a mean-spirited farce:

> [A] paltry cockney newspaper scribbler, had the assurance to address one of the most nobly-born of English Patricians, and one of the first geniuses whom the world ever produced, as "My dear Byron," although it may have been forgotten and despised by the illustrious person whom it most nearly concerned,—excited a feeling of utter loathing and disgust in the public mind, which will always be remembered whenever the name of Leigh Hunt is mentioned.
>
> (*BEM* 2 [October 1817]: 41)

Blackwood's engagements with Byron and Hunt would, as we shall see, become increasingly complex as Lockhart's attitude toward Byron, in particular, evolved, introducing contradictions that disrupted *Blackwood's* seemingly settled opinion of one of the world's "first geniuses." Nevertheless, Lockhart's confident assurance that the public transgression of a "paltry cockney newspaper scribbler" would "always" excite "loathing and disgust" was prescient. By 1823, when the Byron-Hunt friendship came to its bitter conclusion, even Byron was using Lockhart's "Cockney" rhetoric to describe Hunt's circle of friends.[17]

The force of Hunt's dedication to Byron in *Rimini* had also unsettled Byron's closest liberal-minded friends, including his Whig Club associate and Cambridge classmate John Cam Hobhouse. Yet Hobhouse's reaction to the *Rimini* dedication, vividly captured in his diary, also underscores the complexities and contradictions at the center of the Byron-Hunt friendship. On the evening of 3 April 1816, Hobhouse joined Byron for a private gathering at the poet's London residence, where Scrope Berdmore Davies and Hunt were also in attendance. It was Hobhouse's first time meeting Hunt:

> Rode up to London, and settled at Lord Byron's, No 13 Picadilly Terrace. S. B. Davies and Leigh Hunt of the *Examiner* dined with us. Leigh Hunt is Brougham in miniature—a very agreeable man— one-and-thirty—and very unassuming, notwithstanding his dedication to *Rimini* beginning "My dear Byron."
>
> He told us a new story of Johnson. . . . [and] said that the Keeper of Horsemonger Jail, where he was confined for two years, called him "Mister," and seeing him look so ill (he was nearly dead) said "You'll never go out alive, and they don't intend you should." S. B. D. said he could not get in a word between the two authors—he fell down in Byron's room.[18]

Here we see Hunt performing the social role for which intimate friends like Keats and Hazlitt greatly admired him. Indeed, we witness Hunt's talents for storytelling and his Chaucer-like relish of characters of all ranks as he draws meaning from the grim insights of gaolers as well as the polished witticisms of Samuel Johnson. At the same time, we listen to Hobhouse qualify all of this positive impression of Hunt by reminding himself (and future readers of his diary) that the editor of *The Examiner* had recently addressed Byron publicly in the dedication to *Rimini* without giving the poet his title. Hobhouse's conclusion to this revealing vignette nevertheless shows how little the *Rimini* incident, which clearly unsettled *him*, mattered to Byron and Hunt that evening. In fact, Hobhouse is so amused by Scrope Davies's drunken exit that he leaves us with an evocative image of Byron and Hunt—"the two authors"—fully engaged in meaningful conversation. Such conversations form the core substance of the chapters that follow.

The Byron-Hunt friendship can be organized into two phases of equal importance. The first phase, formally considered, covers the period from their first meeting at Horsemonger Lane Gaol to Byron's departure from England at the height of his marriage crisis. In reality, however, the literary acquaintance began much earlier. Byron had read Hunt's popular *Juvenilia* while a student at Harrow, and the volume provided him with a sound model of adolescent authorship for his earliest public offerings: *Hours of Idleness* and *Poems, Original and Translated*. These volumes are the focus of the first chapter, which analyzes the juvenile writings produced and marketed by both authors in the context of an emergent adolescent tradition of literature in Britain. The evidence suggests that Hunt closely followed the formal conventions of this tradition, helping to popularize the genre, while Byron deliberately overturned many of the conventions only to discover the harsh critical realities of Romantic authorship as a consequence.

Hunt, meanwhile, had also taken an early interest in Byron's poetry, particularly his caustic *English Bards and Scotch Reviewers*. Inspired by Byron's satire, Hunt responded with *The Feast of the Poets* in 1812, a similarly themed verse satire on the contemporary poetical scene, which he enlarged (just as Byron had *English Bards and Scotch Reviewers*) and reprinted in new editions in 1814 and 1815. The second chapter looks closely at the private discussions Byron and Hunt had about their early satires while examining their shared aims and targets as well as their stylistic divergences. The stylistic differences in these volumes suggest that the two poets had taken up opposing positions in a wider critical debate about poetic form that had been earlier pursued by Wordsworth in the *Lyrical Ballads*. In particular, the arguments Byron and Hunt put forth in their early satires about the merits of Alexander Pope and his stylistic legacy would become the most contentious of their literary disagreements.

The third chapter, which covers the period of the earliest personal acquaintance of Byron and Hunt, traces Byron's intimate engagements with Hunt's political newspaper: *The Examiner*. The evidence shows that Byron and Hunt frequently engaged each other in its pages during a turbulent period in England between 1812 and 1816. It was a period that witnessed discontent among the laboring classes (including frame workers in Byron's Nottingham), the ascendency of the dissolute Prince of Wales, the future George IV, to the position of Regent, and Napoleon's abdication crisis and final defeat at the Battle of Waterloo. It was largely in response to these events that Byron, who also entered the House of Lords during this period, supplied Hunt with poetic contributions and other materials for his newspaper. Hunt, though sometimes politically and often philosophically at odds with Byron, replied in kind to his friend's submissions, giving them due notice in his political commentaries and literary reviews.

The fourth chapter shifts the focus from politics back to poetry, exploring the shared literary interest Byron and Hunt found in the episode of Paolo and Francesca from Dante's *Inferno*. Hunt's poetical retelling of the episode in *Rimini* sparked a series of epistolary exchanges about Italian literature and English poetry that was crowned by Byron's reading of *Rimini* in manuscript, upon which he also left incisive marginalia. Byron even helped Hunt see the poem through the press, recommending *Rimini* to his publisher, John Murray, in 1815 and thus providing an opportunity for Hunt to reach a larger readership and potentially new heights of poetical celebrity. The chapter shows that Byron's interest in Hunt's most important poem was not superficial as some commentators have deemed it; rather, the evidence reveals that Byron's interest in and engagement with *Rimini* significantly strengthened their literary relationship.

The fifth chapter marks the beginning of the second phase in the Byron-Hunt friendship, covering the period from Byron's departure from England in 1816 to his reunion with Hunt in Italy and their collaboration on *The Liberal* in 1822 and 1823. The focus of this chapter is Byron's reaction to the rise of the "Cockney" poets. Following the publication of *Rimini*, Byron became inevitably linked with Hunt in critical discussions. After tracing depictions of the Byron-Hunt friendship in the Romantic reviews and literary magazines, this chapter looks closely at Byron's reading of and reaction to Hunt's *Foliage*, a volume Cox has described as Hunt's "Cockney Manifesto."[19] Although he was fully aware of Hunt's loose poetic style from having read *The Feast of the Poets* and having annotated *Rimini*, Byron found the contents of *Foliage* alarming. In *Foliage*, he discovered that Hunt had traded the earnest but playful satire of *The Feast of the Poets* and the interesting "Italianism" (*BLJ* 4:326) of *Rimini* for a collection of occasional poems addressed to a diverse and, as Byron thought, highly incongruous group: Byron, Shelley, William Hazlitt, Keats, John Hamilton Reynolds, Benjamin Robert Haydon, and other core members of Hunt's "Cockney School." Moreover, *Foliage* had included a series of original verse translations from Homer that Hunt seemed to suggest had greater merit than any of Pope's translations. Exasperated by Hunt's statements, Byron voiced his anger in private to Moore and Shelley at first but eventually decided to express his thoughts on Hunt and his so-called "Cockney School" publicly. These thoughts were given forceful expression in a series of critical prose writings ("Some Observations Upon an Article in *Blackwood's Edinburgh Magazine*" and unpublished "Addenda" intended for the *Letter to John Murray*) that Byron produced in 1820 and 1821.

In July of 1822, Byron and Hunt, with the assistance of Shelley, reunited in Italy to begin work on a literary miscellany they called *The Liberal*. Shelley's death (less than a week after Hunt arrived) has often been seen as *the* factor that decided the fate of the literary magazine. Yet the evidence reveals that *The Liberal* was undertaken with a great deal of enthusiasm and, as Hunt believed, in a spirit of collaboration. The sixth chapter thus begins by examining Hunt's major contributions to *The Liberal* as deliberate acts of literary engagement with Byron. New manuscript evidence suggests that Hunt and Byron were working closely together on the miscellany, frequently sharing ideas and materials during the assembly of *The Liberal*. The evidence also suggests that the creative dialogue in which they engaged in the early years of their friendship informed many of the editorial and artistic decisions. Only in November of 1822 when Hunt learned of offhand remarks Byron had made about him privately to John Murray did the collaboration on *The Liberal* become irrevocably doomed. While some critics have argued that Byron worked to ensure *The Liberal*'s demise, beginning with the third number, the evidence, in fact, suggests that it may have been Hunt who influenced his friend's decision to withdraw from the miscellany in its final stages. Indeed, the chapter concludes by showing that Byron attempted to rectify the situation through direct acts of literary engagement with Hunt in late works such as *The Age of Bronze* and *The Island*, both written especially for *The Liberal*, that Hunt, in the end, rejected.

Byron's presence remained with Hunt in memory long after the termination of *The Liberal* and Byron's death in Greece in 1824. Hunt would relive his personal and literary engagements with Byron in his *Autobiography* in 1850, but Hunt's most sustained engagement with the poet's memory and their friendship began much earlier with the incendiary *Lord Byron and Some of His Contemporaries* in 1828. The conclusion explores this complex text within the context of the popular market for Romantic biography in the 1820s. Specifically, the conclusion traces the volume's textual history, which shows Hunt to have been a highly reluctant biographer who had regrets about *Lord Byron and Some of His Contemporaries* before it was even published. A discussion of Hunt's return to Byron in the *Autobiography* brings the present study to its conclusion, reminding us that *Lord Byron and Some of His Contemporaries* was not Hunt's final statement on his complex ten-year friendship and literary relationship with Byron.

Notes

1 Percy Bysshe Shelley, *The Letters of Percy Bysshe Shelley*, ed. Frederick L. Jones, 2 vols. (Oxford: Oxford University Press, 1964), 2:442.

2 Clara Tuite, *Lord Byron and Scandalous Celebrity* (Cambridge: Cambridge University Press, 2014), 3.

3 Michael P. Steier, "Lord Byron and the Empress Marie-Louise: A New Letter to Leigh Hunt," *The Byron Journal* 45, no. 2 (2017): 136.

4 Ann Blainey, *Immortal Boy: A Portrait of Leigh Hunt* (New York: St. Martin's Publishers, 1985); Nicholas Roe, *Fiery Heart: The First Life of Leigh Hunt* (London: Pimlico, 2005); Anthony Holden, *The Wit in the Dungeon: The Remarkable Life of Leigh Hunt. Poet, Revolutionary, and the Last of the Romantics* (Boston, MA: Little, Brown and Company, 2005).

5 *Leigh Hunt: Life, Poetics, Politics*, ed. Nicholas Roe (New York: Routledge, 2003); Michael Eberle-Sinatra, *Leigh Hunt and the London Literary Scene: A Reception History of His Major Works, 1805–1828* (New York: Routledge, 2005).

6 Leigh Hunt, *The Selected Writings of Leigh Hunt*, eds. Robert Morrison and Michael Eberle-Sinatra, 6 vols. (London: Pickering & Chatto, 2003).

7 Jeffrey N. Cox, *Poetry and Politics in the Cockney School: Keats, Shelley, Hunt and their Circle* (Cambridge: Cambridge University Press, 1998), 3–5, 46–7.

8 Cox, *Poetry and Politics*, 47. Cox observes that literary magazines like *Blackwood's* attempted "to detach Shelley and Byron, the aristocrats in the group, from the rest of [Hunt's] circle" (27). Elsewhere, Cox says that Byron "clearly came to dislike Hunt" (36). In exile, Byron is only "a kind of corresponding member of [Hunt's] group" (47); and, once Byron and Hunt reunite in Italy in 1822, "the gap between the peer and the plebeian would widen" (49).

9 Byron did, however, claim that some of his juvenile poems were written for his Southwell "social circle" (*CPW* 1:32). Tom Mole also makes a convincing case for *Childe Harold* (Cantos I–II) as a coterie poem in its earliest state. See Tom Mole, *Byron's Romantic Celebrity: Industrial Culture and the Hermeneutic of Intimacy* (New York: Palgrave Macmillan, 2007), 44–59. See also Robert Southey's preface to *A Vision of Judgment* in *Robert Southey: Later Poetical Works, 1811–1838*, eds. Lynda Pratt et al., 4 vols. (London: Pickering & Chatto, 2012), 4:543, 695. Byron attacked Hunt's "Cockney School" in his unpublished "Addenda" to his *Letter to John Murray*; see *CMP* 154–60.

10 Relevant recent studies include: Tim Fulford, *Romantic Poetry and Literary Coteries: The Dialect of the Tribe* (New York: Palgrave Macmillan, 2015); Michelle Levy, *Family Authorship and Romantic Print Culture* (New York: Palgrave Macmillan, 2008).

11 See, for instance, Peter Cochran, *"Romanticism"—and Byron* (Newcastle upon Tyne: Cambridge Scholars Publishing, 2009), 110–50. See also Doris Langley Moore, *The Late Lord Byron* (New York: Harper & Row, Publishers, 1961), 279–87, 408–26. Hunt's financial irresponsibility is a significant factor in Moore's assessment of the relationship.

12 Timothy Webb, "Correcting the Irritability of His Temper: The Evolution of Leigh Hunt's *Autobiography*," in *Romantic Revisions*, eds. by Robert Brinkley and Keith Hanley (Cambridge: Cambridge University Press, 1992), 268–90.

13 Timothy Webb, "Leigh Hunt to Lord Byron: Eight Letters from Horsemonger Lane Gaol," *The Byron Journal* 36, no. 2 (2008): 131–42; "After Horsemonger Lane: Leigh Hunt's London Letters to Byron (1815–1816)," *Romanticism* 16, no. 3 (2010): 233–66.

14 On Byron and *Rimini*, see Timothy Webb, "Stories of Rimini: Leigh Hunt, Byron and the Fate of Francesca," in *Dante in the Nineteenth Century: Reception, Canonicity, Popularization*, ed. Nick Havely (Oxford: Peter Lang, 2011), 32–53; Will Bowers, "Hunt, Byron, and *The Story of Rimini*—A Literary Challenge to 'the Public Mind,'" *Romanticism and Victorianism on the Net* 59–60 (April–October 2011). https://www.erudit.org/en/journals/ravon. On *The Liberal*, see: Jane Stabler, "Religious Liberty in the 'Liberal, 1822–23,'" *Branch: Britain, Representation and Nineteenth-Century History* (January 2015): 1–13; Daisy Hay, "Liberals, *Liberales* and *The Liberal*: A Reassessment," *European Romantic Review* 19, no. 4 (2008): 307–20. William H. Marshall, *Byron, Shelley, Hunt, and "The Liberal"*

(Philadelphia: University of Pennsylvania Press, 1960). See also: Jeffery W. Vail, *The Literary Relationship of Lord Byron & Thomas Moore* (Baltimore, MD: Johns Hopkins University Press, 2001); Ayumi Mizukoshi, *Keats, Hunt and the Aesthetics of Pleasure* (New York: Palgrave Macmillan, 2001); Charles E. Robinson, *Shelley and Byron: The Snake and the Eagle Wreathed in Fight* (Baltimore, MD: Johns Hopkins University Press, 1976).

15 Susan Wolfson's concept of the Romantic "author" as "a literary consciousness" created "in a web of reciprocally transforming and transformative creative subjects," or "interaction," has been especially helpful in shaping this study's thinking about Byron and Hunt as *authors* engaged in complex and relational ways in both the private and public spheres. See Susan J. Wolfson, *Romantic Interactions: Social Being & the Turns of Literary Action* (Baltimore, MD: Johns Hopkins University Press, 2010), 1–13.

16 For the conservative politics of the *Quarterly Review*, see Jonathan Cutmore, *Contributors to the "Quarterly Review"* (London: Pickering & Chatto, 2008), 1–35.

17 See Byron's "Addenda" to the *Letter to John Murray* in *CMP* 154–60.

18 John Cam Hobhouse, "The Separation, January 1st–April 25th 1816," in *The Diary of John Cam Hobhouse*, ed. Peter Cochran. https://petercochran.wordpress.com.

19 Jeffrey N. Cox, "Leigh Hunt's *Foliage*: A Cockney Manifesto," in *Leigh Hunt: Life, Poetics, Politics*, ed. Nicholas Roe (New York: Routledge, 2003), 58–77.

1 Byron, Hunt, and the Juvenile Tradition

When Byron met Hunt at Horsemonger Lane Gaol in May of 1813, the poet called attention to the imprisoned editor's *Juvenilia*, a collection of adolescent verses Hunt had published at age seventeen. Hunt recalled Byron saying "that the sight of my volume at Harrow had been one of his incentives to write verses, and that he had had the same passion for friendship that I had displayed in it." The editor added, "To my astonishment, he quoted some of the lines, and would not hear me speak ill of them" (*LBSC* 2). Hunt published this anecdote at least four times in his life: first, in a poem of farewell "To the Right Honourable Lord Byron, on his Departure for Italy and Greece," which was printed in *The Examiner* on 28 April 1816 and reprinted in *Foliage* in 1818; Hunt later mentioned the anecdote in a sketch of Byron's character printed in *The Examiner* on 29 July 1821 and again in *Lord Byron and Some of His Contemporaries* in 1828. Clearly, Byron's interest in *Juvenilia* had served an important need for the beleaguered editor: the famous creator of *Childe Harold* had acknowledged Hunt as an author of no ordinary ability—a juvenile author—during a period when Hunt's political imprisonment for libelling the Prince Regent had overshadowed his past artistic achievements. Yet *Juvenilia*, as Hunt revealingly shows, had also satisfied an important, early artistic need for Byron, having provided the young aristocrat with "incentive" to begin writing verses during his teenage years. This is not surprising, for Hunt's *Juvenilia*, as Laurie Langbauer has shown, was one of the most popular adolescent volumes published in the first decade of the nineteenth century, moving quickly through four editions and helping to shape an emerging juvenile tradition of literature in Britain.[1]

Critics have generally ignored the juvenile poetry produced by Byron and Hunt, but there has been some recent interest in Hunt's *Juvenilia*, and Jerome McGann's assessment of Byron's juvenile volumes is still incisive.[2] McGann observes that *Hours of Idleness*, in particular, contains many examples of the authorial self-fashioning that would be used to great advantage in *Childe Harold*, a palimpsest of fictionalized biography, which Byron liked to believe had transformed him overnight into a literary celebrity.[3] More specifically, McGann argues that "both the Preface and a majority of the notes scattered throughout [*Hours of Idleness*] are as self-conscious as the verse itself."[4] As Langbauer shows, the juvenile tradition through which Byron and Hunt emerged as authors was itself a highly self-conscious tradition.[5] For Byron, however, the line between self-consciousness and egotism blurred in ways that make *Hours of Idleness* a "naively self-absorbed book," according to McGann.[6] Caroline Franklin sees Byron's "touchy insistence on rank" as a strong mark of this naive self-absorption. Allusions to Byron's "heritage of nobility," Franklin points out, appear throughout *Hours of Idleness*, most obviously in poems such as "On Leaving Newstead Abbey" and "Elegy on Newstead Abbey" but also in poems such as "Stanzas" ("I would I were a careless child").[7] Byron's class posturing famously roused the critical ire of Henry Brougham, who attacked both the poetry and the poet in a review of *Hours of Idleness* for the *Edinburgh Review*. Hunt's *Juvenilia*, on the other hand, was successful, in part, because of the self-conscious but deferential attitude he presented therein. As Hunt later remarked, for a juvenile poet to begin from a place of rank and privilege was unusual, and Byron's public acknowledgment of this privilege is what sets his juvenilia apart from the volumes produced by other adolescent authors in the first decade of the nineteenth century.[8]

When Hunt and Byron published their juvenile volumes, the concept of adolescent genius had not yet gained full critical acceptance: young artists were often just as likely to be criticized as celebrated, thereby making adolescent authorship an unstable venture for those willing to pursue it. As such, the early volumes produced by Byron and Hunt not only reveal significant details about their development as young authors working within a shared tradition, but also about the conditions of Romantic authorship at a transitional moment when the major Romantic reviews (the *Edinburgh Review* and the *Quarterly Review*) were just coming into existence. The literary engagements between young authors and their reviewers, therefore, provide a relevant point of entry for locating the origins of the print politics that would so decisively come to shape the Byron-Hunt literary relationship in the public spaces of Romantic literary culture.

The Cult of Juvenilia

Adolescent genius made a controversial entrance into nineteenth-century British literary culture on the legacy of Thomas Chatterton, the ill-fated boy poet from Bristol.[9] As Daniel Cook has shown, there were complexities that came with juvenile authorship that can be traced to the critical reception of Chatterton's life and works. An article in the *Monthly Mirror* for July 1799 by Robert Fellowes, Curate of Harbury, illustrates the many facets of Chatterton's character under discussion two years before Hunt's *Juvenilia* made its public appearance. Fellowes stated in no uncertain terms that Chatterton was one of the "most extraordinary personages that has appeared in the present century," adding that the young poet had "imbibed a passion for fame, and a thirst for distinction." The curate further observed that in "young Chatterton, the love of pre-eminence was an impetuous and ruling passion," a passion that some, including Wordsworth and Coleridge, saw as a dangerous moral failing and a factor that may have contributed to Chatterton's suicide at the age of seventeen.[10] Fellowes, however, argued that Chatterton had successfully channeled that "passion" into accomplished poetry, including the infamous collection of *Poems, Supposed to have been Written at Bristol, by Thomas Rowley, and Others, in the Fifteenth Century.* For many commentators, the Rowley poems, which generated a lengthy public controversy over their authenticity, exposed Chatterton as a literary fraud. Yet for supporters like Fellowes, the ruse was itself an act of original genius, a "wonderful forgery" that revealed Chatterton's ability to transform himself successfully into a marketable author. Fellowes is astute on this point, suggesting that if Chatterton had published his Rowley poems under his own name, he would have been ignored outside of Bristol. Instead, by creating a complex authorial persona that played upon the period's antiquarian interests, Chatterton had responded ingeniously to the material conditions of the literary marketplace. Of course, Fellowes, like many who had written upon Chatterton in the last decades of the eighteenth century, had also taken Chatterton's age into account in his assessment of the poet's life and art. Indeed, readers were reminded that Chatterton at the "age of sixteen" produced the "tragedy of Ella" (*Ælla: A Tragycal Enterlude*) and that in the "exuberance of [his] juvenile imagination, there are examples of the true sublime."

For Byron and Hunt, Chatterton's "juvenile imagination" was matched, if not surpassed, by that of the English child actor William Henry West Betty ("Master Betty"), styled the "Young Roscius" after the first-century BCE Roman actor. Betty began his acting career at the age of eleven and made his London debut in December of 1804 at Covent Garden where he drew "an immense crowd round all the doors at a very early hour." According to one account of the performance, the boy actor "manifested powers, genius, and discrimination that [was] scarcely creditable."[11] Betty went on to perform hundreds of shows, finding admirers in all quarters of Britain. William Hazlitt, for one, wrote that "Master Betty's acting was a singular phenomenon, but it was also as beautiful as it was singular."[12] Like the boy poet Chatterton, however, the boy actor did not always find mainstream support. In fact, the *Morning Post* for 5 December 1805 criticized the phenomenon of child actors, darkly labeling the performances in which they starred as "Infantine Theatricals." According to the *Morning Post*, "Premature debaucheries, premature decrepitude, or premature death, have usually been the consequence of premature genius and premature abilities." While these remarks may have been a politicized reaction to the recent institutionalization of child actors in Napoleonic France, the idea of "premature death" also recalled the fate of the young Chatterton. Other commentators were less morbid but equally concerned about the popularity of adolescent genius during the Romantic period. The *Chester Chronicle* for 12 March 1802, for instance, stated that it would not accept original "juvenile productions" for inclusion in its columns because they "are not fit for the public," adding that adolescent authorship "generally throws a damp upon the ardour of the young mind, and prevents it in many instances from expanding into maturity."

Despite the debate over Betty's merits in particular and adolescent genius in general, the Young Roscius phenomenon had a decidedly powerful effect on young Byron and Hunt. Byron was fascinated by Betty, attending, "at the hazard of [his] life," several uncomfortably packed performances in London in 1805. Byron's opinion of the boy actor, however, was not a wholly approving one. He wrote to his half-sister, Augusta Leigh (*née* Byron), claiming that Betty was "tolerable in some characters, but by no means equal to the ridiculous praises showered upon him by *John Bull*" (*BLJ* 1:67). The impression also found its way into some of Byron's juvenile poems. Although the poet acknowledged himself to be an "embryo Actor" (*CPW* 1:41, line 16) for his feature role in an amateur production of Richard Cumberland's *Wheel of Fortune*, Byron mocked professional "Infant" actors:

> The House is crammed in every place full
> To see the Boy, of action Graceful;
> While Roscius lends his name to Betty
> Tully must yield the palm to Petty.
>
> (*CPW* 1:196, lines 27–30)

For Paul Elledge, Byron's comments on Betty suggest not disapproval but "unacknowledged or grudging and emulous respect, a mysterious and nagging fascination."[13] Whether Byron's criticisms of the Young Roscius sprang from youthful jealousy or a desire for Betty-like celebrity, Byron had been clearly swept up in the vogue for adolescent genius that had also gripped Hunt.

Hunt, on more than one occasion, explicitly identified himself with Young Roscius and had commented publicly on the young actor's career as early as 1805.[14] When Hunt later reflected on his *Juvenilia* period, he recalled that after the volume appeared, he had been "introduced to literati, and shown about among parties," having become a "kind of 'Young Roscius' in authorship" (*A* 1:194). In an early "Memoir" published in the *Monthly Mirror* in 1810, Hunt referred to himself as a "sort of rhyming young Roscius," adding that he wished to "deprecate these precocious appearances in public, which are always dangerous to the taste, and in general dissatisfactory to the recollection."[15] Despite the embarrassment that Hunt came to feel about his juvenile celebrity, his retrospective assessment is significant, for it reveals that the success of *Juvenilia*, as he came to see it, had depended largely on age, not necessarily talent. As Hunt noted, "it was unusual at that time to publish at so early a period of life" (*A* 1:194). Hunt's commentary on his early poetical success through the lens of Betty's dramatic achievement nevertheless reinforces the idea of authorship—juvenile authorship, in particular—as self-conscious dramatic performance or role-playing: like boy actors on an adult stage, juvenile poets performed roles in a world of letters typically reserved for adults.

The most important aspect of this role, as Hunt and Byron both knew, was the performance of youth. Hunt added a subtitle to his *Juvenilia*, "Written Between The Ages of Twelve & Sixteen," and an "Advertisement" that reassured readers that the poems therein "were the productions of sixteen, and the rest of his intermediate years." David Duff, in fact, argues that Hunt's approach became a common tactic among young, emerging writers at the beginning of the nineteenth century: "the trick" was "to trade on, whilst apparently apologizing for, an author's youthfulness."[16] Several juvenile volumes, all published within a few years of Hunt's maiden volume, followed *Juvenilia*'s example closely, and by the time Byron came to assemble *Hours of Idleness* in 1807, a "cult of juvenilia" had been firmly established with Hunt's book among the earliest and most important examples.

Marketing Juvenilia, Part I: Hunt's *Juvenilia*

In 1801, a seventeen-year-old Hunt, with the help of his father, an ordained minister in the Church of England, and his uncle, the accomplished international painter Benjamin West, published *Juvenilia* by subscription. Hunt managed to secure a significant base of readers from his father's congregation and his uncle's large network of friends in the world of art, literature, and politics. The subscriber list printed with *Juvenilia* is, as Nicholas Roe says, "extraordinary," with over 800 names occupying no less than fifteen pages in the third edition.[17] Early subscribers included John and Arthur Arch, publishers of the first edition of the *Lyrical Ballads*; the poets George Dyer and Henry Pye; and the radical journalist William Cobbett. Politicians are represented by John Horne Tooke, Thomas Erskine, and Rufus King, the "American ambassador in London."[18] Also among the subscribers was John Murray II, Byron's future publisher and the publisher of Hunt's *Story of Rimini*. In addition, Frederick Howard, fifth Earl of Carlisle, Byron's relative and *de facto* guardian, who would refuse his young charge's request for a formal introduction to the House of Lords, appears in Hunt's subscriber list to the third edition. Incidentally, when Byron sent Lord Carlisle a copy of *Hours of Idleness* in 1807, Carlisle, Byron felt, had acknowledged receipt of the volume "before he opened the Book" (*BLJ* 1:133). In need of a dedicatee for his last volume of juvenilia, *Poems, Original and Translated*, Byron must have grudgingly dedicated the book to Carlisle in 1808.

By the first decade of the nineteenth century, however, a book's dedication had become less an expectation than a dignified formality, often of dubious import. Isaac D'Israeli described the dedication as a "species of literary artifice," formerly "an expedient to procure dedicatory fees."[19] Southey agreed, declaring that the "days of dedications are happily well nigh at an end." Yet the author of the revolutionary *Joan of Arc* (a poem issued without a dedication) also knew that a dedication could give a first book, especially the first book from a juvenile author, "consequence in the eyes" of readers.[20] For Henry Kirke White, the young working-class poet Southey admired, championed, and edited after the poet's premature death at age twenty-one, a dedicated patron was a crucial step to public recognition. Not surprisingly, the dedication to Hunt's *Juvenilia* was also a significant feature of the volume's paratext, drawing upon a tradition of dedicating books to members of the nobility that dates back to the time of Elizabeth I. Hunt's volume is formally dedicated to James Henry Leigh, "nephew of the Duke of Chandos," who "was a Privy Councillor, Lord Steward" of the household of George III.[21] Because Hunt's father had tutored the Duke's nephew, *Juvenilia*'s dedication effectively served a dual purpose: it was Isaac Hunt's way of showing formal appreciation to an employer and Hunt's means of connecting with a specific class of polite readers.

The contents of *Juvenilia* were just as important as its apparatus in establishing the book as a public volume to be taken seriously. For one thing, Hunt had included poems of a more ambitious cast than anything he had previously published in the columns of the *Monthly Preceptor, or Juvenile Library*, the literary magazine that had first brought his writerly talents to the public's attention.[22] With lengthy productions such as the Spenserian "Palace of Pleasure" and the didactic "Progress of Painting," *Juvenilia* showcased poetic ambition, imitative though it was, beyond that found in other popular volumes of the time, including Thomas Moore's *Poetical Works of the Late Thomas Little, Esq.* (1801) and Lord Strangford's *Poems, from the Portuguese of Luis de Camoens* (1804), the two "most immediate models" for Byron's early lyrics, according to McGann.[23] The "incentive" that Byron would have found in Hunt's *Juvenilia*, therefore, need not be linked to any one particular poem, or even group of poems, but rather to the conceptual framework of Hunt's volume itself. In addition to imitating a range of verse forms, Hunt positioned his two substantial poems ("The Progress of Painting" and "The Palace of Pleasure") at the end of *Juvenilia*, thus giving the book an internal progression from shorter occasional lyrics to longer didactic poems. The ambition Hunt showcased in these efforts may have inspired Byron to produce the longer and weightier "Oscar of Alva," "The Death of Calmar and Orla," and "The Episode of Nisus and Euryalus" for *Hours of Idleness*. As Byron explained his motives for his first public volume in March of 1807, "I am now preparing a volume for the Public at large, my amatory pieces will be expunged, & others substituted, in their place; the whole will be considerably enlarged" (*BLJ* 1:112). The emphasis on enlargement is important. On the one hand, it suggests Byron's desire to market himself as a poet who could offer more than amatory lyrics in the vein of Moore or Strangford. On the other hand, by declaring the necessity of "expung[ing]" the amatory poems (though Byron would retain several) first printed in the privately published *Fugitive Pieces* and *Poems on Various Occasions*, Byron shows an awareness that such poetry is less suitable, or marketable, for public consumption. And, as McGann points out, "public recognition" for Byron was "a validating condition of achievement."[24] Nevertheless, with a poetic temperament more inclined to challenge than uphold established convention, Byron, as we shall see, made his public debut in *Hours of Idleness* a highly unpredictable experiment in juvenile publication.

Hunt's *Juvenilia*, in the end, had readily succeeded as a public volume. In addition to passing through four editions, each with a swelling new subscriber list, the literary reviews helped secure Hunt's reputation as a juvenile author of great promise. The *Monthly Mirror* reviewed both the first and third editions, asserting of the first that the volume "contains proofs of poetic genius, and literary ability, which reflect great credit on the youthful author, and will justify the most sanguine expectations of his future reputation" (*RR* C2:671). Of the third edition, the reviewer took the opportunity to add, "We think the talents of Mr. Hunt will reflect no small degree of credit on the school [Christ's Hospital] in which he has been educated, and we shall feel ourselves exceedingly happy, if the public commendation we have been the first to offer, should be the means of introducing so promising a bard to the notice of the literary world."[25] All of the reviewers were impressed by the subscriber list. The *Monthly Review* declared that "We are happy in seeing a respectable list of subscribers prefixed to these poems" (*RR* C2:690), and the reviewer for the *European Magazine* echoed the sentiment, stating that "the whole collection is not undeserving of the great encouragement which the numerous list of subscribers shews the Author to have experienced" (*RR* C1:420). In one of the few negative reviews, the writer for the *British Critic* found the subscriber list to be equally commendable but was otherwise disappointed by Hunt's compositions, arguing that the poems proved not "so much genius in poetry as fondness for it" and noting a "superabundance of ornament, without much originality of thought" (*RR* C1:200). Hunt shared this critical opinion later in his life, but at age seventeen, on the strength of the volume's largely positive reception, he had successfully introduced himself to readers and critics who were willing to support an ambitious young poet wanting to play by the rules of juvenile authorship.

Marketing Juvenilia, Part II: Byron's *Hours of Idleness*

As he prepared *Hours of Idleness* for the press early in 1807, Byron had to confront the same pressures of public authorship that Hunt had faced (and surmounted) with *Juvenilia*. However, unlike Hunt, who had made an early leap into print in literary magazines such as the *Monthly Preceptor*, Byron developed as a poet through the more traditional route of private manuscript circulation. Consequently, Byron had limited experience with the juvenile authorship industry just coming into existence.[26] For the young Byron, authorial recognition had been limited to a select group of generally friendly and admiring readers at Southwell in Nottinghamshire, where the poet resided with his mother at various times between 1803 and 1807. An early letter from John Pigot, Byron's closest male companion at Southwell and brother of his closest female companion, Elizabeth Pigot, confirms that in September of 1806 Byron was making an impression on this sleepy provincial town by writing "some very pretty verses."[27] At Southwell, Byron's artistic talents had been stimulated by a precocious circle of young acquaintances, who regularly exchanged books, poems, drawings, and other keepsakes. The Southwell coterie also performed at least two amateur theatricals in which Byron played lead roles.[28] Byron, unsurprisingly, cut the most notorious figure in the circle, boasting of romantic relationships with no less than nine local women; these youthful romances would form the subjects of many of the poems that appeared in the poet's privately published first volume: *Fugitive Pieces*.[29]

As a volume of "Trifles," *Fugitive Pieces* is something quite different than Hunt's *Juvenilia* and Byron's own public volumes: *Hours of Idleness* and *Poems, Original and Translated*. The preface to *Fugitive Pieces* advertises that its contents were "never intended to meet the public eye" and were "printed merely for the perusal of a few friends to whom they are dedicated" (*CPW* 1:363). The published volume thus resembles less a serious volume of poetry assembled for critical approval than a commonplace book of occasional verses to be shared informally with an intimate group. The titles of the poems bear this idea out clearly: "Lines Written in 'Letters of an Italian Nun and an English Gentleman,' by J. J. Rousseau, founded on Facts," one of Elizabeth Pigot's poems, is followed immediately in *Fugitive Pieces* by "Answer to the Foregoing, Address'd to Miss [Pigot]." "On the Death of Mr. Fox" (an "Illiberal Impromptu" that "Appeared in the Morning Post") is printed and answered by Byron in one of the few political poems in the volume.[30] In addition, *Fugitive Pieces* contains several poems about keepsakes, including "The Cornelian," Byron's first significant poem of male love and friendship—a poem about which he came to feel extremely self-conscious.[31] He was, however, notably less self-conscious to promote his passionate relationships in poems such as "To a Beautiful Quaker" and "To Mary, on Receiving her Picture," a poem that might be grouped with "To a Lady, Who Presented to the Author a Lock of Hair, Braided with his Own, and Appointed a Night, in December, to Meet him in the Garden." Other closely linked poems include "Reply to Some Verses of J. M. B. Pigot, Esq. on the Cruelty of his Mistress" and "To the Sighing Strephon," which McGann sees as a "companion piece" to the former (*CPW* 1:381).

Critical reaction to *Fugitive Pieces*, despite its limited circulation, led to early embarrassments. The Reverend J. T. Becher, a friend and advisor, issued Byron his first negative review, objecting to the erotically charged poems included in the volume, particularly those which named, or barely disguised the names of, Southwell women.[32] Byron obliged Becher, destroying the remaining copies of *Fugitive Pieces*, and then issued a revised edition with a new title: *Poems on Various Occasions*. In this new version, Byron removed the offensive "To Mary" and "To Caroline" and replaced names in poems such as "To Julia," which became "To Lesbia," and "Imitated from Catullus. To Anna," which substituted "Ellen" for "Anna." The volume's thematic interest in sensibility had thus been kept largely intact, and Byron seems to have felt confident enough to send a copy of the newly printed book to Henry Mackenzie, the "celebrated author" of *The Man of Feeling*. Mackenzie apparently acknowledged receipt of the volume in a letter that is now lost, but in March of 1807 the young Byron proudly revealed that he had received the author's "Encomiums" (*BLJ* 1:111). It may have been these reassuring remarks from a well-respected literary authority that led Byron to change his mind about his poetic "Trifles" and consider publishing for a larger, unknown and unknowable public audience. Indeed, that same month Byron began making plans for his first public volume: *Hours of Idleness*.

Perhaps the most important consideration Byron had to make in preparing *Hours of Idleness* for the "Public at large" was deciding how to market himself as an author in the volume's preface. For *Poems on Various Occasions*, Byron had reduced the already brief three-sentence preface used for *Fugitive Pieces* to just one sentence: "The only Apology necessary to be adduced, in extenuation of any errors in the following collection, is, that the Author has not yet completed his nineteenth year" (*CPW* 1:364). The emphasis on age shows that Byron was well aware of this fundamental convention of juvenile authorship. For Hunt and other juvenile authors Byron had studied, including Henry Kirke White and Charlotte Dacre, the prefaces to their juvenile volumes shared two common elements: an acknowledgment of minority and deference to the authority of an anonymous (though presumably adult) readership. Hunt's preface ("Advertisement") to *Juvenilia* indeed foregrounded minority as the primary criterion for adolescent authorship:

> The Author thinks it necessary to inform his Readers, as they will undoubtedly perceive how much superior some of the following Poems are to the others, that a few of the first pages, all the Translations but one, the two first Odes, and the first Hymn, were written at a very early age; that the Poem on Retirement, the Pastorals in imitation of Pope and Virgil, Elegy written in Poet's Corner, Ode to Truth, the Progress of Painting, Wandle's Wave, the Hymns for the Seasons, the Palace of Pleasure, and the Funeral Anthem, were the productions of sixteen, and the rest of his intermediate years.[33]

In her short preface "To the Public" in *Hours of Solitude. A Collection of Original Poems, now First Published* (1805), Dacre also presented herself as a juvenile author: "Those Poems in the subsequent collection, where the age at which they were written is not mentioned at the head, are of a recent date. At the age of three-and-twenty, therefore, having no longer extreme youth to plead in extenuation of their errors, I must merely recommend them to mercy."[34] For Dacre, the rhetoric of juvenility, even at a moment when she could no longer be considered a juvenile author, had clearly served a preemptive function as an attempt to ward off hostile critics.

The most significant preface written by a juvenile author before Byron may have been that written by Henry Kirke White for *Clifton Grove* (1803), the only volume the poet would see through the press during his tragically short life. In his preface, White follows Hunt and Dacre by emphasizing his "youth" but is at once more forthright and discursive:

> The following attempts in Verse, are laid before the Public with extreme diffidence. The Author is very conscious that the juvenile efforts of a youth, who has not received the polish of Academical discipline, and who has been but sparingly blessed with opportunities for the prosecution of scholastic pursuits, must necessarily be defective in the accuracy, and finished elegance, which mark the works of the man, who has passed his life in the retirement of his study, furnishing his mind with images, and at the same time attaining the power of disposing those images to the best advantage.[35]

Isaac D'Israeli thought that prefaces were "rarely sincere" and White's preface, though earnest in adopting the expectations of juvenile authorship, seems to support D'Israeli's belief.[36] White's literary talents were indisputable, leading to a sizarship that would allow him to attend Cambridge

a few years after his maiden volume appeared. Yet his adolescent years
were, as he states, without the benefit of "Academical discipline" and, as
a lawyer's apprentice, sufficient time for "scholastic pursuits." The contents of *Clifton Grove*, however, show less "diffidence" than the author's
prose preface would lead the reader to believe. As Richard D. McGhee
has argued, unlike Hunt, who closely imitated earlier English writers in
his *Juvenilia*, White had all the hallmarks of an emergent class of Romantic poets led by Southey and his fellow Lake Poets.[37] The young White
clearly hints at his attraction to this new revolutionary group of poets in
the very first poem in *Clifton Grove*, "To My Lyre, An Ode," in which
the speaker transforms his concerns about his age and his limited educa-
tional experience into a powerful statement of self-identity and artistic
potential. Indeed, for White's speaker "no Academic lore / Has taught, the
solemn strain to pour, / Or build the polish'd rhyme," and yet he remains
confident that his young lyre "to *Sylvan* themes canst soar" (xii).

Byron owned copies of *Clifton Grove* as well as Southey's two-volume
edition of White's poetical *Remains* and expressed great admiration for
this fellow boy poet from Nottinghamshire.[38] It is, therefore, not surprising that Byron may have found White's preface a more attractive
model for *Hours of Idleness* than the brief, conventional prefaces issued
by Hunt and Dacre. The preface to *Clifton Grove*, nevertheless, became
White's first mistake as a young author, just as Byron's preface to *Hours
of Idleness* would become his. As he prepared his first public volume,
Byron was probably not aware of the notice of *Clifton Grove* that had
appeared in the *Monthly Review* for February 1804. The reviewer gave
White no quarter, stating that the volume's ambitious title poem "cannot
be contemplated with any sanguine expectation." Even more damning
was the review's concluding remarks: "The author is very anxious, however, that critics should find in it something to commend, and he shall not
be disappointed; we commend his exertions, and his laudable endeavours
to excel; but we cannot compliment him with having learned the difficult
art of writing good poetry."[39] Like White, Byron placed great stress upon
his preface to *Hours of Idleness*, producing a "much-corrected" working
draft before settling on the final version.[40] In the published version, he
began appropriately enough for a juvenile author, stating that "These
productions are the fruits of the lighter hours of a young man, who has
lately completed his nineteenth year," adding "As they bear the internal
evidence of a boyish mind, this is, perhaps, unnecessary information"
(*CPW* 1:32). As Willis W. Pratt observes, however, Byron had drawn
even more attention to his "boyish mind" in the first draft: the phrase "a
young man" had first been written as "a very young man."[41] Even more
revealing is Byron's revision to lines about his future plans as a writer:
"With slight hopes, and some fears, I publish this first, and last attempt.
To the dictates of young ambition, may be ascribed many actions more
criminal, and equally absurd" (*CPW* 1:34). This sentence appeared in

the draft preface as: "With slight hopes & many Fears, I publish this first, & probably last attempt; to the Desire of *Fame*, may be ascribed many actions more criminal, & equally absurd."[42] In preparing his preface, Byron vacillated between an authorial presentation of himself as a deferential prodigy of ambition, like Hunt, and an author, like White, with a strong sense of self-identity and the "Desire of *Fame*."

Byron's published preface to *Hours of Idleness*, which spans six pages, followed the basic formula of juvenile authorship but retained an exceedingly self-confident and, at times, flippant tone:

> In submitting to the public eye the following collection, I have not only to combat the difficulties that writers of verse generally encounter, but, may incur the charge of presumption, for obtruding myself on the world, when, without doubt, I might be, at my age, more usefully employed. . . . A considerable portion of these poems has been privately printed, at the request, and for the perusal of my friends. I am sensible that the partial, and, frequently, injudicious admiration of a social circle, is not the criterion by which poetical genius is to be estimated, yet, "to do greatly," we must "dare greatly"; and I have hazarded my reputation and feelings in publishing this volume.
>
> (*CPW* 1:32)

For reviewers like Henry Brougham, the bravado Byron displayed in his claims to "'dare greatly'" or, elsewhere, having "pass'd the Rubicon," to "stand or fall by the 'cast of the die,'" was alarming. Histrionics of this kind are altogether absent from Hunt's *Juvenilia*, Dacre's *Hours of Solitude*, and White's *Clifton Grove*. Furthermore, Byron, unlike the deferential Hunt, refused to prostrate himself (beyond the epigraphs printed on the volume's title page and scattered among its contents) before any poetical tradition, asserting instead, "I have not aimed at exclusive originality, still less have I studied any particular model for imitation" (*CPW* 1:33). Whereas Hunt had dutifully drawn attention to his poetical practice as one of imitation in the preface and the subtitle to *Juvenilia*, "Containing: Miscellanies, Translations, Sonnets, Pastorals, Elegies, Odes, Hymns & Anthem," Byron asserted his artistic practice as one of independence.[43] Yet Byronic independence had consequences. The young poet may have introduced *Hours of Idleness* to readers in the manner he thought best suited to his poetic temperament, but, in the end, the volume introduced the poet to the critical realities of Romantic authorship.

Juvenilia and the Romantic Reviewers

Francis Jeffrey's review of Southey's *Thalaba, the Destroyer*, published in the inaugural issue of the *Edinburgh Review* for October of 1802, set a severe but influential tone for the critical treatment of the first-generation

Romantic poets. Brougham, in his review of Byron's *Hours of Idleness* (January 1808), seems to have followed his colleague's lead by treating Romanticism's budding second generation in an equally severe and disapproving manner. Brougham's review of *Hours of Idleness* is ostensibly focused on Byron's juvenile volume, but the personality that Brougham introduced into his criticism anticipates the *ad hominem* arguments that would later be adopted by the writers at *Blackwood's*, who were equally severe on young poets like Keats. As Derek Roper argues, the *Edinburgh Review*, under Jeffrey, actually created a "vogue" for "slashing attacks" that was ultimately "harmful to the development of good criticism."[44] Brougham, a lawyer by profession, seems to have been particularly keen to deliver such attacks. Indeed, among the *Edinburgh* reviewers, as William Christie points out, Brougham was the "most cavalier about simply writing over the top of the book under review,"[45] and the showy opening to his review of Byron's *Hours of Idleness* would seem to illustrate Christie's observation:

> [T]he noble author is peculiarly forward in pleading minority. We have it in the title-page, and on the very back of the volume; it follows his name like a favourite part of his *style*. Much stress is laid upon it in the preface, and the poems are connected with this general statement of his case, by particular dates, substantiating the age at which each was written. Now, the law upon the point of minority, we hold to be perfectly clear. It is a plea available only to the defendant; no plaintiff can offer it as a supplementary ground of action. . . . [but the author] hath no right to sue, on that ground, for the price in good current praise, should the goods be unmarketable.
> (*RR* B2:833)

Brougham's elaborate legal metaphor, facetious as it may seem, arrives at a serious conclusion about juvenile authorship: adolescent publications may have been sacrosanct when Hunt issued his *Juvenilia*, but such productions, as Byron's recent example shows, had become fully integrated into the literary marketplace. Consequently, the commercialization of the genre gives Brougham the authority to evaluate *Hours of Idleness* as a commodity (an "unmarketable" good) and not as a precious gift of literary genius. Brougham's overly severe opinion of Byron's volume, of course, had much to do with the young poet's aristocratic self-fashioning: "It is a sort of privilege of poets to be egoists; but they should 'use it as not abusing it;' and particularly one who piques himself (though indeed at the ripe age of nineteen), of being 'an infant bard'—('The artless Helicon I boast is youth;')—should either not know, or should seem not to know, so much about his own ancestry" (*RR* B2:835). Yet Brougham did not stop there. His mockery of Byron and his juvenilia reaches a climax in another display of verbal dexterity and showy wit as he deconstructs the rhetoric of Byron's preface: "he expects no profit from his publication; and whether it succeeds or not, 'it is highly improbable, from his situation and pursuits hereafter,' that he should again condescend to become an author." The reviewer then concludes on a mocking note: "Therefore, let us take what we get and be thankful. . . . We are well off to have got so much from a man of this Lord's station, who does not live in a garret, but 'has the sway' of Newstead Abbey. Again, we say, let us be thankful; and, with honest Sancho, bid God bless the giver, nor look the gift horse in the mouth" (*RR* B2:835).

In the space of a few columns, and with more personal animus than the *Monthly Review* had shown Henry Kirke White, Brougham may have ended the practice of granting critical leniency to juvenile authors. Much, of course, had changed in the culture of literary reviewing in the six years that had elapsed between the publication of Hunt's *Juvenilia* in 1801 and the appearance of Byron's *Hours of Idleness* in 1807. The *Edinburgh Review* had come into existence in October of 1802, and despite the severity of some of its reviews, it also introduced a more analytical reviewing style. As Roper explains, the *Edinburgh Review* (and later the *Quarterly Review*) developed new standards for literary reviewing. Periodicals not only became more expensive after 1800, but they also became more selective. The "new selectivity made ample space available for original writing" devoted to critical opinion and commentary on matters not necessarily related directly to the work under review.[46] In contrast to Brougham's review of Byron's *Hours of Idleness*, for instance, the reviews of Hunt's *Juvenilia* are all brief, a few paragraphs at most, with an occasional excerpt or two from the poetry. And yet despite the publicity that *Hours of Idleness* received from its appearance in a major Romantic periodical, Byron naturally did not take Brougham's criticism lightly: "As an author, I am cut to atoms by the E[dinburgh] Review, it is just out, and has completely demolished my little fabric of fame" (*BLJ* 1:159).

Wounded deeply by Brougham's remarks, Byron made a deliberate effort to correct the perceived faults of *Hours of Idleness* by issuing a second edition in 1808 with a more conventional title: *Poems, Original and Translated*. This edition, the last of Byron's juvenile publications, has also been the least discussed. But the seriousness with which Byron approached the edition, as we shall see, underscores the anxiety that he must have felt following his first public attempt at authorship. Modern critics have been understandably more interested in *English Bards and Scotch Reviewers*, Byron's powerful early satire written, in part, as a direct response to the *Edinburgh Review*.[47] And although Nicholas Mason may be right to assert that *English Bards and Scotch Reviewers* was Byron's first "adult" attempt at authorship, *Poems, Original and Translated* remains a significant preliminary step in the poet's path to authorial maturity.[48]

In *Poems, Original and Translated*, Byron thoroughly revised the "boyish" presentation of *Hours of Idleness*: he replaced the title, removed the preface, added a formal dedication and frontispiece, and deleted poems in which he had ridiculed former schoolmasters. Hewson Clarke, writing in the *Satirist*, made a point of documenting these changes, asserting with wry approval that Byron's revised edition of juvenilia had been "newly vamped and varnished," adding that "his lordship's art of finesse [appears] to be improved" (*RR* B5:2105). Ultimately, these changes led Clarke to conclude that Byron's new volume showed "His lordship is *somewhat wiser* now" (*RR* B5:2106). Although Byron, at first, had cautioned his publisher, John Ridge, about prematurely issuing a second edition of *Hours of Idleness*, he came to fully endorse the project, giving more attention to matters of presentation and printing than he had with *Hours of Idleness*, which had been left in the capable hands of the Pigots. For *Poems, Original and Translated*, Byron provided Ridge with a complete list of specific instructions: the "size" of the new volume should be that of "Ld. Strangford's & Little's poems"; the title should be changed to "'poems' by Ld. Byron"; the "*Latin Motto*" should be discarded but "the two others can remain"; and finally, the "preface we will omit altogether.—The Dedication I will send in Time." Byron also had second thoughts about reprinting some of the poems from *Hours of Idleness*: "I wish the second poem (Stanzas on a view of Harrow) to be omitted" (*BLJ* 1:137). In another letter to Ridge, Byron listed several more poems to exclude: "To a Beautiful Quaker," "The First Kiss of Love," and "To the Rev. J. T. Becher" (*BLJ* 1:138). He later requested the removal of "Childish Recollections," but decided to keep the cynical "Thoughts Suggested by a College Examination" (*BLJ* 1:154–5). For the frontispiece, he stated: "I will order a design in London, for a plate, my own portrait would perhaps be best, but as that would take up so long a time completing, we will substitute probably a view of Harrow, or Newstead in its stead" (*BLJ* 1:138). Hunt had used a youthful portrait of himself as the frontispiece to the third edition of *Juvenilia*, Dacre included her portrait with *Hours of Solitude*, and Southey used an engraving of Henry Kirke White as the frontispiece in the first volume of his edition of White's poetical *Remains*; in the second volume of that edition, Southey also used an engraving of "Wilford Church near Nottingham," an engraving executed in the same genre as Byron's final choice of frontispiece for *Poems, Original and Translated*: a view of Harrow School in the picturesque style.

For Hewson Clarke, Byron's extensive reworking of *Hours of Idleness* had transformed *Poems, Original and Translated* into an "original work" (*RR* B5:2105) all its own despite carrying the "Second Edition" label on the title page. To be sure, the changes to Byron's new volume confirmed the extent to which the poet had ignored many of the conventions of juvenile publication when he issued his first public volume in 1807. The addition of the frontispiece to *Poems, Original and Translated* alone aligned Byron's volume with those of other juvenile authors, foregrounding the themes of the more conventional poems he retained from *Hours of Idleness*: the poems about Byron's childhood experiences and friendships at school. It is perhaps no coincidence that the most substantial poetical addition to *Poems, Original and Translated* was "To the Duke of D[orset]," a poem that reinforced the volume's celebration of passionate friendship—the theme that Byron had specifically praised in Hunt's *Juvenilia* when the two authors met at Horsemonger Lane Gaol in 1813.

Boyish Minds

Hunt's maiden volume of poems, nevertheless, warns against youthful indulgence in sensibility and passionate engagement. The frontispiece included in the first and second editions of Hunt's *Juvenilia*, for example, was an engraving by Francesco Bartolozzi (after a painting by Raphael Lamar West) that depicts an "emaciated" Chatterton-like figure lying upon a wooden bed in an empty room, "save for the company of rats," as Daniel Cook observes.[49] In subsequent editions, Hunt replaced this engraving with his own portrait and moved the Chatterton-inspired engraving to be bound up with the poem "Retirement, or the Golden Mean," from which the quotation "And, ah! let Pity turn her dewy eyes, / Where gasping Penury unfriended lies" (lines 73–4) that appears beneath the engraving is taken.[50] "Retirement" is one of the longer and more well-known poems in *Juvenilia* and it clearly serves an important didactic function. Written to promote the individual who "cares not where Ambition's maniacs rave" (line 17) and "sinks" not "his manly soul to ruder joys" (line 21), the poem is a celebration of "Retirement," "soother of the wo-worn breast" (line 1). For Hunt, "Retirement" is the virtuous remedy for all human ills, including unmitigated passion. In contrast to dangerously ambitious personalities like Chatterton, the retired man is Hunt's ideal human figure, the being who is "Creation's Lord / Whom all must envy, yet whom all applaud!" (lines 31–2). For Hunt, the retired man "Has learnt to live, and trembles not to die!" (line 34); he is the "Man," above all, who achieves the "Golden Mean" (line 128). The poem's emphasis on manhood (variations of the word "Man" appear no less than nine times over the course of the poem) is significant, for it reinforces the speaker's admiration for mature, rational beings who have "learnt to live." For a juvenile author like Hunt, writing, speaking, and thinking like an adult were important goals, and it is not surprising that he would dramatize these goals, in various ways, in *Juvenilia*.

In "A Morning Walk and View," for instance, Hunt further develops the ideal of the "Golden Mean" by inviting the reader to walk with a knowing guide through "green clad fields" (line 1) and admire the scenes "where Harmony and Peace / Walk hand in hand" (lines 117–8).[51] At one point during the course of this excursion, the speaker reminds us that children are not born with a complete understanding of nature and must learn of its complex and ennobling powers through experience:

> While on the adverse bank the wand'ring boy
> Views the [sun's] bright image, and with hostile stone
> Essays to break the beauteous orb; but, lo!
> He sees it brighten in the sunny ray,
> Wond'ring with vacant stare and open mouth,
> Then plunging, sink within th' unbroken light.
>
> (lines 21–6)

The implication here is that the speaker of the poem has already had the experience of the "wand'ring boy." The speaker, in other words, has given up his "hostile stone," and, like the speaker of "Retirement," has arrived at the point of calm maturity from where he can speak with authority and advise others—a position typically regarded as the purview of adults.

Hunt's insistence on adult role-playing in *Juvenilia* is even more conspicuous in the volume's crowning achievement of imitation: "The Palace of Pleasure." Hunt's "Palace of Pleasure," modeled on Spenser's Bower of Bliss episode and Thomson's *Castle of Indolence*, is replete with a knight errant named Sir Guyon who finds himself enraptured with "Pleasure" in the poem's first canto; in the second canto, the knight loses his way in the dangerously attractive realm of "Pleasure" but is ultimately guided to "Virtue" by "Religion" and her attendant angels. The poem thus traces the maturation of its protagonist, who ultimately rejects youthful pleasures for mature reflections. It is altogether appropriate that "Pleasure" and her attendant vices make their appearance wearing the garb of youthfulness. Guyon encounters "Young Wantonness" (1.36) as well as "Beauty," who appears with Cupid, a "youth enchain'd" and "a lovely little boy" (1.42–3).[52] Other figures likewise arrive in childish guises: "a most delightful train" of "lovely crowned boys" appears, and "after them flew youthful genii high / Cloth'd all in airy robes of streaming light" (1.50–1). Finally, the "last, to close the fine majestic sight, / A lovely chorus, crown'd with laurel green" that resemble "those fair boys at Grecian worship seen / That did in songs their heroes' glories raise" (1.55). All of these youthful visions in Hunt's poem are, however, false visions. This becomes evident early in the first canto when a "beauteous virgin" (1.12) tempts Guyon with the promise that she can "give to youth the knowledge of old age" (1.17). Guyon, as we might expect, readily succumbs to the false promise. In the second canto, "Pleasure's gay veil" (2.20) is suddenly lifted, giving way to a hellish phantasmagoria. Helpless at this point, Guyon requires the aid of a *deus ex machina* to redirect him to the righteous path of maturity: "An angel figure stream'd before the storm!" The "angel," notably unlike the youthful figures associated with "Pleasure" that Guyon had earlier witnessed, is described thus: "Upon her cheek youth's blushes gay and warm / Were mixt with matron gravity" (2.43). It is only through this vision of an angel "mixt" with "youth's blushes" *and* "matron gravity" that Guyon can see with "eye refresh'd upon the sight" (2.48). In the end, the knight marches forth committed to serving the cause of "Religion" (2.52). The thoroughly conventional message that Hunt develops in "The Palace of Pleasure" would have doubtless satisfied the interests of many of *Juvenilia*'s subscribers and helped secure the volume's favorable public reception.

The mature voice of Hunt's "Palace of Pleasure," a reflection of the *Juvenilia* volume as a whole, contrasts sharply with the rebellious voice that appears throughout Byron's *Hours of Idleness*. Indeed, in *Hours of Idleness*, the voice of "George Gordon, Lord Byron, a Minor," as its title page professes, dominates. As Langbauer argues, juvenile authors like Byron and Hunt were both "self-aware and self-fashioning," and Byron's juvenilia, in particular, enact a kind of "doublespeak," which can be "impudent, audacious, outspoken, perhaps downright insubordinate and rebellious."[53] *Hours of Idleness* contains many examples of such juvenile rebelliousness, and Byron himself recognized that the contents of his first public volume were the creations of a "boyish mind" (*CPW* 1:32). Hewson Clarke of the *Satirist* had great fun with such posturing, arguing that the boyishness of *Hours of Idleness* made it a volume fit not for adult readers, but for a readership made up of "*very little* boys and girls" (*RR* B5:2102). In the volume's most memorable homage to childhood, "Childish Recollections," Clarke, unsurprisingly, found the poem to contain "very childish recollections indeed" (*RR* B5:2104). To be sure, there is as much false boy posturing in *Hours of Idleness* as there is unconvincing adult role-playing in Hunt's *Juvenilia*, but Byron's play acting thoroughly disturbed the juvenile conventions that Hunt attempted to uphold. Byron's "boyish mind," for instance, perhaps achieves its most hyperbolic expression in "Damaetas," a poem originally and suggestively titled "My Character" that would have been wholly out of place in a volume like Hunt's *Juvenilia*:

> In law an infant, and in years a boy,
> In mind a slave to every vicious joy,
> From every sense of shame and virtue wean'd,
> In lies an adept, in deceit a fiend;
> Vers'd in hypocrisy, while yet a child,
> Fickle as wind, of inclinations wild.

(lines 1–6)

Byron's character sketch, doubtless exaggerated for effect, projects a "vicious" and "wild" kind of boyishness. One of Byron's early biographers remarked that Byron's juvenile verses had in them "more vigour and warmth than are usually found in the attempts of school-boys."[54] Indeed, unlike Byron, Hunt, in his *Juvenilia*, attempted to convince his readers that even though he was a teenager in years, he saw himself like Wordsworth's ideal poet: as "a man speaking to men."[55]

Hunt's attempt to speak as an adult to the many literary-minded men and women who subscribed to *Juvenilia* can be readily seen in poems that praise English literary traditions. In "Elegy. Written in Poets' Corner, Westminster Abbey," Hunt dutifully surveys the hallowed shrine of England's most venerated poets:

> Live not, where Shakespeare lays his awful dust,
>   The marble records of immortal fame?
> Weeps not the Muse o'er Rowe's beloved bust?
>   And speaks not Truth in Gay's untitled name!
> Who boasts of Kings when bending o'er the shade,
>   Where lies the harp sublime of free-born Gray?
> Who talks of pomp, or who of proud parade,
>   Where modest Thomson drops his spotless lay?
>
> (lines 17–24)[56]

The same poets receive praise in Hunt's ode "To Honour," in which we find "Milton soaring high" (line 33) and we learn that "Gray's terrific hand / Woke to Vengeance Cambria's land," of which "enraptur'd Collins sung" (lines 35–7). England's poets are predictably the heroes of Hunt's maiden volume, and Hunt's recognition of such poets reaffirms his desire to be seen as a poet wholly committed to a native English tradition in both theme and style. In fact, when the young Hunt does venture upon unconventional themes and poetic styles elsewhere in *Juvenilia*, he becomes notably self-conscious. We can see this clearly in "Parody on Dr. Johnson's 'Hermit Hoar, &c.,'" in which a facetious exchange between a "Gentle Lady" (line 1) and an earnest speaker results in a surprisingly playful conclusion:

> "Gentle Lady, on whose cheek
> "Modesty's soft blushes play;
> "Tell, O tell me where to seek
> "Virtue, and her blissful way.
>
> Thus I said, and mournful sigh'd
> As I curs'd beguiling sin;
> When the gentle lady cried,
> *"Come and treat us with some gin!"*
>
> (lines 1–8)[57]

There is, of course, little to suggest indelicacy here, but Hunt, perhaps fearing his readers might have felt otherwise, affixed a note of explanation to the poem: "This is a species of writing imitated from the Italian, the last line of which is made to differ from the foregoing, and produce some ludicrous point from a seemingly grave subject."

Alma Mater Poems

The strategies at work in Hunt's various attempts to write from a mature perspective, and Byron's attempts, *contra* Hunt, to write from the perspective of a rebellious, disaffected youth, naturally pervade the poems concerned with their childhood experiences at school. Both poets drew upon Thomas Gray's well-known *alma mater* poem, "Ode on a Distant Prospect of Eton College," for their own school-themed juvenile poems. In *Juvenilia*, Hunt looked to Gray's "Ode" as a model for "Christ's Hospital" and Byron, in *Hours of Idleness*, did the same for a series of poems that included "On a Distant View of the Village and School, of Harrow, on the Hill," "Granta, A Medley," and "Childish Recollections." For Gray, Eton is a place "where ignorance is bliss" (line 99) and the painful knowledge of the adult world is kept at bay.[58] That adult world, however, persistently invades the pastoral spaces of Gray's Eton, which can protect its young and unsuspecting scholars for only a short period. Gray's rueful message in the "Ode" is stated succinctly in the poem's concluding line: "'Tis folly to be wise" (line 100).

Hunt found Christ's Hospital, the distinguished London charity school he attended from 1791 to 1799, to be a "Sweet spot of innocence and joy" (line 45), but he refused to acknowledge the adult world beyond as the cold place it became for Gray.[59] For Hunt, Christ's Hospital had the power to shape and prepare its students for the challenges of adult life through the useful dissemination of knowledge that Gray mocks as "folly." In this way, Hunt's experience at Christ's Hospital was not an escape from adult concerns but rather a necessary step toward maturation and initiation into the adult world. Just as Byron would mythologize Newstead Abbey as a site of personal and historical importance in *Hours of Idleness*, Hunt idealizes Christ's Hospital as a site with a long and important cultural legacy:

> For she, long time, has lov'd the vaulted arch,
> The gothic window, and the ruin'd pile
> Antique; there, favour'd, has her quiet haunt
> Stood undisturb'd, save by the youthful bards
> That with such praise maintain the Grecian name.

(lines 83–7)

Hunt's "youthful bards" are the school's most distinguished literary graduates: "Could she not sing, beneath whose skilful hand / Bold Dyer and the plaintive Coleridge grew, / Children of poesy?" (lines 91–3). To these distinguished literary contemporaries, Hunt adds other successful graduates, including Britons involved in the continental wars: "the sons of courage, / Of this fam'd school, who early learnt to glow, / With patriot zeal" (lines 110–2). In addition, the speaker praises graduates involved in "Industry, sweet Commerce" (line 141) who gave themselves to careers of trade, vowing to "forsake / Their native home, to seek thy lively form / In distant climates" (lines 145–7). The school's long and distinguished record, in Hunt's estimation, rests firmly upon the example of its graduates who have made the successful transition from the youthful world of Christ's Hospital to the adult world of responsibility. It is with this knowledge that Hunt's speaker can bid farewell to his *alma mater* without regret: "Farewel, ye happy seats of peace and joy" (line 195).

Byron may have remembered Hunt's "Christ's Hospital" when he came to write "Granta, A Medley," one of several poetic tributes to Cambridge in *Hours of Idleness*. In "Granta," Byron's speaker echoes the conclusion to Hunt's poem only to undercut its hopeful message:

> Therefore, farewell, old Granta's spires,
>   No more, like Cleofas, I fly,
> No more thy theme my muse inspires,
>   The reader's tir'd and so am I.
>
> (lines 96–100)

Byron's poem is guided throughout by the disruptive voice of this concluding line. In the poem's eighth and ninth stanzas, for instance, the speaker mocks the student who competes for "college prizes" (line 30) and "Goes late to bed, yet early rises" (line 32):

> He surely well deserves to gain them,
>   With all the honours of his college,
> Who, striving hardly to obtain them,
>   Thus seeks unprofitable knowledge.
>
> (lines 33–6)

In the end, Byron's message is the message of Gray's "Ode" and not that of Hunt's "Christ's Hospital." A similar mocking sentiment pervades Byron's "Thoughts Suggested by a College Examination," another poem about Cambridge whose speaker is relentless in assaulting the "youth, whose scientific pate, / Class honours, medals, fellowships, await" (lines 23–4), who "do not try, by speaking, to convince" (line 32), but rather "to please ourselves" (line 34). The charge of self-interest is one to which Byron frequently recurs in *Hours of Idleness* in order to make his case for casting aside the illusory ideals of youthful romance, friendship, and, in this instance, the pursuit of knowledge. For Byron, the graduates of Cambridge, unlike those who depart and practice useful "modern arts" (line 56), like the graduates of Hunt's "Christ's Hospital," become time-servers, "men" who wear "suppliant smiles" (line 65) to "court the lord of power, / Whether 'tis Pitt or P[e]tty rules the hour" (lines 63–4). The boyish mockery that undergirds Byron's juvenile poems about Cambridge is, however, less apparent in the poems of friendship inspired by his earlier experiences at Harrow.

In his *Autobiography*, Hunt spoke at length of the friendships he formed during his time at Christ's Hospital in "spiritual" terms: "If I had reaped no other benefit from Christ Hospital, the school would be ever dear to me from the recollection of the friendships I formed in it, and of the first heavenly taste it gave me of that most spiritual of the affections," adding that "if ever I tasted a disembodied transport on earth, it was in those friendships which I entertained at school, before I dreamt of any maturer feeling" (*A* 1:143–4). Byron, likewise, in "Childish Recollections" emphasized the spiritual quality in the relationships he had formed at Harrow where "Friendship made [him] blest" (line 56), defining the ideal of friendship as "the dear peculiar bond of youth" (line 57). Elsewhere, the speaker acknowledges that a "stronger impulse vibrates here, / Which whispers, friendship" (lines 213–4), concluding: "Those hearts, dear Ida, have I found in thee, / A home, a world, a paradise to me" (lines 217–8). Some of the strongest attachments Byron and Hunt formed at school resulted from the institutionalized injustices they had witnessed and, in some cases, experienced. For Hunt, friendships at Christ's Hospital often developed out of tense situations, with Hunt finding himself having to protect younger students from the abuses of older boys. Hunt claimed he was an "ultra-sympathizing and timid boy" initially and that the "sight of boys fighting, from which I had been so anxiously withheld, frightened me as something devilish; and the least threat of corporeal chastisement to a schoolfellow . . . affected me to tears" (*A* 1:89). As he advanced to the school's upper forms, however, Hunt said that he gained the "reputation of a romantic enthusiast, whose daring in behalf of a friend or a good cause nothing could put down" (*A* 1:91).[60] Byron earned a similar reputation at Harrow for defending junior classmates from abusive practices, such as fagging, that were routinely inflicted on younger boys by senior students. In his *Letters and Journals of Lord Byron, with Notices of His Life*, Moore recorded an anecdote about Byron defending Harrow classmate George Peel, who had been subjected to an inordinate amount of physical lashings from an older boy. Moore claims that "Byron saw and felt for the misery of his friend" and "advanced to the scene of action" where he proposed that he "would take half" of the lashes.[61] Another early attachment was William Harness, a boy four years Byron's junior. Harness, like Byron, was lame, and Byron "one day, seeing him bullied by a boy much older and stronger than himself, interfered and took his part." The next day

Byron told Harness: "if any one bullies you, tell me, and I'll thrash him, if I can."[62] Byron's actions solidified the friendship, and years later Byron confessed to Harness: "the *first lines* I ever attempted at Harrow were addressed to *you*."[63] More than mere sentimental attachments, the friendships Byron experienced at Harrow, like those Hunt experienced at Christ's Hospital, could be complex, multifaceted experiences.

Classical Sensibility: Virgil and Male Friendship

The most ambitious poems of friendship that Byron and Hunt produced as adolescent authors were inspired by classical models. The classical philosophers of friendship, Plato and Cicero, seem to have been less of an influence on young Byron and Hunt than the classical poets of friendship: Homer and Virgil. In his ode "To Friendship," for instance, Hunt traced the poem's theme specifically to the *Iliad* and the *Aeneid*:

> By all the griefs that rent the vengeful breast
> Of dread Achilles, when the Trojan arm
>> Stretch'd on the clanging earth
>> His bold, his patriot friend;
>
> By all the fire that flash'd from Nisus' eye,
> When the lov'd warrior lay convuls'd in death,
>> His tresses rudely tost
>> On his cold, pallid cheek.
>>> (lines 25–32)[64]

Hunt knew that the intimate friendship of Achilles and Patroclus, his "patriot friend," had initiated a literary tradition of idealized male bonding, but Hunt later recalled that of his required reading at Christ's Hospital the "only classic I remember having any love for was Virgil; and that was for the episode of Nisus and Euryalus" (*A* 1:131). The story of Nisus and Euryalus from the ninth book of the *Aeneid* also had special appeal for Byron, who may have first translated a section of the episode as a school exercise (a short sixteen-line translation appeared in Byron's second privately published volume, *Poems on Various Occasions*).[65] Significantly, however, Byron returned to the translation and enlarged it to include the episode in its entirety, transforming the poem into an impressive 406 lines for *Hours of Idleness*. Not surprisingly, he seems to have taken some pains in the effort. The heavily revised draft, with many textual differences from the final published version, suggests that Byron struggled with translating words such as "love," "affection," and "friendship" as he pondered how to represent the passionate relationship between Nisus and Euryalus for a conservative public audience. The version Byron printed in *Hours of Idleness* adopts, quite provocatively, the phrasings that emphasize romantic feeling and passionate sensibility.[66]

The manuscript thus provides evidence that Byron deliberately and knowingly transformed his translation into something more compelling than a school exercise or a classical "commonplace."[67] As Louis Crompton points out, the classical translations that were marketed for a growing English readership in the late decades of the eighteenth century had taken the opposite tack. Floyer Sydenham, in his translation of Plato's *Symposium*, for example, "took drastic measures to assure that the reader who knew no Greek would not guess at the nature of the love celebrated in the panegyrics of Phaedrus and Pausanias." Crompton further observes that "Achilles, in Sydenham's version, becomes not the lover of Patroclus, but his 'admirer.'"[68]

Byron's translation of Virgil's "Episode of Nisus and Euryalus" appears to have been the juvenile production that he felt was his most important early poetic achievement. Writing to Edward Noel Long on 16 April 1807, Byron proudly explained that he had written a "complete Episode of Nisus & Euryalus" (*BLJ* 1:115). In another letter, Byron declared that the translation was "in [his] opinion the best in point of Versification I have ever written" (*BLJ* 1:118). Byron's evident pride in the accomplishment doubtless derived, in part, from the scope of the effort itself. "The Episode of Nisus and Euryalus" was the longest poem Byron included in *Hours of Idleness* next to "Childish Recollections." Byron clearly found the subject compelling, for he produced a companion piece for the "Nisus and Euryalus" translation in the form of an Ossianic prose retelling of the same story, giving it the title: "The Death of Calmar and Orla." At the same time, Byron was well aware of the controversial sensibility he was promoting with both productions, for he made a point of downplaying classical stories that had idealized male friendship in a note to the cynical "To Romance." Byron's note to line 20, "A Pylades in every friend," is telling:

> It is hardly necessary to add, that Pylades was the companion of Orestes, and a partner in one of those friendships, which with those of Achilles and Patroclus, Nisus and Euryalus, Damon and Pythias, have been handed down to posterity, as remarkable instances of attachments, which in all probability never existed, beyond the imagination of the Poet, the page of an historian, or modern novelist.
>
> (*CPW* 1:373)

For all of his apparent indifference to a tradition of fictionalized male love and friendship, Byron certainly displays a thorough knowledge of the subject. And his public note, of course, contrasts sharply with his private statements to Edward Noel Long about the "Nisus and Euryalus" translation. As such, Byron's note was doubtless an attempt to deflect attention from controversial subject matter that dealt with the theme of same-sex desire in *Hours of Idleness*. However, the self-consciousness of the note seems only to reaffirm the importance of the subject which it seeks to disavow.

In *Juvenilia*, Hunt's poems of male friendship are, on the whole, less ambitious and much more impersonal than those in Byron's *Hours of Idleness* and *Poems, Original and Translated*. The closest Hunt may come to treating the theme with any degree of personal or artistic complexity is, appropriately enough, in a classically inspired poem: an imitation of Virgil's second eclogue. Eva Cantarella observes that early readers of Virgil's second eclogue interpreted the poem autobiographically as a meditation on the passion Virgil (Corydon) felt for a young servant named Alexander (Alexis).[69] Translations of the eclogues available at the beginning of the nineteenth century ignored such potentially troubling biography. Francis Wrangham's annotations included with his translation of the eclogues, for instance, suggested the futility of such biographical reading by dismissively pointing out that the "commentators Servius, Vives, La Cerda, De la Rue, &c., &c. are, as usual divided about the persons supposed to be represented" in the poems.[70] Virgilian biography, however, would have probably mattered less to a teenage Byron and Hunt than Virgilian poetry that had applicability to their own interests and experiences at school. Both clearly found Virgil's treatment of male love and friendship attractive. Ellen Oliensis, in fact, argues that Virgil's language in the second eclogue is suggestive of a "kind of pastoral sexuality—aberrant, unproductive, non-purposive, playful, pre- or extra-marital."[71] Cantarella makes an even stronger case for the message of the second eclogue: the poem transformed physical attraction "into an ethics of love which allowed total freedom in the selection of a love object."[72]

In line with *Juvenilia*'s conventional approach, Hunt chose not to emphasize the provocative Virgilian subtexts in his version of the second eclogue. Hunt's eclogue, titled "Pastoral II," is, however, significant for being one of the few offerings in *Juvenilia* formally addressed to a friend: "Master F. H. Papendieck."[73] Hunt's "Pastoral II" is also one of the more challenging friendship poems in the volume not only for its willingness to engage with a classical tradition of male friendship poetry, but also for the way it pays homage to the tradition of the Virgilian pastoral in English. Hunt must have taken great care in the poem's composition, for in an early letter to the publishers at the *Monthly Preceptor*, the young Hunt reveals a sophisticated understanding of poetical imitation, admitting that "when we attempt a close and literal translation of the poet [Horace, in this case], it is impossible to preserve the poetical and harmonious beauties of the original." Hunt's corollary to this is to allow for a certain creative "freedom" in composition.[74] In "Pastoral II," Hunt indeed took creative liberties with the story of Alexis and Corydon from Virgil's second eclogue. Yet Hunt's changes suggest not a bold attempt at originality but an informed understanding of the pastoral tradition as it had been imitated by Spenser and Pope. Spenser's imitation of Virgil's second eclogue appeared first in order as "Januarye" in the *Shepheardes Calender*. Like Hunt, Spenser had taken liberties with his classical model, substituting the passionate homoeroticism implicit in Corydon's love for Alexis with that of Colin, a "shepheardes boy" and his love for the "countrie lasse called Rosalinde."[75] As Spenser explained in his "Epistle" to the *Shepheardes Calender*, Colin "had long wandred in the common Labyrinth of Love, in which time to mitigate and allay the heate of his passion, or els to warne (as he sayth) the young shepheards . . . of his unfortunate folly."[76] Pope also followed Spenser, retaining Virgil's Alexis character but developing the story through his affection for "Rosalinda." Hunt's imitation follows Pope in presenting something of a hybrid of Virgil's original and Spenser's imitation by adding an explicit biographical element: the voice of young Hunt in *propria persona*:

> Fred'rick, attend; hear one sad lay complain,
> That to our friendship adds this length'ning chain;
> How swains, tho' faithful as thyself, have mourn'd
> Affection scorn'd, or friendship unreturn'd.
> Hear all the griefs, and all the ills of love;
> For thou can'st pity, and may chance approve.
>
> (lines 11–6)[77]

Although Hunt's engagement with the classical tradition of male friendship poetry in *Juvenilia* was filtered through Virgil's conservative English imitators, the autobiographical dimension of "Pastoral II" surely would have had appeal for Byron. As we have seen, the author of *Hours of Idleness* found personal biography to be an attractive source for his juvenile friendship poems, many of which were explicitly addressed to intimate acquaintances: the Duke of Dorset, the Earl of Clare, the Earl of Delawarr, and Edward Noel Long.

In 1801, the effective marketing of Hunt's *Juvenilia*, combined with the young author's deliberate attempt to develop a mature voice that endorsed a life of contentment over childish pleasure, helped establish his maiden volume as a popular model of adolescent verse. Byron, although aware of the conventions required of young authors after reading Hunt's *Juvenilia*, Dacre's *Hours of Solitude*, White's *Clifton Grove*, and perhaps other adolescent volumes, decided to challenge many of these conventions in *Hours of Idleness* with a grandiose preface, a provocative title, and a selection of decidedly "boyish" poems. The volume's public reception, nevertheless, forced the young Byron to reassert himself firmly within the conventional bounds of juvenile authorship in *Poems, Original and Translated*. By the end of the first decade of the nineteenth century, however, Byron and Hunt were no longer the juvenile poets they had, in their divergent ways, attempted to style themselves. Byron transformed himself into a powerful critic of his contemporaries when he adopted a serious poetical genre (neoclassical satire) for *English Bards and Scotch Reviewers*. Hunt, meanwhile, transitioned into a career in journalism as a cultural and theatrical critic—a decision that would soon bring Regency authorship and politics into sharp focus. Hunt would eventually make his return to poetry with *The Feast of the Poets*, a formal satire on the contemporary literary scene that had clear resonance with Byron's popular *English Bards and Scotch Reviewers*.

Notes

1 Laurie Langbauer, *The Juvenile Tradition: Young Writers and Prolepsis, 1750–1835* (Oxford: Oxford University Press, 2016), 129–32.
2 Nicholas Roe, *Fiery Heart: The First Life of Leigh Hunt* (London: Pimlico, 2003), 46–58; Jane Stabler, "Second-generation Romantic Poetry I: Hunt, Byron, Moore," in *The Cambridge History of English Poetry*, ed. Michael O'Neill (Cambridge: Cambridge University Press, 2010): 488–90. Jerome J. McGann, *Fiery Dust: Byron's Poetic Development* (Chicago, IL: University of Chicago Press, 1968), 3–28.
3 McGann, *Fiery Dust*, 5–8. On Byron's "overnight" fame, see Nicholas Mason, *Literary Advertising and the Shaping of British Romanticism* (Baltimore, MD: Johns Hopkins University Press, 2013), 73–80.
4 McGann, *Fiery Dust*, 5.
5 Langbauer, *The Juvenile Tradition*, 52.
6 McGann, *Fiery Dust*, 4.
7 Caroline Franklin, *Byron: A Literary Life* (New York: Palgrave Macmillan, 2000), 19–20.
8 See Hunt's "Sketches of the Living Poets. No. 2.—Lord Byron," E 708, July 29, 1821, 472.
9 Daniel Cook, *Thomas Chatterton and Neglected Genius, 1760–1830* (New York: Palgrave Macmillan, 2013), 160–96.
10 Cook, *Thomas Chatterton*, 169. According to Cook, "Coleridge had failed to monumentalize Chatterton in his anxious monody, and Wordsworth had in verse glibly, though cannily, encapsulated a broad cultural unease with Chattertonian hubris" (194).
11 *The Bury and Norwich Post*, December 5, 1804.
12 William Hazlitt, *The Complete Works of William Hazlitt*, ed. P. P. Howe, 21 vols. (London: J. M. Dent & Sons, Ltd., 1930–4), 8:294.
13 Paul Elledge, *Lord Byron at Harrow School: Speaking Out, Talking Back, Acting Up, Bowing Out* (Baltimore, MD: Johns Hopkins University Press, 2000), 89.
14 Langbauer, *The Juvenile Tradition*, 153. Hunt's early theatrical criticisms appeared in the London-based *News* beginning in May of 1805. See Lois Landré, *Leigh Hunt: Contribution a l'histoire du Romantisme Anglais*. 2 vols. (Paris: Societie D'Edition, 1936), 2:485.
15 "Memoir of Mr. James Henry Leigh Hunt. Written by Himself," *The Monthly Mirror*, April, 1810, 245.
16 David Duff, "The Casket of My Unknown Mind: The 1813 Volume of Minor Poems," in *The Unfamiliar Shelley*, eds. Alan M. Weinberg and Timothy Webb (Farnham: Ashgate Publishing, 2009), 53, 54.
17 Roe, *Fiery Heart*, 52.

18 Roe, *Fiery Heart*, 54.
19 Marvin Spevack, ed., *Isaac D'Israeli on Books: Pre-Victorian Essays on the History of Literature* (London: British Library and Oak Knoll Press, 2004), 76.
20 Robert Southey, ed., *The Remains of Henry Kirke White*, 2 vols. (London: Vernor, Hood, and Sharpe, 1808), 1:15.
21 Roe, *Fiery Heart*, 18–9, 55.
22 Roe, *Fiery Heart*, 49–51. *The Monthly Preceptor* was launched in July of 1800.
23 McGann, *Fiery Dust*, 8. See also Jeffery W. Vail, *The Literary Relationship of Lord Byron & Thomas Moore* (Baltimore, MD: Johns Hopkins University Press, 2001), 14–40.
24 McGann, *Fiery Dust*, 21.
25 *The Monthly Mirror*, July, 1801, 39.
26 Langbauer, *The Juvenile Tradition*, 57–60.
27 Qtd. in *The Works of Lord Byron: Letters and Journals*, ed. Rowland E. Prothero, 6 vols. (London: John Murray, 1898), 1:108.
28 Byron played lead roles in at least two productions: Penruddock in Cumberland's *The Wheel of Fortune* and Tristram Fickle in Allingham's *The Weathercock*.
29 Peter Cochran, "Byron Tests the Freedom of Southwell," in *Liberty and Poetic License: New Essays on Byron*, eds. Bernard Beatty, Tony Howe, and Charles E. Robinson (Liverpool: Liverpool University Press, 2008), 10–1.
30 For a recent discussion of these poems, see Andrew Stauffer, "Byron's Lyrics and the Politics of Publication," in *Byron: The Poetry of Politics and the Politics of Poetry*, eds. Roderick Beaton and Christine Kenyon Jones (New York: Routledge, 2017), 31.
31 Louis Crompton, *Byron and Greek Love: Homophobia in 19th-Century England* (Berkeley: University of California Press, 1985), 99–100.
32 Willis W. Pratt, *Byron at Southwell: The Making of a Poet* (Austin: University of Texas, 1948), 36–9.
33 Leigh Hunt, *Juvenilia; or, A Collection of Poems.* 3rd ed. London: J. Whiting, 1802.
34 Charlotte Dacre, *Hours of Solitude.* Romantic Context: Poetry, ed. Donald H. Reiman (New York: Garland Publishing Inc., 1978).
35 Henry Kirke White, *Clifton Grove, a Sketch in Verse with Other Poems* (London: Vernor and Hood, 1803), vii.
36 Spevack, *Isaac D'Israeli on Books*, 81.
37 Richard D. McGhee, *Henry Kirke White* (Boston: Twayne Publishers, 1981), 48–9.
38 *CMP* 231, 243. These volumes appear in the 1816 "Sale Catalogue" of Byron's library as numbers 3 and 324.
39 White, *The Remains*, 1:18.
40 Pratt, *Byron at Southwell*, 72.
41 Pratt, *Byron at Southwell*, 72.
42 Pratt, *Byron at Southwell*, 76.
43 This subtitle appears in the first and second editions of *Juvenilia*.
44 Derek Roper, *Reviewing Before the Edinburgh: 1788–1802* (Newark, DE: University of Delaware Press, 1978), 46.
45 William Christie, *The Edinburgh Review in the Literary Culture of Romantic Britain: Mammoth and Megalonyx* (London: Pickering & Chatto, 2009), 23.
46 Roper, *Reviewing*, 45.
47 Byron erroneously believed that Francis Jeffrey had written the review of *Hours of Idleness*.

48 Mason, *Literary Advertising*, 68.
49 Cook, *Thomas Chatterton*, 171.
50 The text of "Retirement" is taken from *Juvenilia*, 30–6.
51 The text of "A Morning Walk and View" is taken from *Juvenilia*, 9–14.
52 The text of "The Palace of Pleasure" is taken from *Juvenilia*, 151–211.
53 Langbauer, *The Juvenile Tradition*, 52.
54 *The Complete Works of Lord Byron* (Brussels: Librairie Lecharlier, 1830), x.
55 William Wordsworth, "Preface" to *Lyrical Ballads* (1800), in *The Prose Works of William Wordsworth*, eds. W. J. B. Owen and Jane Worthington Smyser, 3 vols. (Oxford: Oxford University Press, 1974), 1:138.
56 The text of "Elegy" is taken from *Juvenilia*, 93–5.
57 The text of "Parody on Dr. Johnson's 'Hermit Hoar, &c.'" is taken from *Juvenilia*, 7.
58 The text of "Ode on a Distant Prospect of Eton College" is taken from *The Complete Poems of Thomas Gray*, eds. H. W. Starr and J. R. Hendrickson (Oxford: Oxford University Press, 1966), 7–10.
59 The text of "Christ's Hospital" is taken from *Juvenilia*, 17–25.
60 Hunt may be embellishing his "romantic" reputation in this case. See Leigh Hunt, *Leigh Hunt's Autobiography: The Earliest Sketches*, ed. Stephen F. Fogle (Gainesville: University of Florida Press, 1959), 29.
61 Thomas Moore, *Letters and Journals of Lord Byron, with Notices of His Life*, 2 vols. (London: John Murray, 1830), 1:46.
62 Moore, *Letters and Journals of Lord Byron*, 1:47.
63 Moore, *Letters and Journals of Lord Byron*, 1:48.
64 The text of "To Friendship" is taken from *Juvenilia*, 116–8.
65 See *CPW* 1:370.
66 The original manuscript is in the Berg Collection, New York Public Library. See Berg Coll MSS. Byron. See also the collations in *CPW* 1:78 (line 72), 81 (line 165), 89 (line 397).
67 On Byron and the "commonplace," see Hazlitt, *The Complete Works*, 11:76.
68 Crompton, *Byron and Greek Love*, 89.
69 Eva Cantarella, *Bisexuality in the Ancient World*, trans. Cormac Ó Cuilleanáin (New Haven, CT: Yale University Press, 2002), 141.
70 *Virgil*, trans. Francis Wrangham et al., 2 vols. (London: Henry Colburn and Richard Bentley, 1830), 1:37.
71 Ellen Oliensis, "Sons and Lovers: Sexuality and Gender in Virgil's Poetry," in *The Cambridge Companion to Virgil*, ed. Charles Martindale (Cambridge: Cambridge University Press, 1997), 300.
72 Cantarella, *Bisexuality*, 141.
73 See *A* 1:145–6.
74 Qtd. in Roe, *Fiery Heart*, 51.
75 Edmund Spenser, "Januarye," in *The Yale Edition of the Shorter Poems of Edmund Spenser*, eds. William A. Oram et al. (New Haven, CT: Yale University Press, 1989), 29.
76 "Epistle," in *The Yale Edition of the Shorter Poems of Edmund Spenser*, 19.
77 The text of "Pastoral II" is taken from *Juvenilia*, 73–8.

2 Early Satire

English Bards and Scotch Reviewers and *The Feast of the Poets*

Despite the popular success of *Juvenilia*, it would be more than a decade before Hunt issued another volume of poetry. With the help of his well-connected father, the celebrated juvenile author took up employment in Henry Addington's War Office. The work must have seemed appropriate at the time for a writer becoming increasingly interested in public affairs. A temporary break from hostilities with France, the Peace of Amiens (1802–3), had come to an end, and the threat of a Napoleonic invasion had once again become an everyday reality. Hunt had already joined a volunteer regiment in preparation for such an event. And it was through this "unlikely route," as Anthony Holden says, that Hunt first made the acquaintance of London-based actors who inspired him to take the next step in furthering his literary career.[1] Hunt immersed himself in the theater and soon began writing reviews for his older brother John, a publisher who had been issuing a weekly paper called *The News*. Hunt quickly transitioned from part-time critic at *The News* to his role as full-time editor of John Hunt's longest and most successful publishing venture: the reform-driven *Examiner*. By the time *The Examiner* appeared in January of 1808, Hunt had also taken a decisive position with respect to his role as a critic. As he explained it in his farewell message to readers of *The News*: "if I have done nothing else, I have certainly proved what was very generally thought impossible,—that a newspaper critic may be impartial" (*SWLH* 1:22).

The "impartial" criticism that Hunt practiced during his early years as a working journalist has important implications for understanding his friendship and literary relations with Byron. A year before he made Byron's acquaintance, and several years before *The Story of Rimini* became a public scandal, Hunt had already defined the terms of literary engagement through which he would approach Byron and his poetry. Hunt provided an outline of these terms in a review of Byron's "Address, Spoken at the Opening of Drury-lane Theatre" in *The Examiner* for 18 October 1812, a review that Byron had access to and most likely read.[2] At the same time, Hunt repeated and enlarged this criticism in his earliest attempt at original verse satire, *The Feast of the Poets* (hereafter *Feast*), a playful but biting survey of popular Regency poets and critics.[3]

Hunt had composed the first version of his satire for inclusion in *The Reflector* in 1811, the same year Byron's fourth (and last) edition of his own satire on the contemporary literary scene, *English Bards and Scotch Reviewers* (hereafter *English Bards*), appeared.[4] With this context in mind, Clarence DeWitt Thorpe's suggestion that Hunt, with *Feast*, was writing "much under the influence of Byron" is apt and deserves further consideration.[5]

In addition to many thematic similarities between the two satires, as well as many interesting stylistic differences, there is much evidence showing that the poems had served as the basis for an extended literary dialogue between the two friends; this dialogue has been preserved in the correspondence and in the poetry itself. The evidence reveals that Byron and Hunt not only exchanged physical copies of their maiden satires but also intensely debated their contents, disagreeing over the direction British poetry had taken in 1814 and 1815, a period when renewed public interest in Wordsworth had followed a trio of publications: *The Excursion*, *The White Doe of Rylstone*, and the two-volume *Poems*, with its important "Essay, Supplementary to the Preface." Amidst this temporary resurgence of Wordsworthian celebrity, Byron found Hunt's decision to champion the elder Lake Poet in his expanded editions of *Feast* (1814–15) to be especially troubling. Their arguments about Wordsworth deserve more attention than they have received, for their substance would have a significant impact on the literary relationship, guiding Byron's reception of Hunt as a critic and a poet while directing his own thoughts (and writings) on the state of British literature during his years in exile.

Byron's Drury Lane "Address"

In 1811, Byron was still a year away from discovering fame as the author of *Childe Harold*, but he had already become one of the most popular Regency satirists. *English Bards* had just gone into a fourth edition, with combined sales of the published editions totaling at least 4,000 copies.[6] Byron later told Thomas Medwin that his satire had made a "prodigious sensation" when it appeared in 1809, an idea echoed by Byron's distant relative and early literary advisor Robert Charles Dallas, who thought *English Bards* even "rival[ed] the Baviad and Mæviad."[7] Of the subsequent editions, Byron's mother wrote to him in May of 1810 with more than a little maternal exaggeration: the "universal opinion is that since the days of Pope nothing has equaled [*English Bards*]."[8] Byron took the praise approvingly at first but soon grew skeptical: "My Satire it seems is in a fourth edition, a success rather above the middling run, but not much for a production which, from its topics, must be temporary, and of course be successful at first, or not at all" (*BLJ* 2:53). Upon his return to England, following his tour of the Eastern Mediterranean, Byron also became friendly with several of the poets and personages he had attacked in the poem, including Thomas Moore and Lord Holland, and plans for another edition were naturally abandoned. Nevertheless, by the time Hunt came to write his own satire on the contemporary literary scene in *Feast*, Byron's *English Bards* had become one of the most sensational, if not the most popular, verse satires of the day.

Hunt's early awareness of *English Bards* can be established from a note in the fourth issue of *The Reflector*. In the facetious "Project for Making Beaux and Belles Useful," Thomas Barnes, one of Hunt's Christ's Hospital classmates and the future editor of *The Times*, drew attention to Byron's *Hours of Idleness* and offered approving comments on *English Bards*: Byron's "first offering to the public [*Hours of Idleness*] will indeed do no credit to his name; but his 'English Bards and Scottish Reviewers,' [sic] though full of faults, shows a spirit and taste and manliness of thinking, which if well directed may be of service to mankind."[9] As editor of *The Reflector*, Hunt would have read Barnes's article and note on Byron (doubtless with approval), and there is a strong possibility that Byron's poetry had been a topic of private discussion between Hunt and Barnes, just as it would be, a year later, between Hunt and Thomas Mitchell, another Christ's Hospital classmate and *Reflector* contributor. Firm evidence of Hunt's reading of *English Bards* can be found in *The Examiner* for 18 October 1812—published just seven months after *Feast* made its appearance in *The Reflector* alongside Barnes's article.[10] Hunt's "Theatrical Examiner" in the 18 October *Examiner* is a formal review of Byron's "Address, Spoken at the Opening of Drury-lane Theatre, Saturday, October 10th, 1812," an occasional poem written at the request of Lord Holland and first published in the *Morning Chronicle* on 12 October. The majority of Hunt's review, however, is devoted to Byron's two earlier and more substantial poems: *English Bards* and *Childe Harold*.

Although Byron's "Address" had been "coldly received by the public," according to Hunt, the editor was surprised to see a composition "so good" for the occasion (*SWLH* 1:259). Nevertheless, Hunt also stated that he could not "consider it as a very favourable specimen of [Byron's] powers," adding

> His Lordship, we believe, first became known to the public by his ridicule of certain puerile eccentricities, that have latterly degraded our poets, under pretence of restoring it to a native simplicity; and if the poem [*Childe Harold*] which he published the other day was not without eccentricities of its own, and did not altogether come up to the expectations which his detection of the faults of other people had led us to entertain, yet there was a tone about it of thinking for himself both in sentiment and language, and a certain disdain, amounting perhaps to impatience, of appealing to his readers on

any other grounds than those of his own observation founded on a strong natural good sense, which should authorize us at least to expect his undeviating dislike of common-place,—of such lines, in short, as form the greater part of the Address before us.

(SWLH 1:259–60)

Even though *Childe Harold* demonstrated originality and creative strength, Hunt perceived that it still fell short of "expectations" with respect to the strictures Byron had laid out in *English Bards*. Hunt clearly admired Byron's satire, with its interesting mixture of Horatian and Juvenalian elements, and found Byron's "ridicule of certain puerile eccentricities"—his mockery of the Lake Poets—especially noteworthy. Hunt repeated his approval of Byron's maiden satire a decade later, acknowledging that even though the author, as Hunt would learn, had come to "regret" the publication of *English Bards*, it had been written with "feelings of [Byron's] own, [and] it gave a sample of what he was likely to attain to" (*SWLH* 2:344–5). Hunt would, likewise, come to regret publishing *Feast*, but in 1812 the editor of *The Examiner* may have been one of the few critics to resist the "Byromania" that followed the publication of *Childe Harold* by redirecting readers to Byron's early satire and critical attitudes—attitudes that matched Hunt's own developing views on the state of contemporary British poetry.[11]

Elsewhere in his review of Byron's "Address," however, Hunt raised a significant point of disagreement with the poet over the stylistic merits of Pope:

[W]e suspect that Lord Byron did not write this Address con amore . . . he is at all times too much inclined to let his ear and his memory take the place of poetical industry; we do not mean, of industry as opposed to mere indolence, or to a want of poetical ardour and a fondness for writing, but of industry as opposed to a want of regular study and of a systematic search for original excellence. It is owing to want of this study, which such men as MILTON and DRYDEN thought themselves obliged to use before they mastered the niceties of expression, and the capabilities of their native prosody, that our best poets, since the time of POPE, have condescended to use the monotonous flow of verse which he brought into fashion, and which every magazine Strephon can use as well.

(SWLH 1:260)

"[O]riginal excellence" is the standard by which Hunt here defines the success of Byron's published poetry. For Hunt, the mature poetry of Milton and Dryden best exemplified poetic excellence (an idea we will see echoed in *Feast*). Pope's "monotonous flow of verse," on the other hand, suggested stylistic immaturity, an immaturity into which Byron had fallen in adopting the Popeian couplet for the "Address." Hunt also knew, of course, that Byron's *English Bards* had been written in heroic couplets and that its author had called upon Pope's poetic spirit repeatedly throughout the satire. Pope's symbolic and especially his practical importance for second-generation Romanticism would become one of Hunt's chief critical concerns in the years ahead. Hunt, nevertheless, attempted to soften his censure of Byron's style by reiterating that "We like the independence of his opinions,—we like the sturdy good sense, which in spite of some things that occasionally obscure it, looks out from the general features of his poetry; there are certain passages of his more heart-felt effusions, which have even touched our sympathies to the core" (*SWLH* 1:261). The qualities of Byron's writing that most appealed to Hunt ("independence" and "sturdy good sense") were, in fact, two important qualities that the editor had cultivated as he worked to establish his own critical reputation in 1812.[12] The "heart-felt effusions" that Hunt perceived in Byron's poetry, moreover, reflected Hunt's interest in expressive, lyric poetry, which we can trace back to many of the poems in *Juvenilia*. But Hunt's "free observations" on Byron's poetry in his review of the "Address" are of critical significance, for they help clarify the poetic style that Hunt would promote in *Feast*, a satire that attempted to challenge the Byronic model popularized by *English Bards*.

Radical Satire: Sir John Suckling

The popularity of Byron's *English Bards* owed something to the generic links it shared with Popeian satire. The *Gentleman's Magazine* recognized this, remarking that the "Poem before us is unquestionably the result of an impassioned yet diligent study of the best masters, grounded on a fine taste and very happy natural endowments. It unites much of the judgment of the 'Essay on Criticism,' the playful yet poignant smile and frown of indignation and ridicule of the Dunciad, with the versification of the Epistle to Arbuthnot, and the acuteness of the 'Imitations of Horace' of the same Author" (*RR* B3:1076).[13] Hunt, by contrast, composed *Feast* with a "levity" of spirit (an "unwarrantable levity" (*A* 2:85) he later felt) in a style that deliberately opposed the Popeian and thus Byronic mode. Although Hunt's *Reflector* version of *Feast* attracted little critical notice, reviewers of the first separately published edition in 1814 were keenly aware of the challenge the satire presented to a venerated English tradition of Augustan satire. That challenge, the *Satirist* suggested, could be seen in the poem's opening lines:

> T'other day, as Apollo sat pitching his darts
> Through the clouds of November, by fits and by starts,
> He began to consider how long it had been,

Since the bards of Old England had all been rung in.
'I think,' said the God, recollecting, (and then
He fell twiddling a sunbeam as I may my pen),
I think—let me see—yes, it is, I declare,
As long ago now as that Buckingham there.

(lines 1–8)

Of these lines, the reviewer remarked: "We assure our Readers, that we have transcribed these the first eight lines of the *Poem*—*verbatim et literatim*—and that they are a fair sample of the wretched stuff which is spread into 431 lines" (*RR* C2:801). Hunt, in the space of eight lines, had given a provocative alternative to the English heroic couplet as it had been practiced and perfected, as Samuel Johnson believed, by Pope.[14] After the publication of *The Story of Rimini* in 1816, conservative reviewers would regularly describe Hunt's poetic style as "vulgar" for its unorthodox qualities: a preference for colloquial diction, enjambed lines, and irregular rhymes. However, Hunt's loose style, as Rodney Stenning Edgecombe has shown, is in many ways redolent of poetry written by English poets of the seventeenth and eighteenth centuries, including Sir John Suckling, Robert Herrick, and Thomas Gray, poets (all personal favorites of Hunt's) who had, nevertheless, been surpassed as stylists as far as critics like Johnson were concerned.[15]

Hunt's preference for a lighter satirical style during a period of momentous political and social change following the French Revolution was also strikingly at odds with the interests of his contemporaries. Jacobin sympathy, for instance, had been answered forcefully by the conservative satirists who wrote for the *Anti-Jacobin*. For conservative satirists such as William Gifford, George Canning, and John Hookham Frere, the times called for an aggressive poetical style and many, including the politically liberal Byron, looked to the anger-driven tradition of Juvenalian satire and its eighteenth-century imitators, including Pope and Johnson.[16] According to Gary Dyer, Hunt's *Feast*, on the other hand, introduced a different kind of satire in direct response to the popular trend. For Dyer, Hunt's *Feast* reworked a key element of Popeian satire, in particular, through its deliberate use of a loose and unusual "*manner*" of versification. Whereas Pope had used a loose style as a "metaphoric vehicle" for comic purposes, Hunt used the loose style to generate poetic authority. In other words, Hunt infused his satire with a kind of earnest playfulness, often adopting a well-defined persona, in order to oppose what Dyer calls "univocal" satire—satire, like that produced by Byron and Gifford, written in the manner of Pope and Juvenal.[17] In the preface to his 1802 translation of Juvenal's satires, Gifford had defined satire as a genre of "reprobation and scorn," and, taking the Roman satirist as the genre's model practitioner, the translator argued that "vice, like folly, to be restrained, must be overawed."[18] In *Feast*, however, Hunt rejected the idea that satire must "overawe" opponents with "scorn" or *indignatio*. Instead, Hunt promoted a less sublime yet decidedly serious kind of satire that he associated with Sir John Suckling, the seventeenth-century English poet and wit.[19]

Hunt maintained a lifelong interest in Suckling, the Cavalier poet who had also engaged in politics and had a military career under Charles I. Hunt always found such versatility in public characters attractive and he certainly perceived similar qualities in Byron, who would formally enter political life in 1812, the same year he published *Childe Harold*. It was Suckling's poetry that provided Hunt with his authority for using a lighter satiric style in a poem like *Feast*. Writing in *The Companion* in 1828, Hunt acknowledged that Suckling's *Session of the Poets*, Hunt's foundational model for *Feast*, "has been thought to be too careless in its versification." Hunt argued, however, that "its excess that way proves that the carelessness was intentional," concluding that Suckling "seems to have written it while he was dressing, with his stockings down at heel. Regarded in this light, the negligence becomes a beauty, and would be no easy thing to imitate."[20] Despite Johnson's judgment that Suckling "neither improved versification, nor abounded in conceits," Hunt found in Suckling an agreeable stylist who could challenge Pope's poetic and satiric authority.[21] Suckling, nevertheless, did not have major appeal when Hunt first issued *Feast* in 1812. In fact, only one edition of the poet's works appeared during the Regency period.[22] And the first "complete" edition of Suckling's poems had only recently appeared in Robert Anderson's *A Complete Edition of the Poets of Great Britain* (1792–5). By the time Hunt came to write *Feast*, he had probably read Suckling's *Session of the Poets* in Anderson's edition, which did not consider Suckling's achievement to be of much consequence: "[because] he valued himself upon nothing more than the character of a courtier, and a fine gentleman, it is no wonder that he neglected the higher excellencies of genius, and cultivated poetry merely as an amusement."[23] Anderson, like all of Suckling's eighteenth-century editors, however, agreed with Hunt that his *Session of the Poets* was "sufficient to entitle him to the honours of poetry."[24]

For Hunt, Suckling's poetry offered radical potential—something more than "amusement"—at a time when Pope was still seen as the model of poetic excellence and satiric achievement. Guided by Suckling's example, Hunt made a provocative attempt to present an alternative to Pope and perhaps even attract a new audience for Romantic satire. As Edgecombe reminds us, in *Feast*, for "Whatever variations of tone and level there are," these variations "find their sanction in the genre." Edgecombe adds that "when all is said and done, these pleasures remain incidental to the poem's interest as a document of taste, as the response of an important critic towards important contemporaries."[25] Wordsworth, in fact, read *Feast* in this way, remarking that Hunt's criticism even had the power to "affect" the "immediate sale of works." Poetical reputation was, of course, a perennial concern for Wordsworth, and it is not surprising that the elder Lake Poet concluded that "authors who are tender of their own reputation would be glad to secure Mr. Hunt's commendations."[26] Wordsworth, who would make the acquaintance of Hunt in the spring of 1815, may have perceived in Hunt a kindred poet-critic. At the same time, it would not be unreasonable to think that Hunt's *Feast*, in its own way, illustrated Wordsworth's belief that "every author, as far as he is great and at the same time *original*, has had the task of *creating* the taste by which he is to be enjoyed."[27] For Hunt, creative originality meant actively resisting the enduring influence of Pope and the increasing influence of Byron.

Early Criticism: Pope and Dryden

Hunt's argument with Pope was, by his own estimation, the most important critical argument he made during the early stages of his career as a practicing poet and a literary critic. In his *Autobiography*, Hunt confidently remarked of his poetic style that he thought it "succeeded best in catching the variety of [Dryden's] cadences; at least so far as they broke up the monotony of Pope" (*A* 2:171). Hunt's criticism of Pope's "monotony" was by no means original, but it seems to have evolved over many years of deliberate reflection on English versification and the evolution of English poetry since the time of Chaucer.

Hunt's earliest public engagement with Pope, as we have seen, was in *Juvenilia*, where he closely imitated the satirist's youthful pastorals. By 1806, Hunt's admiration for Pope had not changed, but there were hints in his critical writings to suggest he was, like Wordsworth before him, looking forward to a new era for poetry, one guided by alternative models of poetic excellence. In his "Critical Essay" on Oliver Goldsmith, published in the first volume of John Hunt's *Classic Tales* (a series of prose selections from popular English and Continental authors), Hunt offered a lengthy analysis of Goldsmith's poetry, recurring often to Pope as a literary touchstone. Taking his cue from Johnson, who claimed of Goldsmith's *Traveller* that "there had not been so fine a poem since the days of POPE," Hunt agreed, suggesting that the *Traveller* has "all the flow of thought and clear exposition of that exact poet," who still has significant relevance for contemporary poets: "no heroic versifier since the days of POPE has been unchangeably vigorous in a long rhyming poem; SOUTHEY and COWPER, the most original poets of our time, are often unpardonably feeble in this respect, the one through an affectation of simplicity, and the other, singularly enough, of dignity."[28] The implication here is that Hunt has taken originality of style as his critical yardstick for measuring literary merit, just as he would in his *Examiner* review of Byron's Drury Lane "Address." In 1806, Hunt was thus already searching for a contemporary poet—a Byron, a Shelley, or a Keats—to embrace as an emerging versifier of stylistic originality and exemplary poetical vigor to lead a new generation of Romantic authors.

It is noteworthy that throughout his essay on Goldsmith, Hunt paired Dryden and Pope together as the foremost practitioners of poetic style in English. By the time Hunt published *Feast* he had separated the two poets, trading the "monotonous" versification of Pope for the "nobler versification" of Dryden (*A* 1:273). At some point after his essay on Goldsmith appeared, Hunt began to promote Dryden's poetry with purpose. Hunt gave an early indication of this new critical perspective in the first issue of *The Reflector* in 1811. In "Atys the Enthusiast; A Dithyrambic Poem translated from Catullus, with Prefatory Remarks," Hunt offered strong hints about the style that would come to define his own poetry for Regency readers. Hunt began the "Prefatory Remarks" by commenting upon the controversial subject matter of Catullus's poem: a young Greek's rash decision to undergo ritual castration (an action he subsequently regrets) in order to serve the goddess Cybele. Hunt, however, found the Roman poet's handling of the subject to be delicate and exemplary, stating that it was composed "in a manner that might have made Pope himself blush for some parts of his *Eloisa*." Hunt's style in the "Atys" translation was one that blended both English and Continental influences but looked back specifically to the poetry of Dryden. Hunt indeed justified what he called the "irregular" style of his translation by reminding readers that poetic

> irregularity, allowed by modern poetry . . . naturally surpasses all regular metre in *variety* of expression, and has been reckoned by the best writers the most suitable vehicle for the changeful temper of enthusiasm, as may be seen in the two most enthusiastic poems of modern times,—the *Alexander's Feast* of Dryden, and Redi's singular dithyrambic of *Bacco in Toscana*.

Hunt would later translate Francesco Redi in 1825, not long after his collaboration with Byron on *The Liberal* came to an end, but the crucial point here for understanding Hunt's early thoughts on his own poetic style is the idea of poetic "irregularity" as a valid stylistic approach. Dryden's *Alexander's Feast, or the Power of Music,* an experimental ode that dramatizes the interplay of music and poetics, provided Hunt with sound justification for his metrical experimentation in "Atys."[29] Justifying what he feared might be considered a kind of "carelessness" in the style of his translation, Hunt reiterated that "our versification would perhaps be rather improved than injured by looking back to the style of Dryden, particularly with regard to long words at the *end* of a couplet, and the flow of one couplet into another." These features, as we have seen, were two of the formal features of *Feast* that would challenge the poetical sensibilities and the more exacting, polished tastes of the reviewer for the *Satirist* in 1814.[30]

Hunt found support for his observations on Dryden's style in Johnson. As Hunt remarked, he was "very fond" (*A* 1:273) of *The Lives of the Poets* and he may have had Johnson in mind as he worked out his stylistic approach for the "Atys" translation and the near-contemporaneous *Feast*. Hunt knew that Johnson, in general, had preferred Dryden's poetry to Pope's and that the esteemed critic had also described Dryden's style as the essence of variety, one of Hunt's primary stylistic concerns.[31] For Hunt, Dryden was the most important modern practitioner of the English heroic, and the *Feast* was Hunt's most ambitious early attempt to make his case for Dryden's importance. The satire indeed begins with an explicit appeal to Dryden (and Milton). Apollo, Hunt's persona in the poem, has organized a feast for worthy contemporary poets in an age that the satirist perceives to be one of poetic decline: "since Dryden's fine verses and Milton's sublime, / I have fairly been sick of their sing-song and rhyme" (lines 11–2). The reason for the decline is soon made clear:

> But ever since Pope spoil'd the ears of the town
> With his cuckoo-song verses, half up and half down,
> There has been such a doling and sameness,—by Jove,
> I'd as soon have gone down to see Kemble in love.
> However, of late as they've rous'd them anew,
> I'll e'en go and give them a lesson or two.
>
> (lines 17–22)[32]

In omitting Pope from his list of literary exemplars, Hunt has revised Byron's triumvirate of venerable English poets in *English Bards*. Like Hunt, Byron felt that poets such as Dryden and Milton had been usurped by poets like Wordsworth, Coleridge, and Scott: "These are the Bards to whom the Muse must bow: / While MILTON, DRYDEN, POPE, alike forgot, / Resign their hallow'd Bays to WALTER SCOTT" (lines 186–8). For Byron, however, Milton, Dryden, *and* Pope are all of the same caste. In fact, in the first edition of *English Bards*, Byron had foregrounded Pope as the modern English poet *par excellence*: "TIME was, ere yet in these degenerate days / . . . [when] POPE's pure strain / Sought the rapt soul to charm, nor sought in vain" (lines 1–8). In subsequent editions of *English Bards*, Byron expanded the opening section, somewhat obscuring Pope's presence at the satire's outset, but Pope's preeminence is nevertheless emphasized throughout the poem. Hunt's attempt to recast Byron's argument about Pope's importance in *Feast* thus hinges on what Upali Amarasinghe sees as the "most strikingly provocative passage" in the poem: that which explicitly calls Pope's artistic legacy into question.[33] As such, Hunt's rejection of Pope in the opening section of *Feast* appears to be a highly revealing moment of intertextual engagement with *English Bards* and a provocative challenge to Byron.

Jeffrey, Gifford, and the Burlesque

Hunt did share Byron's general attitude toward Romantic periodical culture and the politically motivated critics who had been empowered by the success of the *Edinburgh* and *Quarterly* reviews. Both authors, in fact, had directed much of the satire in *English Bards* and *Feast* at contemporary critics, a decision that highlights their personal and artistic sympathies, as well as some of the complexities that would develop between them after they became formally acquainted in 1813. Therefore, a closer look at the manner in which Byron and Hunt treated the Romantic reviewers in their early satire provides important context for a critical understanding of the friendship and literary relationship.

Believing Francis Jeffrey had written the damaging notice of *Hours of Idleness* for the *Edinburgh Review*, the Byronic speaker of *English Bards* mocks the Scottish editor for his ego-driven criticism, sarcastically declaring that, as a satirist, he will "pursue / The self-same road, but make my own review: / Not seek great JEFFREY's yet like him will be / Self-constituted Judge of Poesy" (lines 59–62). Above all, the reviewers working for Jeffrey are "usurpers on the Throne of Taste" (line 84), who "hail their voice as Truth, their word as Law" (line 86). Byron's uncompromising abuse of Jeffrey in the early sections of *English Bards* is, however, quite different in style and tone from the poem's most sustained attack on the Edinburgh reviewer: that which retraces, in mock-heroic fashion, the abortive duel between Jeffrey and Thomas Moore at Chalk Farm in 1806. Byron clearly delighted in the public sensation generated by the event, explaining in a note that "Messrs. Jeffrey and Moore met at Chalk Farm," but the "duel was prevented by the interference of the Magistracy; and, on examination, the balls of the pistols, were found to have evaporated. This incident gave occasion to much waggery in the daily prints" (*CPW* 1:407). In the poem, the well-known section begins thus:

> Health to great JEFFREY! Heaven preserve his life,
> To flourish on the fertile shores of Fife,
> And guard it sacred in his future wars,
> Since authors sometimes seek the field of Mars!

Can none remember that eventful day,
That ever glorious, almost fatal fray,
When LITTLE's leadless pistol met his eye,
And Bow-street Myrmidons stood laughing by?

(lines 460–7)

The speaker ironically underscores the magnitude of the "eventful day" by observing the "secret shock" that "Dunedin's castle felt" (line 469), adding that the "TWEED ruffled half his waves to form a tear" (line 472). The duel, however, is interrupted when "Caledonia's Goddess hovered o'er / The field, and saved [Jeffrey] from the wrath of MOORE" (lines 490–1). In a reversal of Brougham's arrogant and fallible (human) judgment of *Hours of Idleness*, Byron has the goddess deliver her judgment on Jeffrey with comic deflation, declaring that the critic shall live to become the commander of an "oat-fed phalanx" (line 508), the *Edinburgh Review* itself. Claude M. Fuess and Frederick L. Beaty, alternately, find the section on Jeffrey and Moore to be the "weakest" (Fuess) and "most successful" (Beaty) in the satire.[34] For Fuess, the section lacks the vigor of the poem's Juvenalian sections; for Beaty, the scene offers satire in a different register from that found elsewhere in *English Bards*. Both critics agree, however, that the section can be appropriately classified as an instance of the burlesque, with Byron mocking his subjects in a lighter satirical style.

Hunt, of course, writes comfortably in this lighter satirical mode in the Suckling-inspired *Feast*. And, as one of the more "light yet substantial" moments in *English Bards*, the mock-heroic duel would have had special appeal for Hunt. In a similar deployment of the burlesque in *Feast*, Hunt brings William Gifford, the powerful editor of the Tory *Quarterly Review*, and Apollo together as rivals—not in an epic confrontation on the dueling fields at Chalk Farm but in a banal chance meeting of god and mortal inside of a London tavern. Hunt introduces Gifford as a "sour little gentleman" (line 135) whom Apollo fails to recognize when he first arrives at a feast that has been reserved for poets. Crucially, Hunt achieves his satiric effect here and throughout *Feast* by inverting the "univocal" tactic that Dyer has identified as the style in which Gifford, in the *Baviad* and *Mæviad*, and Byron, in many sections of *English Bards*, deliver their more uncompromising brand of satire. Instead of assailing his opponent from the point of view of a satirical speaker, for instance, Hunt has Gifford satirize himself when Gifford's character addresses Apollo

"And [says], I'm surpris'd that you'll visit this town:—
To be sure, there are one or two of us who know you,
But as for the rest, they are all much below you:
So stupid, in gen'ral, the natives are grown,

They really prefer Scotch reviews to their own;
So that what with their taste, their reformers, and stuff,
They have sicken'd myself and my friends long enough."

(lines 137–43)

Hunt was certainly not the first to find Gifford, as a satirist and a critic, an objectionable figure.[35] Hunt is nevertheless keenly aware of Gifford's critical style, underscoring Gifford's exclusive sense of his classical learning ("there are one or two of us who know you"), his firm rejection of liberal attitudes ("So that what with their taste, their reformers, and stuff"), and his condescending manner of critical judgment ("So stupid, in gen'ral, the natives are grown"). Apollo does give Gifford credit for being the "rod, that got rid of the Cruscas and Lauras" (line 150) and he notes that Gifford's translation of *Juvenal* "stops a gap in one's shelf" (line 152). Yet he adds that this is true "At least in what Dryden has not done himself" (line 153). And Apollo's praise for Gifford's "self-taught example, that conquer'd neglect" (line 155), a reference to the critic's rise from modest beginnings, as described in his biographical introduction to his translation of *Juvenal*, is disingenuous, for the god concludes the interaction with Gifford by undercutting the critic's pretensions to merit and his lack of "modesty, wit" and his "small stock of patience" (line 157). Apollo, having thus declared his judgment upon the *Quarterly* reviewer, excuses Gifford from the feast of the poets, explaining "My visit just now is to poets alone, / And not to small critics, however well known" (lines 158–9).

Hunt's personal objections to Gifford only increased as the *Quarterly Review*, under his editorial watch, waged a merciless campaign of abuse against Shelley, Keats, and other so-called "Cockney" authors who held poetical and political opinions that opposed the high Toryism of the periodical. For Hunt, Gifford typified the problem with Romantic critics who let politics guide their reviews. Byron, in this respect, fully agreed with Hunt about the troubling effects of print politics, but his attitude toward Gifford was more complex. In *English Bards*, Byron had explicitly called upon Gifford to recommence his satirical practice. And with the John Murray-issued *Childe Harold* in 1812, Gifford also became Byron's long-time editor and a "literary father" (*BLJ* 11:117). In contrast, Hunt's engagements with Gifford were guided by deeply rooted differences in politics and poetic taste, and Hunt made it a point to abuse Gifford in later years as well as Kim Wheatley has shown.[36] Hunt's spiteful, book-length attack on Gifford in *Ultra-Crepidarius* (1823), for instance, is a notable example of another verse satire in the burlesque mode that was nevertheless made more severe by the inclusion, at the end of the published volume, of lengthy extracts from Hazlitt's volatile *Letter to William Gifford, Esq.* Byron, meanwhile, would later correspond with Jeffrey and drop any ill will he may have once felt. On the one hand, then, the respective attacks that Byron and Hunt issued in *English Bards* and *Feast* against the leading critical authorities of the period show how closely aligned, in general, their attitudes were toward the Romantic reviews. On the other hand, their disagreements over the merits of Gifford (and Pope) reveal just how far apart Byron and Hunt were in matters of literary taste at the beginning of the second decade of the nineteenth century.

James Cawthorn and *The Feast of the Poets*

The publishing history of the separate editions of *Feast* that appeared between 1814 and 1815 provides additional insight into the literary friendship between Byron and Hunt in 1813. Indeed, with *Feast*, we discover an early example of the practical, material side to the Byron-Hunt literary relationship: the side that involved matters of publishing, reviewing, and annotating. Evidence in Hunt's correspondence strongly suggests that Byron's first visit to Horsemonger Lane Gaol in the spring of 1813 may have provided the imprisoned author with the opportunity (and perhaps the motivation) to republish *Feast* as a separate volume.[37]

On 27 May 1813, a week after Byron met Hunt, the editor wrote to his wife about a visit he had just received from James Cawthorn, a bookseller and the publisher of all four editions of Byron's *English Bards*. Cawthorn's visit to Hunt seems to have been in the capacity of a book buyer, for Hunt informed Marianne Hunt that he had "sold as many of [his] books to Mr. Cawthorn as would fetch £40," an indication of the value of Hunt's private library at the time. Yet Hunt's letter, crucially, also establishes a direct link between Hunt, Byron, and Cawthorn in his capacity as a publisher. Byron, Hunt revealed, had spoken to Cawthorn of his "poetical powers" at some point prior to the publisher's visit. Hunt had apparently asked Cawthorn to recommend a "competent critic" to read a working draft of what must have been the "commencement" of *Rimini* and the publisher had suggested Byron for the purpose. Hunt added that he "had really no intention of giving [Cawthorn] a hint about such a work" and that he did not even remember that he "published at all." The "upshot" of this realization, however, was to prove fortuitous: "[Cawthorn] has agreed, at his own request, to publish it when finished" (*LHOL*). From the end of May until September 1813, Hunt thus appears to have worked in earnest toward the completion of *Rimini*, but he abruptly changed direction in September, realizing that *Rimini* would take additional time to complete. Hunt explained the situation to Moore, to whom he had been sending sections of his poem for comment. In a letter of 20 September, Hunt stated that he had only managed to write an additional "thirty-four lines beyond the place you saw last, and have found it necessary to relieve myself from that intentness of thinking which grave composition requires, by falling in with an old plea, 'the request of friends,' and busying myself in preparing for re-publication the 'Feast of the Poets,' with additional verses and notes."[38] Given his financial needs and his commitments to Cawthorn, Hunt seems to have had few options. The new plan to republish an old work nevertheless appears to have been met with immediate and encouraging approval by the publisher. Cawthorn had already reaped financial rewards from all four editions of Byron's *English Bards* (and would continue to profit from pirated copies) and doubtless saw Hunt's *Feast* as a poem with a comparable likeness to Byron's popular satire. Moreover, the few known titles that Cawthorn, an "outsider" in the trade, according to William St Clair, had published included: John Cam Hobhouse's *Journey through Albania* (1813), a burlesque of Walter Scott's *Lay of the Last Minstrel*, *The Lay of the Scotch Fiddle* (1814), and the *Anecdotes, Hitherto Unpublished, of the Private Life of Peter the Great* (1813). All of these titles represented highly marketable genres—travelogues, satires, and personalities—and so *Feast* would have fit readily into Cawthorn's catalog.[39] More importantly, as noted, Cawthorn had already heard about the imprisoned editor's poetic talents directly from Byron. Therefore, it seems reasonable to conclude that Byron had not only strengthened the acquaintance of Cawthorn and Hunt in a literary sense, but that *English Bards* may have been an important influence on the publisher's decision to proceed with Hunt's *Feast*. In fact, a few days after Cawthorn first visited Hunt in prison, the publisher sent the editor a copy of *Journey Through Albania*, an expensive travelogue (in two volumes quarto) that documented Hobhouse's recently completed Grand Tour with Byron. Such a weighty gift of Byroniana may have served Cawthorn as a way to solidify the new literary partnership with Hunt by gesturing toward their mutual acquaintance with the famous author of *English Bards* and *Childe Harold*.

Thus committed to republishing *Feast*, Hunt finalized revisions to the satire and added lengthy endnotes throughout the fall of 1813. As his first separately published volume of poetry since *Juvenilia*, Hunt's new *Feast* was a significant accomplishment, and Byron and Cawthorn seem to have reenergized Hunt's poetical ambitions during the first year of his political imprisonment. On 4 November 1813, Hunt wrote to Marianne Hunt, confirming that the "verses are printed, & a good part of the notes gone to press:—the book will certainly be out by the first of next month" (*LHOL*). Hunt's newly expanded *Feast* made its appearance in January of 1814 much to the delight of his family and friends. Significantly, Cawthorn had also ensured that the poem would be noticed publicly for the first time, for a ledger written into a copy of the 1814 edition of *Feast* in the Brewer Collection at the University of Iowa shows that a total of thirteen copies "in boards" had been sent off to the "reviews."[40]

The reviews of the first separately published edition of *Feast* were, as Michael Eberle-Sinatra has shown, generally approving.[41] Several reviewers were impressed with the poem's style—a style, as we have seen, that deliberately opposed the Popeian model, employing a loose form of the heroic couplet and other stylistic variations. The *Augustan Review*, for example, found that Hunt "possesses not only a lively and powerful fancy, but a quick perception of metrical excellence" (*RR* C1:33). The *Critical Review* observed that Hunt "endeavours to unite the familiar with the fanciful, and to combine playfulness and humour with sentiment and grace" (*RR* C1:299). The *Eclectic Review* agreed that the poem was "distinguished" by a "playfulness of fancy, and an easy elegance of style" (*RR* C1:320), a sentiment echoed by the *Monthly Review*, which saw the poem "full of [the] most playful imagination" (*RR* C2:696). The *Critical Review*, meanwhile, took Hunt's assessment of Byron's poetry, which we shall soon examine in detail, as a way to assess Hunt's own poetry: "What Lord Byron wants, says Mr. Hunt, is fancy as distinguished from passion; what he himself will probably want, is directly the reverse" (*RR* C1:303). The few wholly negative reviews (in the *British Critic*, the *Satirist*, and the *Critical Review*) were clearly guided by disagreement with Hunt's liberal politics, which had been emphasized on the title page of the 1814 edition: "*The Feast of the Poets, with Notes, and Other Pieces in Verse, By The Editor of the Examiner.*"[42] The Tory *British Critic* declared that in the "poetry there is an affectation of the easy and the familiar style, in which the author has experienced a total failure. A low and vulgar flippancy cannot, except by the readers of the Examiner, be taken for wit" (*RR* C1:205). The reviewer, moreover, lumped Hunt and Byron together as fellow radicals, sarcastically suggesting that the notes "would turn into admirable essays for the Examiner, duly emblazoned in capitals, 'CRITIQUE on LORD BYRON's New POEM,' for the edification of the Sunday beaux" (*RR* C1:206), a reference to Hunt's approval of Byron's recently published *Lara* (1814). In general, however, Hunt's critical notes received high praise from the reviewers. The reviewer for the *Monthly Review*, in fact, stated that the "notes, which occupy the bulk of the volume, contain a variety of strictures which may be read with profit by those persons who are the subjects of them," concluding that "Mr. Hunt's notes may be considered as lectures for the modern school of poetry" (*RR* C2:696).

Critical Notices: Wordsworth and Byron

Byron would have agreed with the reviewers about the quality of Hunt's notes to *Feast*. After receiving a presentation copy of Hunt's new volume, the author of *English Bards* immediately wrote an approving note of receipt: "I have been at your text which has much *good* humour in every sense of the word—and your notes are of a very high order indeed— particularly on Wordsworth" (*BLJ* 4:51). Hunt's major revision to the poem had, in fact, been his formal reconsideration of Wordsworth, and thus the interest Byron had taken in the subject must have fulfilled one of Hunt's chief purposes in issuing a new edition of the satire. Whereas

Wordsworth had been formerly grouped with his fellow Lake Poets as a poet of minor significance in *The Reflector* version of *Feast*, in the revised 1814 version, Wordsworth stood at the head of a new generation of poets. In his lengthy discussion of Wordsworth in the notes, Hunt confirmed the idea: "I do not deny that he is so already, as the greatest poet of the present." To this Hunt added: "we have had no poet since the days of Spenser and Milton,—so allied in the better part of his genius to those favoured men" (*SWLH* 5:65). Hunt continued his notice by praising several of Wordsworth's early poems: "The Female Vagrant," "To a Nightingale," "The Old Cumberland Beggar," "Louisa," "The Happy Warrior," "The World is Too Much with Us," and the "Ode to Duty." Yet Hunt qualified all of this high regard for Wordsworth with several blunt points of criticism: "the question is . . . has Mr. Wordsworth 'attained his object'? Has he acted up to his theory? Has he brought back that natural style, and restored to us those healthy and natural perceptions, which he justly describes as the proper state of our poetical constitutions? I think not." Hunt, rather severely, posited instead that Wordsworth's poetry "gives us puerility for simplicity, affectation for nature; and . . . substitute[s] one set of diseased perceptions for another" (*SWLH* 5:66). Hunt specifically objected to Wordsworth's characters as well as the conclusions, as Hunt saw it, that the poet drew from their solitary perambulations, arguing "I am not objecting to these subjects in behalf of that cowardly self-love falsely called sensibility, or merely because they are of what is termed a distressing description, but because they are carried to an excess that defeats the poet's intention, and distresses to no purpose" (*SWLH* 5:67).

For Hunt, Wordsworth's poetry might ultimately have a harmful effect on readers: it "turns our thoughts away from society and men altogether, and nourishes that eremitical vagueness of sensation,—that making a business of reverie,—that despair of getting to any conclusion to any purpose, which is the next step to melancholy or indifference" (*SWLH* 5:67–8). Hunt thus found Wordsworth projecting an unhealthy egotism and misanthropy. As a corrective, he presented Shakespeare's "morbid abstractions" as examples for Wordsworth to consider: "Shakespeare is full of them; but he has managed to apply them to their proper refreshing purposes; and has given us but one fond recluse in his whole works,—the melancholy Jacques" (*SWLH* 5:68). Hunt, incidentally, would give Byron the nickname "melancholy Jacques,"[43] but the crucial element that emerges in Hunt's discussion of Wordsworth's poetry in the notes to *Feast*, as Jeffrey C. Robinson observes, is that Hunt's apprehensions are rooted in social, not literary, concerns.[44]

Hunt's appraisal of Wordsworth, in many ways, mirrors his final analysis of Byron's poetry in the notes to the 1814 edition of *Feast*, but it is clear that, for Hunt, Byron is a lower order poet than Wordsworth. In Byron's poetry, Hunt perceived a "general vein of melancholy,—a fondness for pithy, suggesting, and passionate modes of speech,—and an intensity of feeling, which appears to seek relief in its own violence." For Hunt, what Byron's poetry "wants in essential poetry" is "fancy as distinguished from passion." Hunt argued that *Childe Harold,* as far as it projected an "intensity of feeling," was "very striking" and "evinced a singular independence and determination of thinking, with little of those fancies, original or borrowed, which are so captivating to young writers in general." In addition, Hunt noted that "The Giaour and Bride of Abydos are two sketches of passion, sparkling and dignified, and abounding in felicitous instances of compression," but added that "They are not free however from common-place verses, and are disfigured besides by a number of strange exotic rhymes" (*SWLH* 5:80).

Hunt concluded his relatively brief discussion of Byron's poetry in the notes to the 1814 *Feast,* tellingly, by praising the "little effusions at the end of the Childe Harold," arguing that "It is here, I think, that the soul of him is to be found, and that he has most given himself up to those natural words and native impressions, which are the truest test of poetry" (*SWLH* 5:80–1). Few readers today who come to Byron through *Don Juan* or *Childe Harold* are likely to agree with Hunt on this point, but Hunt was not wrong in making such a claim for the poet's "little effusions." Indeed, the primary historical evidence we have of Byron's large, everyday readership shows that the lyric poems were those most often shared and copied into commonplace books.[45] Even so, Hunt's claim is suggestive. At the end of the *Childe Harold* volume, Byron included the emotionally powerful "Thyrza poems," which were written after the poet learned of the death of his intimate Cambridge attachment John Edleston. In the "Thyrza poems," Byron, as Bernard Beatty argues, shows great skill and stylistic accomplishment, developing an "adroit but restrained singing voice," the cumulative effect of which is a group of poems that are "adept but not showy."[46] Such poems, in other words, are stripped of the "flash" rhetoric, as Keats described Byron's style, a style that relied more on rhetorical flourish, epigrammatic wit, and classical allusion.[47] The "Thyrza poems" would have also recalled for Hunt the theme of sympathetic friendship that Byron had praised in *Juvenilia* in 1813. Ultimately, in Byron's "little effusions," Hunt perceived a different, more appealing side to Byron's poetic character and public persona. In the notes to *Feast,* Hunt admitted that he found Byron's misanthropy, like Wordsworth's melancholy, to be socially unproductive and suggested that his friend might instead "study society, not only in its existing brilliance or its departed grandeur, but in those middle walks of life, where he may find the most cordial sum of its happiness, as well as the soundest concentration of its intelligence" (*SWLH* 5:79).

Byron was not unappreciative of Hunt's critical commentary in *Feast.* In a letter of 9 February 1814, Byron wrote to thank Hunt for the "very handsome note" but added "I trust—[*Feast*] to be followed by others on subjects more worthy your notice than the works of contemporaries" (*BLJ* 4:49). Byron had been pushing Hunt to complete *Rimini* but found himself reacting with interest to Hunt's strongly worded thoughts on contemporary poetry nonetheless. Byron also conceded, perhaps for the first time, that "Your poem I redde long ago in 'the Reflector' & it is not much to say it is the best '*Session*' we have—& with a more difficult subject—for we are neither so good nor so bad (taking the best & worst) as the wits of the olden time" (*BLJ* 4:50). Byron's reading of the newly published *Feast* seems to have renewed his interest in *English Bards*, for he wrote to his publisher John Murray only a month later, declaring, "yesterday I *reread* E[nglish] B[ar]ds—(bating the *malice*) it is the *best*" (*BLJ* 4:107) poem, Byron felt, he had hitherto produced. Byron, in fact, continued to think deeply about *English Bards* over the course of the next year, specifically in relation to Hunt and his *Feast*, writing to his friend on 1 June 1815 with knowledge of Hunt's intention to publish yet another edition of the satire: "It rejoices me to hear of the well doing and regeneration of 'the Feast' setting aside my own selfish reasons for wishing it success" (*BLJ* 4:295). These "selfish reasons" related to Hunt's decision to introduce Byron properly, for the first time, into the poem itself, where he would make his entrance at Apollo's feast alongside their mutual friend Moore.

One of the curiosities of Hunt's 1814 edition of *Feast* is indeed its failure to include Byron among the guests at Apollo's table. Byron, as we have seen, took his inclusion in the notes as a sufficient gesture of Hunt's goodwill and friendship. Some reviewers, however, perceptively observed the poet's absence. The writer for the *Augustan Review*, aware of Hunt's liberal politics, guessed that "Lord Byron is not mentioned by Mr. Hunt, probably because he did not like his Lordship's rank in society" (*RR* C1:33).[48] The writer for the *British Critic* focused on Hunt's remarks on Byron in the volume's notes, commenting that there "Byron is plentifully bespattered with awkward attempts at flattery and compliment" (*RR* C1:206). The assessment, however, does not accurately capture Hunt's estimate of Byron or his poetry in the notes, which is generally informed, probing, and confident. Yet it remains curious why Hunt chose to leave out the popular poet with whom he had, by 1814, established an intimate personal and intellectual friendship. It may be that the closeness of the friendship itself influenced Hunt's decision to avoid writing publicly on Byron in a satirical work. Furthermore, there had been little positive development in Hunt's critical attitudes toward Byron's poetry since his *Examiner* review of the Drury Lane "Address."

In 1815, however, Hunt must have felt the friendship to have been on a stronger footing, for he decided to include Byron among Apollo's venerable guests in the last separately published edition of *Feast*. The inclusion, nevertheless, is essentially a paraphrase of the position Hunt had already developed in the notes to the 1814 edition. In the poem, Byron follows Moore to Apollo's table with "so kind yet unconscious a face, / So ardent a frankness, yet modest an ease," but the very first question Hunt has Apollo ask the author of the moody *Childe Harold* is critical in nature:

> Pray how came misanthropy into *your* head?
> I suspect (it is true), that in all which you tell us
> Of robbers, and rakes, and such terrible fellows,
> There's something mere scorn could have never devis'd,
> And a sorrow-wise charity roughly disguis'd;
> But you must not be always indulging this tone;
> You owe some relief to our hearts and your own;

Apollo next offers the poet advice that mirrors that which Hunt had given to Byron in the notes to the 1814 edition with a few telling additions:

> So remember; and as to the style of your song,
> And to straight-forward speaking, 'twill come before long:
> But the fact is, that what with your courts and your purses,
> I've never done well with you lords who write verses:
> I speak not of people like Sheffield or Lansdowne,
> Whom some silly Body of Poetry hands down,—
> But Rochester raked himself into his grave;
> A poor sceptred scoundrel slew Surrey the brave;
> And Sackville stopped short of his better ambition,
> And lost a great name in the *shrewd* politician.
> I wouldn't divorce, mind, the muse from the state;
> Great poets have been politicians as great;
> Let both be combined as becomes a true Briton,
> And laurels add weight to the bench that you sit on;
> I love a free spirit; its fancy is free;
> But so much the more you and I must agree.[49]

Hunt presents Byron, like the other poets noticed in the poem, in caricature, comparing him to the noble but unfortunate characters of Rochester, Surrey, and Sackville. This kind of caricature, of course, is appropriate to the playful, Suckling-inspired satire in *Feast*, but it also presents a clear example of Hunt's plain speaking when it came to his friend. Hunt would later come to regret this tactic after speaking of Byron in a surprisingly frank manner in *Lord Byron and Some of His Contemporaries* in 1828. But perhaps the most revealing personal criticism in *Feast* is Hunt's knowledge that the poet has "divorce[d]" himself from actively participating in political life, a decision that Hunt clearly laments and wishes to see reversed.

Despite the personality he injected into the criticism in *Feast*, Hunt did not hesitate to send Byron a finely bound presentation copy of the last separately published edition. Byron appreciated the gesture, reciprocating immediately with a gift of his own: "I send you a thing whose greatest value is it's present rarity" (*BLJ* 4:318). The "thing" was Byron's personal copy of a fourth edition of *English Bards* to which he had added, in holograph, several corrections intended for the suppressed fifth edition of the satire. Hunt acknowledged receipt of Byron's gift on 21 October, stating "I have enough of generous instinct in me to feel at once all the value & delicacy of the gift. . . . In one respect [*English Bards*] has always reminded me of my own early criticisms on actors & dramatists."[50] The Hunt copy of *English Bards*, preserved in the Forster Collection at the Victoria and Albert Museum, is a fascinating relic of the friendship at the height of its first and most congenial phase.[51] Byron's unique gift, to be sure, revealed his awareness of Hunt's interest in and admiration for *English Bards*—an admiration that, as we have seen, can be traced back to Hunt's review of Byron's Drury Lane "Address" in *The Examiner* in 1812. Byron's gift, of course, is also significant as a record of the textual changes he had planned for the suppressed fifth edition of *English Bards*. Perhaps the most important single manuscript alteration in the copy Byron sent to Hunt is that which appears in the prose note on the Chalk Farm duel involving Jeffrey and Moore. In Hunt's gift copy, Byron crossed out the condescending part about the "balls of the pistols" being absent, like "the courage of the combatants," and added an apologetic addendum: "I am informed that Mr. Moore published at the time a disavowal of the statements in the newspapers as far as regarded himself & in justice to him I mention this circumstance as I never heard of it before I cannot state the particulars & was only made acquainted with the fact very lately."[52] For this and like passages in *English Bards*, Byron reminded Hunt that "upon the whole I wish that it had never been written—though my sending you this copy (the only one in my possession unless one of Lady B[yron]'s be excepted) may seem at variance with this statement—but my reason for this is very different—it is however the only gift I have made of the kind this many a day." He added: "You probably know that it is not in print for sale—nor ever will be—(if I can help it)—again" (*BLJ* 4:318). Despite the embarrassment Byron had come to feel about his early satire, his fascination with *English Bards* remained, and that sustained interest was clearly linked to his reading in Hunt's newly published editions of *Feast* in 1814 and 1815.

The Poetical Character: A Literary Dialogue

Despite this friendly exchange of Byroniana, however, the two friends were soon engaged in a more unsettling argument about the poetical character and poetical temperaments. In a letter to Hunt of 22 October

1815, written in response to his friend's express interest in the copy of *English Bards* he had just received, Byron went into great detail about the book's history: "My motive for writing that poem was I fear not so fair as you are willing to believe it—I was angry—& determined to be witty" (*BLJ* 4:320). He added: "I sent you my copy—because I consider your having it much the same—as having it myself—Lady B[ryon] has one—I desire not to have any other and sent it only as a curiosity and a memento" (*BLJ* 4:321). The idea that Hunt's possession of the book equated to joint ownership with Byron is an important admission of the intimacy of the friendship from Byron's point of view. Nevertheless, Hunt may have ventured too far in expressing his own enthusiasm for the friendship at this time. Although he was clearly grateful for the gift, he responded to its receipt with more flattery than he had hitherto shown his friend: "the fact is, it is so rare a thing to meet with a person, who seems, as the phrase is, to jump along with all one's ideas, that one is in danger of paying nothing but compliments to one's self under the guise of ardently approving another."[53] Hunt, crucially, elsewhere in the same letter, admitted that he had taken some of Byron's newly added lines (those on Henry Kirke White) from the hand-corrected copy of *English Bards* and had already published them in a "Round Table" article ("On the Poetical Character") in *The Examiner* for 5 November because they "happened to illustrate some position of mine." The comment, innocent though it may have been, is nevertheless characteristic of the self-serving tone Hunt could sometimes let dominate his correspondence and his social intercourse—a tone upon which many friends, including Keats, would remark with frank disapproval.[54]

Byron responded with typical congeniality, but perhaps sensing that Hunt was becoming too familiar (and perhaps exercising more liberty with the unpublished material than he had anticipated) made a point of reading and objecting to Hunt's argument in the "Round Table" piece to which his attention had been directed. In the article, Hunt had written of the "late excellent" Henry Kirke White as one "who promised to be a poet" had he not died prematurely after becoming a "martyr to study." Hunt reinforced the idea with Byron's manuscript quotation on the boy poet from Nottinghamshire: "The spoiler swept that soaring lyre away, / Which else had sounded an immortal lay. / Oh what a noble heart was here undone, / When Science' self destroyed her favourite son." Hunt then added: "So says of him a noble poet, who is fulfilling the promise of *his* youth, and who had known enough of the pleasures and pains of his nature, to think, we dare say, with us."[55] But Byron, it turns out, did not "think" exactly the same way as Hunt did with respect to the poetical character, the delineation of which was the focus of Hunt's article. Hunt had written the piece, as he explained to Byron, to refute Hazlitt's notion that all poets possess an "*original* poverty of spirit." Hunt suggested instead that poets only occasionally display such despondencies (as he felt was the case with Wordsworth and with Byron as we have seen in the notes to *Feast*). Hunt argued that poetry is the "result of an organization delicate, but not diseased," and that poets have a greater store of "pleasure" than others and so are better equipped to deal with pain and discomfort. Hunt acknowledged, however, that an overindulgence in pleasure could lead to Hazlitt's "poverty of spirit," but reiterated his belief that "health is the great secret" of the "wealth" poets possess.[56] Byron disagreed with Hunt on this point, suggesting that an "addiction to poetry is very generally the result of 'an uneasy mind in an uneasy body'" (*BLJ* 4:332). The "addiction" idea seems to have been Byron's own (the word and the idea do not appear in the "Round Table" articles by Hazlitt or Hunt), but Byron's main point is clear enough: he disagrees with Hunt's theory about the "health" of the poetical mind and agrees with Hazlitt's ideas about the spiritual "poverty" of poets. Whereas Hunt views "diseased" poets like Tasso, Collins, Chatterton, and White as exceptions among a general class of poetical men who have used, and continue to use, "health" to their advantage, Byron sees Hunt's "diseased" poets, instead, as wholly representative of the poetical character. Indeed, Byron stated firmly that "disease or deformity have been the attendants of many of our best—Collins mad—Chatterton *I* think—mad—Cowper mad—Pope crooked—Milton blind—Gray— (I have heard the last was afflicted by an incurable & very grievous distemper—though not very generally known) & others." To underscore his objection to Hunt's more salubrious point of view on the subject, Byron concluded his letter by stating that he had "not time nor paper to *attack* [Hunt's] *system*" but added that it "ought to be done—were it only because it is a *system*" (*BLJ* 4:332).

"The Blind Monarch of the One-Eyed"

Their disagreement over the constitution of the poetical character was only one of several literary arguments developing from their increased intimacy in the late months of 1815. Byron felt less sanguine about Hunt's 1815 edition of *Feast*, primarily, as he stated, on account of Hunt's enthusiasm for Wordsworth. In a letter to Hunt on 7 October 1815, Byron criticized Hunt over his positive opinion of the Lake Poet, mocking Wordsworth as the "blind Monarch of the one-eyed" but noting that "I merely take the liberty of a free subject to vituperate certain of his edicts—& that only in private" (*BLJ* 4:317). In a follow-up letter of 30 October 1815, Byron continued his argument with Hunt, expressing, in no uncertain terms, his disapproval of his friend's position:

> I take leave to differ from you on Wordsworth as freely as I once agreed with you—at that time I gave him credit for promise which is unfulfilled—I still think his capacity warrants all you say of *it*

only—but that his performances since "Lyrical Ballads"—are miserably inadequate to the ability which lurks within him:—there is undoubtedly much natural talent spilt over "the Excursion" but it is rain upon rocks where it stands & stagnates—or rain upon sands where it falls without fertilizing—who can understand him?

(*BLJ* 4:324)

Byron, like Francis Jeffrey, had read Wordsworth's *Excursion* with lackluster enthusiasm, finding it to be a poem that would "never do" (*RR* A2:439). For Byron, Wordsworth was not only the "Arch-Apostle of mystery & mysticism" but he was also, like Hunt, one of the most outspoken contemporary antagonists of Pope: "I have two petty & perhaps unworthy objections in small matters to make to [Wordsworth]—which with his pretension to accurate observation & fury against Pope's false translation of the 'Moonlight scene in Homer' I wonder he should have fallen into" (*BLJ* 4:324–5). To make his case, Byron presented Hunt with an example from *The Excursion* in which Wordsworth had written of Greece's "*fertile* plains—& *sounding* shores" as well as the Mediterranean's "*variegated* sky" (*BLJ* 4:325). Byron, who had travelled to Greece with Hobhouse, responded with wry matter-of-factness to Wordsworth's romantic descriptions: "The rivers are dry half the year—the plains are barren—and the shores *still* & *tideless* as the Mediterranean can make them—the Sky is anything but variegated" (*BLJ* 4:325).

Byron also revealed to Hunt his awareness of Wordsworth's "Essay, Supplementary to the Preface" to *Poems*, in which the Lake Poet, agreeing with Hunt, had argued that Pope had "bewitched the [English] nation by his melody, and dazzled it by his polished style."[57] More provocative was Wordsworth's claim that

the poetry of the period intervening between the publication of the Paradise Lost and the Seasons does not contain a single new image of external nature; and scarcely presents a familiar one from which it can be inferred that the eye of the Poet had been steadily fixed upon his object, much less that his feelings had urged him to work upon it in the spirit of genuine imagination. To what a low state knowledge of the most obvious and important phenomena had sunk, is evident from the style in which Dryden has executed a description of Night in one of his Tragedies, and Pope his translation of the celebrated moonlight scene in the Iliad. A blind man, in the habit of attending accurately to descriptions casually dropped from the lips of those around him, might easily depict these appearances with more truth.[58]

Recalling Hunt's notes on Wordsworth in *Feast*, Byron explained: "both he & you go too far against Pope's 'so when the Moon &c.' it is no translation I know—but it is not such *false* description as asserted" (*BLJ*

4:325). But rather than turn his assault on Wordsworth into a personal attack on Hunt, Byron, thinking better of the situation, concluded the argument by adopting one of Hunt's own critical techniques: an offering of poetic advice. Indeed, Byron concluded by inquiring about *Rimini*, a move clearly designed as a hint for Hunt to give up his interest in Wordsworth and develop, instead, his own *"original"* (*BLJ* 4:330) voice in a poem for which Byron had genuinely high expectations.

Yet it must also be observed that in this important series of epistolary exchanges about Wordsworth, Byron was seriously questioning Hunt's attitudes about Pope. In the separately published editions of *Feast*, Hunt's opinion of the author of *The Dunciad* had become even more transparent. In the preface to the 1814 edition, for instance, Hunt hinted at a work (*Rimini*) that would update the Popeian couplet for a new generation of readers. In the meantime, Hunt implied, *Feast* must serve as a preview of that more serious and original work that "would attempt to reduce to practice his own ideas of what is natural in style, and of the various and legitimate harmony of the English heroic" (*SWLH* 5:32). In the notes, Hunt reiterated the idea: "the public ear has been excited to expect something better; and perhaps there never was a more favourable time than the present, for an attempt to bring back the real harmonies of the English heroic, and to restore to it half the true principle of its music,—variety" (*SWLH* 5:44). For Hunt, Pope remained popular because of the "indolence" of readers, who "care not to enquire why [they are] satisfied" with his poetry. If the

> attention, however, of more poetical readers is once roused to this point, they will find our author not merely deficient on the score of harmony, but to a degree apparently so obvious and at the same time so surprising, that they will be inclined to wonder how they could have endured so utter a want of variety, and will not be willing, in future, to listen to a poet of any pretensions, who shall come before them without a new stop or two to his lyre.
>
> (*SWLH* 5:46)

What Pope ultimately lacks and what Hunt ultimately endorses is "that proper mixture of sweetness and strength,—of modern finish and ancient variety" (*SWLH* 5:48). Hunt's views on Pope, as he admits and as we have seen, were not new. Besides Wordsworth, critics from the Wartons to Johnson and poets from Cowper to Burns had carried on or noticed similar arguments against Pope's style.[59] Nevertheless, Hunt's commentary on Pope in *Feast* is unique in that it appears outside of the pamphlet war that would constitute the Romantic period's so-called "Bowles/Pope Controversy." Hunt's entry into this famous controversy, as Amarasinghe shows, was through *Feast*, with the attack on Pope therein made even more explicit in the critical apparatus subjoined to the 1814 and 1815 editions. In this way, Hunt's approach has clear similarities to Wordsworth's approach in the second and subsequent editions of the *Lyrical Ballads*, in which the poetry had served as an illustration of the theories developed in that volume's preface.[60]

Hunt made an effort to qualify his strongly worded attitudes about Pope and Pope's style in the first separately issued edition of *Feast*: "I am not here joining the cry of those, who affect to consider Pope as no poet at all. He is, I confess, in my judgment, at a good distance from Dryden, and at an immeasurable one from such men as Spenser and Milton." Hunt added that he was "only considering his versification; and upon that point I do not hesitate to say, that I regard him, not only as no master of his art, but as a very indifferent practiser, and one whose reputation will grow less and less, in proportion as the lovers of poetry become intimate with his great predecessors, and with the principles of musical beauty in general" (*SWLH* 5:44). Despite Hunt's attempt to soften his remarks, his statements on Pope were provocative and clearly meant to provoke critical interest. Hunt's *Feast* is perhaps one of the foremost critical statements on an emerging style of second-generation Romantic poetry. Both *Feast* and *English Bards*, in fact, advance, in divergent ways, one of the primary issues at stake for the poets of the preceding generation. For Byron, the formally conceived and executed *English Bards* was a ringing endorsement of the Popeian tradition of satire. For Hunt, *Feast*, by contrast, urged a formal break from the Popeian model by looking back to Suckling and other earlier English writers. As Richard Marggraf Turley has rightly observed, Hunt's *Rimini*, with its "manifesto-like preface," which furthered the stylistic arguments of *Feast*, was the "logical continuation of Wordsworth's own" in the *Lyrical Ballads*.[61] We also need to remember, however, that Hunt's poetic theories owe much to his reading in Johnson and especially his interest in Dryden, interests that suggest there is more continuity with these earlier authors than recent critical discussions of Hunt's poetry have indicated. Hunt's most important practical test of his poetical philosophy was, of course, still to come. Byron continued to think highly of *Rimini*, but with Hunt's progress on that poem moving slowly between 1813 and 1815, the two friends looked to carry on their conversations by addressing new topics in an altogether different context: *The Examiner*.

Notes

1 Anthony Holden, *The Wit in the Dungeon: The Remarkable Life of Leigh Hunt. Poet, Revolutionary, and the Last of the Romantics* (New York: Little Brown and Company, 2005), 27.

2 Lady Melbourne brought Hunt's review to Byron's attention and offered to send her copy of *The Examiner*. Byron replied: "Thanks for your 'Examiner[.]' Hunt is a clever man & I should like to know his opinion—pray send it, it will be very acceptable." See *BLJ* 2:233.

3 Hunt later referred to *Feast* as the "earliest of [his] grown productions in verse." See the preface to *The Poetical Works of Leigh Hunt* (London: Edward Moxon, 1832), xlvii.

4 The satire first appeared in Hunt's *Reflector: A Quarterly Magazine, on Subjects of Philosophy, Politics, and the Liberal Arts.* 2 vols. (London: John Hunt, 1811), 2:313–23. See Kenneth E. Kendall, *Leigh Hunt's Reflector* (The Hague: Mouton & Co., 1971), 50–2.

5 Clarence DeWitt Thorpe, "Leigh Hunt as Man of Letters," in *Leigh Hunt's Literary Criticism*, eds. Lawrence Huston Houtchens and Carolyn Washburn Houtchens (New York: Octagon Books, 1976), 33.

6 See William St Clair, *The Reading Nation in the Romantic Period* (Cambridge: Cambridge University Press, 2004), 163–4.

7 Thomas Medwin, *Medwin's Conversations of Lord Byron*, ed. Ernest J. Lovell Jr. (Princeton, NJ: Princeton University Press, 1966), 144. A. R. C. Dallas, *Correspondence of Lord Byron*, 3 vols. (Paris: Galignani, 1825), 1:25.

8 Qtd. in Doris Langley Moore, *Lord Byron: Accounts Rendered* (New York: Harper & Row, 1974), 122.

9 Hunt, *The Reflector*, 2:373. For the attribution, see Kendall, *Leigh Hunt's Reflector*, 96.

10 The fourth issue of *The Reflector* had been ready in late 1811, but it appeared on 23 March 1812. See Kendall, *Leigh Hunt's Reflector*, 28.

11 On "Byromania," the contemporary term used to describe the Byron phenomenon after the publication of *Childe Harold*, see Ghislaine McDayter, *Byromania and the Birth of Celebrity Culture* (Albany: The State University of New York Press, 2009).

12 Hunt later spoke of these qualities as affectations: "I too often got into a declamatory vein. . . . I wrote, though anonymously, in the first person, as if, in addition to my theatrical pretensions, I had suddenly become an oracle in politics; the words philosophy, poetry, criticism, statesmanship, nay, even ethics and theology, all took a final tone in my lips." See *A* 2:2.

13 See also the *Critical Review*: "It would be much for the advantage of literature, that every ten or twenty years should produce a new Dunciad to expose the ravings of folly, the coxcombry of learning, and the aberrations of genius." *RR* B2:607.

14 Of Pope, Johnson wrote: "New sentiments and new images others may produce, but to attempt any further improvement of versification will be dangerous. Art and diligence have now done their best, and what shall be added will be the effort of tedious toil and needless curiosity." See Samuel Johnson, *The Lives of the Poets. A Selection*, ed. Roger Lonsdale (Oxford: Oxford University Press, 2009), 436.

15 Rodney Stenning Edgecombe, *Leigh Hunt and the Poetry of Fancy* (Madison, NJ: Fairleigh Dickinson Press, 1994), 153–64.

16 Gary Dyer, *British Satire and the Politics of Style, 1789–1832* (Cambridge: Cambridge University Press, 1997), 46–51.

17 Dyer, *British Satire*, 67–8, 87.

18 Juvenal, *The Satires of Decimus Junius Juvenalis,* trans. William Gifford (London: W. Bulmer and Co., 1802), xlviii.

19 Leigh Hunt, *The Companion*, February 27, 1828, 84–8. See also Hunt's *Wit and Humor* (London: Smith, Elder, and Co., 1856), 218. According to Hunt, Suckling's "Constant Lover" is "the perfection of easy, witty, light yet substantial writing."

20 Hunt, *The Companion*, February 27, 1828, 88.

21 Johnson, *Lives*, 17.
22 Thomas Clayton lists two editions: *The Works of Sir John Suckling. Containing His Poems, Letters, and Plays* (1709), which was reprinted in 1719 and again in 1766 and 1770 (in two volumes); and *Selections from the Works of Sir John Suckling. To Which is Prefixed a Life of the Author, with Critical Remarks on His Writings and Genius*, which was not issued until 1836. See Sir John Suckling, *The Works of Sir John Suckling: The Non-Dramatic Works*, ed. Thomas Clayton, 2 vols. (Oxford: Oxford University Press, 1971), 1:lxxix–lxxx.
23 Robert Anderson, ed. *A Complete Edition of the Poets of Great Britain*, 13 vols. (London: John & Arthur Arch, 1792–5), 3:728.
24 Alexander Chalmers, ed. *The Works of the English Poets, from Chaucer to Cowper*, 21 vols. (London: J. Johnson; J. Nichols and Son, 1810), 6:487.
25 Edgecombe, *Leigh Hunt*, 164.
26 William Wordsworth, *The Letters of William and Mary Wordsworth: VIII. A Supplement of New Letters*, ed. Alan G. Hill (Oxford: Oxford University Press, 1993), 144–5.
27 William Wordsworth, "Essay, Supplementary to the Preface," in *The Prose Works of William Wordsworth*, eds. W. J. B. Owen and Jane Worthington Smyser, 3 vols. (Oxford: Oxford University Press, 1974), 3:80.
28 Leigh Hunt, *Classic Tales, Serious and Lively. With Critical Essays on the Merits and Reputations of the Authors*. 5 vols. (London: John Hunt, 1806–7), 1:41–3.
29 For an informed analysis of the Catullan elements in "Atys," see Henry Stead, *A Cockney Catullus* (Oxford: Oxford University Press, 2016), 257–65.
30 Hunt, *The Reflector*, 1:166–9.
31 Johnson wrote: "Dryden's page is a natural field, rising into inequalities, and diversified by the varied exuberance of abundant vegetation." In his comparison of Dryden and Pope, Johnson further argued: "Of genius, that power which constitutes a poet; that quality without which judgement is cold and knowledge is inert; that energy which collects, combines, amplifies, and animates; the superiority must, with some hesitation, be allowed to Dryden." See Johnson, *Lives*, 420.
32 In the first published edition of *Feast* in *The Reflector*, line 11 had originally been printed thus: "That since Dryden's true English and Milton's sublime." See Hunt, *The Reflector*, 2:314.
33 Upali Amarasinghe, *Dryden and Pope in the Early Nineteenth Century* (Cambridge: Cambridge University Press, 1962), 166.
34 Claude M. Fuess, *Lord Byron as a Satirist in Verse* (New York: Columbia University Press, 1912), 56. Frederick L. Beaty, *Byron the Satirist* (DeKalb: Northern Illinois University Press, 1985), 38.
35 Roy Benjamin Clark, *William Gifford: Tory Satirist, Critic, and Editor* (New York: Columbia University Press, 1930), 52–3, 60–1.
36 Kim Wheatley, "Conceiving Disgust: Leigh Hunt, William Gifford, and the *Quarterly Review*," in *Leigh Hunt: Life, Poetics, Politics*, ed. Nicholas Roe (New York: Routledge, 2003), 180–97.
37 *Feast* was published as a single volume in 1814 by Cawthorn and then republished in 1815 by Gale and Fenner.
38 See Thomas Moore, *Memoirs, Journal and Correspondence of Thomas Moore*, ed. Lord John Russell, 8 vols. (London: Longman, Brown, Green, and Longmans, 1853–56), 8:156.
39 Little seems to be known of Cawthorn beyond his involvement with Byron's *English Bards* and Hunt's *Feast*. See St Clair, *Reading Nation*, 163–4.

40 MS. Brewer 828/H941f. The ledger, which is not in Hunt's hand, seems to be a final statement of account with Hunt for the 1814 edition of *Feast*. The details can be summarized as follows: "1,000" copies were initially printed by "Mr. Reynell" for Cawthorn but at some point "260" of these copies were given over to "Gale & Curtis," who published *Feast* in 1815; the "260" (presumably unsold) copies of the 1814 *Feast* must have been those included as a "*bonus*" for the *Rimini* contract Hunt signed with "Gale & Curtis." See *LHLL* 77. The venture with Cawthorn for *Feast* appears to have produced modest financial returns. According to the ledger, Hunt earned just over £20.

41 Michael Eberle-Sinatra, *Leigh Hunt and the London Literary Scene: A Reception History of His Major Works, 1805–1828* (New York: Routledge, 2005), 33–42.

42 Hunt's name was added to subsequent editions of *Feast*.

43 See Hunt's letter to John Cam Hobhouse of 30 July 1816. NLS MS. 43449.

44 Jeffrey C. Robinson, "Hunt and the Poetics and Politics of Fancy," in *Leigh Hunt: Life, Poetics, Politics*, ed. Nicholas Roe (New York: Routledge), 161–3.

45 See Corin Throsby, "Byron, Commonplacing, and Early Fan Culture," in *Romanticism and Celebrity Culture, 1750–1850*, ed. Tom Mole (Cambridge: Cambridge University Press, 2009), 235–6.

46 Bernard Beatty, "'Accomplished Verse' and 'Awakened Hearts': Byron's 'Thyrza Poems,'" *The Byron Journal* 33, no. 2 (2005): 81, 85.

47 John Keats, *The Letters of John Keats*, ed. Hyder Edward Rollins, 2 vols. (Cambridge, MA: Harvard University Press, 1958), 2:192.

48 The review is of the first of two 1815 editions of *Feast*.

49 The text is from the "Second Edition, Amended and Enlarged" of *The Feast of the Poets* (London: Gale and Fenner, 1815), 11–3.

50 The text is from Timothy Webb, "After Horsemonger Lane: Leigh Hunt's London Letters to Byron (1815–16)," *Romanticism* 16, no.3 (2010): 244.

51 Forster 1267. The half-title page is signed "Byron" and dated 31 December 1811 in the poet's hand. Hunt's receipt of the book is acknowledged on the verso of the half-title, where the following note appears in his hand: "Given me by the author on my birthday. October 19 1815. Leigh Hunt." Beneath this, Hunt has heavily (and suggestively) crossed out what must be the Latin: "Ea denique firma amicitia est." See Webb, "After Horsemonger Lane," 244 and note.

52 The text is from Hunt's copy of *English Bards and Scotch Reviewers*. (London: Cawthorn, 1811), 36–7. Forster 1267. Byron's holograph note is printed (with slight differences) by McGann in *CPW* 1:407.

53 Webb, "After Horsemonger Lane," 245.

54 Nicholas Roe, *Fiery Heart: The First Life of Leigh Hunt* (London: Pimlico, 2005), 150.

55 See Hunt's "On the Poetical Character," in *The Round Table*, ed. William Hazlitt, 2 vols. (Edinburgh: Archibald Constable, 1817), 1:188.

56 Hazlitt, *The Round Table*, 1:176–7, 189.

57 Wordsworth, *Prose Works*, 3:72.

58 Wordsworth, *Prose Works*, 3:73.

59 Robert J. Griffin, *Wordsworth's Pope: A Study in Literary Historiography* (Cambridge: Cambridge University Press, 1995), 6–7.

60 Amarasinghe, *Dryden and Pope*, 222.

61 Richard Marggraf Turley, *The Politics of Language in Romantic Literature* (New York: Palgrave Macmillan, 2002), 35.

3 The Politics of Intimacy

Byron and *The Examiner*

On 21 April 1816, Byron became the subject of discussion in *The Examiner* at a decidedly tense moment: the height of his marriage crisis. Annabella Milbanke left the poet in January but the separation did not become official until late April. By then rumors and gossip had filled the columns of the dailies and weeklies, which did not hesitate to publish Byron's private drama and capitalize on the darker realities of literary celebrity in the age of "Byromania."[1] In response to the sensational reporting, Hunt attempted to defend Byron's private character in *The Examiner* in a piece he titled "Distressing Circumstance in High Life." The depth of the poet's personal despondency over the separation and his legal settlement with Lady Byron has been discussed at length by Leslie Marchand and Malcolm Elwin, but the supporting role Hunt and his *Examiner* played during the proceedings has been overlooked.[2] It was a role, however, that Byron would not soon forget, recalling several years later that no other friend was willing to defend him publicly during his marriage crisis.[3]

Yet the fact that Hunt's defense appeared in the pages of a radical newspaper, the paper that had sent the Hunt brothers to prison in 1813, highlights a recurring theme in Hunt's public engagements with Byron: a willingness to challenge the literary establishment and even the limits of social decorum. In this case, Hunt chose to treat publicly an especially private matter: the separation proceedings of a lord and his wife. What is more, Hunt's article was written with characteristic familiarity—a familiarity that had already roused the ire of the conservative reviewers who had labeled *The Story of Rimini* a socially and morally transgressive poem and its author a "vulgar" opportunist (*RR* C2:756). As critics have long recognized, however, it was the familiar style of Hunt's journalism that generated so effectively a powerful illusion of sincerity and confidentiality, or what Jane Stabler neatly describes as an "aesthetics of intimacy."[4] This "intimacy," in fact, becomes an important theme in Hunt's *Examiner* defense of Byron:

> We have the honour of knowing the Noble Poet; and as friendship is the first of principles in our theory, involving as it does the final purposes of all virtue itself, we do not scruple to confess, that whatever

silence we may have thought ourselves bound to keep with regard to qualities which he could not have possessed, had he been such as the scandal-mongers represented him, we should nevertheless, if we thought our arm worth his using, have stood by him and his misfortunes to the last. But knowing him as we do, one fact at least we are acquainted with; and that is, that these reckless calumniators know nothing about the matter;—and we know further, that there have been the vilest exaggerations about it;—and that our Noble Friend with all his faults, which he is the last man upon earth to deny, possesses qualities, which ought to crumble the consciousness of these men into dust.

(*E* 434 [21 April 1816]: 248–9)

Hunt here generates his authority to write about Byron by having the "honour of knowing" him, and, knowing him as he does, the editor is in a position to offer readers seemingly much more than groundless gossip like that being offered by "scandal-mongers" such as John Scott at the *Champion*. To reassure readers of this, Hunt heightens the effect with physical metaphors, extending his "arm" for Byron's use while standing firmly by the beleaguered poet's side. The editor, moreover, sets a high standard for his journalistic reporting of the marriage scandal, declaring that in writing publicly on a delicate topic he is guided by a philosophical "theory," what he calls "the first of principles"—that of friendship.

Hunt's engagements with Byron in *The Examiner* elsewhere reveal a related political dimension to the textual intimacy Hunt created for his readers. As Payson G. Gates has shown, private debates of a political nature can be found in many of the miscellaneous "Round Table" essays written by Hunt and William Hazlitt and published in *The Examiner* between 1815 and 1817.[5] In fact, Hunt's "Day by the Fire," a "Round Table" number reprinted from *The Reflector*, has been seen as a principal example of the editor's conversational mode and a prototype for the Romantic familiar essay.[6] Yet, before this celebrated essay was politically repurposed and the "Round Table" series itself was installed, Hunt had already been engaging in political conversations in the columns of *The Examiner* with Byron. In 1812, Hunt began following Byron's political career in Parliament and by the time Napoleon abdicated in April of 1814 the two friends were fully engaged in dialogue in the pages of *The Examiner*. And still later, by the time Hunt published his defense of Byron's character during the marriage crisis, Byron had provided Hunt with several poems on Napoleonic themes as well as several private letters on Napoleonic topics, all of which Hunt proceeded to publish and discuss in *The Examiner*. Crucially, in these early conversations, we witness Hunt both testing and being tested by the textual intimacy that he cultivated and helped popularize as a journalistic style.[7] In some cases, Hunt finds the Byronic materials to be antithetical to his own political and philosophical positions, and thus a challenge to his editorial self-confidence and authority. In other cases, the editor is fully and sympathetically engaged with the poet, using his columns to publicly strengthen the bonds of their private friendship.

"The Wit in the Dungeon"

John and Leigh Hunt introduced themselves as warm partisans in the cause of parliamentary reform when they launched *The Examiner* in January of 1808. In the pages of this political weekly, the Hunt brothers made it their social mission to detail, critique, and censure, when necessary, the activities of the Prince of Wales, the future King George IV, and his father, the declining King George III. In an early article, "A Letter of Strong Advice to His Royal Highness the Prince of Wales on His Character and Connections," Hunt set the tone for his treatment of the younger George with a quotation from Bolingbroke's *Idea of a Patriot King*: "Let not Princes flatter themselves. They will be examined closely in private as well as in public life." From the beginning, *The Examiner* regarded the intimate details of private life to be just as important as those of public life, and Hunt displayed a willingness to speak to "Princes" seemingly on a personal level: "I am endeavouring to gain a difficult reputation, that of the honest Editor of a Journal; and . . . it becomes every man in my situation to be content with advising you as a friend though he may be regarded as your enemy" (*E* 34 [21 August 1808]: 529–30). When the Prince assumed control of the government on 5 February 1811, officially establishing his Regency, Hunt was nevertheless willing to suspend his critical judgment, believing that the Prince could, as he himself had hinted, be a catalyst for governmental reform. Yet when it became clear that the Prince would not pursue a reformist agenda, Hunt, as one recent commentator puts it, became "acutely critical of the Prince's political apostasy" (*SWLH* 1:215) and responded appropriately.

What made the situation so frustrating for Hunt and liberal-minded friends like Byron and Thomas Moore was the fact that the Prince had courted prominent reformers such as Charles James Fox and had spoken openly of a Whig-run ministry in the decades leading up to his Regency. Hunt must have known, however, that a transition of political power would have been difficult for a number of reasons. For one thing, the Whigs had not had consistent backing from the Crown since George III had been installed in 1760 and, as political historians have shown, the Whigs themselves had failed to achieve internal unity as a party during the Georgian period.[8] Meanwhile, the Tories presented a formidable obstacle to reform in the wake of the French Revolution and the on-going war with Napoleonic France. There were also personal reasons for the Prince Regent to reject a formal transition of power. The day before he officially became Regent, the Prince informed Spencer Perceval, the acting prime minister, that there would be no Whig coalition. The official reason given by the Prince was "filial duty."[9] George III, ailing but alive, became the son's convenient excuse, and the argument went that a political uprooting of the kind Byron, Moore, and the Hunts were seeking could affect the elder George's fragile condition. In response, the Hunts went on the offensive, working aggressively to expose the Regent's double-dealing in the pages of *The Examiner*. Their tactics—though applauded by Moore, Byron, and a young Shelley—soon brought libel charges. In December of 1812, the brothers were prosecuted and sentenced to two years imprisonment; a £1,000 fine (£500 for each prisoner) to be paid on exit would give the brothers additional cause for anxiety.[10]

The basis for the libel conviction was Hunt's lead article in *The Examiner* for 22 March 1812, "The Prince on St. Patrick's Day," in which the editor offered a sarcastic critique of a "set of wretched common-place lines" (a panegyric addressed to the Prince Regent) published in the *Morning Post*. For Hunt, the verses had with insupportable presumption deemed the Prince the "*Glory of the People*" and "*Protector of the Arts*." Hunt responded accordingly:

> What person, unacquainted with the true state of the case, would imagine, in reading these astounding eulogies, that this . . . *Adonis in Loveliness*, was a corpulent gentleman of fifty! In short, that this *delightful*, *blissful*, *wise*, *pleasurable*, *honourable*, *virtuous*, *true* and *immortal* PRINCE, was a violator of his word, a libertine over head and ears in debt and disgrace, a despiser of domestic ties, the companion of gamblers and demireps, a man who has just closed half a century without one single claim on the gratitude of his country or the respect of posterity!
>
> (*E* 221 [22 March 1812]: 179)

The rhetoric was provocative but just in Hunt's estimation, and the overall evaluation was not unlike that which *The Examiner* had printed in previous years. As early as 1809, Hunt had issued an attack on the Prince's private character: "If you object to a Prince, who is an acknowledged spendthrift and adulterer, you would overthrow all the Princes in Europe" (*E* 58 [5 February 1809]: 82). Even then, such commentary would have seemed unexceptional to a British public long aware of the Prince's dissolute past. Unfortunately for the Hunts, the Prince had a long and antagonistic relationship with the press. Nearly two decades before *The Examiner* came into existence, a much younger Prince of Wales expressed outrage when the radical pamphleteer Charles Pigott published his *Jockey Club, or a Sketch of the Manners of the Age* (1792), a scurrilous pamphlet satirizing the future Prince Regent that avoided libel charges only because it had been published anonymously.[11] The openly defiant Hunts would find no quarter from the middle-aged Prince.

Hunt's imprisonment, however, brought him immediate celebrity. Social visits from friends (new and old) became a daily event at the famous prison cell that Hunt converted into a colorful poetic bower. Byron, for one, made Hunt's acquaintance only a few months after the editor entered Horsemonger Lane Gaol. Byron brought with him a shared sympathy for parliamentary reform and a shared antipathy toward the Prince Regent—factors that immediately helped solidify the friendship. Indeed, the day before he met Hunt, Byron sent Moore these spirited lines:

> To-morrow be with me, as soon as you can, sir,
> All ready and dress'd for proceeding to spunge on
> (According to compact) the wit in the dungeon—
> Pray Phoebus at length our political malice
> May not get us lodgings within the same palace!
>
> (*CPW* 3:88, lines 6–10)

Wryly sympathizing with the "political malice" Hunt had been issuing against the Prince Regent in *The Examiner*, Byron was clearly eager to meet the celebrated "wit in the dungeon." Byron, like Moore, found much to admire in Hunt's fiercely independent approach to politics. As Hunt later reflected, the "*Examiner*, though it preferred the Whigs to the Tories, was not a Whig of the school then existing. Its great object was a reform in Parliament, which the older and more influential Whigs did not advocate" (*A* 2:77). Hunt proudly asserted his political independence from the Tories and the Whigs in *The Examiner* and distanced himself from mainstream political associations, including the epicenter of aristocratic Whig activity at Holland House. Although Byron would become associated with Holland House, his own politics in 1812 and 1813 were, like Hunt's, essentially reformist. At Cambridge, however, Byron had been engaged in conventional politics, joining the Whig Club founded by his Cambridge classmate John Cam Hobhouse. The plan for both men had been to prepare for parliamentary careers; yet Byron confessed his fears on this score to Francis Hodgson, another classmate: "I wish parliament were assembled, that I may hear, and perhaps some day be heard;—but on this point I am not very sanguine" (*BLJ* 2:141). Byron would, in fact, make three speeches in the House of Lords, and each one would be covered with interest by Hunt in *The Examiner*.

Manufacturers and Radicals

Byron delivered his first speech to the House of Lords on 28 February 1812. The topic chosen was the "Frame Work Bill," which would have made frame-breaking, an on-going threat among the skilled weavers of Byron's Nottingham, a capital offense. According to Robert Charles

Dallas who had accompanied Byron to Parliament for the occasion, the young parliamentarian's first speech had been a success, receiving "many compliments from the Opposition Peers."[12] Byron was certainly not alone in speaking against the bill, joining Lord Holland and other prominent Whigs. Hunt, from a distance, had also joined the effort, observing Byron's parliamentary debut approvingly in *The Examiner* for 1 March 1812. The editor had been using the newspaper at this time to address the Prince Regent, but made a point of inserting a comment about Byron's debut, stating that the young politician in his "maiden speech, delivered some strong opinions against the [Frame Work Bill]" (*E* 218 [1 March 1812]: 132). On 20 March, the Tory-sponsored bill was ratified (as expected), but Byron's appearance in Parliament had clearly caught Hunt's attention. As we saw earlier in his review of Byron's Drury Lane "Address" in *The Examiner*, Hunt had been attracted to the "sturdy good sense" (*SWLH* 1:261) of the poet's critical opinions in *English Bards*, and here the notice of Byron's "strong opinions" on the Frame Work Bill suggests a similar level of interest and a clear recognition of Byron's political promise. Hunt's ability to discover and promote young talent is, of course, generally discussed in relation to friends such as Keats, for whom Hunt would advertise indefatigably in later years. Yet several years before he met Keats, and one week before Byron became famous as the author of *Childe Harold*, Hunt issued what seems likely to be his first public notice of the talented young aristocrat and rising poet in the pages of *The Examiner*.[13]

The discontent over working conditions for England's frame workers soon spread to other areas and into other sectors of manufacturing, prompting Hunt to address the growing crisis. Hunt's coverage of the issue is worth considering next to Byron's maiden speech, for in addition to showing general solidarity with Byron's view of Britain's working classes, it reveals the limits of the editor's radical politics and establishes a firm basis for political agreement with Byron. When the rioting Byron had witnessed in January and February spread north to Manchester and its environs, the army had been called in, just as it had in Nottingham, to quell the rioting manufacturers (See *E* 225 [19 April 1812]: 254–5; and *E* 227 [3 May 1812]: 276–7). These were most likely the specific circumstances that led Hunt to take a firm stance on the discontented manufacturers and the measures being taken to suppress them. In *The Examiner* for 10 May 1812, Hunt lamented the conditions of the workers and declared England's inept government and its on-going war against Napoleonic France as the primary causes of the unrest. Importantly, Hunt also voiced his opinion of the military's role in suppressing the uprisings:

> [T]here are times and occasions, in which, whatever may be the *first* cause of the misfortune, and however unattributable to the people, a

recourse to military interference is absolutely and indispensably necessary for the commonest security of property and life; and the present occasion is one of them. There is no alternative:—either force must be threatened by force, or insurrection must do as it pleases.

(*E* 228 [10 May 1812]: 289)[14]

The remarks may appear surprising, for Hunt had earlier voiced strong opposition to the British military in a series of important *Examiner* articles that exposed military corruption and abusive practices.[15] But in this instance, as Hunt states, the army had acted justly because "there [was] no alternative."

Hunt's fear of a total "insurrection," an underlying idea in his 10 May *Examiner* article, was a fear that Byron shared and had also raised in his maiden speech in Parliament, reminding his fellow parliamentarians of the short distance between Nottingham and London:

All this has been transacting within 130 miles of London and yet we "good easy men! have deemed full sure our greatness was a ripening" & have sate down to enjoy our foreign triumphs in the midst of domestic calamity.—But all the cities you have taken, all the armies which have retreated before your leaders, are but paltry subjects of self-congratulation, if your land divides against itself.

(*CMP* 25)

Privately, Byron reiterated his fears in more explicit terms, telling Lord Holland in a letter of 25 February that the weavers' "excesses may be condemned, but cannot be subject of wonder.—The effect of ye. present bill would be to drive them into actual rebellion" (*BLJ* 2:165). Byron, *contra* Hunt, nevertheless argued that "the Sword is the worst argument that can be used, so should it be the last"; yet, in Nottingham, "it has been the first" (*CMP* 25). Though disagreeing on the use of military force to stop the rioting manufacturers in various parts of England, Hunt and Byron were both clearly apprehensive about the prospect of an "actual rebellion."

This apprehensiveness is consistent with attitudes maintained by both men throughout their lives and is suggestive of a fundamentally "cautious," Whiggish approach to politics.[16] Byron and Hunt had also approached the designation "radical" with caution.[17] Both men associated radicalism, in its most extreme form, with social leveling, which inevitably recalled the worst excesses of the French Revolution. Byron spoke openly against radical politics, including those he later thought were being promoted by popular "blackguards" (*BLJ* 7:81) such as Henry Hunt (no relation to Leigh Hunt), a radical who had been active and, in some cases, highly successful in rousing the discontented masses. The occasion for the Peterloo Massacre, it will also be recalled, had been Henry

Hunt's speaking on parliamentary reform before a crowd of 60,000 on St. Peter's Field in Manchester on 16 August 1819. Friends like Hobhouse, meanwhile, had been leaning farther to the left in their support of reform, and Byron wrote an angry letter to his publisher, John Murray, in response to the severity of the changing political climate: "I am out of all patience to see my friends sacrifice themselves for a pack of blackgaurds—who disgust one with their Cause." In the same letter, however, Byron reiterated that he had "always been a friend to and a Voter for reform" (*BLJ* 7:44). It was through this lens of aristocratic liberalism that Hazlitt, as James A. Houck argues, viewed the poet as a poor player when it came to politics: "The liberal poet defends freedom for all and courts revolution, while the aristocrat shelters behind his title and fears the rabble."[18] Byron himself, in a lengthy note appended to the *Two Foscari* (1821), confirmed his aristocratic sensibilities and their effect on his politics, reiterating his fear of revolution in England: "I look upon such as inevitable, though no revolutionist: I wish to see the English constitution restored and not destroyed. Born an aristocrat, and naturally one by temper, with the greater part of my present property in the funds, what have *I* to gain by a revolution?" (*CPW* 6:223). Unlike the more radically inclined Shelley, though an "agrarian reactionary" by birth and temperament, as Donald H. Reiman reminds us, Byron was open about his aristocratic "temper" and the limitations, he felt, it placed upon his politics.[19] At the same time, Byron's "wish to see the English constitution restored and not destroyed," a vestige of the Whiggism Malcolm Kelsall has traced in the poet's political writings, was a wish that was fully shared by the editor of *The Examiner.*

Hunt's approach to party politics comes into focus as early as 1811 with the publication of a list of politicians who, Hunt believed, might effectively lead a parliamentary coalition for reform.[20] Hunt's list is telling; it included old Whig constitutionalists such as Samuel Whitbread as well as more radical-leaning players like Francis Burdett and Major John Cartwright. Hunt was savvy enough to perceive that political extremism, in any form, was not the way to gain influence and achieve meaningful ends. For that purpose, a more balanced coalition of conservative and radical Whigs would be necessary. Hunt's position comes into even sharper focus two years later, when he refers to his politics as those of a "Constitutional Reform[ist]" (*E* 266 [31 January 1813]: 65), rejecting the more extreme principles of famous levelers like Cromwell or Washington. Accordingly, Carl Woodring describes Hunt as a "Constitutional meliorist" who preferred a "mixed government in the form of limited monarchy."[21] Like Byron, Hunt also openly opposed radicals such as Henry Hunt, remarking in 1812 that the radical orator was only "injur[ing] the cause of Reform by his vulgar and turbulent proceedings" (*E* 238 [19 July 1812]: 449). Hunt remained chary of extreme forms of radicalism in later years as well, even after coming under the influence of Shelley and the poet's influential father-in-law, William Godwin. In the wake of the horrifying events of Peterloo, for example, Hunt refused to print Shelley's *Masque of Anarchy* in *The Examiner*, fearing any additional violence the poem might engender. When Hunt ultimately did go to press with the poem in 1832, soon after the passing of the Reform Act, he did so while retaining some anxieties about Shelley's radical attitudes, marking provocative sections in the poem for possible omission as he revised the proofs for the publisher Edward Moxon.[22]

Personal Politics

Although Byron and Hunt naturally disagreed on certain particulars in political matters, their politics were, in the main, aligned in 1812. This is certainly evident in the positions they held on the issue of Catholic rights, the focus of Byron's second parliamentary speech. Byron delivered his speech on the Roman Catholic claims before the House of Lords on 21 April 1812 in support of Catholic enfranchisement and the removal of "Civil Disabilities" (*CMP* 295) long suffered by this religious minority in England and their Irish Catholic neighbors, who were now politically joined through the recent Act of Union. In his speech, Byron rarely generalized, grounding his discussion in specific and sometimes brutal examples of Catholic oppression.[23] None of the speakers that followed, however, referenced the poet's speech, and the Catholic petition itself failed to reach a majority decision just as it had in previous years. In his second speech in the House of Lords, Byron had spoken his politics clearly and deliberately but seemingly to little purpose.

In the 26 April issue of *The Examiner*, Hunt was more optimistic about the prospects for Catholics, writing this brief summary of Byron's speech: "Lord Byron also supported the motion, being of opinion that the Roman Catholics had an equal right with their Protestant Brethren to serve God and the King in their own way" (*E* 226 [26 April 1812]: 261). As mutual friends of the Irish Catholic Moore, Byron and Hunt viewed the issue of Catholic enfranchisement in personal terms, and Hunt featured the Catholic question in *The Examiner* on more than one occasion. Taking issue with institutionalized religion in British society in general, Hunt argued instead for "a system of philosophic morals," suggesting that "a love of the general good, founded on a well-educated conscience and a trust in the wisdom of DEITY, is a much more useful as well as noble principle of conduct than any which involves a dereliction of reason and shock to humanity" (*E* 227 [3 May 1812]: 275). Guided by eighteenth-century rationalists such as Locke, skeptics such as Voltaire, and utilitarians such as Bentham, Hunt "embodied the rational faith" of "liberal beliefs" that developed from the Enlightenment.[24] It was no coincidence that in 1812 *The Examiner* offices moved to 21 Maiden Lane, Covent Garden, the address at which Andrew Marvell once resided and Voltaire once lodged.[25]

As far as Byron's own brief experience with parliamentary politics went, it was difficult to relate to the optimism that Hunt promoted in *The Examiner*. Desponding over what he perceived to be his own inability to promote real change in Parliament, Byron made the following confession to his half-sister, Augusta Leigh, in March of 1813: "my parliamentary schemes are not much to my taste—I spoke twice last Session—& was told it was well enough—but I hate the thing altogether—& have no intention to 'strut another hour' on that stage" (*BLJ* 3:32). In January of 1816, Byron suggested to Hunt that it was the "corruption" of the political system itself that turned him away from politics: "if you knew what a hopeless & lethargic den of dullness & drawling our hospital is—during a debate—& what a mass of corruption in it's patients—you would wonder—not that—I very seldom speak—but I ever attempted it—feeling—as I trust I do—independently" (*BLJ* 5:19).

Byron's last appearance in Parliament on 1 June 1813 did little to convince him of the value of his political endeavors, even though his speech had been urged by a personal association with Major John Cartwright. Hunt had long supported Cartwright, a veteran advocate for liberal causes, in *The Examiner,* and Byron became acquainted with the reformer through his association with Cartwright's own London Hampden Club in the summer of 1812.[26] Byron's Cartwright speech was a presentation of Cartwright's petition on the abuses and obstructions that liberal petitioners, in general, faced. Byron delivered the speech with force and purpose, and, importantly, it also marked a significant development in *The Examiner*'s handling of the poet's parliamentary career, for it was the first of Byron's speeches to be printed in full in the columns of Hunt's paper.[27] Ultimately, however, Byron came to see his endorsement of Cartwright as yet another futile attempt at politics. When Moore asked Byron about the subject of Cartwright's grievance, the poet, who had been speaking "in a state of most humorous exaltation" afterward, replied, "The grievance? . . . Oh, *that* I forget."[28] The petition, it turns out, had been rejected on the basis of a technicality: a requisite concluding statement in the form of a one-line "prayer" (*CMP* 314) had been left off the document.

For as much as Hunt and other politically minded friends such as Moore and Hobhouse had urged Byron to pursue parliamentary activity beyond his three speeches, the poet never felt his efforts served or could serve to make change or produce meaningful action. David Erdman attributes this attitude to Byron's psychic need for an intimacy that might have provided encouragement, noting Lady Oxford's departure from England in the fall of 1813 as the crucial factor in Byron's growing indifference to politics.[29] In his private journal, Byron may have confirmed the idea: "I presented Cartwright's [petition] last year. . . . But 'I am not i' th' vein' for this business. Now, had [Lady Oxford] been here, she would have *made* me do it. *There* is a woman, who, amid all her fascination, always urged a man to usefulness or glory. Had she remained, she had been my tutelar genius" (*BLJ* 3:228–9). Left to his own devices, without personal support and encouragement, Byron found himself instead practicing a kind of "willful nihilism," as Malcolm Kelsall says, when it came to his political career.[30]

It is nevertheless remarkable that in the very same journal entry in which he lamented Lady Oxford's departure and recorded his disgust with his parliamentary efforts, Byron also recorded his impressions of "Leigh Hunt (an acquisition to my acquaintance—through Moore—of last summer)." The detailed entry makes it clear that Byron thought highly of Hunt during this early phase of their friendship. In fact, Byron has left us a description of Hunt's character that is certainly one of the more probing and balanced evaluations of Hunt by a contemporary:

> Hunt is an extraordinary character, and not exactly of the present age. He reminds me more of the Pym and Hampden times—much talent, great independence of spirit, and an austere, yet not repulsive, aspect. If he goes on *qualis ab incepto*, I know few men who will deserve more praise or obtain it. I must go and see him again;—the rapid succession of adventure, since last summer, added to some serious uneasiness and business, have interrupted our acquaintance; but he is a man worth knowing; and though, for his own sake, I wish him out of prison, I like to study character in such situations. He has been unshaken, and will continue so. I don't think him deeply versed in life;—he is the bigot of virtue (not religion), and enamoured of the beauty of that "empty name," as the last breath of Brutus pronounced, and every day proves it. He is, perhaps, a little opinionated, as all men who are the *centre* of *circles*, wide or narrow—the Sir Oracles, in whose name two or three are gathered together—must be, and even as Johnson was; but, withal, a valuable man, and less vain than success and even the consciousness of preferring "the right to the expedient" might excuse.
>
> (*BLJ* 3:228)

It is tempting to think that Hunt might have taken Lady Oxford's place in spurring Byron to political activity during his remaining years in London. But where Moore and Hobhouse had already failed, there seems little reason to think Hunt could have succeeded. Besides, there were complications. As Byron admitted, other pursuits and personal dilemmas had "interrupted" the "acquaintance." The friendship had commenced a year too late to have any impact on Byron's decision to cast off the "parliamentary mummeries" (*BLJ* 3:206) he had come to detest by the summer of 1813.

Napoleon and *The Examiner*

Carl Woodring once suggested that it would be "instructive to have a close chronological comparison of Hunt's assessments [of Napoleon] with those of Byron."[31] A comprehensive comparison of this kind would, of course, be a daunting task given *The Examiner*'s weekly coverage of Napoleon. As John Clubbe and Simon Bainbridge have shown, the list of known statements that Byron made about Napoleon is also extensive.[32] Napoleon, to be sure, was a figure of great importance to Byron and Hunt. In fact, the French emperor became the explicit focus of an extended dialogue between them—a dialogue that was carried out in the pages of *The Examiner* through private letters, poetic exchanges, and literary reviews. The conversation spans a dramatic two-year period between 1814 and 1816 during which Byron and Hunt witnessed Napoleon's abdication and exile, the Hundred Days, and his final defeat at the Battle of Waterloo. To provide context for their extended dialogue about Napoleon, it will be useful to begin with an overview of the Napoleon character that Hunt constructed for the readers of *The Examiner*.

Hunt had many political heroes, but Napoleon was not one of them. The political heroes Hunt championed in *The Examiner* were liberal-minded men and women with the ability to hold multiple, often conflicting, viewpoints. They were individuals with the ability to act disinterestedly for the social good. In short, they were individuals who possessed what Hunt called "philosophical" talent—figures such as Sydney Smith, Henry Brougham, and Byron, Hunt felt, all possessed this talent.[33] The most important historical touchstone for Hunt's philosophical hero worship, however, was the ninth-century English King Alfred. Alfred, though a highly successful military leader, was committed to governmental reform and the advancement of learning and education. As Hunt saw it, Alfred was proof that a politician could govern as a philosopher. Napoleon was undoubtedly the most important political figure of the Romantic age, but for Hunt he came to resemble other disreputable historical personages of a similar stature. To Hunt, historical leaders from Caesar to Charlemagne, though unquestionably talented, had too much of the military sense about them and lacked the imaginative sympathies and philosophical talents that the editor regarded as the ideal criteria for effective leadership.

In the early years of *The Examiner*, Hunt nevertheless developed a dual attitude toward Napoleon, carefully separating the French emperor's useful leveling of Europe's tyrannical dynasties from his relentless exercising of what Coleridge called the "commanding genius."[34] Indeed, in July of 1809, Hunt asserted his independence from the polarizing popular political positions on Napoleon's character: "For my part, I can admire the talents of this wonderful man, his activity in prosperity, his prudence in adversity, his encouragement of the fine arts, and his freedom from luxury and effeminacy, without having the least respect for his bad temper, his bad passions, or his bloodshed" (*E* 81 [16 July 1809]: 449–50). A year later, Hunt reiterated: "I am willing to steer properly between extremes in the estimation of character, and for that reason I have always admired the talents of BONAPARTE, as I would have done those of FREDERICK, of ALEXANDER, of GENGHIS KHAN, or any other illustrious slaughterer of mankind." Hunt qualified the idea, once again, by noting that "not the less have I deprecated the abuse of those talents,—not the less have I deprecated his ambition, his bloodshed, his manifestations of meanness, and all the other traits in his character which have cut him off from true greatness" (*E* 134 [22 July 1810]: 450). Hunt's sympathy for the "illustrious slaughterer[s] of mankind" may seem uncharacteristic, but, as Philip Shaw has suggested, the utilitarian side of Hunt's liberalism "enable[d] him, despite his avowed hatred of war, to rationalize its long-term effects."[35] Hunt confirmed the idea in blunt terms: "it is a truth which posterity will acknowledge, that the nations [Napoleon] overthrows are usually in want of such a conqueror" (*E* 23 [5 June 1808]: 362).

Yet, over the course of 1810, Napoleon's military ambitions, as well as a series of repressive measures taken to limit the freedom of the press in France (a topic Hunt highlighted in *The Examiner* in September of 1810), made the editor increasingly skeptical of the French emperor's willingness to follow a virtuous path to governance. The following spring, Hunt's commentary on Napoleon acquired a mocking aspect generally reserved for favorite *Examiner* targets like the Prince Regent. In his lead article for 28 April 1811, Hunt argued that "The evil that [Napoleon] has done is his own,—the result of his own bad passions—the perversion of his own talent" (*E* 174 [28 April 1811]: 260). Hunt supported the idea with a caricature of the French emperor: "he has founded a new dynasty, married into the first House in Europe, made kings of his brothers and his servants, and has just had his last wishes crowned by an heir: in a word, he has grown fat, and that is a sure sign of being in comfortable condition." To complete the portrait, Hunt offered several unflattering comparisons: "That this cutter up of flesh may look well and jolly, as the phrase is, may be very true; it is a common case with butchers; but Nero was fat, and at the same time miserable; William the Conqueror was fat, and his jollity was nothing but disease" (*E* 174 [28 April 1811]: 259).

Near the end of 1812, Hunt's attitude toward the French emperor showed no fundamental change, but the Napoleon phenomenon had clearly taken a toll on the editor: "The world wants repose, in order to enjoy the means of that improvement, which, amidst all the evils it has suffered, Providence has been working out for its future good" (*E* 246 [13 September 1812] 579). The appeal to a Providential plan, a new idea for Hunt and one to which he infrequently alludes, nevertheless hinted at his disillusionment with Napoleonic ambition.[36] The following year, Hunt continued to think in larger and more abstract ways about the French emperor's actions; at the same time, he continued to write about the state of Europe in a vivid and intimate style:

> [P]erhaps at this very moment, while our readers are turning over these pages in the stillness and bosom-peace of their families, thousands of human creatures, in the fate of every one of whom a family's happiness may be involved, are being bruised, and slashed, and scattered to pieces,—and all on account of one man's ambition, created by the vices and fostered by the weakness of bad Courts.

At this time, Hunt also continued to voice his general detestation of war, an attitude he would develop more fully several years later in *Captain Sword and Captain Pen* (1835):

> We have no wish to soften the minds of people needlessly, or to declaim about evils to no purpose; neither are we believers in the perfectibility of human nature; but we do think, that the succession of miseries which any despot who happens to be cleverer than his neighbours has it in his power to inflict upon mankind, may some time or another be found to be an absurdity too melancholy for tolerance; and that some limit, at least, may be put to that puerile and vain passion for war.
>
> (*E* 280 [9 May 1813]: 295)

In 1813, Hunt's resistance to philosophical extremes kept him from fully endorsing the Godwinian "perfectibility" that the young Shelley fervently championed. And later that same year, Hunt, from his own corner in Horsemonger Lane Gaol, had finally joined the choir of Britons urging Napoleon's defeat: "without indulging in dreams of earthly perfectibility, [we] believe that something may be done, and every thing ought be tried, for reducing the food and appetite of ambition" (*E* 304 [24 October 1813]: 674).

Despite Hunt's disillusion with and near dismissal of the French emperor at the end of 1813, one unexpected event gave the editor pause: Napoleon's abdication in April of 1814. Hunt not only welcomed the news but the situation presented a new and encouraging line of inquiry for *The Examiner*. Hunt now asked: could Napoleon's exile and imprisonment be a path to philosophical reformation? Hunt was quick to embrace the idea, and the thought of Napoleon's imprisoned condition on the Isle of Elba suddenly seemed similar to his own situation a thousand miles away in London. Hunt even found he could write with renewed optimism upon the "illustrious slaughterer" for whom he had long held mixed feelings of admiration and disgust: "If he can stand all this, and turn it into any thing like philosophy, he will be a greater man than he ever shewed himself in prosperity" (*E* 328 [10 April 1814]: 238). Hunt continued in this vein throughout the month:

> If such a man can bear the burden of solitude we shall certainly be inclined to give him credit for greater qualities than we ever before thought he possessed; for we are not of opinion with some persons, that it would have shewn a braver spirit in him to have fled and fought it out to the last, dying perhaps like another CATILINE, under a heap of slain, and with his face grinning upwards: such a death might have been more of a piece with his violent and disdainful life, but it certainly would not have redounded so much to his credit for real courage, which consists in patience and not in desperation.
>
> (*E* 329 [17 April 1814]: 243)

Although exile had provided Napoleon with an opportunity for philosophical renewal, as Hunt believed, it had also effectively disproved Hunt's early prediction for the French emperor's fate:

> Like all men who have risen into greatness by trampling on the forms and civil intercourse of the times, he has no point to which he can recede in case of failure: he has no contemporaries to whose level he can sink without disturbing their repose and their passions: he cannot retreat, like a common monarch, to the peaceful enjoyment of his throne after defeat: he has too violently outraged the *"noble race of established potentates"* to hope for the least forbearance from their jealousy and revenge: his hopes exist upon their hopelessness; he has been too great ever to be little; and if he falls he will fall, like SAMPSON, in the last indignant effort of his strength, bringing down on his head the mighty structures and the mighty men of the age.
>
> (*E* 36 [4 September 1808]: 562)

The comparison of Napoleon to the larger-than-life Samson was the closest Hunt would come to predicting a sensational end for Napoleon. For Byron, however, such an end for Napoleon was an expectation.

Although Byron's attitude toward the French emperor fluctuated between moments of intense idolatry, bitter frustration, and serious depression (sometimes all at the same time), the poet had exceedingly high expectations for Napoleon. In fact, Peter Cochran's claim that the "world of art is where Byron's Napoleon belongs" provides an apt basis of comparison of Byron's attitudes toward Napoleon with those held by Hunt. For Byron, as Cochran explains, "to bring [Napoleon] into the dull, oppressive world of English politics would spoil the effect, and prick the dream-bubble."[37] For Hunt, as we have seen, Napoleon came to be a figure who was firmly grounded in the "dull" world of politics and history, where he was subject to the common pitfalls of mortal men and judged accordingly. Byron's early interest in Napoleon had already revealed the French emperor's alluring, mythical quality for the young poet. Indeed, Byron's well-known defense of his Napoleonic bust at Harrow, though full of showy bravado, was symbolic.[38] Byron had literally defended Napoleon as a work of art. The poet, of course, would soon discover the fragility of the clay with which his hero had been molded. Yet, for Byron, Napoleon would always represent imaginative possibility: he was neither the Satanic tyrant that the Tory press made him out to be nor the military dictator that Hunt had eventually presented him as in the pages of *The Examiner*. Byron refused to see Napoleon as anything but a larger-than-life character, even if that character was doomed to be "nothing, save the jest of Fame" (*CPW* 2:90, line 328). In short, Byron saw Napoleon as a figure worthy of poetry. If there were flaws in his character, there was still an irresistible "fire / And motion of the soul which will not dwell / In its own narrow being" (*CPW* 2:91, lines 371–3).

Two Napoleonic Odes

When it was first published on 16 April 1814, Byron's *Ode to Napoleon Buonaparte* joined a market already crowded with extemporaneous verses inspired by the news of the French emperor's abdication. Offerings included, among others, Stratford Canning's *Buonaparte, a Poem*, an "Ode" by John Hamilton Reynolds, and Hunt's "Ode for the Spring of 1814."[39] Hunt's "Ode" appeared in *The Examiner* on 17 April and Byron must have been pleased with it, for he promptly sent it to John Murray, praising the poem's sentiments but criticizing the style: "the thoughts are good—but the expressions *buckram* except here & there" (*BLJ* 4:98).[40] One reason Byron may have wanted his publisher to see Hunt's "Ode" was to offer a basis of comparison with his own recently published *Ode*, for there are indeed "thoughts" in Hunt's production that resonate with Byron's own. At the same time, as Timothy Webb has shown, Byron and Hunt had already been engaged in an intense private discussion about Napoleon's character in their correspondence at the beginning of April. Byron, therefore, came to Hunt's "Ode" with a keen interest in Hunt's ideas about the French emperor. In fact, many of the issues the friends were debating in private were made public in their respective odes.

Byron's *Ode* portrays Napoleon as a character that, in many ways, is close in likeness to the Napoleon Hunt came to develop in the preceding years in *The Examiner*. For Byron, Napoleon, fallen from sublime heights, is an "Ill-minded man!" (line 10) and the source of his own ruin: "By gazing on thyself grown blind, / Thou taught'st the rest to see" (lines 12–3). In his "Ode," Hunt similarly draws Napoleon as one who has been "Swept in his own careering blast" (*E* 329 [17 April 1814]: 251, line 3). Furthermore, at the start of Byron's *Ode*, a series of heavy pauses heightens the description of Napoleon's sudden and dramatic change:

> 'Tis done—but yesterday a King!
>   And arm'd with Kings to strive—
> And now thou art a nameless thing
>   So abject—yet alive!
>
> (lines 1–4)

Hunt, likewise, proceeds in his "Ode" with an effective use of rhetorical balance. Napoleon's fall from power, introduced in the compact opening lines, "THE vision then is past, / That held the eyes of nations (lines 1–2), is enlarged and reinforced by the anaphora that concludes the first stanza: "We look'd, and saw the wonder on his throne; / We rais'd our eyes again, and lo, his place was gone" (lines 10–1). Hunt's "Ode" contains other rhetorical flourishes that Byron would have likely admitted. For example, Hunt's aphoristic "Experience, Truth, and Conquest of the Will, / These took the troubler's place, and bade the plague be still" (lines 21–2) surely would have pleased the poet who would later write: "There is the moral of all human tales; / 'Tis but the same rehearsal of the past, / First Freedom, and then Glory—when that fails, / Wealth, vice, corruption,—barbarism at last" (*CPW* 2:160, lines 964–7).

At the same time, there are significant stylistic differences between the two odes. Hunt's poem is composed of six stanzas of eleven lines each, a sharp reduction from Byron's fifteen stanzas of nine lines each in its first edition. Metrically, Hunt's poem varies with more frequency than Byron's *Ode*, which primarily utilizes more compact lines. In addition, Byron's *Ode* develops unfavorable comparisons between Napoleon and historical or mythical figures, such as Prometheus, Sulla, and Timour, in order to dramatize the significance of the French emperor's fall. Hunt's "Ode," on the other hand, shows no obvious interest in historical allusion, employing instead images relating to the natural world, including a sustained metaphor of seasonal change befitting the poem's title: "And lo, how earth and sky, / As if the charm completing, / From winter's other tyranny / Revive, and give us greeting" (lines 34–7). In these images and the related image of the "bee, that rings the basking hour, / Comes for his kiss from flow'r to flow'r" (lines 41–2), we can perceive stylistic differences between the two odes. We can also perceive such differences in Hunt's preference for figurative devices such as synesthesia, which he employs frequently in his "Ode," observing "Never did sweeter sound / From discord drop resolving" (lines 23–4) and "With frank eyes listening to the glassy spheres; / The Eagles of the North were seen" (lines 29–30).

The essential philosophical differences the two friends developed with respect to Napoleon's fallen condition become evident in the conclusions to their odes. Hunt, as we have seen, held a profound hope for Napoleon's philosophical rehabilitation in his isolation. Beginning with the final stanza of his "Ode," however, Hunt transforms the setting into that of his own prison cell, using the conceit, paradoxically, to celebrate his own liberation:

> O Liberty! O breath
>   Of all that's true existence!
> Thou, at whose touch the soul at death
>   But leaps to joy and distance;
>   Before thy present call
>   The very captive's wall,
> If wrongly round him, like a curtain flies;
>   The green and laughing world he sees,
>   Waters, and plains, and waving trees,
> The skim of birds, and the blue-doming skies,
> And sits with smile at heart, and patience-levell'd eyes.
>
> (lines 56–66)

In the end, Hunt's "Ode" shows little overt concern with Napoleon, becoming instead a prayer to "Liberty" from the perspective of the imprisoned editor himself. With Napoleon suffering the same fate, Hunt can rest contentedly knowing that when the iron "curtain flies" his eyes will meet a "green and laughing world," not a stern, inhospitable world ruled by war and Napoleonic ambition. Patience in adversity becomes a virtuous rallying point for Hunt: Napoleon's literal imprisonment becomes Hunt's metaphorical freedom. Byron, on the other hand, concludes his *Ode* not with Hunt's philosophical contentment but in a great fervor of perplexity and agitation. Pursuing Napoleon to the last, Byron poses a series of unresolved and increasingly vexed questions: "Thou Timour! in his captive's cage / What thoughts will there be thine, / While brooding in thy prisoned rage?" (lines 127–9). Is Napoleon, like Timour, without his "sceptre" to be with "All sense . . . gone" (line 132), or will the fallen emperor "like the thief of fire from heaven, / . . . withstand the shock?" (lines 136–7). Either way, the situation, as Byron sees it, is hopeless. In the poem's final stanza, the speaker addresses Napoleon, observing pointedly that even Satan "in his fall preserv'd his pride, / And if a mortal, had as proudly died!" (lines 143–4). The final message of the *Ode*, implying the necessity of heroic death, would become a serious cause of concern to Hunt and a topic for discussion in *The Examiner.*

Napoleon and the Human Context

By 24 April, Hunt had read Byron's *Ode*, deciding that its message of despair required an immediate response, and his *Examiner* provided the opportunity to capitalize on the immediacy of the subject. In his lead article "Bonaparte" for that Sunday, Hunt began by reiterating the optimistic message from his "Ode":

> [P]eace, in short, after an interval of twenty years, suddenly throwing open the intercourse between nations, and a new reasonableness of expectation given to the hopes of all lovers of improvement and happiness,—all these things, coming too at a time when the whole of christendom is keeping holiday, and when spring has returned with double luxury after a winter of unexampled severity, naturally carry people beyond their usual limits of enjoyment, and throw the common-places of life and business into the back-ground.

Elsewhere, Hunt elaborated upon his hope for general "improvement and happiness" by explaining that he now felt free to indulge his imagination: "Thus the world out of doors is represented to us as exhibiting a kind of perpetual fair; and luckily we can easily form a picture of it in our minds; for Attorney-Generals cannot commit one's fancy to custody" (*E* 330 [24 April 1814]: 257). The ability to "form a picture" of a "perpetual fair" of spring was, of course, a basic survival mechanism for the imprisoned Hunt. Keats celebrated the idea in a poetic display of political solidarity with the editor: "Think you he nought but prison walls did see, / Till, so unwilling, thou unturn'dst the key?" (lines 6–7).[41] As Anthony Holden points out, even the wax seal Hunt applied to the correspondence he sent from prison carried the Latin expression *Ego solus sum liber*, a tag that served the dual purpose of promoting Hunt's philosophical resolve while reassuring correspondents of his well-being.[42] The occasion of Napoleon's abdication was thus an exceedingly joyous one for Hunt, and his mood, if not his health, had taken a turn for the better.

Perhaps the most revealing aspect of Hunt's "Bonaparte" article for 24 April, however, is the illustration from Napoleon's domestic life that Hunt provided in order to make his case against Byron's *Ode* and convince his friend to view the situation in a more human context. Hunt introduced Napoleon's private character by surveying a series of anecdotes, commenting approvingly upon eyewitness reports that Napoleon wept publicly when he announced his abdication. Anticipating objections on this point, Hunt argued that such display of emotion should not be seen as a sign of weakness (Byron had argued the same in support of the Princess Charlotte in his "Lines to a Lady Weeping"), but rather as proof that even in a hardened soldier like Napoleon there exists the "kindliness of human nature" (*E* 330 [24 April 1814]: 258). Hunt went so far as to suggest that some "declamatory persons" wishing to object to such a notion might consider the classical authority of Homer whose Achilles and Odysseus were both men prone to tears. There is a strong suggestion here that Hunt, in fact, had the classically minded author of the *Ode* in mind, for Hunt proceeded in the next section of the article to address Byron directly, criticizing his *Ode* for its portrayal of Napoleon as weak-minded for choosing life over death.

In their private discussion of Napoleon's character at the beginning of April, the focus, seemingly provided by Byron, had been on the Napoleonic character in a historical and political context, with Byron comparing the French emperor to figures as diverse as Richard III and the Byzantine Emperor Palaeologus.[43] In his analysis of "Bonaparte" (and Byron's *Ode*) in the 24 April *Examiner*, however, Hunt provided a new context for the continuation of their early April discussion: the intimate domestic spaces of Napoleon's private life. Concluding his selection of Napoleonic chitchat with a "terrible anecdote" about Napoleon and a "favourite" servant, Hunt related that the latter was said to have presented his "master" with a "carefully sharpened sword" soon after the abdication proceedings concluded. Hunt heightened the effect for readers by presenting the anecdote in dialogue form, with the servant inquiring about the lethal weapon he has brought: "Will you use it yourself, or shall I put it through your body?" When Napoleon replies that he thinks neither option will do, favoring life instead, the servant asks Napoleon to slay *him*, for he would no longer be able to "live under such *disgrace.*" Hunt rejected the story outright, citing a false understanding of social custom: "unfortunately, domestics do not talk in this way to their masters." Nevertheless, the notion of heroic death that the anecdote raised was a way for Hunt to segue into his discussion of Byron's *Ode*: "We have been induced to say a word or two more upon this point by the publication of an Ode to NAPOLEON, attributed to a celebrated young Nobleman, and bearing indeed evident marks of his strong way of putting things." Hunt specifically targeted the "strong" import of the following lines: "If thou hadst died as honour dies, / Some new Napoleon might arise" (lines 95–6). Hunt asked: "what is to be understood by dying 'as honour dies?' Is it in battle, or on the scaffold, or by his own hand?" Acknowledging such possibilities, Hunt added that

> honour has also made its exit very quietly on occasion, and by which of these deaths was NAPOLEON to perform what he promised, and prove that *adversity was not too much for him?* There is the point. We confess we were rather surprised to find this opinion coming

from the Noble Lord, to whom the above lines are attributed, as in his other productions, he appears to have a fine apprehension of affliction, and of the courage necessary to bear it.

(*E* 330 [24 April 1814]: 258)

Hunt, in contrasting the message of Byron's *Ode* with the "fine apprehension of affliction" found in "his other productions," may have been recalling the title character of *Childe Harold* who, though gloomy to the last, "learn'd to moralize" with "conscious Reason" (*CPW* 2:21, lines 319, 321). But Hunt's immediate purpose is not to make comparisons between the *Ode* and Byron's previously published poetry, but rather to convince Byron to reconsider his bleak opinion of Napoleon in his fallen condition by drawing a more humane picture of the situation. Indeed, Hunt proceeded to ask of those who think as Byron does on the subject: "is not the chief secret of their opinion—this,—that they have formed rather too fine a notion of a conqueror like BONAPARTE in the first instance, and then thought that he was bound to keep up to it to the last in a striking, rather than a proper manner?" Hunt desires Byron to see Napoleon's seemingly cowardly response in defeat as one that was both human and noble. Hunt thus concluded by offering Byron an alternative to consider: "[Napoleon's] not putting himself to death in the first instance, makes him something better in our minds than a mere CATILINE or MAKIMINUS; and if he leads a reasonable life in his exile, and does what little he can to make those about him comfortable, in recompense of all the misery his soldiership has inflicted, we shall say, not that he was a great man when he was Emperor, but that he gave some symptoms at last that he *might have been*" (*E* 330 [24 April 1814]: 259).

Hunt was not alone in opposing Byron's *Ode* for promoting the "desperate flash-out of a man's career."[44] The reviewer for the *Reasoner*, for instance, made a "single objection to the morality" of Byron's poem, arguing that to "talk of the bravery of suicide sounds too much of the Roman." The reviewer, echoing Hunt, instead posited that "it is a far higher, a far more noble, a far more magnanimous species of courage, which enables a man to bear the evils of life without repining; to suffer patiently the sorrows of adversity; to prove that the darts of adverse fortune are too blunt to wound him" (*RR* B5:2009). The reviewer for the *Scourge* lamented that "Lord Byron, living in a Christian country, should have neglected a noble opportunity of alluding to the influence of religion, and that he should not have reprobated the act of suicide rather than have taunted Napoleon with not committing it" (*RR* B5:2231). The *Theatrical Inquisitor* gave perhaps the most scathing overall assessment, calling the poem a "collection of trite reflections upon ambition, and the vanity of sceptres, and triumphs, and victories, eked out with common-place allusions drawn from Milton and the Roman History" (*RR* B5:2248). In any event, Hunt's firm rejection of the

Ode's message of despair did not dissuade Byron from supplying the editor with additional Napoleonic material of a notably private character for his next *Examiner.*

Domestic Politics: Napoleon and Marie-Louise[45]

While Hunt and Byron were debating the fate of Napoleon, John Cam Hobhouse, as ardent an admirer of the French emperor as Byron, had rushed off to Paris to witness the dramatic events as they unfolded. He wrote to Byron on 20 April, complaining of "bad lodgings" and noting that "not a single thing in Paris" had answered his "expectation[s]."[46] Hobhouse's letter nevertheless forms a crucial link to the on-going conversation between Byron and Hunt about Napoleon in the spring of 1814. After receiving Hobhouse's letter, Byron promptly sent the missive on to Hunt, who gladly took "extracts" for inclusion in that Sunday's *Examiner.*[47] The printing of private correspondence (real or fictitious) in the pages of Hunt's newspaper was an established practice and one that would be repeated, but Byron's willingness to share a letter from Hobhouse, Byron's close acquaintance whom Hunt had not yet met, sent a clear message of political solidarity to the imprisoned editor.[48] Hunt would later interpret Byron's openness in such matters to be a singular lack of discretion. Yet by publishing extracts from Hobhouse's letter in *The Examiner* on 1 May, Hunt showed no apprehension, at the time, about his friend's epistolary openness, using the intimacy of the letter format as a way to continue their Napoleonic dialogue while publicly reinforcing the value that he placed on his friendship with Byron.

In fact, Byron's policy of open intelligence sharing seems to have emboldened the editor to take additional liberties. In addition to printing a large section of Hobhouse's letter, Hunt appears to have included a major section, if not the whole, of Byron's own letter of late April that had been sent with the Hobhouse correspondence. Though Hunt did not name Byron as the author, the content of the letter readily suggests Byron, for we know from Hunt's reply of 27 April that Byron had written to him with reflections on the Austrian-born Empress Marie-Louise, Napoleon's second wife: "I quite agree with you about the Empress," Hunt stated, but added: "you are getting upon dangerous with an editor. Do you know, I was half tempted to extract the arguments of your last [letter] (the best that are to be found for that side of the question), & answer them in my next Examiner, as a correspondent's,—with permission, of course." Hunt must have prepared the 1 May *Examiner* over the next several days, deciding in the end to incorporate his friend's thoughts on the Empress with or without his express "permission." That he did so, however, should not be surprising, as a discussion of Marie-Louise in *The Examiner* would have continued the general theme of their April correspondence. Moreover, the inclusion of Byron's private letter presented Hunt with an opportunity to further develop the illusion of intimacy that had already been used to great effect in the pages of *The Examiner*. The letter, embedded in Hunt's lead article, "Louis XVIII.—The Emperor Napoleon," is prefaced thus: "Upon this subject we cannot forbear quoting the words of a friend, whose burst of feeling is always worth listening to, and who is certainly no friend to NAPOLEON, as his name, if we thought ourselves at liberty to mention it, would abundantly testify" (*E* 331 [1 May 1814]: 275). The designation "friend," once used with strong political import by Southey, Wordsworth, and Coleridge, had an equally powerful public suggestiveness for Hunt. And Hunt's claim that the "friend" who supplied the letter is "certainly no friend to NAPOLEON" was appropriate, for the editor knew, having read Byron's *Ode* the previous week, that Byron had little, if any, sympathy for Napoleon in his fallen condition.

The letter from Byron that Hunt printed in *The Examiner* makes it clear that the two friends also had disagreements about Marie-Louise:

> What think you of the *Empress*? Her abandonment of him has destroyed my *philoguny*—I have in one part of the world or another observed something of life—and have generally remarked that though men almost always to a man fall away from the *falling*—no degradation of rank or even of character—nothing but a gross personal ill-conduct towards *herself*—and often not even *that*—will tear away a woman from the object of her duty or attachment. Of course I put the passions out of the question:—if there is another and professed lover in the case, original sin may prevail;—but I mean a cold-blooded, interested desertion—a calculating abandonment—a bias to the stronger side—no—no—hitherto *that* was a *masculine* vice, and now it ought to be a feminine infamy. 'Sdeath—she should have followed him with her boy in her arms to "date obolum Belisario," were it necessary.
>
> (*E* 331 [1 May 1814]: 275)

Byron had written to Annabella Milbanke on 20 April about Marie-Louise, repeating some of the ideas that were included in the letter Hunt printed in *The Examiner* on 1 May.[49] In the letter to Annabella, Diego Saglia points out that Byron's discussion of Napoleon and Marie-Louise presents a pressing political issue (Napoleon's abdication) as being just as important as a domestic issue (Napoleon's marital relations).[50] Hunt, of course, found both the public and private concerns of such men and women to have social relevance, for it reinforced his belief that there was a direct correlation between the private habits of public figures and their ability to govern effectively. Indeed, in 1808, in the first year of *The Examiner*'s existence, Hunt had written: "I do not think that a minister, or any other great officer of Government, who is privately vicious, can be a proper guardian of the public" (*E* 30 [24 July 1808]: 465). The idea was repeated in Hunt's response to Byron's comments on Napoleon and Marie-Louise in the letter printed in *The Examiner*:

> We are persuaded this will be the first impression with every body of right feelings; but till we know more of the private qualities both of MARIA LOUISA and her husband, the conclusion against a woman under such circumstances will become too painful to one's contemplations; and the "philoguny" of our friend in question will, we are very certain, after a death of some thirty seconds, start up again at the first glance of a fair English face, and not be behind hand in *imagining* every possible excuse for the Empress.

We know from Hunt's 27 April letter to Byron that he had agreed, in theory, with the poet's strongly worded opinion of the Empress's apparent failing, what Byron calls her "feminine infamy," for "refus[ing]" to follow her husband into exile. Hunt, however, had qualified the idea, not knowing enough about the private characters of the married couple. After making light of Byron's exaggerated despair over the loss of his "philoguny," Hunt offered a more balanced appraisal of the situation, questioning Byron's ideas about the Empress's requisite fidelity to her husband and rejecting the idea that even a husband's "gross personal ill-conduct" might not "tear away a woman from the object of her duty." Hunt speculated instead that if the Empress had abandoned Napoleon, then it may be justified, in the event that his private character was found to have been as "brutal" as his public character. Should Napoleon be cleared from private misconduct, Hunt suggested that he was ready to follow Byron's lead, noting that the Empress's refusal would "exhibit the unnatural spectacle of a wife and mother deserting a man in his misfortunes."

Although Hunt's decision to print his friend's private thoughts on Marie-Louise in the pages of *The Examiner* may have been made without explicit approval, Byron seems to have willingly tolerated, and likely encouraged, the editorial actions taken by the imprisoned journalist. This, of course, would not be the last instance in which Hunt was to take liberties with Byron's correspondence, as Hunt's later printing of several private letters in *Lord Byron and Some of His Contemporaries* reveals. Importantly, in 1814, Hunt clearly saw the publication of Byron's letter in *The Examiner* as a way to publicly acknowledge the strength of their friendship while continuing their on-going debate over Napoleon's abdication crisis.

Two Napoleonic Lyrics

Between April 1815 and April 1816, Hunt published four Byron-authored lyrics in *The Examiner*: "Oh! Snatched Away in Beauty's Bloom" (23 April 1815); "Bright Be the Place of Thy Soul" (11 June 1815); "Napoleon's Farewell (From the French)" (30 July 1815); and "On the Star of 'The Legion of Honour' (From the French)" (8 April 1816). At least two of these, "Napoleon's Farewell" and "On the Star of 'The Legion of Honour,'" were presented to Hunt with Byron's express permission and special directions for printing. Details concerning Hunt's receipt of the two non-Napoleonic lyrics, "Oh! Snatched Away in Beauty's Bloom" and "Bright Be the Place of Thy Soul," are not forthcoming, but both poems were also published in other editions by Isaac Nathan and John Murray. The two Napoleonic lyrics, however, form an integral part of Byron's on-going creative engagements with the French emperor and an equally important part of the poet's political engagements with the editor of *The Examiner*.

Hunt had been following Napoleon's activities closely at the beginning of 1815, insisting in his lead article for the 1 January *Examiner*, "The Bonapartes," that it was difficult to do otherwise: "Bonaparte still forces himself upon your mind as himself; he depends upon nothing unconnected with the direct personal idea of him to give him importance; he is watched in imagination." In the same *Examiner* issue, Hunt was also glad to make the happy announcement of his friend's approaching nuptials. The "great pleasure" Hunt took in reporting on Byron's private activities ("a poet's honeymoon is something worth mentioning") agreed with his generally festive mood at the beginning of the new year (*E* 366 [1 January 1815]: 1, 8). Hunt's release from prison was only a month away, and throughout the fall of 1814 he had been readying for publication a new political poem called *The Descent of Liberty*, his first major offering since *The Feast of the Poets* had been reissued in 1814.

Written in the summer of 1814 but not published until 1815, *Descent* is a poetical "Mask" and a fanciful allegory of restored peace to the British Isles following Napoleon's exile to Elba. *Descent* enlarged upon the hopes for peace Hunt had described in his "Ode for the Spring of 1814" in a more elaborate poetical dress. As Hunt explained in the preface to his new poem:

> THE following piece was written, partly to vary the hours of imprisonment and ill health, partly to indulge the imagination of the author during a season of public joy when he could realize no sights for himself, and chiefly to express the feelings of hope and delight, with which every enthusiastic lover of freedom must have witnessed the downfall of the great Apostate from Liberty.[51]

In *Descent*, Hunt presented Napoleon in allegorical costume as an "Enchanter," who was "foil'd in his attempt to force / His art beyond its limits" (lines 16–7). Now in exile, he

> Sits wrapp'd in double gloom, listening at times,
> With half fear, to catch the expected sound
> Of numbers coming in their fresh revenge
> To dash him from his height.
>
> (Prologue, lines 24–7)

According to "Liberty," the poem's heroic savior, "This is the hour / I look'd for" (lines 27–8) and will "Descend in lustre through the freshen'd air, / Met by the flowering Spring" (lines 34–5) to "Summon the triumphs and the joys about me, / And lead a lovelier period for mankind" (lines 37–8).

On 12 March 1815, however, less than two months after he had presented Byron with a gift copy of *Descent*, doubtless wanting his friend to read its message of hope for a "lovelier period," Hunt's vision of liberty had gone. In his lead article for *The Examiner* "Bonaparte in France Again," Hunt gave his first public reaction to the news of Napoleon's escape from Elba: "WE want nothing now, to finish the romantic history of the present times, but a visit from the Man in the Moon, or an invasion from a hitherto undiscovered people who shall be to us what the Spaniards were to the Mexicans. BONAPARTE has taken his flight from Elba" (*E* 376 [12 March 1815]: 161). As the shock settled, Hunt followed Napoleon's "flight" over the next several weeks. On 19 March, he concluded the two-part "Bonaparte in France Again," and on 26 March he claimed that "[n]ever, in it's character and results, was there a more extraordinary journey than this," a thought that echoed Byron's own comments from late March to Moore: "It is impossible not to be dazzled and overwhelmed by [Napoleon's] character and career" (*BLJ* 4:284). Not until 7 May did Hunt relieve himself of Napoleonic coverage. For two weeks straight, he reported on the subject of "Italian Independence," but, as the Battle of Waterloo neared, the editor returned his focus firmly to Napoleon in a run of lead articles from 28 May's "Approaching Contest with Bonaparte" to 2 July's "Victory of Waterloo—Bonaparte's Abdication." The first half of 1815 was, as Hunt reiterated, an extraordinary time.

It was at this moment that Byron put new pressure on the editor and his *Examiner* by revisiting their Napoleonic debate of the previous spring. In July, Byron sent Hunt "Napoleon's Farewell." Byron knew that Hunt invited debate on topics of political interest but was nevertheless open about the "position" expressed in his new Napoleonic lyric, writing to his friend: "My dear Hunt . . . I send you a scrawl in rhyme which—if you use it—I would wish to be inserted *anonymously*—it certainly does not contain your political sentiments nor indeed my own altogether—but I have endeavored to adapt them to the person speaking or *singing*—if he can ever be supposed to do so simple a thing as *ye last*" (*BLJ* 4:306–7). Hunt replied the same day, but said little about Byron's poetic gift: "Pray accept my thanks for your poetry, which will, of course, be inserted, & without a name."[52] The brevity of the reply was perhaps the first sign of the anxiety the editor felt about the poem's political message, for Hunt would have perceived that there was still a great distance between his feelings about Napoleon and Byron's.[53]

"Napoleon's Farewell" is formally divided into three stanzas, an organization that mirrors that of other poems in the recently published *Hebrew Melodies* (1815). Furthermore, "Napoleon's Farewell" installs a character speaker, a tactic that can be seen in other lyrics in the *Hebrew Melodies* volume, including "Jephtha's Daughter," "Song of Saul before his Last Battle," "Were My Bosom as False as Thou Deem'st It to Be," "Herod's Lament for Mariamne," and "On the Day of the Destruction of Jerusalem by Titus." "Napoleon's Farewell" also shares identifiable features with other, little known but near contemporary, lyrics such as "Golice Macbane," which concludes the fourth line in each of its seven stanzas with a refrain that praises Macbane, who was urged to an act of "desperate resolution and heroism" at the Battle of Culloden (*CPW* 3:474). Byron always had strong, nostalgic feelings for his Scottish heritage and his praise for Macbane must have rekindled those feelings and provided yet another example of heroic death. As with many of the lyrics included in *Hebrew Melodies*, and indeed within the Biblical tradition of songs upon which they were founded, the speakers of "Golice Macbane" and "Napoleon's Farewell" sing laments not for individual, private suffering, but rather for the larger cultural groups the speakers represent. In this way, both poems can be classified as "national song[s]" and thus part of a genre that had become increasingly popular during the Napoleonic wars.[54] "Napoleon's Farewell," as Byron described it, was meant to be sung and accompanied by music. As such, the basic repetition in the first line of each of the three stanzas reinforces the song-like quality of the lyric: "Farewell to the land" (line 1) becomes "Farewell to thee, France!" (lines 9, 17) in the second and third stanzas. The Napoleonic speaker also proudly declares that "I have warred with a world which vanquished me only" (line 5) and have become the "last single Captive to millions in war!" (line 8). The speaker does momentarily realize, however, that his fallen position came "When the meteor of Conquest allured me too far" (line 6), an idea with which Hunt would have agreed. Yet the second stanza not only intensifies the speaker's lament, but it also shifts the focus from Napoleon's defeated position to that of France itself. The speaker now argues: "I made thee the gem and the wonder of earth,— / But thy weakness decrees I should leave as I found thee, / Decayed in thy glory, and sunk in thy worth" (lines 10–2). The thought only serves to enhance the speaker's resolve: "Oh! for the veteran hearts that were wasted / In strife with the storm, when their battles were won" (lines 13–4). Since fault lies with France and not with the speaker, the latter becomes emboldened, speaking more defiantly in the third stanza: "when Liberty rallies / Once more in thy regions, remember me then" (lines 17–8). Taking a tack opposite that which Hunt had taken in *Descent*, Byron ultimately portrays France, not England, as the potential site of reawakened "Liberty." The lyric's central shift, emphasized in the concluding line, also leaves the emperor's future unwritten: "And yet may thy heart leap awake to my voice— / There are links which must break in the chain that has bound us, / *Then* turn thee and call on the Chief of thy choice!" (lines 22–4).

Hunt, however, was in no mood to celebrate France or its political future in the summer of 1815. In *The Examiner* for 25 June 1815, the editor wrote with a profound sense of melancholy about the recent Battle of Waterloo:

> [L]et us hope that good will come out of the evil, though of a different complexion from what the Allied Sovereigns may contemplate. In one point of view, nothing but affliction and disgust present themselves to the mind at the sight of so many lives destroyed, so many public burdens increased, and so much misery of all sorts occasioned to families; but in another point, the very excess of the thing produces a hope of better days.
>
> (*E* 391 [25 June 1815]: 413)

In the same issue, Hunt printed a new poem on the late Allied victory titled simply "A Song." The poem's incantatory quality resembles that found in similar verse passages from *Descent*, but the poem's message perhaps takes its inspiration from earlier staples of British patriotism such as Collins's "Ode to Liberty" and Thomson's "Rule Britannia." Like these earlier poems, "A Song" extols England as the "Queen of the West / With thy fair swelling bosom and ever-green vest" (lines 1–2). Hunt's poem, however, acquires a radical political meaning—not for what it praises, but for that which it refuses to praise: Arthur Wellesley, first Duke of Wellington. Wellington had been the subject of much eulogy in the Tory press after the Battle of Waterloo. The decorated hero, though, is conspicuously absent from Hunt's "Song." At the same time, "Song" clearly shows that its author was eager to assert that the seat of liberty remained firmly in England and not in France as Byron had argued in "Napoleon's Farewell." Byron sent his lyric to Hunt just over a month after "Song" appeared, which leaves open the possibility that Byron may have read Hunt's poem and decided to answer it with a national song of his own. In any case, it is not surprising that Hunt added the following headnote to "Napoleon's Farewell" when it appeared in *The Examiner*: "We scarcely need remind our readers, that there are points in the following spirited Lines, with which our opinions do not accord; and indeed the Author himself has told us, that he rather adapted them to what may be considered as the speaker's feelings, than his own" (*E* 396 [30 July 1815]: 491). In the spirit of political engagement and open intellectual debate, Hunt was still willing to publish Byron's latest lyrical experiment in *The Examiner*. Hunt also acknowledged his friend's request to remain anonymous by creating the false impression that the poem was a "Translation" from a French lyric and thus written by an anonymous French author. The strategy may seem simplistic from our modern vantage point, but it was an effective way for Hunt to distance himself from the poem's pro-Napoleonic message and perhaps a way to keep unwanted scrutiny from hostile readers at bay. In fact, Hunt's editorial approach with "Napoleon's Farewell" transformed the lyric into something of a private poetical ruse known only to Byron and Hunt.[55]

Hunt's willingness to engage Byron on the subject of Napoleon in *The Examiner* did not end with the emperor's defeat at Waterloo or the publication of "Napoleon's Farewell." Less than a year later Byron gave Hunt yet another lyric with Napoleonic sympathies: "On the Star of 'The Legion of Honour.'" In the weeks leading up to Byron's departure from England, at the height of the public scandal over the poet's marriage separation, the two friends had been in close contact. And it was during one of Hunt's visits to Byron's Piccadilly residence, as Jerome McGann speculates, that the poem was likely given to the editor. As McGann also notes, however, "On the Star" was probably composed at an earlier period in 1814.[56] The poem clearly links thematically to their on-going Napoleonic conversations, and thus would have been a fitting parting gift from Byron just before he left England. There is also the possibility that Byron and Hunt may have jointly seen the poem as a fitting response to Wordsworth and his recently published sonnets on Waterloo that had appeared in John Scott's *Champion*. Besides the fact that they both objected strongly to Wordsworth's post-Waterloo poetry, Scott had become a personal target for Byron at this time for being one of the first journalists to sensationalize his marriage crisis. Hunt, too, once on friendly terms with Scott, was outraged by the coverage of the poet's separation.

Nevertheless, Byron would have known that the sentiments in "On the Star," like those in "Napoleon's Farewell," once again, did not accord with Hunt's political opinions and would likely give the editor further cause for anxiety. In fact, the conclusion to "On the Star" explicitly recalled the "flash-out" argument about heroic death that Byron had promoted in the *Ode* of 1814. True heroism, as Byron presented it to Hunt's readers, was still reserved exclusively for those "Who proudly fall in [Freedom's] array" (line 40). Not surprisingly, when he printed the poem in *The Examiner*, Hunt included another prefatory note that attempted to downplay the poem's political message:

> The friend who favoured us with the following lines, the poetical spirit of which wants no trumpet of our's, is aware that they imply more than an impartial observer of the late period might feel, and are written rather as by [a] Frenchman than [an] Englishman:—but certainly neither he, nor any other lover of liberty, can help feeling and regretting, that in the latter time, at any rate, the symbol he speaks of was once more comparatively identified with the cause of freedom.
>
> (*E* 432 [7 April 1816]: 218)

Hunt's willingness to publish this last of Byron's Napoleonic lyrics reveals the extent to which their political engagements, even on issues toward which both men held strong and divergent opinions, were powerful and shaping forces behind their intellectual friendship. At the same time, Byron's Napoleonic lyrics had clearly tested Hunt's editorial confidence on the phenomenon of Bonaparte. By 1816, Byron's presence in *The Examiner*, as intimate as Hunt made it out to be, hinted at the complexities of public friendship in post-Napoleonic British literary culture—a culture in which the popularity of the literary magazine was on the rise along with new reviewers and diverse readerships. For Hunt, the complexities of navigating these readerships as well as his private friendships would be fully realized after the publication of *The Story of Rimini*.

Notes

1 Ghislaine McDayter, *Byromania and the Birth of Celebrity Culture* (Albany: State University of New York Press, 2009), 1–9.
2 Leslie A. Marchand, *Byron: A Biography.* 3 vols. (New York: Alfred A. Knopf, 1957), 2:563–608. Malcolm Elwin, *Lord Byron's Wife* (New York: Harcourt, Brace & World, Inc., 1962), 339–471.
3 Thomas Medwin, *Medwin's Conversations of Lord Byron*, ed. Ernest J. Lovell, Jr. (Princeton, NJ: Princeton University Press, 1966), 48.
4 Jane Stabler, "Leigh Hunt's Aesthetics of Intimacy," in *Leigh Hunt: Life, Poetics, Politics*, ed. Nicholas Roe (New York: Routledge, 2003), 96–7.
5 Payson G. Gates, *William Hazlitt and Leigh Hunt: The Continuing Dialogue* (Essex, CT: Falls River Publications, 2000), 39–40.
6 Gregory Dart, *Metropolitan Art and Literature, 1810–1840* (Cambridge: Cambridge University Press, 2012), 2.
7 David Stewart, *Romantic Magazines and Metropolitan Literary Culture* (New York: Palgrave Macmillan, 2011), 120–1.
8 B. W. Hill, *British Parliamentary Parties, 1742–1832* (London: George Allen & Unwin, 1985), 119–20, 156–9, 193–4.
9 Qtd. in Saul David, *Prince of Pleasure: The Prince of Wales and the Making of the Regency* (New York: Atlantic Monthly Press, 1998), 318.
10 Nicholas Roe, *Fiery Heart: The First Life of Leigh Hunt* (London: Pimlico, 2005), 181.

11 David, *Prince of Pleasure*, 132–3.

12 R. C. Dallas, *Recollections of the Life of Lord Byron* (London: Charles Knight, 1824), 204.

13 *Childe Harold* was published on 10 March 1812.

14 See also *E* 241, 8 August 1812, 497.

15 Roe, *Fiery Heart*, 97–9.

16 Malcolm Kelsall, *Byron's Politics* (Sussex: The Harvester Press, 1987), 37.

17 There has been much discussion of the term "radical" during the Romantic period but little consensus about its meaning. Carl Woodring suggests that in "the context of journalism before the Reform Bill, the word *radical* implied uprooting in an indirect way; not necessarily even the way of the demagogue in inciting the masses to uproot, but dangerously enough (the Tories thought) in encouraging or rousing the demagogues." See "Leigh Hunt as Political Essayist" in *Leigh Hunt's Political and Occasional Essays*, eds. Lawrence Huston Houtchens and Carolyn Washburn Houtchens (New York: Columbia University Press, 1962), 35. Hunt applied the word retrospectively to this early period in his *Autobiography*. See *A* 2:98, 107–8. Byron wrote to Hobhouse that he had never heard the word "radical" until after he left England in 1816. See *BLJ* 8:81.

18 James A. Houck, "Byron and William Hazlitt," in *Lord Byron and His Contemporaries*, ed. Charles E. Robinson (Newark, DE: University of Delaware Press, 1982), 72.

19 Donald H. Reiman, "Shelley as Agrarian Reactionary," in *Romantic Texts and Contexts* (Columbia: University of Missouri Press, 1987), 260–74.

20 Michael Roberts, *The Whig Party, 1807–1812* (London: Franck Cass & Co. Ltd., 1965), 281–6.

21 Woodring, "Leigh Hunt," 32, 37.

22 See Percy Bysshe Shelley, *The Manuscripts of the Younger Romantics. Vol. II: The Mask of Anarchy*, ed. Donald H. Reiman (New York: Garland Publishing Inc., 1985), 104.

23 *CMP* 35.

24 Woodring, "Leigh Hunt," 9, 42.

25 Roe, *Fiery Heart*, 170.

26 Marchand, *Byron*, 1:390. See also *CMP* 312.

27 *E* 284, June 6, 1813, 358.

28 Thomas Moore, *Letters and Journals of Lord Byron, with Notices of His Life*, 2 vols. (London: John Murray, 1830), 1:402.

29 David V. Erdman, "Lord Byron and the Genteel Reformers," *PMLA* 56, no. 4 (1941): 1092–4.

30 Malcolm Kelsall, "Byron's Politics," in *The Cambridge Companion to Byron*, ed. Drummond Bone (Cambridge: Cambridge University Press, 2004), 50.

31 Woodring, "Leigh Hunt," 47.

32 See John Clubbe, "Between Emperor and Exile. Byron and Napoleon, 1814–1816," *Napoleonic Scholarship* 1 (1997): 70–84. See also Simon Bainbridge, *Napoleon and English Romanticism* (Cambridge: Cambridge University Press, 1995), 134–52.

33 Hunt described Smith as a "wit who abounds in delightful combinations, and is at once unrelentingly orthodox and engagingly tolerant." See *E* 227, 3 May 1812, 275. On Brougham, see Hunt's letter to Byron of 23 December 1813: "I need not say I am sorry to lose your society this evening, & still more that I cannot bring two minds into collision, like your Lordship's and Mr. Broughams, which I am sure would enjoy each other; for Brougham, though he appears to the world as a politician only, is something still more, & has a fine taste & a hearty relish of poetry,—or rather, I should

say, he is a true politician, who has a taste for every thing that makes us social as well as free." See Timothy Webb, "Leigh Hunt to Lord Byron: Eight Letters from Horsemonger Lane Gaol," *The Byron Journal* 36, no. 2 (2008): 135–6. According to Kenneth Neil Cameron, Hunt's "ideal grouping of political talent would have been led by Brougham in the Commons and Byron in the Lords." See *Shelley and his Circle*, eds. Kenneth Neil Cameron, Donald H. Reiman, and Doucet Devin Fischer, 10 vols. (Cambridge, MA: Harvard University Press, 1961–2002), 4:647.

34 Samuel Taylor Coleridge, *Biographia Literaria. The Collected Works of Samuel Taylor Coleridge*, eds. James Engell and W. Jackson Bate, 2 vols. (Princeton, NJ: Princeton University Press, 1983), 1:31–2.

35 Philip Shaw, "Leigh Hunt and the Aesthetics of Post-War Liberalism," in *Romantic Wars: Studies in Culture and Conflict, 1793–1822*, ed. Philip Shaw (Aldershot: Ashgate Publishing, Ltd., 2000), 192.

36 See also *E* 306, November 7, 1813, 705: "if [Napoleon] would summon up a true magnanimity, he might shew himself the ruling mind still, by declaring his errors from the throne, and confessing that Providence has pointed out his path to a better and more peaceful ambition."

37 Peter Cochran, *Byron's Romantic Politics: The Problem of Metahistory* (Newcastle upon Tyne: Cambridge Scholars Publishing, 2011), 12.

38 See *BLJ* 3:210.

39 Jeffrey N. Cox, *Romanticism in the Shadow of War: Literary Culture in the Napoleonic War Years* (Cambridge: Cambridge University Press, 2014), 160–1.

40 The *OED* cites William Hazlitt's use of "buckram" in 1822 to mean "Stiffness; a stiff and starched manner; that which gives a man a stiff exterior." Hunt's poetry, however, is more typically described as being flexible and social.

41 John Keats, "Written on the Day That Mr. Leigh Hunt Left Prison," in *The Poems of John Keats*, ed. Jack Stillinger (Cambridge, MA: Harvard University Press, 1978), 32.

42 Anthony Holden, *The Wit in the Dungeon: The Remarkable Life of Leigh Hunt. Poet, Revolutionary, and the Last of the Romantics* (Boston, MA: Little, Brown and Company, 2005), 83.

43 See Hunt's letter of 2 April 1814 in Webb, "Leigh Hunt to Lord Byron" 136–8.

44 Webb, "Leigh Hunt to Lord Byron," 137.

45 Portions of this section have been reproduced by the kind permission of the editor of *The Byron Journal*. See Michael P. Steier, "Lord Byron and the Empress Marie-Louise: A New Letter to Leigh Hunt," *The Byron Journal* 45, no. 2 (2017): 135–40.

46 John Cam Hobhouse, *Byron's Bulldog: The Letters of John Cam Hobhouse to Lord Byron*, ed. Peter W. Graham (Columbus: Ohio State University Press, 1984), 122.

47 See Hunt's letter of 27 April 1814 in Webb, "Leigh Hunt to Lord Byron," 138.

48 Roe, *Fiery Heart*, 214–5.

49 See *BLJ* 4:101–2.

50 Diego Saglia, "Matrimonial Politics: Two References to Marie Louise of Austria in Byron's Poetry," *The Byron Journal* 26 (1998): 113.

51 Text of the preface is from Leigh Hunt, *The Descent of Liberty, A Mask* (London: Gale, Curtis, and Fenner, 1815), v. The text of the poem is taken from *SWLH* 5:87–8.

52 See Hunt's letter of 28 July in Timothy Webb, "After Horsemonger Lane: Leigh Hunt's London Letters to Byron (1815–1816)," *Romanticism* 16, no. 3 (2010): 242.

53 See Peter Cochran, *Byron, Napoleon, J. C. Hobhouse, and the Hundred Days* (Newcastle upon Tyne: Cambridge Scholars Publishing, 2015), 266.

54 See Isaac Nathan and Lord Byron, *A Selection of Hebrew Melodies, Ancient and Modern by Isaac Nathan and Lord Byron*, eds. Frederick Berwick and Paul Douglass (Tuscaloosa: University of Alabama Press, 1988), 14–7.

55 For a discussion of similar insider games in *Blackwood's Edinburgh Magazine*, see David Stewart, *Romantic Magazines and Metropolitan Literary Culture* (New York: Palgrave Macmillan, 2011), 131.

56 *CPW* 3:475–6.

4   *The Story of Rimini*
Annotating, Publishing, Reviewing

By 1816, Hunt's libelous prose in *The Examiner* had solidified his reputation as a writer of dangerous political sensibility. The editor was thus already a target of the conservative press when *The Story of Rimini*, his poetical retelling of the episode of Paolo and Francesca from Dante's *Inferno*, appeared in February. Hunt's *Rimini*, however, inflamed the Tory press in an unprecedented way. John Wilson Croker of the *Quarterly Review* savaged the poem and its author for challenging Pope's literary authority, (allegedly) promoting incest, and transgressing social decorum with a dedication to a lord that began: "My Dear Byron." Croker's review, in short, ensured that personality and politics would be the critical standard for treating Hunt and his work. The radically experimental author of *Rimini* was inseparable from the ex-prisoner and libeler of the Prince Regent.

Before *Rimini* appeared in print, Byron was well aware of the poem's subversive qualities and experimental style. At the same time, Byron greatly admired the poem's "Italianism," its foundation in Italian literary history, as well as the "originality" (*BLJ* 4:326) of Hunt's design. Byron first learned of *Rimini* when he met Hunt at Horsemonger Lane Gaol and soon began providing Hunt with books from his personal library to assist with the poem's composition. In the late months of 1815, as the poem neared completion, Byron read all four of its cantos in manuscript, leaving incisive comments on Hunt's choice of diction and poetic style. At the same time, Byron forged an unlikely alliance between Hunt and the conservative publisher John Murray, who agreed to publish the poem despite finding that it "differ[ed] so much from any that [he had ever] published."[1] When the poem finally appeared in February of 1816, Byron urged Thomas Moore to review it in the *Edinburgh Review* because he believed that doing so would "set it up before the public eye where it ought to be" (*BLJ* 5:35). Later, writing to Moore from Italy in April of 1817, Byron described an excursion he wished to make to the environs of Rimini specifically for Hunt, "who will be glad to hear of the scenery of his Poem" (*BLJ* 5:211). It thus becomes evident that if *The Examiner* had secured Hunt's friendship with Byron on the basis of shared political feeling and liberal sentiment in 1813, then *Rimini* would serve to reinforce the strength of the friendship on the grounds of shared poetical interest. Indeed, although they had sparred mightily over the merits of Pope and Wordsworth, they managed quite easily to find common ground in their appreciation of Italian literature. As Byron encouragingly reminded Hunt on 30 October 1815, "you have 2 excellent points in [*Rimini*]—originality—& Italianism—I will back you as a bard against half the fellows on whom you throw away much good criticism & eulogy" (*BLJ* 4:326).

The publication of *Rimini*, however, was more than just the literary *ne plus ultra* of the Byron-Hunt friendship. Hunt's poem was, according to Jeffrey N. Cox, a watershed moment for Romantic literature in England: "Hunt taught a generation of poets how to raid the Italian cultural archive in order to remake British poetry."[2] In his foundational study *Italy and the English Romantics*, C. P. Brand provides support for the idea, noting that the Italian comic tradition, with its playful mixing of the "conversational style and comic rhymes" is apparent in early works such as *The Feast of the Poets*. Italian verse forms, moreover, had little appeal for the first-generation Romantics but were "employed readily" by the likes of Byron, Shelley, and Keats—poets, as Cox argues, who were directly inspired by Hunt's example.[3] Nevertheless, Byron's engagement with Hunt's *Rimini* in the years before and after its publication has only recently become the subject of critical interest.[4] Indeed, commentators and bibliographers have long viewed Byron's approving statements about Hunt's *Rimini* as "polite" or "fulsome."[5] Yet the evidence shows that Byron not only held a deep interest in Hunt's poem before and after he left England in 1816, but that he had a genuine interest in its success as a document of taste—as a work that could showcase the "Italianism" he admired and would later adopt for his own poetic purposes in experimental works such as *Beppo* and *Don Juan*.

Rimini, Dante, and the Romantic Author

Comprised of only four slim "Cantos," *Rimini* remains Hunt's most ambitious poem. Hunt's retelling of Dante's famous story of an illicit and ill-fated romance is lavishly told and embellished with colorful description, but the retelling itself is built upon a single moment from Canto V of Dante's *Inferno*: a fatal kiss exchanged between a married woman, Francesca of Ravenna, and her brother-in-law, Paolo of Rimini, who is Anglicized as "Paulo" in Hunt's retelling.[6] Hunt's *Rimini* begins, however, with auspicious nuptial preparations, as Francesca is to be wedded to Giovanni of Rimini. The characters, both of noble stock, have been matched by prior arrangement: Francesca is "to crown the comfort of the land" (Canto I, line 31) as the bride of "bold Giovanni" (line 36), whose "victories have obtained her hand" (line 32). Hunt makes it clear that no love exists or can exist between bride and bridegroom in such an arrangement, for we also learn that

> [Francesca] had stout notions on the marrying score,
> And where the match unequal prospect bore,
> Might pause with firmness, and refuse to strike
> A chord her own sweet music so unlike.
>
> (Canto II, lines 28–31)

Although we are already made to believe that the marriage of Francesca and Giovanni will not be a happy one, Hunt builds anticipation for the wedding day, describing the city of Ravenna and its inhabitants in great detail before bringing the romance that develops between Francesca and Paulo into focus. The basis for the attraction between the two characters begins with a ruse gone awry. At the suggestion of Francesca's father, Giovanni asks his amiable and attractive brother Paulo to stand in for him as his "proxy" (line 19) at the wedding. The ruse fails spectacularly when Francesca and Paulo become infatuated with each other. The climax of the poem is Hunt's rewriting of the conclusion to Canto V of the *Inferno*. In Canto III of *Rimini*, Paulo joins Francesca in a secluded bower, her site of private retreat from Giovanni's watch. Following Dante's storyline closely, Hunt has the pair lock eyes and exchange a fatal kiss while engaged in reading the story of Lancelot and Guinevere in the romance of *Lancelot du Lac*. Giovanni soon learns of the incident after Francesca calls out Paulo's name (in her sleep) and the Duke of Rimini vows revenge. The denouement of the tale in Canto IV involves a duel between Paulo and Giovanni, in which Paulo takes his own life by impaling himself upon Giovanni's sword. Francesca, meanwhile, dies of grief, albeit with notable stoic resolve and an unshaken commitment to Paulo. The poem concludes with an elaborate funeral train—an inverted image of the wedding train that opens Canto II—for the two young lovers, who are carried back to Ravenna and buried together at a site where "on fine nights in May / Young hearts betrothed used to go there to pray" (Canto IV, lines 519–20).

Cox has recently elucidated the cultural moment in post-Napoleonic Britain that exists behind the romance that Hunt created in *Rimini*, suggesting that Hunt's poem "offers a new style of writing in order to imagine a world of peace arising from love."[7] For readers like Byron, the Dantean qualities of *Rimini* also gave the poem significance at a time when few writers were working with Italian authors and literary traditions. Several years after encountering *Rimini*, Byron would look to Dante the exile for political purposes, composing the "Prophecy of Dante" (1821), in part, as a political statement in support of Italian independence. But Byron was also, like Hunt, deeply interested in Dante as an artist and an innovator. In fact, William Hazlitt's description of the author of the *Commedia* as the "father of modern poetry" highlights some of the essential characteristics in Dante's writing that the Romantics found so appealing:

> His mind lends its own power to the objects which it contemplates, instead of borrowing it from them. He takes advantage even of the nakedness and dreary vacuity of his subject. His imagination peoples the shades of death, and broods over the silent air. He is the severest of all writers, the most hard and impenetrable, the most opposite to the flowery and glittering; who relies most on his own power, and the sense of it in others, and who leaves most room to the imagination of his reader. Dante's only endeavour is to interest; and he interests by exciting our sympathy with the emotion by which he is himself possessed.[8]

Hunt and Byron would have agreed with Hazlitt that one of Dante's strengths was his ability to generate "sympathy" by interesting readers in the "emotion" of the author himself. As the first "modern" poet, in other words, Dante was a prototype of the self-reflective Romantic author.[9] Hunt, in fact, said that he first turned to Dante in a self-reflective moment of his own "a year or two before" he entered prison while vacationing at Hastings with his wife and new-born son: "I was very happy; and looking among my books for some melancholy theme of verse, by which I could steady my felicity" (*A* 2:170). The author of *Rimini*, however, did not share Dante's "melancholy" moods nor did he agree with Dante's judgment of Paolo and Francesca. Hunt called Dante's *Inferno* a "sublime nightmare" (*SWLH* 5:165), and on more than one occasion criticized the excess of gloom, bigotry, and intolerance he saw as the poem's defining features: "one is astonished and saddened at the cruelties in which the poet allows his imagination to riot." Hunt added that if "Dante had erred only on the side of indulgence, humanity could easily have forgiven him—for the excess of charity are the extensions of hope; but, unfortunately, where he is sweet-natured once, he is bitter a hundred times." Nevertheless, Hunt, like Hazlitt, believed that "when Dante is great, nobody surpasses him," declaring "I doubt if anybody equals him, as to the constant intensity and incessant variety of his pictures."[10]

In the years leading to *Rimini*'s publication, Hunt found Dante's "intensity" and "variety" featured prominently in the story of Paolo and Francesca. As Hunt explained it in the preface to *Rimini*, the episode "has long been admired by the readers of Italian poetry, and is indeed the most cordial and refreshing one in the whole of that singular poem the Inferno." The effect of the episode was such that Hunt concluded: "We even lose sight of the place, in which the saturnine poet, according to his summary way of disposing both of friends and enemies, has thought proper to put the sufferers; and see the whole melancholy absurdity of his theology, in spite of itself, falling to nothing before one genuine impulse of the affections" (*SWLH* 5:165). Simply put, Hunt had discovered in Dante's story of Paolo and Francesca a "flesh-and-blood" (*CLH* 1:123) moment governed by the "genuine impulse of the affections." As Hunt saw it, it was Dante's "system of religious terror" that had ordered the lovers into the second circle of hell.[11] Byron, according to Ralph Pite, firmly aligned himself with Hunt on this point, reading Dante not strictly as a theological or a political poet, but as a poet who could, at times, infuse his religious understanding and his politics with "tender" emotion.[12] Byron also agreed with Hunt's sympathetic reading of the doomed lovers in the *Inferno*, defending Dante from the charge of a want of "gentle feelings" (*BLJ* 8:39) by specifically citing the Francesca and Paolo episode. In fact, as Frederick L. Beaty suggests, "Not until Leigh Hunt pointed the way did Byron seem to have any partiality for a specific story in the *Commedia*."[13]

Annotating *Rimini*: The Evidence of Marginalia

The depth of Byron's interest in Hunt's poetical retelling of the story of Paolo and Francesca can still be discerned in the handwritten marginalia he left in the poem while it was just a working manuscript. The manuscript, written out neatly in ink by Hunt on octavo-sized leaves, is now housed in small green folding boxes and stored within the recesses of the British Library.[14] In 1816, Hunt had been keen to preserve the manuscript for his own purposes. At some point, he carefully applied small red wax letter seals to each page with Byron's marginalia and then affixed sheets of thin paper to the seals to create temporary protective layers. Today the thin sheets of protective paper are gone, only pieces of the red wax remain, and Byron's penciled annotations are faint and sometimes almost illegible. An amateur attempt at manuscript preservation, Hunt's effort nevertheless remains a testament to the high value he placed upon *Rimini* and Byron's critical comments.

Hunt's careful treatment of the *Rimini* manuscript, however, was not always so apparent. On 7 November 1815, as he was preparing to send it to John Murray, Byron's publisher, Hunt wrote to Byron: "shall you have any objection to his reading the M.S. with your pencil marks?" Hunt also added this revealing comment: "My first impulse was to take them out, as I had already done with the first canto, which was going to press under the other booksellers."[15] As an expedient, Hunt seems to have used the manuscript of Canto I with Byron's marginalia as review copy for a potential publisher ("the other booksellers" were Gale, Curtis, and Fenner). It follows that had Byron's annotations appeared in the margins of the manuscript, their presence would have made the document less-than-presentable and in all likelihood in need of explanation.

If Byron's annotations, moreover, were of a critical nature, then they would have obviously made for a poor gloss upon a poem in need of a publisher. Byron, at any rate, must have replied in the affirmative to Hunt, for the pages with his marginalia were eventually used as press copy for Murray's edition of the poem. In fact, one gets the impression that Hunt may have deliberately wanted to leave Byron's approving marginalia in Cantos II and III, doubtless believing that if Murray could see that Byron had endorsed *Rimini*, then the publisher would have little reason to deny its value.

It is not clear whether Byron provided annotations in Canto IV of *Rimini*, but Hunt sent him the last canto, seemingly entire, for review on 1 February 1816.[16] A few days earlier, Byron had returned an "extract" (*BLJ* 5:18), which may have been a revised section from one of the earlier cantos upon which he had already left comments. In any case, the surviving manuscripts with Byron's marginalia, comprising part of Canto II and the whole of Canto III, capture Byron's earliest thoughts on Hunt's poetical style—a style that would become, as Richard Cronin says, the "single most important influence" on a young Keats and a new generation of Romantic authors.[17] At the same time, the marginalia provide a unique window into Byron's reading habits. While Beth Lau cites over one hundred and fifty known examples of books with Hunt's marginalia, books with Byron's marginalia exist but are rare.[18] Consequently, far less attention has been given to Byron's reading and annotative practice. And although there is available evidence showing Byron's practice of editing his own works for publication, there is no comparable example of his having annotated the working manuscript of a poetical contemporary—in this case, a friend. For this reason, however, the marginalia must be interpreted cautiously. As H. J. Jackson reminds us, even when we think a reader's annotations may provide a secure way into his or her private thoughts, there are still many external, circumstantial factors to consider.[19] The most obvious factor here is that Byron was annotating for Hunt's edification. Even so, the dearth of comparable examples from Byron makes the poet's marginalia in Hunt's *Rimini* an especially important instance of Romantic annotation.

Andrew Nicholson has described some of the known examples of Byron's marginalia in published books. These include comments in Hobhouse's *Imitations and Translations from the Ancient and Modern Classics*, a note in Boswell's *The Life of Samuel Johnson*, remarks in D'Israeli's *The Literary Character*, two notes in Foscolo's *Jacapo Ortis*, and comments in Madam de Staël's *Corinne*. In general, Byron wrote very little in these books, sometimes scribbling only a single remark, and, on the whole, his annotative practice is typical of other annotators of the Romantic period.[20] In some cases, Byron criticized or praised select passages as he read (Hobhouse's *Imitations* and Madam de Staël's *Corinne* fit this category). In other instances, especially in books not authored by friends or acquaintances, Byron annotated when the content related, directly or indirectly, to his life or his work, and his response is often personal (D'Israeli's *Literary Character*, Foscolo's *Jacapo Ortis*, and Boswell's *Life of Samuel Johnson* are all relevant here). Perhaps Byron's most well-known marginalia, however, are those he left in his own published works. There are several examples, including the marginalia found in two different copies of *English Bards and Scotch Reviewers*: the copy of the fourth edition presented to Hunt as a gift in 1815 and another copy of the fourth edition that Byron annotated in 1816 (*CPW* 1:396). Other notable examples include an early printed copy of *Fugitive Pieces* and Galignani's edition of *Don Juan*.[21] In these instances, Byron annotated in order to correct or reject what had been published—sometimes the corrections are in response to printer error (in *Fugitive Pieces*, for instance), but more often the corrections represent substantive changes due to an altered perspective as is the case in the two annotated copies of *English Bards and Scotch Reviewers*.

The majority of the comments that Byron left in pencil on Hunt's *Rimini* manuscript treat sections of the poem that we might expect the author of *Childe Harold* and the Turkish Tales to be drawn. For instance, in Canto II, Byron responded approvingly to Hunt's energetic description of the animal world:

> A moment's trouble find the knights to rein
> Their horses in, which, feeling turf again,
> Thrill, & curvet, & long to be at large
> To scour the space & give the winds a charge,
> Or pulling tight the bridles, as they pass,
> Dip their warm mouths into the freshening grass.
> But soon in easy rank, from glade to glade,
> Proceed they, coasting underneath the shade,
> Some baring to the cool their placid brows,
> Some looking upward through the glimmering boughs.
> (Ashley 906, f. 3r)[22]

To the left of this section, Byron drew a long vertical line and added in large letters, "Very good—indeed" (f. 2v). In contrast to the opening canto, in which Hunt had slowly built up anticipation for the wedding ceremony, Canto II celebrates the conclusion of the preceding day's nuptials with a great store of unleashed energy, captured vividly in the actions of the horses that bound toward Rimini with Paulo and Francesca in tow. That Byron would have been attracted to these creatures that "Thrill, & curvet, & long to be at large" is not surprising, for he too felt great sensitivity for the animal world, especially creatures exploited for human entertainment. In the Cadiz bull-fighting scene in the first canto of *Childe Harold*, Byron meditated, sympathetically, upon the bloody spectacle from the bull's perspective (lines 747–91). In a more under-stated way, Hunt has accomplished the same kind of cultural critique in *Rimini* by describing an entire scene from the perspective of the horses, who proceed "in easy rank" as if they were prisoners freed from the chains of the previous day's events. Animal rights were, in fact, a press-ing topic for Byron and Hunt, who seem to have found common ground on the subject on at least one more occasion in Italy in 1823 when they probably discussed Izaak Walton's *Compleat Angler*.[23]

Byron also found the beginning of *Rimini*'s third canto, titled "The Fatal Passion" in the manuscript, worthy of notice in the marginal spaces of Hunt's poem:

> Now why must I disturb a dream of bliss,
> Or bring cold sorrow 'twixt the wedded kiss?
> [*Two lines heavily canceled by Hunt*]
> Sad is the strain, with which I cheer my long
> And <u>caged</u> hours, & try my native tongue,
> Now too while rains autumnal, as I sing,
> Thrash the dark bars, chilling my sicklied wing,
> And all the climate presses on my sense;
> But thoughts it furnishes of things far hence.
>
> (Ashley 906, f. 4r)

The author of the brooding *Childe Harold* doubtless saw the "cold sor-row" of *Rimini*'s third canto as an appropriate and appealing shift in the poem's dramatic focus, balancing the description of the wedding events in the first two cantos against that of the tragic events that follow Fran-cesca's affair with Paulo in the two remaining cantos. Byron also found merit in *Rimini*'s lone biographical reference to Hunt's political impris-onment. Byron underscored "<u>caged</u> hours" and wrote "very excellent verse" alongside. Soon after meeting Hunt in prison in 1813, Byron half-jokingly recorded that even though he wished his new friend "out of prison" he liked "to study character in such situations" (*BLJ* 3:228). The singular course of study is confirmed by Byron's interest in other famous prisoners, including Prometheus, Torquato Tasso, and François de Bonnivard, who would each become subjects of shorter poems Byron produced after 1815.

Byron also left important marginal comments on *Rimini*'s antagonist, penciling approving remarks next to Hunt's description of Giovanni, a character who "whelm'd you with a weight of scorn" yet "made, 'twixt virtue & defect, / A sort of fierce demand on your respect" (Ashley 906, f. 9r). Byron called the description "Capital—& true to Nature" (f. 8v). In fact, according to Hunt, Lady Bryon, who read and admired *Rimini*, once "compared [Byron's] temper to that of Giovanni" (*LBSC* 5). Hunt found the claim baseless, but Malcolm Elwin has shown that Byron did indulge in a kind of dark playacting with his wife, rehearsing lines from works of Gothic fiction apparently for shock effect.[24] What may have been a harmless activity on Byron's part, however, seems to have become a serious cause of concern to Annabella, who would, after their separation in 1816, cite Byron's role-playing as evidence of his insanity. Hunt rejected this, concluding that the "excess of his moods, which out of the spleen, and even self-reproach of the moment, he indulged in perhaps beyond what he really felt, were so terrifying to a young and mortified woman, that she began to doubt whether he was in possession of his senses" (*LBSC* 6). Although the impression we gather from Hunt is that Annabella could not or would not differentiate Byronic performance from sincerity, deliberate mystification of this kind appears to have been a part of Byron's personality that close friends like Moore also found peculiar, if not alarming.[25]

As a published critic, Byron also knew that a judicious reviewer, or annotator in this case, must balance praise with criticism.[26] For Byron, Hunt's faults in *Rimini* were faults of style. In Canto II, for example, next to "the swarming insects fry, / Opening with noisome din, as you go by" (Ashley 906, f. 3r), Byron scribbled "prosaic" (f. 2v). In response, Hunt did little more than take a second look at the lines, replacing "you" with "they," ignoring Byron's overall objection to the prose-like quality of the couplet. Similarly, Hunt left "The worst of Prince Giovanni, as his bride" (f. 8r) unchanged, even though Byron thought the phrase "worst of" here "Colloquial." Byron suggested instead the more resonant phrase "sin of" (f. 7v), a phrase that appears often in his own poetical romances.[27] Perhaps for that reason, Hunt, wishing to preserve his artistic independence while avoiding what he considered a gothic commonplace, ignored his annotator's advice. Hunt did, however, make changes elsewhere in response to Byron's concerns. Hunt revised "somewhat stouter" in the description of Giovanni and Paulo, "the one / Was somewhat stouter, t'other finelier spun," to incorporate Byron's penciled suggestion of "more robust, the other" (f. 5r). Hunt also carefully considered Byron's objection to "A nose of taste was his" (f. 6r) in the lengthy description of Paulo's physical features. Next to this, Byron implored, "Say—Grecian—Roman—what you will—but not 'of taste'" (f. 5v). Hunt conceded and substituted "a graceful nose was his." In such instances, we see Byron demanding a strong and direct adjectival phrase where Hunt seems to want a more impressionistic phrase. Among the many florid descriptions of Francesca, Byron thought the balanced phrasing of "Society her sense, reading her books, / Music her voice, every sweet thing her looks" (f. 17r) to be particularly "Beautiful.—" (f. 16v). He paused only at "her fancy was / Of sunbeams mingling with a tuft of grass" (f. 20r), praising the conceit with reservation: "This sounds like a concetto—but yet it is too good to part with" (f. 19v). Byron also questioned what appeared to him to be a false comparison between Paulo's benevolent character and the fallen angels in Milton and Tasso: Paulo "could put on / A glowing frown, as if an <u>angel</u> shown" (f. 6r). Looking for precision of meaning in the use of "angel," Byron suggested "spirit" instead and reminded Hunt that "the common idea of Angelic is benignant—notwithstanding your authority from Tasso & Milton" (f. 5v).

With its many colloquial phrases and experimental stylings singled out for critical remark, *Rimini*'s more traditional poetic techniques were often overlooked by contemporary reviewers. Byron was interested in some of these techniques, including Hunt's use of the triplet. Hunt, as we saw in the second chapter, had studied Dryden's poetry closely and was particularly struck by the novelty and irregularity of *Alexander's Feast*. The triplet is one of the more obvious techniques that Hunt may have also learned from the author of *Absalom and Achitophel*, a poem in which Christopher Ricks identifies several strategic deployments.[28] Hunt employed the triplet frequently in *Rimini* to break the monotony of the regular Popeian couplet, but Hunt's placements are often predictable. In no less than twenty triplets spread out across *Rimini*'s four cantos, each triplet appears at the end of a verse paragraph, and in three instances at the end of a canto (Canto III being the one exception). Byron may have tried to warn Hunt about overusing the device when he annotated the following lines about Paulo's face being "<u>A morning glass of unaffected nature</u>,— / Something, that baffled every pompous feature,— / The visage of a glorious <u>human</u> creature" (f. 7r). Byron noted that the "first & last" lines of the "triplet" were "Excellent," but added, "I would cut out the second not because bad but unequal to the other two" (f. 6v). Hunt, firmly devoted to stylistic experimentation with Dryden as his authority, kept the triplet fully intact.

After he finished annotating Canto III ("The Fatal Passion") in manuscript, Byron summarized his marginalia in a letter on 22 October 1815. Byron began by emphasizing the delight he had discovered in reading Hunt's latest canto: "You have excelled yourself—if not all your Contemporaries in the Canto which I have just finished—I think it above the former books—but that is as it should be—it rises with the subject." Byron continued: "the conception appears to me perfect—and the execution perhaps as nearly so—as verse will admit.—There is more originality than I recollect to have seen elsewhere within the same compass" (*BLJ* 4:319). With the merits of *Rimini* established, Byron then considered its faults: "there are not many—nor such as may not be easily altered being almost all *verbal* . . . occasional quaintness—& obscurity—& a kind of harsh & yet colloquial compounding of epithets—as if to avoid saying common things in the common way—'difficile est proprie communia dicere' seems at times to have met with in you a literal translator" (*BLJ* 4:320). Byron had translated the Latin in *Hints from Horace* as "'Tis hard to venture where our betters fail, / Or lend fresh interest to a twice-told tale" (lines 181–2). And, in his letter to Hunt, Byron invoked the

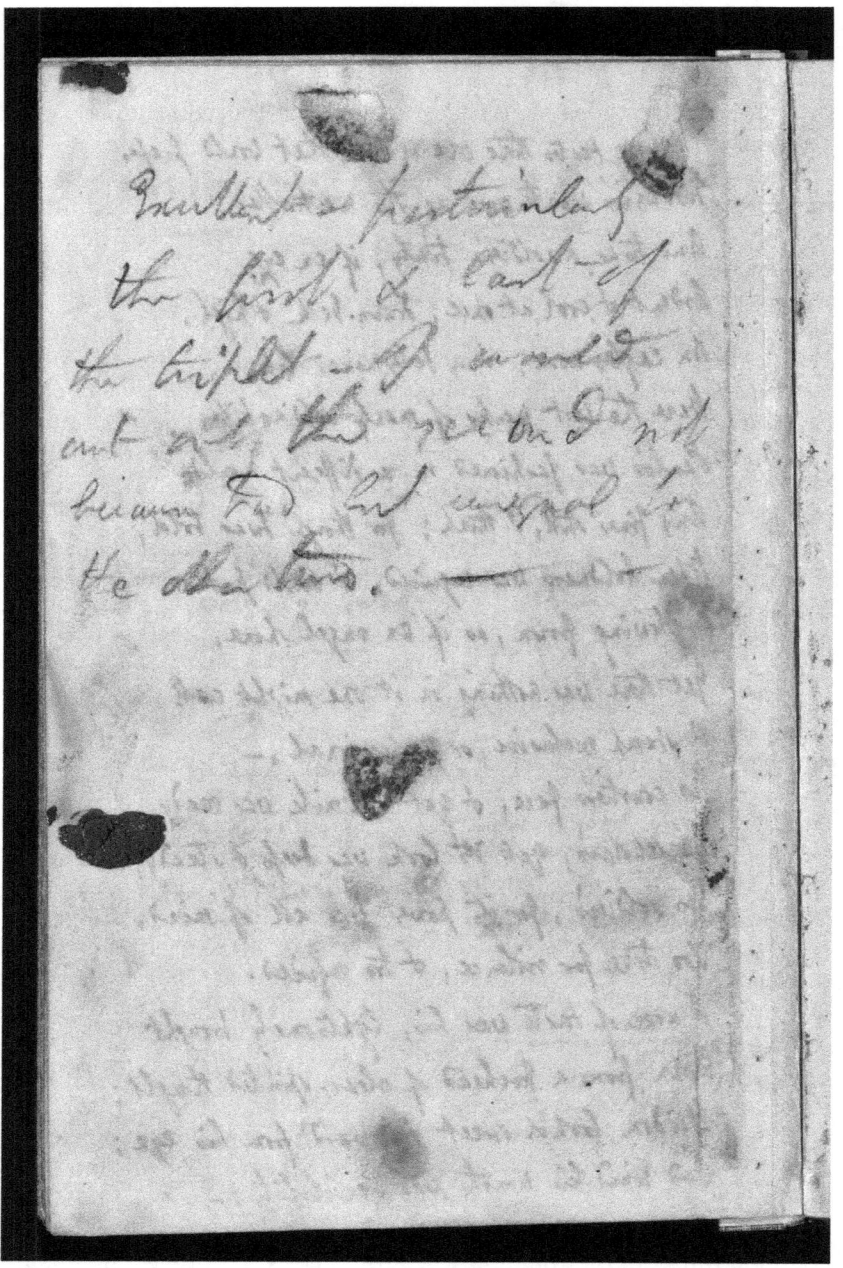

Figure 4.1 The Story of Rimini. Leigh Hunt's Holograph Manuscript. © The British Library Board. Ashley 906 f. 6v.

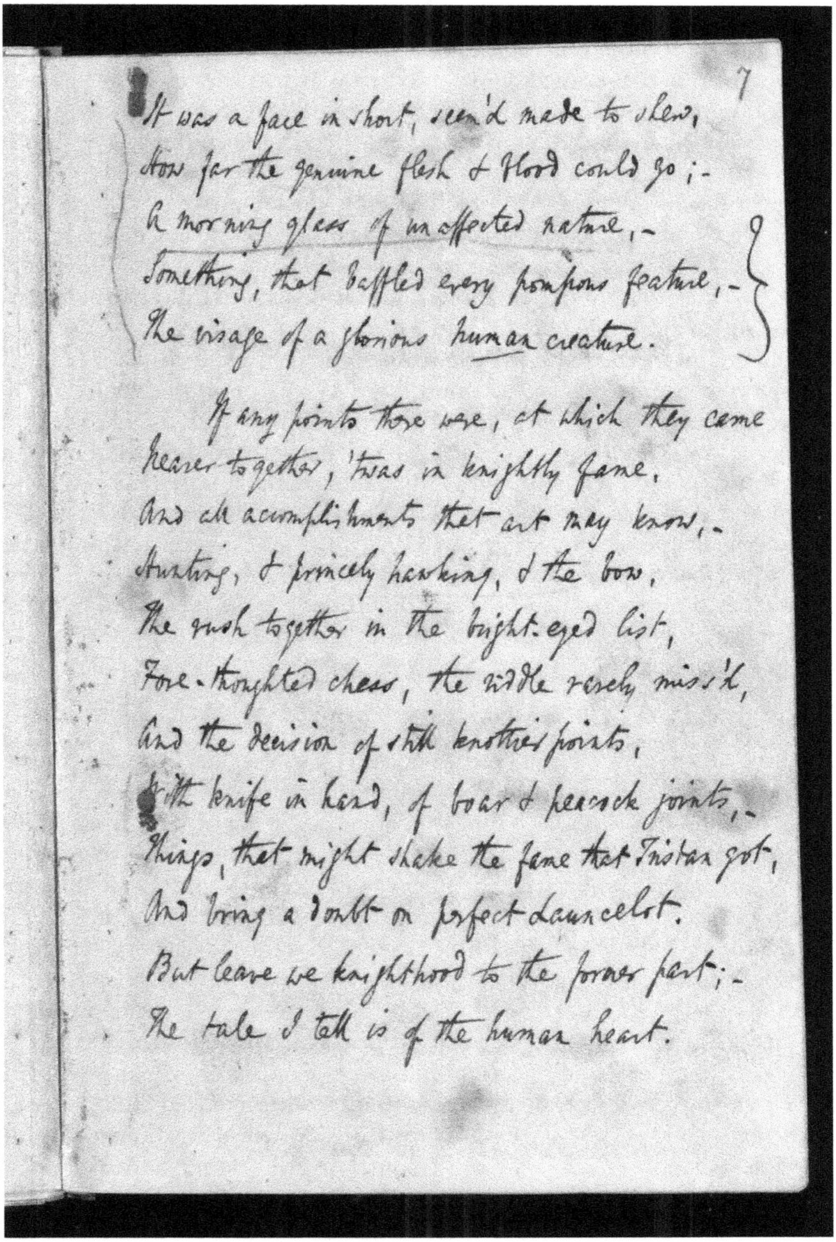

It was a face in short, seem'd made to shew,
How far the genuine flesh & blood could go ; –
A morning gleam of unaffected nature, –
Something, that baffled every pompous feature, –
The visage of a glorious human creature.

If any points there were, at which they came
Nearer together, 'twas in knightly fame.
And all accomplishments that art may know, –
Hunting, & princely hawking, & the bow,
The rush together in the bright-eyed list,
Fore-thoughted chess, the riddle rarely miss'd,
And the decision of still knottier points,
With knife in hand, of boar & peacock joints, –
Things, that might shake the fame that Tristan got,
And bring a doubt on perfect Launcelot.
But leave we knighthood to the former part ; –
The tale I tell is of the human heart.

Figure 4.2 *The Story of Rimini.* Leigh Hunt's Holograph Manuscript. © The British Library Board. Ashley 906 f. 7r.

Horatian dictum as a warning, reiterating the difficulty of trying to "lend fresh interest" to the venerable "twice-told tales" of tradition like Dante's story of Paolo and Francesca. Moreover, as Byron saw it, Hunt did not make the most convincing case for renewing Dante's story in English by deliberately "avoid[ing] saying common things in the common way" with appropriate diction and stylistic polish. Hunt's experimental use of language in *Rimini*, of course, is precisely that which he wished to showcase. Hunt later came to accept Byron's criticism of *Rimini*, but he may have underestimated his achievement when he reflected upon it thus: "I unfortunately chose the subject of Dante's famous episode. I did not consider, indeed at the time was not critically aware, that to enlarge upon a subject which had been treated with exquisite sufficiency, and to his immortal renown, by a great master, was not likely, by any merit of detail, to save a tyro in the art from the charge of presumption" (*A* 2:170). The stylistic concerns that *Rimini* had raised for Byron when he read through the poem in manuscript would remain with him in later years. It is perhaps not coincidental that the Horatian advice that Byron offered Hunt in 1815 became a guiding theme of *Don Juan* in 1819: "Difficile est proprie communia dicere" (*CPW* 5:1) was the motto Byron chose, after rejecting others, for the first two published cantos, thus foregrounding the idea that language and poetic style were of central importance to the *Don Juan* project.

"Leafiness & Alarm": A Defense of *Rimini*

On 30 October 1815, Hunt confirmed receipt of the "packet" containing Canto III of *Rimini* with Byron's annotations.[29] Anxious to learn Byron's opinion of his poem, Hunt was obviously pleased with his friend's overall approval. At the same time, he was just as anxious to answer Byron's criticisms and justify the poem's unique style. Hunt's 30 October letter, in fact, provides a highly detailed explanation of and justification for *Rimini* by drawing attention to the "Italianism" that had piqued Byron's interest from the very beginning.

Hunt acknowledged Byron's objections to the poem's "obscurities" and "occasional quaintness": "you will do me justice enough to believe that it is not from mere vain rejection, but in vindication of a theory which I have got on the subject, & by which it appears to me that the . . . original part of my style,—if the attempt to bring back an idiomatic spirit in verse,—can be so called—must stand or fall." Hunt added: "Upon the 'obscurities' pray have no mercy," and "It shall be the same with the 'occasional quaintness,'—that is to say, if they are deviations from recognized & natural modes of speaking, & not merely from . . . some of the politer forms of versification." Hunt's confidence in his "theory" was made especially apparent in the line that followed: "for here is the point in question; and I am vain enough to think, that you who are carried so instinctively, in your own poems, to native & undisguised emotion, will, of all writers, think with me before long." This is a surprisingly forthright assertion, not uncharacteristic, but one that is suggestive of the intimacy Hunt must have felt he had achieved with Byron over the course of 1814 and 1815. In 1813, Hunt had justified the experimental style of *Rimini* to Moore, who, like Byron, appears to have been skeptical of Hunt's loose style. Hunt justified his poetical experimentation to Moore with reference to Wordsworth, "a great poet" with a "command of the very identical words which he requires."[30] By late 1815, however, Hunt knew from his many private exchanges with Byron about *The Feast of the Poets* that the author of *English Bards and Scotch Reviewers* had little enthusiasm for Wordsworth or his poetry. As such, Hunt needed to redefine the context in which his critical terms would be cast, and he did so by drawing Byron's attention to the great writers of the Italian romance tradition:

> You [Byron] have the complete thing in point of feeling & charac-
> ter,—why not, always, in point of words? The plain matter is this:—
> it appears to me that we often hurt the effect, in modern poetry,
> of very true feelings & descriptions by putting them in false lan-
> guage,—that is to say, we accommodate ourselves to certain habit-
> ual, sophisticated phrases of <u>written</u> language, & thus take away
> from real feeling of any sort the only language <u>it ever actually uses</u>,
> which is the <u>spoken</u> language. Does this not constitute the main
> difference, in point of style, between the higher & middle species of
> <u>drama</u>, for instance,—English drama? And what is that <u>charm</u> we
> speak of as finding in the Italian writers, particularly <u>Ariosto</u>,—&
> in Ariosto too as contrasted with <u>Tasso</u>? Doubtless the greater part
> of it is in nativeness of feeling, but then this is completed & made to
> have it's proper charm by nativeness of language.[31]

Hunt clearly felt comfortable enough with Byron to tell him plainly that, as a poet, he is wrong "in point of words." The style that Byron should pursue, Hunt suggested, should be, in theory, naturalistic: poetical language should capture "<u>spoken</u>" language and not imitate the "false language" of modern poets like Pope and Johnson. And yet Hunt's critical terms here and elsewhere, as P. M. S. Dawson rightly points out, can be quite "slippery."[32] What exactly does Hunt mean by a "nativeness of feeling"? And what relation does this feeling have to a "nativeness of language"?

There are perhaps no wholly satisfying answers to these questions in Hunt's letter, but we can always derive hints about Hunt's meaning by listening to his objections to the poetical practices of his contemporaries. In a revealing letter to John Murray from 18 December 1815, for instance, Hunt offered the following remarks on the style of his poem: "I wish [*Rimini*], if possible, to afford a specimen of a well-felt, natural style of writing;—to shew a departure from those common, set styles of poetical artifice which most persons can imitate, to a language of natural passion & reasonable familiarity, in which <u>things</u> are superior to <u>words</u>;—in short, to be a sound specimen of sheer English writing & feeling, . . . free alike from the poetical cant of magazines, & from that <u>eccentricity</u>, which is the rock that Southey & others split upon."[33] Hunt provided additional perspective on this "natural style" in the preface to *Rimini*:

> [T]he proper language of poetry is in fact nothing different from that of real life, and depends for its dignity upon the strength and sentiment of what it speaks. It is only adding musical modulation to what a fine understanding might actually utter in the midst of its griefs or enjoyments. The poet therefore should do as Chaucer or Shakespeare did,—not copy what is obsolete or peculiar in either, any more than they copied from their predecessors,—but use as much as possible an actual, existing language,—omitting of course *mere* vulgarisms and fugitive phrases, which are the cant of ordinary discourse, just as tragedy phrases, dead idioms, and exaggerations of dignity, are of the artificial style, and yeas, verilys, and exaggerations of simplicity, are of the natural.
>
> (*SWLH* 5:167–8)

Hunt's interest in "adding musical modulation" to his verse has recently been discussed as one of his unique strengths as a stylist.[34] Hunt's main objection to modern stylists, however, drew heavily upon a tradition of critical reaction to the concept of poetic diction and anything that resembled "the artificial style." In this, as critics have noted, Hunt's ideas are closely aligned with Wordsworth's.[35] This is not to say that Hunt provided few insights into the subject of poetic diction and style. One of Hunt's primary contributions to the development of second-generation Romantic poetry, as Cox has suggested, is his "Italianism," the element that made *Rimini* so appealing to Byron in the first place. Unlike Hunt, Wordsworth did not emphasize Italian literary traditions in his poetic theorizing, looking instead to the Bible, the early English poets, and the ballads collected by Thomas Percy.[36] Percy himself, in fact, had observed that Italian literary traditions had much to offer English readers: "Should the publick encourage the revival of some of those ancient Epic Songs of Chivalry, they would frequently see the rich ore of an Ariosto or a Tasso."[37]

Percy's comment would not have been lost upon Hunt, who was well aware of the importance of the *Reliques of Ancient English Poetry* to the development of modern verse.[38] Echoing Percy's praise for the writers of Italian romance, Hunt discussed Ariosto in the same breath as Shakespeare with great purpose in his 30 October letter to Byron: "I endeavour to think, first of what is natural & what I have observed of nature, & secondly, of such writers as Ariosto . . . [and] Shakespeare." Specifically, Hunt explained that the "whole of Lear is a glorious specimen, particularly perhaps in the scene with Cordelia, & that speech, which always makes me sink within me, 'Pray do not mock me. / I am a very foolish fond old man, Fourscore <u>& upward</u>,—&c.'"[39] This celebrated speech from *King Lear* is characterized, in Hazlitt's words, by the benevolent feeling that Lear, in his most "desolate state," is able to rekindle through "the tender care of Cordelia."[40] For Hunt, a father of three in 1815, the experience of the scene was visceral. Hazlitt would further observe of *King Lear* that "The passion which [Shakespeare] has taken as his subject is that which strikes its root deepest into the human heart."[41] So, too, for Hunt, Lear's tragedy represented another "flesh-and-blood" story not unlike that which he had discovered in the fifth canto of Dante's *Inferno* when he first encountered Paolo and Francesca in their passionate, albeit fatal, embrace.

Similar "natural" moments, Hunt suggested to Byron, were to be found in Ariosto's great epic poem the *Orlando Furioso*. The examples from Ariosto that Hunt introduced in his 30 October letter to Byron are especially important, for by drawing Byron's attention to them Hunt established himself as a veritable poet-scholar who had gone back to Ariosto's original text for his authority. As a corollary to this, Hunt told Byron that he had little respect for the *Orlando Furioso*'s English translator John Hoole, describing him as "a very poor creature in every respect." Though Byron may have agreed with Hunt on this point, Hunt could not resist making a similar remark about Pope that would have probably unsettled his correspondent: "but Pope, I fear, in the instance before us, should have done as badly." Despite lapsing momentarily into territory that he must have realized would do little to convince Byron of *Rimini*'s stylistic merits, Hunt produced several examples from Ariosto's *Orlando Furioso* to illustrate the qualities he found most appealing therein. For instance, he directed Byron's attention to the "exquisite description of Angelica's flight in the first book," highlighting Stanzas 33 and 34, "in which one seems to go through nothing but leafiness & alarm."[42] Angelica's "flight" had first taken hold of Hunt's imagination as a child when he visited Benjamin West's London studio and encountered a painting of this famous scene. With time, Hunt came to reflect on the episode in terms of its language and its poetry as a convincing and effective mixture of pathos and suspense. Indeed, according to Deanna Shemek, "the imagery of octave 34, as distinct from that of the preceding lines, is not playful but archetypally terrifying," serving to heighten the sense of danger and the effects of fear on Angelica as she flees Rinaldo.[43] Hunt reinforced the idea by drawing Byron's attention to a similar moment later in the same canto: the famous simile of the flying fawn, "one of those thousand natural little touches, both in idea & description," Hunt said, "with which [Ariosto] enchants one":[44]

> Come after her he did. A fight between the rivals ensued; and the beauty, taking advantage of it, again fled away—fled like the fawn,

that, having seen its mother's throat seized by a wild beast, scours through the woods, and fancies herself every instant in the jaws of the monster. Every sweep of the wind in the trees—every shadow across her path—drove her with sudden starts into the wildest cross-roads; for it made her feel as if Rinaldo was at her shoulders.[45]

This prose translation from the *Orlando Furioso*, produced by Hunt for *Stories from the Italian Poets* (1846), shows his ability to capture another instance of Ariosto's "leafiness & alarm," drawing nature with great energy and detail while describing its most terrifying aspects. Hunt would later comment that the "secret of Ariosto's greatness" was, like Shakespeare's, "in going all lengths with Nature as he found her, not blinking the fact of evil, yet finding a 'soul of goodness' in it, and, at the same time, never compromising the worth of noble and generous qualities."[46] The idea seems to bear itself out in the simile of the flying fawn, which vividly captures a natural sympathy between a mother and child violently torn asunder. The examples from Ariosto to which Hunt drew Byron's attention in the 30 October letter clearly showcased the depth of Hunt's reading in the Italian romance tradition. And there can be little doubt that the display helped to convince Byron of *Rimini*'s merits as a work of art and a document of taste.

With his discussion of the poem's Italian influences out of the way, Hunt turned from an informed defense of his poem to a friendly plea for its publication. He did so by employing an epistolary joke he often used in his correspondence with Byron: an apology for length. Yet there is a particular irony to the joke in this instance, for Hunt produced two additional pages in which he explained his former embarrassments with publishers and booksellers. After confessing a great deal on this score, Hunt finally made his appeal to Byron: "what do you think of the situation in which I find myself with this poem of mine,—this poem, which Moore encouraged in the commencement, & which Byron has flattered during it's progress?" Hunt clearly wished for Byron to see *Rimini* as a statement of poetic solidarity, calling to mind the role that their mutual friend Moore had played in supporting the poem in its earliest stages. With this in mind, Hunt then asked his correspondent "[i]n plain prose": "my dear Byron, would it be quite agreeable to you . . . still to mention to your bookseller that I have a poem of 1400 lines drawing to a close, & that I would come to terms with him about it."[47] Interestingly, Hunt seems to imply here that Byron may have initially (perhaps in conversation) proposed the idea of Murray's involvement. At any rate, Byron replied immediately to Hunt's four-page missive, acknowledging that he had sent a note of endorsement to Murray. The response was exactly what Hunt could have wanted. There was no objection to the poetic "theory" that *Rimini* promised to illustrate and, more importantly, a letter of introduction to a prominent London publisher—Byron's publisher—had been secured.

Hunt and John Murray: Publishing *Rimini*

Hunt acted on the strength of Byron's endorsement, writing to the veteran publisher John Murray on 8 November. "Sir," Hunt began, "Lord Byron informs me that you will be willing to treat with me for the poem which he was good enough to mention to you" (*LHLL* 69). Murray had been preparing himself for Hunt's letter since early November, informing Byron that he was "very anxious to receive Mr. Hunts poem of which your Lordships opinion is perfectly satisfactory" (*LJM* 145). The Murray-Hunt partnership would develop quickly, for less than two months later Hunt had agreed to terms with the publisher for *Rimini*.

Hunt still had much to do before the complete manuscript could be placed in the publisher's hands. The first canto was still with Gale, Curtis, and Fenner—a matter which had given Hunt "some trouble to get it back again." There was a "gap in the second canto," which Hunt had "filled up" with a prose synopsis that would "enable [Murray] to understand the story." The third canto still required some adjustments and the fourth canto was not yet written due to "a good deal of illness & perplexity." Hunt nevertheless informed Murray that he had "given" himself "to the end of the month to finish it," for his goal was to have the poem "out" in the "height of the book-season."[48] Yet when the self-imposed deadline arrived, the fourth canto of *Rimini* still required attention, and there were other practical matters yet to be resolved. Hunt wrote again on 18 December to settle payment details, suggesting two different asking prices, either £500 or £450, a "sum I happen to want just now," for *Rimini* and pleading ignorance as to whether such a sum could be considered "a modest proposal" or "an impudent one."[49] To settle the money question properly, Hunt, in fact, asked Murray to come "down here some day" for he was "not in the habit just now of going out of the neighborhood." As Nicholas Roe points out, Hunt's agoraphobia was still a real matter less than a year after his release from Horsemonger Lane Gaol.[50] Hunt had already been forced to reject invitations from Byron to visit him at his lodgings in Piccadilly. Still, Murray, knowing little of Hunt's psychological profile, must have been perplexed, if not seriously taken aback, by Hunt's request that he venture from Albemarle Street to settle the contract for *Rimini*. Perhaps sensing that such a request, coupled with his blunt asking price of £450 (or £500), was likely to raise the publisher's eyebrows, Hunt concluded his letter with the confident observation that *Rimini*'s value—whatever it might be—had, in a sense, already been decided by Byron and his high "praise" of the poem: "If this looks very vain, pray remember that I have not wanted praises calculated to make me so. You know to whom I more pa[r]ticularly allude; & the praise was the more delightful to me, inasmuch as that personage, of all of the modern writers I know, <u>promises</u>, I think, to carry this style of writing [i.e., Hunt's], by & by, to it's <u>perfection</u>."[51]

But Murray did not respond favorably. By 27 December, nearly two months after Hunt had initiated contact with the publisher, Murray had finally read *Rimini* in the fragmented form that Hunt had managed to provide, and he did so with lackluster interest. The publisher began his reply to Hunt in no uncertain terms: the poem "differs so much from any that I have published, that I am fearful of venturing upon the extensive speculation to which your estimate would carry it." Murray's first thought was that Hunt should look elsewhere for a publisher: "I therefore wish that you would propose its publication and purchase to such houses as those of Cadell, Longman, Baldwin, Mawman, &c—who are capable and most likely to become purchasers." Still, knowing that he was dealing with Byron's friend upon Byron's recommendation, Murray concluded: "should you not have found any arrangement to your mind, I would undertake to print an Edition of 500 or 750 Copies, as a trial, at my own risk and give you one half of the profits; after this edition the Copyright shall be entirely your own property." Murray seems to have been aware of Hunt's anxiousness about the poem, for he also reassured Hunt that if the "trial" edition proved successful then he would "find no difficulty in procuring purchasers."[52] Murray, however, also knew that his offer differed greatly from the terms Hunt had originally presented. And yet Hunt, it turns out, was satisfied with the publisher's proposal, making no objection whatsoever in his reply of 29 December. Hunt felt, in fact, that Murray's offer had united the "natural caution of a tradesman with the feelings of a gentleman." Perhaps encouraged by Murray's talk of *Rimini*'s probable success, but most certainly desperate to clear past debts and provide financial support for his family, Hunt declared, "I am therefore very willing, if you have no objection, to close in at once with the alterior offer you make me, without giving myself any further trouble & anxiety in removing from one bookseller to another."[53]

Hunt's decision to accept Murray's reduced terms for *Rimini* probably surprised the publisher, who had at that moment written to Byron, describing the terms of the offer to Hunt and asking for Byron's advice. Murray, notably, left out the suggestion he made that Hunt should first consider publishing elsewhere. The publisher instead told Byron that Hunt had asked £450 for *Rimini*, which would "presuppose a sale of, at least 10,000 Copies." Murray justified his rejection of Hunt's asking price by stating, "if I may trust to my own experience in these matters, I am by no means certain that the sale would do more than repay the expenses of Paper & Print—but . . . the Poem is peculiar & may be far more successful, in which event, the proposition which I have made to the author will secure to him all the advantages of such a result." Byron, as we shall see, did not share Murray's confidence in his ability to judge the success of a prospective author in this instance. Yet Murray continued, "I trust that your Lordship will see in this an anxious desire to serve Mr. Hunt although, as a mere matter of business, I can not avail myself of his offer. . . . I am really uneasy as [sic] your feelings in this affair but I think I may venture to hope that your Lordship knows . . . me sufficiently to allow me to trust my decision entirely to your usual kindness" (*LJM* 149). The publisher made it clear that he was only dealing with Hunt out of a desire to please Byron, and he now sought confirmation of Byron's actual "feelings in this affair." Byron strongly disagreed with Murray's offer to Hunt, informing his publisher that he thought the terms for *Rimini* unreasonable, but, by this time, Byron's objections could do little to influence the terms of the contract.

Murray replied to Hunt on 1 January 1816 without mentioning having written to Byron. Instead, the publisher declared that he was now ready to "serve" Hunt according to his wishes. To satisfy these, Murray suggested that he would "print one Edition of [the] Poem to consist of 750 Copies at [his] own expense" and then "give [Hunt] half the profit when these are sold." The "Copyright," Murray continued, would then "be entirely your own property." With these financial details out of the way, Murray next offered Hunt a first glimpse of what his published poem would look like: "I propose to print your Poem in the same form . . . as the last edition of your friend Lord Byrons [sic] works." Hunt must have been pleased to learn that *Rimini* would be printed uniformly in the same size as Byron's four-volume collected edition of poetical works— the same edition which Byron had made a presentation of to Hunt several months earlier. It was a smaller octavo size (foolscap) than the size in which Byron's Turkish Tales had been printed. Murray reassured his new author on this score, noting that the smaller size was the "most prosperous form" for publication.[54] Hunt would have had no objections to Murray's proposal, for Byron had warned his friend about publishing *Rimini* in a larger format, especially an expensive quarto edition, the "worst size possible for circulation" (*BLJ* 4:326).

After he sent off his reply to Hunt, Murray immediately set *Rimini* up in proof. It was in Hunt's hands by 4 January 1816, for Hunt replied in a brief note—a significant contrast to his lengthy missives to Murray of 9, 18, and 29 December—to say that he was "much pleased with the size & general appearance of the proof." Hunt also took the opportunity to enclose a new "passage that was wanting to fill up a gap in the second canto, together with another which I wish to be printed instead of one in the third, as marked." Hunt also promised to "send . . . the concluding canto by the middle of next week" (*LHOL*). By the end of the month, however, Hunt still had not finished the poem, for on 29 January Byron returned an "extract with thanks for the perusal." Crucially, in the same letter, Byron also informed Hunt that he was "just at present in no good humour" (*BLJ* 5:18–9) with Murray. One reason for this, Byron explained, was that he "differ[ed] entirely" with the "*terms* of [Hunt's] agreement" with Murray for the publication of *Rimini*.

Byron and John Murray: Publishing *The Siege of Corinth* and *Parisina*

While Hunt had, to his satisfaction, managed to see *Rimini* through the press in the early months of 1816, Byron was at the same moment at loggerheads with Murray over terms for the publication of two new poems: *Parisina* and *The Siege of Corinth*. Along with the publisher's handling of Byron's *Corsair* and *Ode to Napoleon Buonaparte*, Murray's attempt to dictate the appearance of *Parisina* and *The Siege of Corinth* is another less-than-congenial episode in the history of the Byron-Murray partnership.[55] *Parisina* and *The Siege of Corinth* are generally seen as the culmination of Byron's highly successful run of verse tales, which had commenced with *The Giaour* in 1813. *The Bride of Abydos* (1813), *The Corsair* (1814), and *Lara* (1814) all followed. On 2 January 1816, the day after he finalized the terms with Hunt for *Rimini*, Murray sent Byron his opinion of *The Siege of Corinth* manuscript, which the publisher had just received: "My Lord, I tore open the packet you sent me and have found in it a Pearl—it is very interesting—pathetic beautiful—do you know I would almost say Moral—I am really writing to you before the billows of the passions you have excited are subsided" (*LJM* 150). Murray had also sent a £1,000 advance for the poem, which Byron promptly tore up and returned to his publisher. The poet's actions should have come as no surprise, for in the summer of 1812, soon after *Childe Harold* became a commercial success, Byron transferred the copyright to Robert Charles Dallas. Byron routinely refused money for his poetical labors in the early years of his career, and Murray would have probably also remembered the accusations made by the *Courier* in 1814 that Byron had been receiving "large sums of money for his work." The rumors, as Mary O'Connell explains, so "infuriated" Byron that he was eventually driven to write to Murray "to put an end to their association."[56] Tensions, of course, eased and Byron and Murray were in partnership again in the spring of 1815 when the publisher brought out his edition of the *Hebrew Melodies*. But the episode involving *Parisina* and *The Siege of Corinth* in the early months of 1816 shows that tensions persisted between Byron and his publisher, and Murray's less-than-handsome treatment of Hunt at the same moment had much to do with Byron's uneasiness.

Byron's reply to Murray's letter of 2 January, which included the torn pieces of the £1,000 advance, did not reveal the extent of the disappointment he felt at the publisher's recent treatment of Hunt. Byron instead began his letter with what seems a half-joking reference to Murray's dealing with his friend for *Rimini*: "Dear Sir—Your offer [for *Parisina* and *The Siege of Corinth*] is *liberal* in the extreme—(you see I use the *word to* & *of* you—though I would not consent to your using it of yourself to Mr. H[unt]) & much more than the two poems can possibly be worth." Knowing the political divisions that existed between the liberal

Hunt and the Tory Murray, Byron emphasized the disparity between Murray's conservative financial dealing with Hunt for *Rimini* and the publisher's generous offer for *Parisina* and *The Siege of Corinth*: "I cannot accept it—nor will not." Byron added, however, that the publisher was "most welcome to them as additions to the collected volumes without any demand or expectation on my part whatever." Byron made his reasoning clear: "I do not like to risk my fame (whether merited or not) which I have been favoured with—upon compositions which I do not feel to be at all equal to my own notions of what they should be" (*BLJ* 5:13). In the days that followed, Murray nevertheless pursued the idea of publishing the poems separately in order, presumably, to maximize profits before he would consider burying two substantial new works within a collected edition as Byron suggested. Murray went to see Byron on 4 January 1816, and the meeting seems to have paid off, for the publisher came away believing that Byron "will yet allow their separate publication" (qtd. in *LJM* 152). To shore up matters, Murray sent Byron flattering comments about *Parisina* and *The Siege of Corinth* from individuals with whom he had shared the manuscripts. Among these individuals was Isaac D'Israeli, one of Byron's favorite living authors, who, Murray informed Byron, had been "perfectly overcome by [*Parisina*]" (*LJM* 153). By 10 January, the publisher had succeeded in persuading Byron to go forth with the two poems for separate publication, for on or around that date, he sent Byron the proof of *Parisina* and promised to do the same with "a revise of Corinth—this night or tomorrow" (*LJM* 154).

New developments, however, soon threatened to undo Murray's plan. Samuel Rogers had learned from Sir James Mackintosh that William Godwin was in financial trouble—a common situation for the author of *An Enquiry Concerning Political Justice*—and thereupon engaged Byron, at Mackintosh's bidding, about Murray's offer for *Parisina* and *The Siege of Corinth* as a source of aid to Godwin. Byron agreed, telling Murray that he wished now to accept the offer for the poems.[57] Murray immediately put Byron's missive into William Gifford's hands. Gifford felt just as nonplussed as Murray about Byron's intentions, lamenting the "officious friends" who had gotten Byron into "a most *unlordly* scrape" (qtd. in *LJM* 156). Though Gifford did not say it directly, Byron's support for the radical Godwin was antithetical to his (and Murray's) political sensibilities. Thus reassured by Gifford that Byron was making a terrible mistake, Murray responded to the poet thus:

> Your Lordship will pardon me if I cannot avoid looking upon it as a species of cruelty, after what has passed, to take from me so large a sum . . . to cast it away on the wanton and ungenerous interference of those who cannot enter into your Lordship's feelings for me, upon persons who have so little claim upon you, and whom those who so

interested themselves might more decently and honestly enrich from their own funds, than by endeavouring to be liberal at the cost of another, and by forcibly resuming from me a sum which you had generously and nobly resigned.

(LJM 155–6).

Murray had a point, but he also made sure that Byron knew his "feelings" about funding radicals such as Godwin: "I am no rich man, abounding, like Mr. Rogers, in superfluous thousands, but working hard for independence, and what would be the most grateful pleasure to me if likely to be useful to you personally, becomes merely painful if it causes me to work for others for whom I can have no such feelings" (LJM 156).

Byron answered Murray's letter on 22 January with notable coolness, reminding the publisher of the transfer of the Childe Harold copyright to Dallas as being "in no respect different" from that which he proposed to do for Godwin with the advance for Parisina and The Siege of Corinth. Having explained the matter plainly, Byron concluded: "The things in question shall not be published at all—& there's an end of the matter" (BLJ 5:17). Revealingly, Byron may have also made Murray now feel the full force of his anger over the publisher's recent treatment of Hunt: "The truth of the matter seems this—you offered more than the poems are worth—I said so—& think so:—but you know—or at least ought to know your own business best." Byron has here adopted Murray's sentiments, ironically it would seem, from the publisher's letter of late December, in which he had justified his cautious offer for Hunt's Rimini thus: "I think your Lordship will not be displeased at a determination founded upon the best judgment I can form of my own business" (LJM 149). In the early months of 1816, Byron's personal associations were paramount.

Reviewing *Rimini*: The *Quarterly* and The *Edinburgh*

By the end of February, Hunt was understandably eager to learn the fate of the poem that had taken him nearly five years to complete. Byron, whose feelings about Murray had now cooled, wrote encouragingly to Hunt to report that "Murray tells me it is going on well." And he added a reassuring note about *Rimini*'s long-term success: "you may depend upon it there is a substratum of poetry which is a foundation for solid & durable fame." Nevertheless, Byron reminded Hunt that the "objections (*if* there be Objections—for this is a *pre*sumption & not an *as*-sumption) will be merely as to the mechanical part—& such as I stated before—the usual consequence of either novelty or revival." Byron also offered his opinion of Hunt's controversial "My Dear Byron" dedication: "Your prefatory letter to 'Rimini' I accepted as it was meant as a public compliment & a private kindness." He added: "I am only sorry that it may perhaps operate against you—as an inducement & with some a pretext—for attack—on the part of the political & personal enemies of both" (*BLJ* 5:32). Byron was, of course, right on both accounts. What Byron could not foresee, however, was the extent to which Hunt's dedication was to be used as a "pretext" for "attack" from the reviewers, particularly the attacks issued by *Blackwood's Edinburgh Magazine* the following year as well as those that came from the members of the Murray circle—Gifford, John Wilson Croker, William Stewart Rose, John Taylor Coleridge, and even Murray himself.

Nevertheless, Hunt must have been pleased with the first signs of *Rimini*'s success. Already emboldened by Byron's encouraging remarks, Hunt received the first round of reviews (letters of congratulations) from long-time friends. Hazlitt was in raptures over *Rimini*: "I have read the story of Rimini with extreme satisfaction. It is full of beautiful and affecting passages. You have I think perfectly succeeded." Among his favorite lines, Hazlitt listed "Formed in the very poetry of nature," and among the "most elegant" lines, Hazlitt named those beginning "And she became companion of his thought / Silence her gentleness before him brought." Hazlitt further stated that he found the "description of the death of Francesca better than any," adding with a wry glance at the opening of Francis Jeffrey's review of Wordsworth's *Excursion*: "*This will do.*"[58] A few days later, Haydon sent remarks that were characteristically hyperbolic but vivid: "I have read, and reread your exquisite pathetic tale, till my Soul is cut in two—and every nerve about me pierced with trembling needles."[59] Moore also sent his congratulations, adding a phrase from Wordsworth's "Lines Composed a Few Miles above Tintern Abbey" that he knew would have pleased Hunt: "There are many of the lines of Rimini that 'haunt me like a passion.'" Moore cited one of the poem's regular couplets as his favorite: "The woe was earthly, fugitive, is past; / The song that sweetens it, may always last" (Canto IV, lines 23–4). To this he added, "I am afraid *you* will set this down among your regular, sing-song couplets—to me it is all music."[60] That Moore felt the need to qualify his praise of a "regular" couplet in *Rimini* reveals not only his awareness of his friend's sensitivity to matters of style but also just how much Hunt's systematic attempt to weaken the regularity of the Popeian couplet had become a friendly matter of dispute between them. Thomas Mitchell, Hunt's Christ's Hospital classmate and future translator of Aristophanes, in fact, thought *Rimini*'s style a masterful blend of the old and the new, the "progress of a new mind bearing between Byron, Wordsworth, and Dryden—catching from each, and winding itself up into a whole of its own" (*CLH* 1:100). Mitchell's characterization perhaps gets at the essence of what Hunt had wanted to achieve stylistically with *Rimini*. A letter from Charles Lamb also arrived: he stated that he and his sister had read *Rimini* "with great delight," quipping "We congratulate you most sincerely on the fruit of your prison hours."[61] And finally, additional reaction came in from Byron at some point between 26 February and 3 April. Only fragments of this correspondence, which had been "mutilated or lost" (*LBSC* 163), according to Hunt, have survived. But the remnants provide further evidence of Byron's keen interest in the success of Hunt's poem. Byron informed Hunt that "Sir Henry Englefield (a mighty man in the *blue* circles & a very clever man any where) sent to Murray in terms of the highest eulogy:—and with regard to the common reader—my *sister* and *cousin* (who are now all my family—and the last gone since away to be married) were in fixed perusal & delight with it—& they are 'not critical' but fair—natural—unaffected—& understanding persons.——Frere—and all the Arch-literati—I hear—are also very unanimous in a high opinion of the poem" (*BLJ* 5:58–9). Soon enough, however, the encomiums gave way to the criticisms that Hunt and Byron had both been expecting. Reviews in the *Quarterly*, the *Edinburgh*, and many other periodicals began to appear throughout the spring and summer of 1816. Only some of these reviewers, however, made a deliberate effort to attack Hunt's person and his friendships, while the majority of the reviewers, as John O. Haydon puts it, only "had reservations of one kind or another."[62]

The earliest published reviews of *Rimini* reveal that Byron's approval of the poem's "Italianism" as well as his concerns about the poem's loose style were generally shared by the reviewers. The *Literary Panorama*, for instance, noted that "Chaucer studied the poets of Italy" and that "Shakespeare made their tales the foundation of some of his noblest efforts." On this score, the reviewer declared approvingly that with *Rimini* "Mr. H. treads in their steps" (*RR* C2:546). And yet the same reviewer knew that "Mr. Hunt *will* not be a perfect poet, but retains imperfections easily pointed out, by men who possess no proportion of his powers" (*RR* C2:544). One of these "men" was the reviewer at the *Monthly Review*, who "wish[ed] that Mr. Hunt had attended to his own precept of '*omitting mere vulgarisms*' in diction." Elsewhere, the reviewer went so far as to list over fifty examples of Hunt's use of "Hudibrastic double endings" on the "most improper occasions" (*RR* C2:701). Most of the reviewers also noted Hunt's slighting remarks on Pope in the preface and responded accordingly. The *Monthly Review* agreed with Hunt's "opinion of the great superiority of Dryden over Pope," but added: "we disapprove [of] some of his degrading phrases applied to Pope, even as a versifier" (*RR* C2:700). The *Augustan Review*, likewise, took Hunt to task for his depreciation of Pope, objecting to Hunt's idea of a "natural" poetic style: "some degree of elevation of expression as well as of sentiment, some abstinence from ordinary words and ordinary phrases, may be essential to the dignity of the muse" (*RR* C1:38). These and like protests against Hunt's style in *Rimini* were, however, largely echoes of the most important early review to pass judgment upon Hunt's poem: that which appeared in Murray's *Quarterly Review* in May of 1816.

In the *Quarterly Review* for January 1816 (published 18 May 1816), John Wilson Croker, Secretary to the Admiralty and Tory reviewer, wrote mercilessly of *Rimini*: "it is written on certain pretended *principles*, and put forth as a pattern for imitation, with a degree of arrogance which imposes on us the duty of making some observations on this new theory, which Mr. Leigh Hunt, with the weight and authority of his venerable name, has issued, ex cathedra, as the canons of poetry and criticism" (*RR* C2:753). Hunt's system of "pretended *principles*," according to Croker, was above all a "disease":

> Mr. Hunt's *first* canon is that there should be a *great freedom of versification*—this is a proposition to which we should have readily assented; but when Mr. Hunt goes on to say that by *freedom of versification* he means something which neither Pope nor Johnson possessed, and of which even "they knew less than any poets perhaps who ever wrote," we check our confidence; and, after a little consideration, find that by freedom Mr. Hunt means only an inaccurate, negligent, and harsh style of versification, which our early poets fell into from want of polish, and such poets as Mr. Hunt still practice from want of ease, of expression, and of taste.

Although Croker's criticism is cast in much harsher language, such criticism of Hunt's style was, in many ways, an echo of that Byron had already issued privately to Hunt in 1815. But Croker took his criticisms one step further by making them personal.

The most damaging aspect of Croker's review was his use of personality. The *ad hominem* approach would become standard practice for conservative critics treating Hunt's works, and Croker's review of *Rimini* played no small part in establishing the critical discourse.[63] Croker generalized about the inadequacy of Hunt's learning: "We shrewdly suspect that Mr. Hunt, with all his affectation of Italian literature, knows very little of Ariosto; it is clear that he knows nothing of Tasso" (*RR* C2:753). We have already seen evidence to the contrary in Hunt's letter of 30 October 1815 to Byron. Yet much more damning was the way Croker concluded his review: with a pointed attack on Hunt's friendship with Byron. Of *Rimini*'s dedication, Croker claimed: "we never, in so few lines, saw so many clear marks of the vulgar impatience of a low man, conscious and ashamed of his wretched vanity, and labouring, with coarse flippancy, to scramble over the bounds of birth and education, and fidget himself into the *stout-heartedness* of being familiar with a LORD" (*RR* C2:756). It is this brief but biting charge that guided many subsequent observations about the Byron-Hunt friendship in the Romantic press. Hunt would never convince Britain's literati that his friendship with Byron was acceptable on personal or artistic grounds. *Blackwood's Edinburgh Magazine*, just over a year later, would begin its campaign of abuse against Hunt and his so-called "Cockney School," ensuring that Croker's charge remained firmly before the public. But none of this should be surprising. By 1816, the politically conservative reviewers at the *Quarterly* had conveniently forgotten that Hunt had once been a celebrated prodigy, the author of *Juvenilia*, or more recently the author of the well-received *Feast of the Poets* and *Descent of Liberty*. For the *Quarterly*, Hunt was a former prisoner, a libeler of the Prince Regent, and the radical editor of *The Examiner*, who would not be permitted access to a literary culture dominated by Walter Scott (soon to become Sir Walter Scott) and Lord Byron. Hunt later wrote in his *Autobiography* that *Rimini* "would have met with no such hostility, or indeed any hostility at all, if politics had not judged it" (*A* 2:172–3). Hunt may have been right but it would have been naïve to think it could have been otherwise. As Mark Parker reminds us, the conservative reviewers had not forgotten (or forgiven) Hunt's "'Fat Adonis' caricature of the Prince Regent," a powerful symbol of the personality Hunt himself had used against his political enemies in *The Examiner*.[64]

Although the *Quarterly* had issued a strong message to the author of *Rimini*, two talented reviewers from the *Edinburgh Review*—Francis Jeffrey and William Hazlitt—attempted a formal defense of Hunt and his poem. The review nevertheless came too late to have any impact on Hunt's poetic reputation.[65] Hazlitt's role as the primary author of the review, moreover, ensured that it would not be taken seriously by the conservative press.[66] The situation Hunt had found himself in with respect to the *Edinburgh Review* and *Rimini* is not dissimilar to that in which Keats had found himself in 1820 when Jeffrey's belated review of *Endymion* did little to offset Croker's infamous attack on Keats's volume. Yet the *Edinburgh*'s defense of *Rimini* still had great significance for Hunt for many reasons. In the first place, several prominent writers had been lined up for the review, making its appearance a highly anticipated event. Byron, *Rimini*'s foremost champion, had initially wanted to write the review, which is remarkable when we consider that he wrote very few reviews during his life. But after Byron had been named by Hunt in the poem's dedication, Byron prudently asked Moore to undertake the review to avoid charges of partiality. Moore, however, never shared Byron's enthusiasm for *Rimini*, explaining that with "respect to Hunt's poem, though it is, I own, full of beauties, and though I like himself sincerely, I really could not undertake to praise it *seriously*. There is so much of the *quizzable* in all he writes, that I never can put on the proper pathetic face in reading him."[67] In any event, Hazlitt, while Moore and Byron were deliberating, had already been making preparations for placing his review of *Rimini* in the hands of Jeffrey.[68]

Hazlitt's review shows that he was clearly enthusiastic about *Rimini* and recognized its importance and originality. Echoing some of Byron's earliest remarks on the poem, Hazlitt declared that "THERE is a great deal of genuine poetry in this little volume; and poetry, too, of a very peculiar and original character." Placing the poem in the pre-Popeian literary context that meant so much to the second-generation

Romantics, Hazlitt added that "It reminds us, in many respects, of that pure and glorious style that prevailed among us before French models and French rules of criticism were known in this country, and to which we are delighted to see there is now so general a disposition to recur" (*RR* C1:377). Hunt must have been highly pleased with Hazlitt's observations, for they reinforced his stated aims to reintroduce earlier English authors and alternative literary traditions to Romantic readers. In line with other reviewers, however, the *Edinburgh* clearly took issue with the poetic style in which *Rimini* had been written: "we think there is a good deal of affectation in his homeliness, directness, and rambling descriptions. He visibly gives himself airs of familiarity, and mixes up flippant, and even cant phrases, with passages that bear, upon the whole, the marks of considerable labour and study" (*RR* C1:378). Jeffrey, who Duncan Wu thinks was responsible for this particular criticism of *Rimini*, would continue to speak of Hunt's style in such terms in later years, telling Hunt privately in 1844 that he could still be "too careless and colloquial in expression," adding, however, that his "*idioms* in general are most graceful and elegant, as well as soft and natural" (*CLH* 2:36).[69] In 1816, the *Edinburgh Review*, with Hazlitt's influence, was still willing to promote a rising new generation of Romantic authors with Hunt and his "little volume" leading the way.

If the *Edinburgh*'s review of *Rimini*, with Jeffrey's additions, had nevertheless come to the same conclusion about Hunt's style as the *Quarterly* had, Hazlitt and Jeffrey did so, importantly, by directing the focus away from Hunt's personality. In the *Quarterly*, besides emphasizing the defects of Hunt's private character, Croker distracted readers by quarreling with Hunt's preface and his "pretended *principles*," drawing out words, phrases, and short excerpts to illustrate his specific objections to Hunt's style. In so doing, Croker constantly intruded upon the poetry with his critical observations and commentary. Only two extracts of uninterrupted verse of substantial length were provided: the section that begins "'Twas Lancelout of the Lake, a bright romance"; and the section that begins "But noble passion touch'd Giovanni's soul" (*RR* C2:755–6). In total, these two extracts, respectively, print 36 lines and 18 lines of uninterrupted text. In contrast, Hazlitt and Jeffrey made it a point to emphasize the reader's role in coming to terms with the merits of Hunt's poem by reprinting long, deliberately uninterrupted, extracts with the longest extract, beginning "So now you walked beside an odorous bed," amounting to 76 lines of verse (*RR* C1:382). Most of the other extracts, meanwhile, average about 50 lines of uninterrupted verse. Although the reprinting of lengthy extracts in reviews and literary magazines during the Romantic period was commonly perceived as a form of puffing or a way to fill out a review, the *Edinburgh* reviewers were keenly aware that the *Rimini* extracts were a particular matter of importance: "We have given these extracts at length, that our readers might judge of the story of Rimini, less on our authority, than its own merits" (*RR* C1:385). Hazlitt had clearly read Croker's review and deliberately responded to it by avoiding its critical fallacies. In fact, the other notable difference between the treatment of *Rimini* in the *Edinburgh* and the *Quarterly* was that the former did not venture one word upon Hunt's dedication to Byron or upon Hunt's friendship with the noble poet—both were facets, Hazlitt and Jeffrey knew, that could only distract readers from forming their own appraisal of the artistry of Hunt's poem.

The Murray-Croker-Gifford Conspiracy

With two major and several minor reviews of *Rimini* available, Hunt had much to reflect upon, but it was Croker's hostile *Quarterly* article that stayed uppermost in his mind for the remainder of 1816. Hunt became convinced that Murray had ordered Croker's review, thus undermining any chance that *Rimini* may have had of finding mainstream approval. Hunt's belief on this score, though unsubstantiated, first becomes apparent in Hunt's letters from May of 1816, when the author seems to have accused the publisher of raising the agreed-upon selling price of *Rimini* after the contract had been settled and the volume had appeared on bookseller shelves.[70] The implication, as Hunt appears to have suggested, was that Murray was making additional, unauthorized profit from the sale of *Rimini*. In a letter to Moore on 21 May 1816, Hunt added a political dimension to the conspiracy he believed was being waged against his poem: "I was prepared, of course, for a reasonable carbanado from the Government quarters, and even for a good deal of stout objection perhaps from more friendly ones, as far as difference of theory was concerned; but this assault is mere foaming at the mouth."[71] On 19 August 1816, Hunt also remembered the following detail about *Rimini*'s publication: "A very few days afterwards,—I think not above three or [four], if so many,—the Quarterly Review was advertised for publication" with *Rimini* included "in the list of books criticised" (*LHLL* 76).

Hunt was not the only one to believe that Murray and the *Quarterly* reviewers had made a deliberate attempt to prevent *Rimini* from succeeding. Byron's friend John Cam Hobhouse, for one, thought that the poem had been "bedivilled" by the *Quarterly Review*.[72] Byron repeated this intelligence in a letter to Moore on 11 April 1817, knowing that "There was a devil of a review of [Hunt] in the Quarterly, a year ago" (*BLJ* 5:211). Hazlitt, meanwhile, placed the blame directly upon the *Quarterly Review*'s chief editor, William Gifford.[73] Despite the concerns of Hunt and his friends, there is no firm evidence to support Hunt's belief that Murray had any direct involvement. For one thing, Murray denied having any influence over the reviewers at the *Quarterly*. Writing to Byron, the publisher confessed: "What they choose to say of you in the Quarterly—I can not always prevent—but may the judgment of God fall upon me if I would publish any work containing a line against one for whom independent of my devoted affection for this persevering friendship—I am on so many accounts under everlasting obligation" (*LJM* 344). At the same time, Murray was not above enjoying "a line against" Byron's closest friends or relishing a negative review in the pages of the *Quarterly*. In another letter to Byron from September of 1817, for example, the publisher seems to take pleasure in the fact that the radically inclined Hobhouse had been "marvelously [sic] ill used in the Quarterly just published—where he is called a <u>Bone-grubber</u>" (*LJM* 246). Of all of Byron's friends, however, Hunt had the unfortunate distinction of becoming the main target of ridicule within the Murray circle.

In fact, there was a genuine fear among Murray's associates that Hunt and his politics were detrimental to Byron's literary celebrity. Writing to Murray on 26 March 1820, Croker opined:

> What interest can Lord Byron have in being the poet of a party in politics or of a party in morals or of a party in religion—why should he wish to throw away the suffrages . . . of more than half the nation—He has no interest in that direction & I believe has no feeling of that kind.—In politics he cannot be what he appears, or rather what M^{essrs}. Hobhouse & Legh [sic] Hunt wish to make him appear[;] a man of his birth, a man of his taste, a man of his talents, a man of his habits can have nothing in common with such miserable creatures as we now call <u>radicals</u>.
>
> (qtd. in *LJM* 316–7)

Croker clearly felt confident enough, despite knowing Byron only through his writings and through conversation with Murray, to make such personal claims for the poet. Nevertheless, the burden of having to deal with Hunt—still the formidable voice of *The Examiner*—eventually took its toll on the reviewer of *Rimini*. Croker seems to have been turned off by the thought of having to treat Hunt a second time in the *Quarterly*. In a revealing letter to Murray written in July of 1819, Croker admitted: "Mr. Gifford has set me Leigh Hunt as a *task*. He asks but two or three pages, and I shall see what I can do this evening, but I had rather have let it alone."[74] The letter is vague in its particulars. The "*task*" may have been a review of Hunt's recently published edition of poetical works offered by Charles and James Ollier, but, if so, no review of these volumes ever appeared. What Croker's letter makes clear, however, is that Murray's reviewers at the *Quarterly* did communicate directly, at least on occasion, with the publisher about their work. So while it does seem reasonable to think that Murray may have played a part in Croker's damaging review of *Rimini* in 1816—by having an awareness of it and doing nothing to alter or prevent the review—the idea must remain conjecture until new evidence comes forth to support Hunt's belief that there was, in fact, a Murray-led conspiracy against *Rimini*.

Having exiled himself from England in April of 1816, Byron had little awareness of Hunt's on-going interactions with Murray. He was probably also unaware that Hunt had satirized Murray in *The Examiner* in the spring of 1817 during the *Wat Tyler* scandal involving Southey.[75] In the midst of this quarrel, in a letter to Byron on 13 May 1817, Murray wrote: "Your friend Hunt, because I could not give him £500 for his Rimini—has had the baseness to enter upon a Series of Abuse [sic] of me—which I really regard no further than that I never did give my name to the Public, except in a business advertisement" (*LJM* 229). Even without knowing the details of the quarrel, Byron was only half sympathetic, remembering well enough that Murray's actions in the early months of 1816, as the *Rimini* and *Parisina* volumes were moving through the press, had left much to be desired. Byron replied to Murray on 4 June 1817 thus: "I am sorry to hear of your row with Hunt—but suppose him to be exasperated by the Quarterly—& your refusal to *deal*—& when one is angry—& edit[s] a paper I should think the temptation too strong for literary nature—which is not always human" (*BLJ* 5:234). It is clear that Byron was still willing to defend his talented friend, whom he knew to be, like himself, possessed of a "literary nature"—a nature that did not always take kindly to Romantic reviewers or Romantic publishers.

During his years of exile, Byron would continue to hear of the quarrels of authors, publishers, and reviewers, with Murray serving as the primary conduit for such information. Stories and rumors about Byron's connection with Hunt, however, increasingly became a public matter of debate and a serious cause of concern for the exiled poet. Byron would become decidedly vexed in the spring of 1818 when he received a copy of Hunt's *Foliage* and, afterward, encountered a series of literary reviews and lampoons written by a new cast of conservative voices with an eager inclination to pick up where Croker had left off with his attack on Hunt and *Rimini*. John Taylor Coleridge of the *Quarterly Review* and John Gibson Lockhart of *Blackwood's Edinburgh Magazine* began a sustained campaign of abuse against Hunt and his so-called "Cockney" friends—Keats, Shelley, and Hazlitt—that would have significant consequences for the Byron-Hunt friendship and literary relationship, for it was inevitable that Byron, the dedicatee of *Rimini*, would be dragged into Hunt's outspoken critical writings on the state of modern poetry. Although Byron voiced his concerns privately at first, he eventually joined the public outcry against Hunt and his circle of friends in a series of critical prose writings of his own that came to a head when Byron made his formal entry into the "Bowles/Pope Controversy." The prolonged outcry against Pope, Byron believed, was a sure sign of a new and uncertain direction for English poetry.

Notes

1 The National Library of Scotland (hereafter NLS) ACC. 13264, f. 25v.
2 Jeffrey N. Cox, "Re-Visioning Rimini: Dante in the Cockney School," in *Dante and Italy in British Romanticism*, eds. Frederick Burwick and Paul Douglass (New York: Palgrave Macmillan, 2011), 185.
3 C. P. Brand, *Italy and the English Romantics* (Cambridge: Cambridge University Press, 1957), 85–7.
4 See Timothy Webb, "Stories of Rimini: Leigh Hunt, Byron and the Fate of Francesca," in *Dante in the Nineteenth Century: Reception, Canonicity, Popularization*, ed. Nick Havely (Oxford: Peter Lang, 2011), 31–53; see also Will Bowers, "Hunt, Byron, and *The Story of Rimini*—A Literary Challenge to 'the Public Mind,'" *Romanticism and Victorianism on the Net* 59–60 (April–October 2011). www.erudit.org/en/journals/ravon.
5 See Peter Cochran, "Byron and Leigh Hunt: 'The Wit in the Dungeon,'" in *"Romanticism"—and Byron* (Newcastle upon Tyne: Cambridge Scholars Publishing, 2009), 116. See also T. A. J. Burnett, *The British Library Catalogue of the Ashley Manuscripts*. 2 vols. (London: The British Library, 1999), 1:46.
6 For a discussion of the historical figures behind the characters in *Rimini*, see Dante Alighieri, *The Divine Comedy: Inferno*, trans. Charles S. Singleton, 2 vols. (Princeton, NJ: Princeton University Press, 1970), 2:83–95.
7 Jeffrey N. Cox, *Romanticism in the Shadow of War* (Cambridge: Cambridge University Press, 2014), 178.
8 William Hazlitt, *The Complete Works of William Hazlitt*, ed. P. P. Howe, 21 vols. (London: J. M. Dent and Sons, Ltd., 1930–34), 5:17.
9 See Joseph Luzzi, *Romantic Europe and the Ghost of Italy* (New Haven, CT: Yale University Press, 2008), 147–8.
10 Leigh Hunt, *Stories from the Italian Poets*. 2 vols. (London: Moxon, 1846), 1:55, 63, 66.
11 Hunt, *Stories*, 1:52.
12 Ralph Pite, *The Circle of Our Vision: Dante's Presence in English Romantic Poetry* (Oxford: Oxford University Press, 1994), 199–200.
13 Frederick L. Beaty, "Byron and the Story of Francesca da Rimini," *PMLA* 75, no. 4 (1960): 396.
14 MS. Ashley 906. These cantos are Hunt's *"autograph fair copy."* See Burnett, *The British Library Catalogue of the Ashley Manuscripts*, 1999, 1:45–6. See also Clarice Short's "The Composition of Hunt's *The Story of Rimini*," *Keats-Shelley Journal* 21 (1972): 207–18.
15 Timothy Webb, "After Horsemonger Lane: Leigh Hunt's London Letters to Byron (1815–1816)," *Romanticism* 25, no. 2 (2015): 249–50.
16 Webb, "After Horsemonger Lane," 250.
17 Richard Cronin, *The Politics of Romantic Poetry: in Search of the Pure Commonwealth* (London: Macmillan Press, Ltd., 2000), 190–1. See also Walter Jackson Bate, *The Stylistic Development of Keats* (London: Routledge & Kegan Paul, 1958), 1–42.
18 Beth Lau, *Keats's Paradise Lost* (Gainesville: University Press of Florida, 1998), 10.
19 H. J. Jackson, *Marginalia: Readers Writing in Books* (New Haven, CT: Yale University Press, 2001), 99–100.
20 Jackson, *Marginalia*, 81–100.
21 *The Manuscripts of the Younger Romantics: Lord Byron IV: Miscellaneous Poems*, eds. Alice Levine and Jerome J. McGann (New York: Garland Publishing Inc., 1988), 1–80; 217–25.

22 All references to MS. Ashley 906 are hereafter cited parenthetically. Transcriptions of Byron's marginalia have been made from the manuscript and have been compared to Andrew Nicholson's transcriptions in *CMP* 213–7.

23 Compare lines 165–72 in Hunt's "The Choice" (first published in *The Liberal*, No. IV, in 1823) on angling to Byron's attack on anglers in stanza 106 of Canto XIII of *Don Juan* and its accompanying note (*CPW* 5:759). Byron had written Canto XIII in February of 1823, the same month in which Hunt was preparing material for the last two numbers of *The Liberal*, including "The Choice," and it seems probable that they had discussed fish rights together at this time.

24 Malcolm Elwin, *Lord Byron's Wife* (New York: Harcourt, Brace & World, Inc., 1962), 258, 456.

25 Thomas Moore, *Letters and Journals of Lord Byron, with Notices of His Life*. 2 vols. (London: John Murray, 1830), 1:120.

26 Byron published reviews of William Wordsworth's *Poems* (1807), William Spence's *Poems* (1811), and William Ireland's *Neglected Genius* (1812). See *CMP* 8–19.

27 Childe Harold, for instance, "through Sin's long labyrinth had run" (Canto I, line 37). See also *The Giaour*: "The curse for Hassan's sin was sent / To turn a palace to a tomb" (lines 280–1).

28 Christopher Ricks, "Dryden's Triplets," in *The Cambridge Companion to John Dryden*, ed. Steven N. Zwicker (Cambridge: Cambridge University Press, 2004), 94.

29 Webb, "After Horsemonger Lane," 245. All quotations from Hunt's 30 October letter hereafter are taken from Webb's edition.

30 Hunt's letter from 20 September 1813 is printed in Thomas Moore, *Memoirs, Journal, and Correspondence of Thomas Moore*, ed. Lord John Russell, 8 vols. (London: Longman, Brown, Green, and Longmans, 1853–56), 8:157.

31 Webb, "After Horsemonger Lane," 245–6.

32 P. M. S. Dawson, "Byron, Shelley, and the 'New School,'" in *Shelley Revalued: Essays from the Gregynog Conference*, ed. Kelvin Everest (Leicester: Leicester University Press, 1983), 98.

33 NLS MS. 43449.

34 Jane Stabler, "Second-generation Romantic Poetry I: Hunt, Byron, Moore," in *The Cambridge History of English Poetry*, ed. Michael O'Neill (Cambridge: Cambridge University Press, 2010), 490–1.

35 Dawson, "Byron, Shelley, and the 'New School,'" 95–8; see also Richard Margraff Turley, *The Politics of Language in Romantic Literature* (London: Palgrave Macmillan, 2002), 76–9.

36 William Wordsworth, *The Prose Works of William Wordsworth*, eds. W. J. B. Owen and Jane Worthington Smyser, 3 vols. (Oxford: Oxford University Press, 1974), 1:162; 3:75–6. For a discussion of artistic affinities between Dante and Wordsworth, see Luzzi, *Romantic Europe*, 143–4.

37 Thomas Percy, *Reliques of Ancient English Poetry*. 3 vols. (London: John Nichols, 1794), 3:xxiv.

38 See *A* 1:89. "Percy's 'Reliques' were preparing a nobler age, both in poetry and prose."

39 Webb, "After Horsemonger Lane," 246.

40 Hazlitt, *The Complete Works*, 4:258, 269.

41 Hazlitt, *The Complete Works*, 4:258.

42 Webb, "After Horsemonger Lane," 246.

43 Deanna Shemek, "That Elusive Object of Desire: Angelica in the 'Orlando Furioso,'" *Annali d'Italianistica* 7 (1989): 124.

44 Webb, "After Horsemonger Lane," 246.

45 Hunt, *Stories*, 2:178.
46 Hunt, *Stories*, 2:161–2.
47 Webb, "After Horsemonger Lane," 247.
48 Hunt to Murray, 9 December 1815. NLS MS. 43449. For the "prose synopsis," see Ashley 906, f. 1v.
49 NLS MS. 43449.
50 Nicholas Roe, *Fiery Heart: The First Life of Leigh Hunt* (London: Pimlico, 2005), 224–5.
51 NLS MS. 43449.
52 NLS ACC. 13264, f. 25v.
53 NLS MS. 43449.
54 British Library (hereafter BL) Add. MS. 38523, ff. 23–4.
55 Mary O'Connell, *Byron and John Murray: A Poet and His Publisher* (Liverpool: Liverpool University Press, 2014), 123–31. See also Andrew Nicholson, "Napoleon's 'Last Act' and Byron's Ode," *Romanticism* 9, no. 1 (2003): 68–81.
56 O'Connell, *Byron and John Murray*, 131–2.
57 Byron wanted "six hundred pounds" to go to Godwin and the "remainder" to be used for "other purposes," which Marchand explains: "Byron intended to divide the remainder . . . between Coleridge and [Charles] Maturin." See *BLJ* 5:16.
58 William Hazlitt, *The Letters of William Hazlitt*, eds. Herschel Moreland Sikes et al. (New York: New York University Press, 1978), 153.
59 BL Add. MS. 38108, f. 155.
60 Thomas Moore, *The Letters of Thomas Moore*, ed. Wilfred S. Dowden, 2 vols. (Oxford: Oxford University Press, 1964), 1:390.
61 Charles Lamb, *The Letters of Charles and Mary Anne Lamb*, ed. Edwin W. Marrs, Jr., 3 vols. (Ithaca, NY: Cornell University Press, 1975–78), 3:209–10.
62 John O. Hayden, *The Romantic Reviewers: 1802–1824* (London: Routledge & Kegan Paul Limited, 1969), 179.
63 For a discussion of the treatment of Hunt's personality in *Blackwood's Edinburgh Magazine*, for instance, see David Higgins, *Romantic Genius and the Literary Magazine: Biography, Celebrity, Politics* (New York: Routledge, 2005), 55–9.
64 Mark Parker, *Literary Magazines and British Romanticism* (Cambridge: Cambridge University Press, 2004), 108.
65 Duncan Wu has recently argued that "most of the published text is [Hazlitt's]." See William Hazlitt, *New Writings of William Hazlitt*, ed. Duncan Wu, 2 vols. (Oxford: Oxford University Press, 2007), 1:178.
66 "On the Cockney School of Poetry. No. 1." *BEM* 2, October 1817, 41.
67 Moore, *Letters and Journals of Lord Byron*, 1:644.
68 Hazlitt, *New Writings*, 1:177.
69 Hazlitt, *New Writings*, 1:178.
70 See Murray's letter to Hunt. BL Add. MS. 38523, f. 31.
71 Moore, *Memoirs, Journal and Correspondence of Thomas Moore*, 8:215.
72 John Cam Hobhouse, *Byron's Bulldog: The Letters of John Cam Hobhouse to Lord Byron*, ed. Peter W. Graham (Columbus: Ohio State University Press, 1984), 222.
73 Hazlitt, *The Complete Works*, 9:26.
74 John Wilson Croker, *The Croker Papers. The Correspondence and Diaries of the Late Right Honourable John Wilson Croker*, ed. Louis J. Jennings, 3 vols. (London: John Murray, 1885), 1:146.
75 See *E* 485, April 13, 1817, 236–7; *E* 489, May 11, 1817, 299–303.

5 Byron and the Cockney School

One purpose of the sensational "On the Cockney School of Poetry" series in *Blackwood's Edinburgh Magazine*, in which Hunt held a prominent position as the school's founder, was to separate Cockneys from patricians, radicals from patriots, and, more specifically, to persuade readers to reject the idea that a creative sympathy or private friendship between figures like Hunt and Byron could, in reality or in print, ever exist. With the publication of *Rimini*, such social divisions were routinely emphasized in public discussions of the Byron-Hunt friendship. As Jeffrey N. Cox points out, however, such divisions were also apparent in Hunt's private circle, for the author of *Childe Harold* did not always fit comfortably alongside Hunt's friends—a group that included, among others, Keats, Shelley, Hazlitt, and Benjamin Robert Haydon.[1]

Hunt, in many ways, had his own difficulty placing Byron within his sphere of influence and convincing the poet to fully accept his ideas for remaking modern poetry. At first, after several months of private collaboration on *Rimini* in the late months of 1815, Hunt believed that he had found a leading role for Byron to play, boldly announcing in the preface to that poem that Byron would be *the* modern poet to perfect the system upon which *Rimini* had been written.[2] Hunt may have been presumptuous in thinking that Byron would adopt his poetic theories for creative ends, but he was prescient in predicting that the author of *Don Juan* would become the most important poetic innovator of the Romantic age. The hostile critical reaction to *Rimini*, however, seems to have forced Hunt to rethink his decision to enfold Byron within his creative plans in such a decidedly self-assured manner. Less than a year after *Rimini* appeared, Hunt's "Young Poets" article was published in *The Examiner*, revealing that the editor had already reconsidered his plans for reforming modern poetry. In this well-known article, Hunt introduced a new group of young, generally unknown authors: Shelley, Keats, and John Hamilton Reynolds. In the same article, Hunt also found space to express his "delight" with Byron's recently published third canto of *Childe Harold*, an installment that reaffirmed for Hunt the idea that Byron had "taken his place where we always said he would be found,—among the poets who have a real feeling for numbers, and who go directly to Nature for inspiration" (*E* 466 [1 December 1816]: 761). Yet it was clear that Byron, no longer a young poet, had been replaced in Hunt's poetical schemes by Shelley, Keats, and Reynolds. Although Byron was still to have a role to play in Hunt's plans, that role became less defined after Byron's departure from England in April of 1816.

For Byron, on the other hand, Hunt's increasingly outspoken views as a cultural and literary critic came into sharp focus during his years in exile. In particular, Byron's reading of Hunt's *Foliage*, a volume Cox has described as Hunt's "Cockney Manifesto," would raise unexpected new concerns about Hunt's creative theories, associations, and motivations.[3] Byron also continued to read widely in the Romantic periodicals, including the Tory *Quarterly Review* and *Blackwood's*, the dynamic, politically conservative newcomer. The ill-natured treatment of Hunt's private character in these publications, as well as the attention they were giving to Hunt's private friendships, would be an additional cause for concern to the exiled poet. Byron's angry response to this attention, along with his thoughts on the "Cockney School," would emerge in a series of critical prose writings, including his formally conceived defense of Alexander Pope, the *Letter to John Murray* (1821). In exile, Byron, as we shall see, came to discover that his celebrity and his poetry were being subjected to new distortions and political abuses that derived, in part, from his association with Hunt and the "Cockney School."

"A Considerable Sympathy": *Parisina* and *Rimini*

A series of advertisements that ran in the *Morning Post* at the beginning of February 1816 announced that Byron's *Siege of Corinth* and *Parisina* volume had just been published, perhaps on the same day, or shortly after, Hunt's *Rimini* appeared.[4] The simultaneous or near-simultaneous publication of the last installment of Byron's verse tales and Hunt's major new poem ensured that the two poets would be linked together before a large portion of the reading public. That link would have also been apparent to readers who bought unbound copies of *The Siege* and *Parisina* volume, for in the book catalogs that John Murray had included with Byron's latest production we also find Hunt's *Rimini* being advertised. Perhaps the most important link between the *Siege* and *Parisina* volume and Hunt's *Rimini* at the beginning of 1816, however, was that created by the Romantic reviewers. Indeed, the two volumes came to occupy the same columns in the *Chester Chronicle* in March, the *British Review* in May, and *Blackwood's* in November of 1817, with each periodical providing joint reviews. This critical pairing marked a significant development in the Byron-Hunt literary relationship, for it initiated a trend that would persist until the last reviews of *The Liberal*, the miscellany jointly authored by Byron and Hunt in Italy in 1822 and 1823, appeared.

For Byron, the critical attention given to *Rimini* and *The Siege* and *Parisina* volumes, notwithstanding the potential benefit to Hunt's poetical career, must have been unwanted. In the first place, Byron, as we saw in the last chapter, said that he cared little for *The Siege* or *Parisina*. Furthermore, despite the number of copies that sold (9,500 through four editions), the reviewers reacted to *The Siege* and *Parisina* volume with notable hostility.[5] Yet two major reviewers noticed that *Parisina*, in particular, made for a strong literary pairing with *Rimini*. William Roberts of the *British Review*, in fact, believed that there was "a considerable sympathy between them in the choice of their subjects" (*RR* B1:434). That subject was incest. It is not without a critical foundation, then, that we might ask what, if any, creative influence had Byron and Hunt been exerting on each other in the late months of 1815 as *Rimini* and *The Siege* and *Parisina* volumes were both being prepared for publication.

The domestic tragedy in *Parisina*, like that in the story of *Rimini*, is set in motion by an incestuous affair, and echoes of Hunt's *Rimini* are immediately apparent in Byron's tale. *Parisina* begins, for example, at "Este's bower" (line 19), a "trysting-place" (line 60) surrounded by "foliage thick" (line 23), to which Parisina, wife of Azo, Marquis of Este, goes to evade her husband's watch and pursues an illicit affair with Hugo, Azo's "bastard son" (*CPW* 3:358). *Parisina*'s opening scene would have reminded readers of Francesca's "accustomed bower" (Canto III, line 508), a "summer-house so fine in such a nest of green" (line 485), where the heroine of Hunt's *Rimini*, as we have seen, escapes Giovanni's oversight and eventually exchanges her fatal kiss with Paulo. In fact, following Hunt's storyline closely, Byron has Parisina call out Hugo's name in her sleep, revealing her secret affair in the presence of her husband. Startled by the confession, Azo acts swiftly and remorselessly, sentencing Hugo to death by public execution. In his *Autobiography*, Hunt later claimed that Byron had taken the idea for Parisina's nocturnal revelation directly from *Rimini* (*A* 2:171). Whether Byron did take the hint from Hunt, or whether, as some commentators suggest, he took it from Shakespeare, Byron would have certainly known that Hunt had used the plot device in *Rimini*, having recently annotated the poem in manuscript.[6]

And yet despite their shared features, *Parisina* and *Rimini* are quite different in the way they treat the theme of incest. The relationship pursued by Hugo and Parisina in Byron's tale leads to bleak consequences for both characters, who, according to Daniel P. Watkins, are subjected to a complex web of social, religious, and political forces "relentlessly exerting their power to preserve social order and individual morality at the expense of individual life."[7] While a similar argument might be made for the deadly consequences of the transgressive relationship pursued by Paulo and Francesca in *Rimini*, Hunt appears to present the relationship in attractive ways. Reviewing *Rimini* for *Blackwood's*, John Gibson Lockhart (writing as "Z.") observed that "Many a one reads Rimini as a pleasant romance, and closes it without having the least suspicion that he has been perusing a tale pregnant with all the horrors of most unpardonable guilt" (*BEM* 2 [November 1817]: 201). Francesca, moreover, dies stoically, fully committed to Paulo, who impales himself upon Giovanni's sword, refusing to allow his own brother to slay him. Although Paulo and Francesca might be seen as victims of the cruel and unjust strictures of the societies they inhabit, both characters still retain the ability to accept death on their own terms. In *Parisina*, on the other hand, Byron refuses to grant such agency to Parisina and Hugo, leaving his heroine to live out her days in madness, for her "life began and closed in woe!" (line 529). Hugo, meanwhile, dies at the scaffold without protest or struggle.

In the May 1816 issue of the *British Review*, William Roberts reviewed Byron's *Siege* and *Parisina* volume and Hunt's *Rimini* together, praising Hunt's offering while condemning Byron's. Roberts attacked Byron outright, briefly treating the "wretched Parisina" by categorizing it thus: "To the same limbo of inanity we would gladly consign all those unholy images of slaughter, sensuality, incest, and infidelity, which have taken such poetical possession of Lord Byron's brain" (*RR* B1:429). Roberts concluded that the "subject is not more objectionable than the poetry is contemptible" and provided a mere snippet from the poem's final scene, fearing that Byron's treatment of the incest theme in no way mirrored that of the "lofty writers of ancient tragedy [who] so managed the subject as to convey nothing to tickle the ear of lust, or shock the sentiment of modesty" (*RR* B1:434). Most reviewers followed Roberts's lead and chose not to discuss *Parisina*, focusing their comments instead on *The Siege*. And yet few critics hesitated to explore the particulars of *Rimini*'s incest theme. Most did so, of course, in order to condemn Hunt for appearing to sanction the illicit behavior. Roberts, however, clearly admired Hunt's *Rimini* and treated the poem in detail not to condemn it, but to hold it up as a model for how to transform controversial subject matter into art—how to accomplish, in other words, that which Byron, according to Roberts, had failed to do in *Parisina*. This is not to say that Roberts's attitude toward *Rimini* was wholly accepting, for he began his review, like most other reviewers of Hunt's poem, by attacking Hunt's poetic theories: "We have hopes . . . that one day or other we shall see Mr. Hunt emancipated from these very silly prejudices, and acknowledging in every language a diction of common use, and a diction of poetry." At the same time, Roberts found in *Rimini* "a richness of expression, a vivacity in the colour of his words, and a chaste use of appropriate ornament, which show [Hunt] to feel that poetry is an art, notwithstanding his industrious affectation to hide it." Perhaps most surprising of all,

Roberts found Hunt's treatment of the incest theme to be "touched with as much decency, as the conduct of the story would admit" and that the consequences of the crime had been painted "in the language of virtue" (*RR* B1:435).

John Gibson Lockhart's review of *Rimini* and *Parisina* in *Blackwood's*, on the other hand, rejected *Rimini* outright on moral, political, and artistic grounds. Although Lockhart's review appeared in November of 1817, over a year after the two poems had been published, the belated review served an important purpose for the new literary magazine. By making *Parisina* and *Rimini* the focus of the second installment of the "Cockney School" series, Lockhart could develop his politically conservative narrative against Hunt and his circle by reviewing *Rimini*, a work Lockhart thought epitomized Hunt's "Cockney" radicalism, against Byron's seemingly moral and righteous *Parisina*. Taking this approach, Lockhart not only turned Roberts's appraisal of *Parisina* and *Rimini* on its head, but Lockhart also, as we shall see, deliberately and narrowly read Byron's poem in a way that fit the "Cockney" narrative *Blackwood's* was developing—a narrative that firmly rejected the idea that Byron and Hunt were (or could be) poetical or social equals.[8]

Lockhart began his review of *Rimini* and *Parisina* by suggesting that Hunt, in adopting the theme of incest from Dante, "might also have enumerated the two best dramatists that have appeared within our own recollection, Schiller and Alfieri" (Byron had referred the reader to these two dramatists in his preface to *Parisina*).[9] Lockhart also suggested that Hunt, in pursuing the incest theme, might have considered another well-known author, the "first of all living poets, Lord Byron" (*BEM* 2 [November 1817]: 195). As Lockhart argued, "To none of these poems, however, does the subject of Rimini bear so great a resemblance as to Parisina, and it is this very circumstance of likeness which brings before us, in the strongest colours, the difference between the incest of Leigh Hunt and the incest of Byron." Lockhart, however, proceeded to offer a reading of *Parisina* that ignored the contextual details Byron had included in his preface to the poem. Lockhart argued that because *Parisina* apparently drew its creative inspiration from the ancient Greek dramatists, Byron had the "same desire to represent incest as a thing too awful to spring up of itself, without the interference of some revengeful power—the same careful avoidance of luxurious images—the same resolution to treat unhallowed love with the seriousness of a judge, who narrates only that he may condemn the guilty and warn the heedless" (*BEM* 2 [November 1817]: 196–7). Lockhart thus presented Byron's *Parisina* as a cautionary tale, a narrative of moral retribution, ignoring the domestic complexities of the tragedy and, importantly, the uncertain historical record of the events dramatically rendered in the poem. Edward Gibbon, Byron's source for the *Parisina* story, had condemned outright the actions of the historical Nicholas III (Azo in *Parisina*). In the passage from Gibbon that Byron chose to reprint in the preface to *Parisina*, we learn: "[Azo] was unfortunate, if [Hugo and Parisina] were guilty; if they were innocent, he was still more unfortunate: nor is there any possible situation in which I can scarcely approve the last act of the justice of a parent" (*CPW* 3:358). It thus follows that Byron, by reprinting Gibbon's remarks, was, first and foremost, aware of the incompleteness of the historical record and that he, like Gibbon, either believed or was willing to entertain the belief that the severe punishments Azo inflicted upon Parisina and Hugo were not justifiable on moral, and perhaps even legal, grounds given the insufficiency of the historical evidence.[10] Yet Azo, in Lockhart's reading of *Parisina*, is not an "unfortunate" husband and parent, but a righteous judge, a "revengeful power" who swiftly and remorselessly punishes Hugo and Parisina for their transgression.[11] Lockhart's argument, of course, was *the* argument that needed to be made if he were to effectively separate Byron's creative achievement in *Parisina* from Hunt's radical experiment in *Rimini*.

To enforce this separation, Lockhart declared forcefully that "It was reserved for the happier genius of Leigh Hunt, to divest incest of its hereditary horror—to make a theme of unholy love the vehicle of trim and light-hearted descriptions of courtly splendours and processions." Following this line of analysis, Lockhart concluded that "Mr. Hunt seems, all through his poem, to imagine that he is writing a mere ordinary love-story." Through this critically reductive lens Lockhart placed Hunt before the public as a weak poetic rival to Byron: "As, in the subject and passion of his Poem, Mr. Hunt has the desire to compete with Lord Byron, so here, in the more airy and external parts of his composition, he would fain enter the lists with the Mighty Minstrel" (*BEM* 2 [November 1817]: 197–8). Lockhart's assertion has little foundation in fact. Given what we know of the composition histories of *Parisina* and *Rimini*, it is much more likely that Byron's *Parisina* was inspired, in part, by his reading of Hunt's *Rimini* in late 1815 and early 1816.[12] Hunt, presumably, did not encounter *Parisina* until Byron sent him a gift copy of the volume in February.[13] Byron, of course, had known of *Rimini* for some time and had recently annotated the poem in manuscript. But Byron's private admiration for and engagement with *Rimini* were facts beyond the reach of Lockhart. They were facts, moreover, that would not have fit *Blackwood's* narrative of the literary relationship and private friendship that existed between Byron and Hunt.

Blackwood's Cockneys and Lockhart's Byron

John Gibson Lockhart's "On the Cockney School of Poetry" series, launched in October of 1817, was one of the most controversial features in *Blackwood's* during its early years. As Tom Mole has shown, among other journalistic strategies, the magazine used personalities in effective but pernicious ways, bullying authors and critics, real or imagined, with heavy doses of *ad hominem* arguments.[14] Ridicule, caricature, and satire sold especially well in Romantic Britain, and Hunt had the unfortunate distinction of becoming one of *Blackwood's* earliest targets for its relentless satire and cartooning. In the first number of the "Cockney School" series, Lockhart ("Z.") gave himself the "honour" of "christening" Hunt and his poetical (and political) followers with the "Cockney School" label, while Hunt himself was awarded the highest honor as the school's "chief Doctor and Professor," a "Professor" nevertheless with "vulgar modes of thinking and manners in all respects" (*BEM* 2 [October 1817]: 38). Lockhart also discussed *Rimini* at some length, arguing, facetiously, that the poem was "not wholly undeserving of praise." This surprising statement was a direct response and a challenge to John Wilson Croker's damning review of *Rimini* in the *Quarterly*, a review that Lockhart called "illiberal." With a desire to make *Blackwood's* a powerful, if controversial, addition to Romantic review culture, William Blackwood's methods included strategically placed attacks on rival reviews and reviewers.[15] The *Quarterly*, therefore, was fair game for censure in the pages of *Blackwood's* even though the two periodicals were ostensibly aligned politically and were certainly in agreement about Hunt's poetic vulgarities and radical politics. For this reason, Lockhart also implicated Jeffrey, Hazlitt, and the *Edinburgh Review*, claiming that Hazlitt's review of *Rimini* was, in fact, the reason for the creation of the "Cockney School" series: "It was chiefly in consequence of [Jeffrey's] allowing Leigh Hunt to pass unpunished through a scene of slaughter, which his execution might so highly have graced, that we came to the resolution of laying before our readers a series of essays on *the Cockney School*" (*BEM* 2 [October 1817]: 41).

Lockhart's discussion of *Rimini* in the first "Cockney School" number also stressed the interchangeable qualities of the poem and the author: "Leigh Hunt [is] a man certainly of some talents, of extravagant pretensions both in wit, poetry, and politics, and withal of exquisitely bad taste." No critical analysis of *Rimini* was offered nor were any extracts provided. Instead, Lockhart relied on generalizations: "Every thing is pretence, affectation, finery, and gaudiness." Hunt's "writings," moreover, could be dismissed for political and religious reasons since the "two great elements of all dignified poetry, religious feeling, and patriotic feeling, have no place in his writings." In all of this, the reader senses that Lockhart's lack of critical insight and nuance is of little importance, for his primary purpose is to draw a caricature of Hunt. Indeed, taking the *ad hominem* approach a step further than Croker had in his *Quarterly* review of *Rimini*, Lockhart set up Hunt as a poetical pretender of the lowest order next to his friend Byron: "All the great poets of our country have been men of some rank in society, and there is no vulgarity in any of their writings; but Mr. Hunt cannot utter a dedication, or even a note, without betraying the *Shibboleth* of low birth and low habits. He is the ideal of a Cockney Poet" (*BEM* 2 [October 1817]: 38–9). Lockhart's most damning comments in the first number of the "Cockney School" series related specifically to Hunt's private friendships:

> The Founder of the Cockney School would fain claim poetical kindred with Lord Byron and Thomas Moore. Such a connexion would be as unsuitable for them as for William Wordsworth. The days of Mr. Moore's follies are long since over; and, as he is a thorough gentleman, he must necessarily entertain the greatest contempt for such an under-bred person as Mr. Leigh Hunt. But Lord Byron! How must the haughty spirit of Lara and Harold contemn the subaltern sneaking of our modern tuft-hunter. . . . We dare say Mr. Hunt has some fine dreams about the true nobility being the nobility of talent, and flatters himself, that with those who acknowledge only that sort of rank, he himself passes for being the *peer* of Byron. He is sadly mistaken. He is as completely a Plebian in his mind as he is in his rank and station in society.
>
> (*BEM* 2 [October 1817]: 40–1)

Using class as a criterion for denying Hunt the right to public authorship and private friendship, Lockhart reinforced what Robert Morrison and Daniel S. Roberts describe as the "harsh conservative agenda" that *Blackwood's* espoused in its early years.[16]

Despite the apparent commercial effectiveness of Lockhart's class-based approach to Hunt and his circle of friends, the publication of *Beppo* (1818), Byron's early poetic experiment with the Italian comic style he would perfect in *Don Juan*, threatened to undo the Byron character that Lockhart had constructed in the early numbers of the "Cockney School" series.[17] In the June 1818 issue of *Blackwood's*, it seems probable that Lockhart, writing under the pseudonym "ANGLICANUS," presented readers with a radically different version of Byron from that which had appeared previously in the pages of *Blackwood's*. Indeed, the "first of all living poets" (*BEM* 2 [November 1817]: 195) was suddenly numbered among the last, occupying a new position in the magazine. Because Lockhart's review of *Beppo* was *Blackwood's* first negative review of Byron's poetry and personality, Lockhart was cautious about the presentation; rather than presenting a formal review, which had been *Blackwood's* standard practice for treating Byron's works, Lockhart presented his review of *Beppo* in the guise of a "Note to the Editor, *Enclosing a Letter to the Author of Beppo.*" In this "Note," which was presumably also Lockhart's creation, the author admitted that the contents of the "Letter" will, in fact, startle *Blackwood's* long-time readers:

> THE mode in which the critics of your Journal have, on all occasions, expressed themselves concerning the poetry of Lord Byron, convinces me, that they have not as yet considered its tendency in the same point of view with myself. Borne away by a pardonable enthusiasm in favour of its genius, they have overlooked, for otherwise I do not imagine your correspondents would have failed to condemn, the effect which it is likely to produce upon readers of superficial attainments, or unsettled principles.

Lockhart stated that the "notion which I had long ago formed of Lord Byron's true character, has lately received confirmation, more than I ever looked for, from the publication of his Beppo," adding that the "baseness of his principles is there represented in a manner not indeed more open, but, I doubt not, infinitely more dangerous than before." Echoing his earlier remarks on the beginnings of the "Cockney School" series, Lockhart also claimed that the mock "Letter" to Byron would not have been published had not Jeffrey in the *Edinburgh Review* praised *Beppo* "without thinking himself bound to express a single feeling of indignation" (*BEM* 3 [June 1818]: 323).

The six-page letter "To the Author of Beppo" that follows the prefatory "Note" praised Byron's genius before lamenting Byron's fall from poetic superiority. To emphasize the seriousness of this fall, Lockhart contrasted Byron with other "noble" authors of the past and concluded his new appraisal of Byron's character in blunt terms: "Your predecessors, in one word, my Lord, have been the friends—you are the enemy of your species" (*BEM* 3 [June 1818]: 325). After reading *Beppo*, Lockhart confirmed that now "We look below the disguise which has once been lifted, and claim acquaintance, not with the sadness of the princely masque, but with the scoffing and sardonic merriment of the ill-dissembling reveller beneath it. In evil hour did you step from your vantage-ground, and teach us that Harold, Byron, and the Count of Beppo are the same" (*BEM* 3 [June 1818]: 329). In the space of six pages, *Blackwood's* had overturned its former presentation of Byron, making it clear that Byron's poetry and his personality would be held to a new moral standard. Lockhart, as we have seen, had been willing to convince himself in his early appraisal of the Byron-Hunt literary relationship that a poem like *Parisina*, modeled, in part, on a classical tradition of tragedy, was morally pure in its treatment of incest. However, the shockingly nonclassical *Beppo*, with its unfamiliar Italian style and its light-hearted treatment of infidelity, marked a significant turning point for *Blackwood's* and its treatment of Byron.[18]

In the July 1818 issue, Lockhart pursued a wider course of attack against the Cockneys, assaulting Hunt, Hazlitt, and Francis Jeffrey in the third number of the "Cockney School" series:

> One wicked Cockney will not again be permitted to praise another in that journal, which, up to the moment when incest and adultery were defended in its pages, had, however openly at war with religion, kept at least upon decent terms with the cause of morality. It was indeed a fatal day for Mr. Jeffrey, when he degraded both himself and his original coadjutors, by taking into pay such an unprincipled blunderer as Hazlitt.
>
> (*BEM* 3 [July 1818]: 456)

The "journal" Lockhart has in mind here is the *Edinburgh Review*, and the "wicked Cockney" is Hazlitt, who had reviewed *Rimini* in 1816. And while Hazlitt is the specific target of Lockhart's attack in this section, it is significant that Lockhart also takes aim at Jeffrey, knowing that the *Edinburgh Review* had treated Hunt's *Rimini* (and more recently Byron's *Beppo*) with approval.[19] Indeed, in an article ostensibly aimed at Hunt and his Cockney circle, Lockhart's latest attack on Jeffrey, like his recent attack on Byron, underscores the challenge *Blackwood's* faced in attempting to separate Cockneys from non-Cockneys. By July of 1818, both groups were clearly entrenched in the same columns of the magazine.

Although neither Lockhart nor any other *Blackwood's* reviewer would ever explicitly label Byron as a Cockney author, Lockhart, using the more playful satirical persona "William Wastle, Esquire," hinted at the idea in the August 1818 issue. In "The Mad Banker of Amsterdam; or the Fate of the Brauns," a satirical poem that facetiously adopts the *ottava rima* of *Beppo*, Byron is implicitly grouped with Hunt and Keats for writing poetry in a form that *Blackwood's* saw as Cockney in origin. In the poem's conclusion, for example, we learn that "They made [Mynheer] Braun's spousy,"

> Tho' far from thin, you'll recollect, appear
>   A perfect skeleton—the reverse of frowsy.
> (I don't defend this rhyme—'tis very bad,
> Tho' used by Hunt, and Keats, and all that squad.)
>
> (*BEM* 3 [August 1818]: 533)[20]

Byron is not directly named here, but Lockhart's criticism of Wastle's imperfect and "very bad" rhyme, which has nevertheless been put to ironic use in the "Mad Banker," becomes a formal critique of the poetical style of *Beppo*—a style, Lockhart argues, "used" by Hunt, Keats, and their Cockney "squad." *Blackwood's* was not the only magazine to suggest that Byron was, after the publication of *Beppo*, showing veritable signs of Cockney-ism. A year later, the *Literary Journal* issued a burlesque "in the manner of Leigh Hunt, Esq." entitled "Pleasant Walks; A Cockney Pastoral." In this humorous periodical piece, written in mock imitation of Hunt's own manner and style, the anonymous author reconstructs a one-way conver-sation between "Hunt" and "K[eats]," in which the former pontificates about typical Cockney themes: the classical "Castalian springs" waiting to be discovered just outside of London in "Hampstead's up-and-down pathy spot" as well as the "silky Pope-like tethers" of the heroic measure that Hunt believed still hindered the progress of modern poetry. The most significant feature of the satire, however, is the author's signature line boldly presented at the end of the poem: "Beppo." By 1819, Byron, in more than one corner of the periodical market, was being constructed as an author with Cockney interests and associations.[21]

Byron, Moore, and *Foliage*

Hunt's preface to *Foliage*, subtitled "Cursory Observations on Poetry and Cheerfulness," continued to develop the poetic theories and ideas that had already been established in *The Feast of the Poets*, the preface to *Rimini*, and the "Young Poets" article in *The Examiner*. With *Foli-age*, a collection of dedicatory sonnets, occasional poems, and original translations, several of which had been previously published in *The Ex-aminer*, Hunt also demonstrated that he wished to continue to incorpo-rate Byron into his critical discussion of modern poetry:

> The three living poets, who may chiefly be said to have characters of their own, have found their advantage in it, especially Byron and Moore, experience being the principal ground on which the former goes, and natural disposition the latter. The remaining one, Words-worth, whose ground is morals, has not succeeded so well as either in one sense of the word; but taking every thing into consideration, the novelty of his poetical system, and the very unattractive and in my opinion mistaken nature of his moral one, he has succeeded still more; and is generally felt among his own profession to be at the head of it.[22]

In a gift copy of *Foliage* that Shelley delivered to Byron on Hunt's behalf in the spring of 1818, Byron read Hunt's latest remarks about Word-sworth with anger and frustration, believing not only that Wordsworth's poetry still had little merit, but also that the practice of poetry itself could never be considered a "profession," as Hunt had suggested. After reading through the rest of the contents in Hunt's *Foliage*, Byron wrote to Thomas Moore on 1 June 1818: "Did you read his skimble-skamble about [Wordsworth] being at the head of his own *profession*, in the *eyes* of *those* who followed it? I thought that Poetry was an *art*, or an *attribute*, and not a *profession*" (*BLJ* 6:47). Byron must have been equally confounded by other remarks in Hunt's preface where Hunt wrote confidently about his two poetical friends: "Among the poets who were bred up in the French school, Moore, who is a real musician also, has lately given a valuable proof of his approbation of a different system of verse in the new-modelled heroic numbers of his Lalla Rookh." Of Byron, Hunt argued, "my noble friend, Lord Byron, who waits as little for his own genius to be admired, before he admires that of others, does justice, I know, to the new school, though his charity inclines him to say what he can for a falling one."[23] To Hunt, the "falling" school of poetry in 1818 meant the French or Popeian school. Not surprisingly, Byron was particularly incensed by Hunt's remarks on Pope's Homeric translations elsewhere in the preface to *Foliage*. Indeed, in his letter of 1 June, Byron pointedly asked Moore: "Did you look at the translations of his own [in *Foliage*] which he prefers to Pope and Cowper, and says so?" Hunt had argued that Cowper had suffered in his work as a translator from the "over timidity of his constitution." He had also called Pope's translation of the *Iliad* an "elegant mistake" in "two volumes octavo," adding that "it is impossible for any studier of Homer's words, and their infinite varieties of meaning, not to be struck with the gratuitous and vague talking which prevails in [Pope's] translations."[24] At the same time, Hunt declared that his own translations provide "a stronger sense of the natural energy of the original," a comment that specifically drew forth Byron's ire. *Foliage*, unbeknownst to Hunt, had become a catalyst for Byron's reassessment of his friend's critical posturing and his poetry in 1818.

Byron's letter to Moore of 1 June revealed in no uncertain terms the negative impression that Hunt's *Foliage* had made upon him. Byron's letter (likely no longer extant) was first published in Moore's *Letters and Journals of Lord Byron, with Notices of His Life* (1830) in an incomplete state, with words, phrases, sentences, and whole sections omitted by Moore.[25] The fragmented letter is nevertheless of primary importance for our understanding of the state of the Byron-Hunt friendship as well as that of the Moore-Hunt friendship in the spring of 1818, for the letter constitutes Byron's first known expression of raw anger toward Hunt and his poetry. This hostile feeling, however, seems to have been the consequence of two related factors: Byron's reading of Hunt's *Foliage* and Byron's awareness of Hunt's critical remarks on Moore's *Lalla Rookh* (1817), which Hunt had included in a letter to Moore on 24 March 1818. Moore had clearly been angered by Hunt's remarks on his poem. And in a letter to Byron (probably also now lost) to which Byron's letter of 1 June 1818 was the reply, Moore had apparently disclosed Hunt's criticism of *Lalla Rookh*.

In his letter to Moore of 24 March 1818, Hunt confessed that he had delayed writing to his friend about the highly anticipated *Lalla Rookh*, a long narrative poem on an Eastern theme written in the manner of Byron's Turkish Tales, because of the poor impression it had made upon him:

> "Lalla Rookh," to be sincere with you, appeared to me to be too florid in its general style; but there are exquisite passages, and you have so truly a poetical character of your own—you are so truly, by birth, a poetical animal, out of the pale of book-associations, and a free inhabitant of the most Elysian parts of nature—that the more you resolved to speak and to feel out of the sincerity of your own impulses, without thinking it necessary to search for ideas, the more to your advantage, I am persuaded, it would be.

Moore should not have been surprised at Hunt's candid criticism of *Lalla Rookh*, for candidness had long been an element in their literary friendship, going back to Hunt's published criticism of Moore's early comic opera, *M. P.; or, The Blue-Stocking* (1811).[26] Hunt's appraisal of *Lalla Rookh*, however, seems to have struck a nerve with Moore. For one thing, Moore, as Jeffery Vail reminds us, had spent several years writing *Lalla Rookh*, and there can be little doubt that he felt personally wounded by Hunt's "sincere" remarks about an ambitious poetical undertaking.[27] Moore, in the winter months of 1818, had also been mourning the recent loss of an infant daughter and, as many of his existing letters from the period show, Moore was operating under great duress and emotional strain. In turning to Byron—a trusted friend and poetical ally—soon after receiving Hunt's letter of 24 March, Moore was thus probably seeking sympathetic relief on more than one level.

Although the letter that Moore sent to Byron about Hunt and Hunt's criticism of *Lalla Rookh* is not forthcoming, the evidence of its existence and the general thrust of its contents can be reasonably inferred from Byron's reply of 1 June. Therein Byron began the long section on Hunt by responding specifically to what Moore had written about a certain Hunt "letter," which, as William Keach suggests, was doubtless Hunt's letter of 24 March "criticizing" *Lalla Rookh*.[28] Byron wrote to Moore thus:

> Hunt's letter is probably the exact piece of vulgar coxcombry you might expect from his situation. He is a good man, with some poetical elements in his chaos; but spoilt by the Christ-Church Hospital and a Sunday newspaper,—to say nothing of the Surry [sic] Jail, which conceited him into a martyr. But he is a good man. When I saw "Rimini" in MSS., I told him that I deemed it good poetry at bottom, disfigured only by a strange style. His answer was, that his style was a system, or *upon system*, or some such cant; and, when a man talks of system, his case is hopeless: so I said no more to him, and very little to any one else.
>
> (*BLJ* 6:46)

Byron did not stop there. "[Hunt] believes his trash of vulgar phrases tortured into compound barbarisms to be *old* English; . . . He (Leigh H.) is an honest Charlatan, who has persuaded himself into a belief of his own impostures, and talks Punch in pure simplicity of heart, taking himself (as poor Fitzgerald said of *himself* in the Morning Post) for *Vates* in both senses, or nonsenses, of the word." Byron also revealed the full extent of his anger with the contents of *Foliage*. Unlike the playful satire in *The Feast of the Poets* and the interesting "Italianism" of *Rimini*, *Foliage* was stylistically and thematically at odds with Byron's poetic sensibilities. As such, Byron's exceedingly sarcastic appraisal of the volume's occasional poems and their author is not surprising: "But Leigh Hunt is a good man, and a good father—see his Odes to all the Masters Hunt;—a good husband—see his Sonnet to Mrs. Hunt;—a good friend—see his Epistles to different people;—and a great coxcomb and a very vulgar person in every thing about him. But that's not his fault, but of circumstances" (*BLJ* 6:46–7).

Byron's reference to Hunt's "circumstances" may suggest that Moore had, in addition to disclosing Hunt's criticisms of *Lalla Rookh*, summarized for Byron the first part of Hunt's 24 March letter, which included a long apology for not writing more often and, specifically, for not having noticed *Lalla Rookh* in *The Examiner*:

> I had not forgotten you, believe me,—I neither could, nor ought; but we happened not to hear from each other for some time before your large poem came out, and then a most villanous [sic] habit of delay, which want of occupation in early youth, and sickness afterwards, conspired to fix into the very bones of me, made me so creep on from week to week without paying it the proper attention in the "Examiner," which I nevertheless used to swear to myself, week after week, to do, that at last I fairly became ashamed of noticing the book at all, much more of writing to yourself. One or two similar *circumstances*, which other real friends have tolerated in the kindest manner, but which have induced another of a more doubtful complexion, in spite of greater infirmities of his own of the same sort, to read me a very hot lecture upon, have made me think very seriously of this habit of mine. It is certainly very much against my theories of friendship, and, I think I may say, not at all compatible with the rest of my practice of it, which has ever been accounted somewhat romantic and over-zealous. (italics mine)[29]

It becomes clear why Moore, after reading this opening section, as well as the unfavorable criticism of *Lalla Rookh* that followed, would have found Hunt's "letter" to be exasperating. Despite Hunt's positive intentions and his eagerness to reaffirm his "theories of friendship," Moore was unconvinced and seems to have thought it appropriate to bring the critical reflections of a mutual friend to Byron's attention. And having just read through Hunt's *Foliage* and becoming frustrated with its contents, Byron readily sympathized with Moore about Hunt's 24 March "letter." While Timothy Webb is right to suggest that it would be unwise to overemphasize Byron's "harsh" remarks on Hunt in his 1 June correspondence with Moore, the letter is nevertheless of great significance as a record of Byron's critical opinion of *Foliage*.[30] The letter shows that Byron's anger had indeed been largely directed at Hunt's latest collection of poems and poetic theories. Although we might speculate how Byron would have reacted to *Foliage* had Hunt not written to Moore about *Lalla Rookh* in the critical manner that he did, it seems likely that Byron's low opinion of Hunt's "Cockney Manifesto" would not have been altered in any significant way, for the poet had other, more pressing reasons to be angry with Hunt and his latest volume of poetry.

Byron's frustration with Hunt for his treatment of Moore's *Lalla Rookh* soon cooled, but his uneasiness with *Foliage* persisted throughout 1818. Sometime after 9 June, Byron read John Taylor Coleridge's politically motivated synopsis of Hunt's *Foliage* in the *Quarterly Review*.[31] Byron mistakenly believed that the review had been written by Robert Southey, which only increased Byron's anger. The poet expressed his frustration in a letter of 24 November 1818 to John Murray: "I have read his review of Hunt, where he has attacked Shelley in an oblique and shabby manner" (*BLJ* 6:83). Southey, Byron thought, had also been responsible for spreading rumors that he, the Shelleys, and Claire Clairmont were involved in a "League of Incest," dating from their time together in Geneva in the summer of 1816. In Coleridge's review of *Foliage*, the "oblique" reference Byron observed, however, related specifically to a rumored guest "album" (*RR* C2:760) that Southey apparently encountered by chance in 1817 while traveling through the Alps. The album, discovered by Southey at a mountain lodge, contained the names of Shelley, Mary Shelley, and Claire Clairmont, and next to their names were various expressions, in Greek characters, of atheism and godlessness. Byron apparently also encountered this (or another) album containing the names of the Shelley group during an excursion he made to Chamonix with John Cam Hobhouse.[32] The significance of this Shelley gossip for Byron, however, was that Coleridge's review of *Foliage* made it clear that Shelley's controversial philosophies and religious attitudes, which Byron never accepted, were now being linked publicly to Hunt and his Cockney associates. Knowing this, and because of his personal friendships with both Hunt and Shelley, Byron seems to have felt his reputation to have become particularly vulnerable in the fall of 1818:

> Southey would have attacked me, too, [in the review of *Foliage*], if he durst, further than by hints about Hunt's friends in general; and some outcry about an "Epicurean system," carried on by men

of the most opposite habits, tastes, and opinions in life and poetry (I believe), that ever had their names in the same volume—Moore, Byron, Shelley, Hazlitt, Haydon, Leigh Hunt, Lamb—what resemblance do ye find among all or any of these men? and how could any sort of system or plan be carried on, or attempted amongst them?

(*BLJ* 6:83)

Byron's remarks, like those he had made in his 1 June letter to Moore, show how closely he had read through the contents of Hunt's *Foliage*, for the "men of the most opposite habits" that "ever had their names in the same volume" are the addressees of several of the sonnets and occasional poems found in the *Foliage* volume. With *Foliage*, Hunt had proudly assembled a group of Cockneys and non-Cockneys, as Cox suggests, in order to present the public with a veritable "roster of the Hunt circle" to promote group strength and solidarity in response to the on-going abuses coming from *Blackwood's*.[33] It is thus significant that Byron's renewed anger at Hunt's *Foliage* after reading Coleridge's review was now being directed at Hunt's promotion of what Byron perceived to be a fundamentally incompatible group of authors. Whereas Byron had been willing, at an earlier point in time, to tolerate Hunt's public expressions of friendship and gratitude in *The Feast of the Poets*, and even in the dedication to *Rimini*, Byron was, two years later, unnerved by Hunt's insistence on enfolding him publicly within a larger, incongruous circle of authors.

The impact that the *Foliage* volume had on Byron and his thinking on the state of English poetry was reaffirmed by another significant literary conversation Byron had had in 1818. On the authority of Shelley, who delivered Hunt's presentation copy of *Foliage* to Byron in the spring of 1818, we know that the two poets had discussed Hunt and his "Cockney Manifesto" on or around 22 August. Shelley informed Mary Shelley on 23 August that during his recent visit with Byron, they had "talked of literary matters," including "his fourth Canto [of *Childe Harold*] which [Byron] says is very good, & . . . Foliage which he quizzes immoderately."[34] Shelley's notice of Byron's immoderate criticism of *Foliage* is revealing, for in expressing his animus toward Hunt's book to Shelley, Byron seems to have spoken candidly about Hunt and his poetry even with an awareness of Shelley's personal friendship with the author of *Foliage*. In fact, Byron reiterated his feelings about *Foliage* and its Cockney associations two years later, reminding Shelley on 26 April 1821: "You know my opinion of *that second-hand* school of poetry" (*BLJ* 8:103).

Clearly, *Foliage* had been much on Byron's mind throughout the spring and summer of 1818. As Byron intimated in his letters to Moore of 1 June and Murray of 24 November, as well as in his private discussions with Shelley in late August, Hunt's continued assault on Pope, his unjustified regard for Wordsworth, and his insistence on bringing together before the public every name—Cockney and non-Cockney—that came within his sphere of friendship and influence were deeply troubling acts. Although Byron did not publicly address Hunt's actions in 1818, *Foliage* had strongly impressed upon him the idea of needing to do so. The opportunity soon came when *Blackwood's* attacked Byron and his experimental new poem *Don Juan* in August of 1819.

Byron's "Observations" on Hunt and the Cockneys

Byron's "Some Observations Upon an Article in *Blackwood's Edinburgh Magazine*" was written as a direct response to *Blackwood's* hostile "Remarks On Don Juan" (published in the August 1819 issue). Yet Andrew Nicholson's acknowledgment of the pamphlet's wider relevance is apt: "Some Observations," Nicholson suggests, "is best regarded as a precursor to the 'Bowles/Pope Controversy.' . . . although the target of [Byron's] attack is not Bowles, the cause he here champions is that of Pope against his then-current detractors (such as Wordsworth and Keats), and his arguments and criticisms anticipate those he deploys in the later controversy" (*CMP* 360). Among Pope's "then-current detractors," Hunt, of course, should be added, for the author of *Foliage* was one of the poets who had been uppermost in Byron's thoughts during the period immediately preceding that in which *Don Juan* and "Some Observations" were produced. In fact, Hunt's importance to the development of "Some Observations" is confirmed by the textual evidence that has survived. As we shall see, the holograph draft manuscript shows that Byron's treatment of Hunt in the first version of "Some Observations" was far more complex than that given in the version eventually set up in proof in the spring of 1820. Indeed, the heavily revised sections of the draft manuscript that specifically discuss Hunt and his poetry show that Byron had great difficulty writing about Hunt for a public audience. In the manuscript, Byron vacillated between expressing feelings of frustration and issuing statements of critical complaint.

Byron began writing "Some Observations" on 15 March 1820 and on 29 March, the poet sent the completed draft with an additional note on Pope to Murray. At that time, he also made his intentions with respect to the pamphlet clear:

> I have at last lost all patience with the atrocious cant and nonsense about Pope, with which our present blackguards are overflowing, and am determined to make such head against it, as an Individual can by prose or verse—and I will at least do it with good will.——— There is no bearing it any longer, and if it goes on, it will destroy what little good writing or taste remains amongst us.———I hope there are still a few men of taste to second me, but if not, I'll battle it alone—convinced that it is in the best cause of English literature.
> (*BLJ* 7:61)

Byron's strongly worded phrase "present blackguards" provides useful information, for it separates some of Pope's Romantic detractors from others. The Reverend William Lisle Bowles, despite his prominent part in the so-called "Bowles/Pope Controversy," would probably not have been given the label "blackguard" by Byron, but a "Cockney" poet like Keats certainly would have been. Nevertheless, the forceful rhetoric may have led Byron to reconsider "Some Observations" shortly after he sent the draft to Murray, for on 23 April Byron informed his publisher that he did not intend to move forward with his prose pamphlet "*at present*" (*BLJ* 7:83). The communication, however, reached Murray after "Some Observations" had already been set up in proof, and when Byron subsequently received the proofs, he again changed his mind, declaring in another letter to Murray that "the prose (the Edin. Mag. answer) looks better than I thought it would," adding "*you may publish it*—there will be a row—but I'll fight it out—one way or another" (*BLJ* 7:102). At this point, John Cam Hobhouse, who read Byron's draft of "Some Observations," seems to have written to his friend about the pamphlet, suggesting that Byron again reconsider his plans for publication. On 8 June Byron replied to Hobhouse thus: "You are right—the *prose* must not be published—at least the merely *personal part*" (*BLJ* 7:114). In his letter, which is now missing, Hobhouse may have used the same argument against the publication of "Some Observations" that he had used earlier against the publication of the first two cantos of *Don Juan*. Hobhouse's primary objection to *Don Juan* was that it would be damaging to Byron's public "reputation." In a letter from 5 January 1819 to Byron, Hobhouse had indeed argued that the "immoral turn of the whole and the rakish air of the half real hero will really injure your reputation both as a man and a poet."[35]

Hobhouse apparently succeeded in convincing Byron to reconsider aspects of "Some Observations," for Byron told his friend that he was willing to withhold the "*personal part*" of his attack on *Blackwood's* from the prose pamphlet. However, Byron remained adamant about publishing the section on Pope.[36] In fact, the "*personal part*" of "Some Observations" (Byron's defense of *Don Juan*) ends where the section on Pope begins, and it is at this point that Byron also brings Hunt into the fabric of his argument:

> [T]he Edinburgh Reviewers, and the Lakers—and Hunt and his school, and every body else with their School, and even Moore—without a School—and dilettanti lecturers at Institutions—and elderly Gentlemen who translate and imitate,—and young ladies who listen and repeat—Baronets who draw indifferent frontispieces for bad poets, and noblemen who let them dine with them—in the Country, the small body of the wits and the great body of the Blues—have latterly united in a depreciation [of Pope] of which their fathers would have been as much ashamed as their Children will be.

Byron continued in "Some Observations" in the same heated manner, asking of his contemporaries: "what have we got instead?" (*CMP* 107). Byron's answer would have probably surprised his critics and his friends alike, for all of them were responsible, in Byron's estimation, for the "Decline of English Poetry" (*CMP* 104). Byron, in no uncertain terms, blamed this decline on

> The lake School . . . a deluge of flimsy and unintelligible romances imitated from Scott and myself who have both made the best of our very bad materials, and erroneous System . . . Hunt who had powers to have made "the Story of Rimini" as perfect as a fable of Dryden—has thought fit to sacrifice his Genius and his taste, to some unintelligible notions of Wordsworth—which I defy him to explain.——Moore has—but why continue?
>
> (*CMP* 107)

Byron's anger at the Romantic devaluation of Pope is given its fullest expression in this section of "Some Observations," and that anger is directed most conspicuously at Hunt. Hunt's "unintelligible notions" about Wordsworth, of course, had long-been a topic of disagreement between the two friends. But, significantly, Byron here suggests for the first time that Hunt's *Rimini*—a poem Byron once greatly admired— was ultimately an artistic failure. Although it would be wrong to see this as a firm statement of disapproval of the artistry of *Rimini*, or its author, Byron's comments clearly suggest strong feelings of disappointment with Hunt's most important poem.

It is notable that next to the pointed criticisms of Hunt and his poetry, and to a lesser extent Moore and his poetry in "Some Observations," Byron's many references to the Lake Poets in the section on Pope can seem enervated and even dated at times. In some cases, the criticism Byron directs at Wordsworth, Coleridge, and Southey repeats arguments that had already been made over a decade earlier in *English Bards and Scotch Reviewers*. In "Some Observations," for example, we hear of Southey and the Lake School, which began "with an Epic poem 'written in Six weeks' (So Joan of Arc proclaimed herself)" (*CMP* 107). And in *English Bards*, we find an earlier version of the same joke. There the satirist longs for the time when "An Epic scarce ten centuries could claim" (line 191) before Southey brought forth his "annual strains" (line 204) in epic: "First in the ranks see Joan of Arc advance" (line 205). In the same section of *English Bards*, Byron had attacked Wordsworth, "the dull disciple of [Southey's] school" (line 235), by mocking the poet in a note for "labour[ing] hard to prove that prose and verse are much the same" (*CPW* 1:404). And in "Some Observations" Byron repeats what was, by 1820, a commonplace criticism of Wordsworth, who "thinks that he has been all his life writing both prose and verse, and neither of what he conceives to be such can be properly said to be either one or the other" (*CMP* 105). To be sure, Byron's anger at the Lake School had increased after reading Wordsworth's *Excursion* (1814) and the supplemental essay in *Poems* (1815), two significant offerings from Wordsworth published after *English Bards*. Byron's reading of Coleridge's *Biographia Literaria*, as McGann has argued, had also been a significant factor in renewing Byron's hostility toward the Lake Poets during the period of his exile.[37] As we have seen, the rumor about the "League of Incest," for which Byron held Southey directly responsible, was also a factor in Byron's critical return to the Lake Poets in "Some Observations" (and *Don Juan*). And yet in "Some Observations," Byron was willing to admit that "Southey—Wordsworth, and Coleridge had all of them a very natural antipathy to Pope, and I respect them for it—as the only original feeling or principle—which they have contrived to preserve." Byron added: "But they have been joined in it by those who have joined them in nothing else,—By the Edinburgh Reviewers, by the whole heterogeneous Mass of living English Poets—excepting Crabbe, Rogers, Gifford and Campbell—who both by precept and practice—have proved their adherence; and by me,—who have shamefully deviated in practice" (*CMP* 106). It thus becomes clear that the force of Byron's argument in "Some Observations" has, in part, been generated by a much more pressing (and confounding) problem than the Lake Poets: how to interpret his own body of work along with the work produced by friends like Moore and Hunt, two of the most significant figures in the "Mass of living English Poets."

Byron's position with respect to Hunt in "Some Observations," however, is more complex than it may seem on the surface, for despite Hunt's "inexplicable" notions about Wordsworth and *Rimini*'s artistic faults, Hunt was still a friend and *Rimini* was one of the few contemporary works that Byron clearly felt had great potential. Byron's high estimation of Hunt's poetical abilities as well as his firm acknowledgment of Hunt's artistic failings are reinforced in the pamphlet's section on Keats, a poet for whom Byron held Hunt personally responsible. Byron begins his discussion of Keats by discussing the well-known lines from "Sleep and Poetry" that implicitly attack Pope and his poetic legacy:

> —But ye were dead
> To things ye knew not of, were closely wed
> To musty laws lined out with wretched rule
> And compass vile; so that ye taught a School
> Of Dolts to SMOOTH, *inlay*, and *clip*, and *fit*,
> Till, like the certain words of Jacob's wit,

Their verses tallied.—Easy was the task:
A thousand handicraftsmen wore the mask
Of Poesy.

(*CMP* 113–4)

"The writer of this," Byron observes, "is a tadpole of the lakes, a young disciple of the six or seven new Schools, in which he has learnt to write such lines and such sentiments as the above" (*CMP* 116). However, the implication, as the draft of "Some Observations" makes clear, is that Keats's failures as a poet are the direct result of his association with Hunt, from whom Keats "has learnt to write such lines." The draft shows that Byron had intended to make the Hunt-Keats association explicit in this section of the text. In the draft, Byron had first written the line beginning "The writer of this" thus: "The writer of this is a young disciple of ~~Leigh Hunt~~ Mr. Leigh Hunt, who at least knows better."[38] Byron then canceled the entire line in the draft, removing the comment about Hunt's knowing "better," and rewrote the sentence so as to remove any explicit reference to the author of *Rimini*. The revision clearly suggests that Byron was struggling with his characterization of Hunt; Byron appears to want to criticize Hunt without directly attacking him. Byron also deliberately avoided naming Hunt in the section on Keats by speaking of "those" who were responsible for leading Keats astray: "As Mr. K. does not want imagination nor industry—let those who have led him astray look to what they have done;—surely they must feel no little remorse in having so perverted the taste and feelings of this young man, and will be satisfied with one such victim to their Moloch of Absurdity" (*CMP* 116). Byron's manuscript draft of "Some Observations," however, makes it apparent that he believed Keats has had only one teacher.

The "Addenda" to the *Letter to John Murray*

Although "Some Observations" did not appear during his lifetime, Byron remained committed to issuing a formal prose defense of Pope. A second opportunity presented itself when Thomas Campbell published his seven-volume edition of *Specimens of the British Poets* (1819). In the general introduction to *Specimens* ("Essay on English Poetry"), Campbell took issue with contemporary arguments about Pope's understanding and treatment of "Nature." He argued for a wider understanding of the concept and Pope's interpretation of it by suggesting that "Nature, in the wide and proper sense of the word, means life in all its circumstances— nature moral as well as external. As the subject of inspired fiction, nature includes artificial forms and manners" (qtd. in *CMP* 402). In his introduction, Campbell also issued pointed remarks about William Lisle Bowles, whose prefatory essay to his edition of Pope's *Works* (1806) had included an attack on Pope's moral character. Bowles is credited with initiating the Romantic period's so-called "Bowles/Pope Controversy," which was revived in 1819 when Bowles responded to Campbell with a prose pamphlet entitled *The Invariable Principles of Poetry* (1819). Not long after this, Byron "entered the fray," as Nicholson says, with his *Letter to John Murray* (1821) and "instantly defused the issue," restoring "to the controversy its principal poetical focus" (*CMP* 404–5). In the *Letter*, Byron famously observed that the "grand 'primum mobile' of England is *Cant*—Cant political—Cant poetical—Cant religious—Cant moral—but always *Cant*." And, for Byron, the worst illustration of the "fashion" for "Cant" was the "hysterical horror of poor Pope's not very well ascertained—& never fully proved amours" (*CMP* 128). And while Byron's *Letter* may have refocused the controversy, turning it away from a focus on Pope's personal character, the published pamphlet was rather restrained in its treatment of the modern poets, projecting an air of urbanity that the more personal sections in "Some Observations" on Hunt, Moore, and the "Decline of English Poetry" lacked.

It was perhaps on account of its manner of argumentation and its appearance (two years after Campbell's *Specimens* had been published), however, that Byron's *Letter* found little support among British readers and reviewers. Hunt, for one, thought that the Pope controversy had long been settled and that Byron's pamphlet was out of date when it appeared in the spring of 1821. As Hunt wrote in *The Examiner*:

> The question about Pope has surely been settled long ago, never to be revived again to any purpose, by friend or foe. It is not the Wartons alone that settled it, or Mr. Bowles, or Mr. Wordsworth, or any other critic or poet, however critical; but the great re-opening of the intellectual world by changes and revolutions, when mens' minds found the drawing-room of the French school of poetry insufficient for them, and broke forth again into the regions of passion and imagination.
>
> (*RR* B3:1008)

In fact, Hunt seems to have had little regard for Byron's *Letter*, in general, for he assigned formal review duties to another writer at *The Examiner*.[39] Hunt claimed that he was suffering from illness at the time. Still, Hunt clearly felt that he needed to say something on the subject of Pope, a poet, as we have seen, who had been of great importance to the development of Hunt's critical thoughts on modern poetry and the heroic couplet. Hunt's comments on Byron's *Letter* appeared in a lengthy postscript to *The Examiner*'s review. In his postscript to the review of the *Letter*, Hunt pointedly remarked of Byron's latest production: "I conceive, with all due deference to Lord Byron and his great talents, that he has written on the present occasion a very amusing pamphlet, a good, jovial, after-dinner effusion, a something between banter and gravity, wilfulness and real opinion,—any thing, in short, but an argument." Hunt's dismissive remarks in *The Examiner*, which Byron likely never saw, are certainly not surprising given what we know of Hunt's opinions with respect to Pope and his poetry. Yet Hunt also seems to have been put off by the manner in which the *Letter*, he felt, had been cast. Indeed, he thought that Byron, in the *Letter*, had "played the patrician a little; which is a thing he can so well afford to dispense with" (*RR* B3:1008). Hunt's thinking on this score was probably influenced by Hazlitt's review of the *Letter* in the *London Magazine*, which Hunt had seen as the most convincing public statement on the Pope controversy and a fair assessment of Byron's contribution to it (*LBSC* 116). Nevertheless, Hunt seems to have been genuinely surprised by the appearance of Byron's *Letter*, explaining to the readers of *The Examiner* that he felt the need to retrieve some of Byron's correspondence from 1815 in order to clarify exactly what his friend had once told him privately about Wordsworth, who is disparagingly alluded to in Byron's *Letter*.[40] The fact that Hunt still had such correspondence in his possession confirms the high value that he continued to place on his friendship with Byron. More importantly, despite the number of years and the physical distance separating them in 1821, Byron's entry into the Pope controversy, and Hunt's published response to Byron's *Letter* in *The Examiner*, reveal the extent to which both friends were still very much engaged in dialogue about the state of modern poetry.

The section of Byron's *Letter* that would have had the most appeal for Hunt, however, never appeared in print. The unpublished "Addenda" was a lengthy additional section that specifically focused on Hunt and the Cockney poets. In this unpublished section, Byron also rekindled the anger and frustration that had appeared in "Some Observations" in the sections on Hunt and the "Cockney School." Byron's ostensible purpose in the "Addenda" was to answer a charge made by Isaac D'Israeli in his review of Bowles's *Invariable Principles*. In his review, D'Israeli had observed that "Pope preferred *in-door* to *out-door* nature," but D'Israeli then asked, "did this require inferior skill or less of the creative faculty than Mr. Bowles's *Nature*?" (qtd. in *CMP* 443). In the "Addenda," Byron attempted to refute the charge that Pope knew nothing of real "Nature" with language he seems to have absorbed from his reading of *Blackwood's* "Cockney School" articles: "Now is it not a shame after this to hear our Lakers in 'Kendal Green' and our Bucolical Cockneys crying out (the latter in a Wilderness of bricks and mortar)—about 'Nature' and Pope's 'artificial indoor habits.'——Pope had seen all of Nature that *England* alone can supply" (*CMP* 154). The term "Cockney" does not appear in "Some Observations" or in any of the published editions of the *Letter*. The "Addenda" thus seems to be the first time that *Blackwood's* Cockney rhetoric had found its ways into Byron's critical vocabulary. And for this reason, perhaps, Byron does not appear to be completely sure about how to employ the new terminology. Elsewhere in the "Addenda," for instance, he speaks of the phrase "Cockney School" as one of unwarranted derision:

> In the present rank fertility of "great poets of the Age"—and "Schools of poetry" a word which like "Schools of Eloquence" and "of Philosophy" is never introduced till the decay of art has increased with the number of it's Professors—in the present day then,—there have sprung up two Sects of Naturals—the Lakers—who whine about Nature because they live in Cumberland—and their *under-Sect*—(which some one has maliciously called the "Cockney School")—who are enthusiastical for the country because they live in London.——It is to be observed that the rustical founders are rather anxious to disclaim any connection with their metropolitan followers—whom—they ungraciously review—& call Cockneys—Atheists—foolish fellows—bad writers and other hard names not less ungrateful than unjust.
>
> (*CMP* 155–6)

Like Byron's draft of "Some Observations," the draft manuscript of the "Addenda" provides additional evidence of the deliberateness he had taken in crafting his portrait of Hunt therein. We see this, for example, in Byron's note that "some one" (Lockhart) had "maliciously" attacked Hunt, labeling him and his friends as members of the "Cockney School." The manuscript shows that Byron had originally wanted to end the related next line beginning "It is to be observed" after "bad writers" with "and what not."[41] Byron, however, went back to this line and added the long concluding phrase: "other hard names not less ungrateful than unjust." The addition was perhaps intended to strike an even more sympathetic tone in a section of the "Addenda" that was clearly meant to defend Hunt's character.

Yet, in other sections in the draft of the "Addenda," Byron modified or canceled intended criticisms of Hunt that he seems to have realized would have been too strong for publication. The following section is a useful illustration of Byron's process of revision in the "Addenda":

> When he was writing his "Rimini"—I was not the last to discern it's beauties long before it was published.—Even then I remonstrated against it's ~~vulgar [?points]~~ vulgarisms—which are the more extraordinary—because the Author is anything but a vulgar man.—Mr. ~~Hunt~~ Hunt's answer—was that he wrote them upon principle—they made part of his "System—,"—I then said no more. When a man talks of his System—it is like a woman talking of her Virtue— —^I let them talk on.^ ~~they are both pretending to something which they have not in them—by way of [?deluding] themselves as well as others.~~[42]

After momentarily struggling with how to address Hunt's "vulgarisms" in *Rimini*, Byron wrote several additional lines explaining his objections to Hunt's "System" and to system-makers in general. In the draft, the line that begins "they are both pretending" is heavily canceled, suggesting that Byron perhaps felt he had already gone far enough in upbraiding Hunt for the stylistic infelicities of *Rimini* and thus wished to soften his overall criticism in this section of the "Addenda." Byron simply went back to the series of dashes after "Virtue" and added the short concluding statement: "I let them talk on." The next section of the "Addenda," on the other hand, shows Byron addressing Hunt and his "System" of poetry with less reluctance. In the draft, Byron added a series of emphatic dashes to end a line that criticizes Hunt for influencing a new generation of writers: "To be sure he has 'led his ragamuffins where they will be well peppered'— — — — —." The extended series of dashes appear to suggest a firm break in thought in anticipation of a new line of inquiry. Yet Byron, in uncharacteristically tiny script, went back to the dashes and added this additional criticism of Hunt in the small space available: "But a system-maker must receive all sorts of proselytes."[43]

Byron's criticism of Hunt and his "System" in the "Addenda," however, seems to have grown more severe over the course of drafting the entire piece. For early in the "Addenda," Byron made a point of issuing a genuine defense of Hunt's character, providing a significant statement of "friend[ship]" with Hunt—a statement that, in many ways, echoed the earliest impressions that Byron had formed about Hunt and recorded in his private journal in 1813. Indeed, in 1821, Bryon revealed that his opinion of Hunt's character had not, in any fundamental way, changed:

> The most rural of these Gentlemen is my friend Leigh Hunt—who lives at Hampstead.—I believe that I need not disclaim any personal or poetical hostility against that Gentleman.—A more amiable man in society—I know not—nor—(when he will allow his sense to prevail over his Sectarian principles)—a better writer. . . . Whether there are writers who could have written "Rimini"—as it might have been written I know not—but Mr. Hunt is probably the only poet who would have had the heart to spoil his own—Capo d'Opera.
>
> (*CMP* 156–7)

Byron's description of Hunt as a "Gentleman" as well as his high praise of "Rimini" are clear attempts to defend his friend from the class-based personalities that had been constructed and used with ill intentions against Hunt by *Blackwood's* and the *Quarterly Review*. Nevertheless, Byron was firm, just as he always had been, about asserting his skeptical opinion of Hunt's stylistic choices and poetical theories: "Even then I remonstrated against [*Rimini's*] vulgarisms." Yet Byron was still willing to promote the potential of *Rimini*, acknowledging it as Hunt's "Capo d'Opera." For all of his hesitation about Hunt's poetic "System," Byron's defense of Hunt's character in the unpublished "Addenda" remains a powerful statement of solidarity and friendship a year before the two men would reunite in Italy.

And yet perhaps because of its incongruities and its strongly worded sections, especially its concluding remarks about the *"vulgar"* poets (Hunt excepted) and an *"Aristocracy of Poets"* (*CMP* 159), the "Addenda" to the *Letter* never appeared in print. Byron wrote to John Murray in March of 1821, requesting that the publisher either rework the concluding remarks (with clarifying statements Byron provided) or withhold the section altogether, calling it an unnecessary "digression" (*BLJ* 8:93). By this point in time, Byron was, moreover, fully anticipating Hunt's arrival in Pisa to begin collaborative work on *The Liberal*. As such, a public attack on Hunt and his friends, no matter how carefully worded, would have surely been alarming to the author of *Rimini* as he was making plans to reunite with Byron after six years. Byron also knew that Hunt now had the opportunity to make up for his past poetical sins and his critical errors by leaving Cockney London for cosmopolitan Italy, where the most important literary engagement in their ten-year friendship would commence with great enthusiasm and end in bitter regret.

Notes

1 Jeffrey N. Cox, *Poetry and Politics in the Cockney School: Keats, Shelley, Hunt and Their Circle* (Cambridge: Cambridge University Press, 1998), 47–9.

2 *SWLH* 5:168. "There are narrative poets now living who have fine eyes for the truth of things, and it remains with them perhaps to perfect what I may suggest." Hunt named Byron as *the* "narrative" poet "now living" who would be the poet to fulfill this task in his letter to John Murray of 18 December 1815. See NLS MS. 43449.

3 Jeffrey N. Cox, "Leigh Hunt's *Foliage*: A Cockney Manifesto," in *Leigh Hunt: Life, Poetics, Politics*, ed. Nicholas Roe (New York: Routledge, 2003), 58–77.

4 In the *Morning Post* for 5 February 1816 the following advertisement appears: "In a few days will be published . . . STORY OF RIMINI: A POEM. By LEIGH HUNT." On 14 February, the following advertisement appeared: "This day is published" Byron's "The SIEGE of CORINTH, a Tale; PARISINA, a Tale"; in the same advertisement, under the same heading, *Rimini* also appears. Jerome McGann says that Byron's volume appeared on 13 February. See *CPW* 3:481.

5 William St Clair, *The Reading Nation in the Romantic Period* (Cambridge: Cambridge University Press, 2004), 587.

6 See Peter Cochran, "'The Wit in the Dungeon,'" in *"Romanticism"—and Byron* (Newcastle upon Tyne: Cambridge Scholars Publishing, 2009), 118. See also Nicholas Roe, *Fiery Heart: The First Life of Leigh Hunt* (London: Pimlico, 2005), 244.

7 Daniel P. Watkins, *Social Relations in Byron's Eastern Tales* (Madison, NJ: Farleigh Dickinson Press, 1987), 129.

8 Cox, *Poetry and Politics*, 27: "As one sees particularly in reviewers' attempts to detach Shelley and Byron, the aristocrats in the group, from the rest of the circle, there is behind the *Blackwood's* assaults a premise that poetry is best left to gentlemen."

9 See *CPW* 3:358.

10 In a recent analysis of *Parisina*, Piya Pal-Lapinski, in fact, argues that "the major part of Byron's poem draws out the cruelty and violence of the state. . . . to examine the problem of sovereignty poised on the brink of transition from an absolutist to a modern state." See Piya Pal-Lapinski, "From Risorgimento to Fascism: The Politics of *Parisina*," in *Byron: The Poetry of Politics and the Politics of Poetry*, eds. Roderick Beaton and Christine Kenyon Jones (New York: Routledge, 2017), 213.

11 Compare with Watkins, *Social Relations*, 134.

12 See *CPW* 3:488–91.

13 *BLJ* 5:32.

14 Tom Mole, "*Blackwood's* 'Personalities,'" in *Romanticism and Blackwood's Magazine*, eds. Robert Morrison and Daniel S. Roberts (New York: Palgrave Macmillan, 2013), 89–99.

15 Robert Morrison and Daniel S. Roberts, eds. *Romanticism and Blackwood's Magazine* (New York: Palgrave Macmillan, 2013), 2–3.

16 Morrison and Roberts, *Romanticism and Blackwood's Magazine*, 3–4.

17 Robert Morrison, "Blackwood's Byron: The Lakers, the Cockneys, and the 'Throne of Poetical Supremacy,'" *Romanticism* 23, no. 3 (2017): 277–8.

18 John Wilson, however, would challenge Lockhart's new presentation of Byron in later reviews of the poet's works. See Morrison, "Blackwood's Byron," 278–9.

19 See Francis Jeffrey's review of *Beppo* in *RR* B2:888–93.

20 For the attribution of the poem and a discussion of its significance to the development of periodical poetry in *Blackwood's*, see Thomas Richardson, "John Gibson Lockhart and *Blackwood's*," in *Romanticism and Blackwood's Magazine*, eds. Robert Morrison and Daniel S. Roberts (New York: Palgrave Macmillan, 2013), 40–1.

21 The poem is reprinted in Lewis M. Schwartz, *Keats Reviewed by His Contemporaries: A Collection of Notices for the Years, 1816–1821* (Metuchen, NJ: The Scarecrow Press, Inc., 1973), 152–5.

22 The text is taken from Leigh Hunt, *Foliage; or Poems Original and Translated* (London: C. and J. Ollier, 1818), 13–4.

23 Hunt, *Foliage*, 14.

24 Hunt, *Foliage*, 31–2.

25 Moore made it clear that he printed Byron's letter to shame Hunt for *Lord Byron and Some of His Contemporaries*, stating in a note accompanying the printed letter that he "had, in first transcribing the above letter for the press, omitted the whole of this caustic and, perhaps, over-severe character of Mr. Hunt; but the tone of that gentleman's book having, as far as himself is concerned, released me from all those scruples which prompted the suppression, I have considered myself at liberty to restore the passage." Thomas Moore, *Letters and Journals of Lord Byron, with Notices of His Life*. 2 vols. (London: John Murray, 1830), 2:177.

26 Thomas Moore, *The Letters of Thomas Moore*, ed. Wilfred S. Dowden, 2 vols. (Oxford: Oxford University Press, 1964), 1:157–9.

27 Jeffery W. Vail, *The Literary Relationship of Lord Byron & Thomas Moore* (Baltimore, MD: Johns Hopkins University Press, 2001), 103–14.

28 See William Keach, *Arbitrary Power: Romanticism, Language, Politics* (Princeton, NJ: Princeton University Press, 2004), 77.

29 Thomas Moore, *Memoirs, Journal, and Correspondence of Thomas Moore*, ed. Lord John Russell. 8 vols. (London: Longman, Brown, Green, and Longmans, 1853–56), 8:235.

30 Timothy Webb, "'Unshadowing the Rialto': Byron and the Patterns of Life," *The Byron Journal* 39, no. 1 (2011): 21. Webb points out that Byron was "prone to pleasing Moore by simplifying the complexities of his early relationship with Hunt and the intimacy of their poetic relations" (21).

31 For the attribution, see Jonathan Cutmore, *Contributors to the "Quarterly Review"* (London: Pickering & Chatto, 2008), 150. The January 1818 issue of the *Quarterly Review* was published on 9 June 1818. See Coleridge's closing remarks on Hunt's personality: "He possesses talents, which might have made him a useful citizen, and a respectable writer; but he wants sound principle and Christian humility; and the want of them has made him as a citizen what we do not like to name, and as a writer only not contemptible because he is sometimes pernicious. Had he been thoroughly well principled . . . he might still have been anxious to improve the taste and manners of his countrymen as well as to correct the abuses of their government" (*RR* C2:763).

32 See Peter Cochran, *Byron and Bob: Lord Byron's Relationship with Robert Southey* (Newcastle upon Tyne: Cambridge Scholars Publishing, 2010), 71, 75.

33 Cox, "Leigh Hunt's *Foliage*," 60.

34 Percy Bysshe Shelley, *The Letters of Percy Bysshe Shelley*, ed. Frederick L. Jones, 2 vols. (Oxford: Oxford University Press, 1964), 2:37.

35 See Peter W. Graham, *Byron's Bulldog: The Letters of John Cam Hobhouse to Lord Byron* (Columbus: Ohio State University Press, 1984), 258.

36 *BLJ* 7:114.

37 "The famous attack on the Lake School [in *Don Juan* I–II] was in fact initially inspired by Byron's reading of Coleridge's *Biographia Literaria*." See *CPW* 5:666.

38 GEN MSS. 892. Series 1. Beinecke Rare Book and Manuscript Library, Yale University.

39 See Reiman's note in *RR* B3:1006.

40 *CMP* 135.

41 National Library of Scotland (hereafter NLS) MS. 43491, f. 18r.

42 NLS MS. 43491, f. 18v.

43 NLS MS. 43491, f. 18v.

6 Byron and Hunt in Italy
The Art of *The Liberal*

Byron and Hunt reunited in Italy in July of 1822. Despite a lapse in correspondence on both sides, the writings they produced during a long six-year interval of separation clearly show that the two men maintained a keen interest in each other's lives and work. Even though Byron remained critical of *Rimini*'s "System," he defended Hunt's character in his various prose writings on Pope and the "Cockney School." Hunt, meanwhile, discussed Byron with Shelley and continued to review Byron's poetry and prose in *The Examiner*.[1] In many ways, the reunion in Italy was a natural development in the friendship and a fitting culmination to the literary relationship. Italian literature, after all, had been the strongest creative link between Byron and Hunt since the period of their earliest acquaintance in England.

A Radical New Kinship

Since December of 1820, Byron had been expressing interest in the idea of a literary collaboration. He had first written to Thomas Moore with the thought of producing a literary magazine suitable for both original poetry and liberal politics, but Moore did not share Byron's enthusiasm for the project.[2] In August of 1821 at Ravenna, Byron revisited the idea of a collaborative project in conversation with Shelley, who suggested Hunt's involvement. Byron, by all accounts, agreed that Hunt would be an excellent fit for the scheme, and Shelley eagerly communicated Byron's thoughts to Hunt. In charge of a large family and suffering from ill health at the time, Hunt was intrigued but forced to refuse the initial Shelley-Byron request to travel to Italy to begin work on a project that had not yet been clearly defined. However, when Shelley persisted and Byron agreed to finance the voyage, Hunt eventually accepted the offer and prepared to leave England in late September of 1821.[3] Although the logistics of bringing Hunt, his wife, and their several children out to Italy would prove particularly challenging, the three collaborators were, for the moment, united by a strong sense of purpose and fraternity.

From the beginning, the Byron-Hunt reunion and literary collaboration on a miscellany they eventually called *The Liberal* had been guided by an encouraging combination of Shelley's high-minded philosophical idealism, Byron's keen interest in collaborative experimentation, and Hunt's journalistic talent and experience. As Jeffrey N. Cox sees it, there was an added benefit for Shelley in bringing the Hunts out to Italy: it was an opportunity to reestablish the community that had been lost when the Shelleys departed Great Marlow, where the Hunts had lived with them for a brief but creative period in 1817.[4] In Italy, as Shelley saw it, *The Liberal* could also serve as the public voice of a radical new kinship that would now firmly include Byron among its members. And there are hints that Shelley's vision for such a community might have been realized, for it was at Byron's Casa Lanfranchi, a historic palazzo in Pisa with connections to Dante and Michelangelo, that Hunt came to live during July, August, and most of September of 1822. In the gardens there, Hunt and Byron, sometimes accompanied by Byron's "last attachment," Teresa Guiccioli, would meet for daily conversations on literature and politics as they made plans for their new miscellany.[5] However, the idealism that had brought the two friends back together at Byron's Pisan bower would be held in check by the tragic events that soon followed.

On 8 July, less than a week after Hunt arrived at Pisa, Shelley and his friend Edward Ellerker Williams were drowned on their return voyage from Leghorn to Lerici, where the Shelleys had been living at the time of the Hunts' arrival. The tragedy would have serious personal, material, and artistic consequences for the collaboration on *The Liberal*. Nicholas Roe, however, rightly observes that there are two different ways to view Hunt's situation with Byron in Italy after Shelley's unexpected and untimely death. One approach is to view the events that followed through the grim lens of the Shelley tragedy. This approach, Roe says, "dwells on the failure of the *Liberal*; [Hunt's] ill-feelings about Byron and Mary Shelley; his intractable money problems; his quarrel with his brother John; his wife's illness; the bleak Tuscan winters; and his separation from [his sister-in-law] Elizabeth Kent." Yet another way to view the situation is to see how "Hunt turned the grief and isolation occasioned by Shelley's death to creative gain."[6] Taking Roe's alternative as a starting point, this chapter looks closely at the "creative gain" that came out of the Byron-Hunt collaboration in the year that followed Shelley's death. Contrary to the long-standing critical view that *The Liberal* was a collaborative "failure," new evidence, combined with a fresh look at the contents of the early numbers of the miscellany, suggests that the Byron-Hunt collaboration in Italy, despite a series of mounting domestic and private tensions, was more durable and creatively meaningful than has been generally perceived.[7]

Recent discussions by Daisy Hay and Jane Stabler have helpfully acknowledged this fact. Stabler even observes that "a fuller recognition of [*The Liberal*'s] collaborative achievement might suggest that the project was more consistent, coherent, and successful than previous critics have allowed."[8] The recovery of primary evidence may lend support to Stabler's suggestion. Such material has long provided useful context for understanding the work Byron and Hunt produced in Italy. William H. Marshall's *Byron, Shelley, Hunt, and "The Liberal"* (1962), for example, drew upon unpublished correspondence of Hunt and John Hunt to help explain, among other developments, Byron's complex publishing relations after his long-standing partnership with John Murray broke down in the late months of 1822. In addition to this correspondence, Marshall gathered all of the available published evidence and traced the events and material causes that led to the creation and dismantling of *The Liberal*. Timothy Webb's more recent study "Arrival of Don Juan at Shooter's Hill: The Politics of Romance," meanwhile, shows that there is still primary evidence waiting to be recovered that can deepen our understanding of the Byron-Hunt collaboration in Italy. Not only has Webb drawn attention to Hunt's article on *Don Juan* Canto XI (published in *The Examiner* on 5 January 1823), but he has also described the complex personal engagements between Byron, Hunt, and Mary Shelley in 1822 and 1823, with reference to unpublished correspondence dating to Hunt's time with Byron in Italy. The personal engagements, however, constitute only a portion of Webb's study. Taking Hunt's *Examiner* article and Byron's *Don Juan* Canto XI as a point of departure for exploring their literary relations in Italy, Webb also suggests that the "conjunctions" between *The Examiner* article and Byron's unpublished canto "indicate a particular closeness of opinion." He adds that although "it would be unwise to suggest that either writer 'influenced' the other . . . their shared concerns and the coincidence of their interests at this point suggest that, for all their differences and for all Byron's evident exasperation with Hunt and his family, there was a significant coming together of the disaffected aristocrat and the reforming newspaper editor."[9] Extending Webb's assessment of the Byron-Hunt relationship in its last phase, this chapter recovers additional primary evidence and offers close readings of the work Byron and Hunt produced in Italy to show that the "shared concerns" they had may not have been "coincidence[s]" after all, but rather deliberate acts of literary engagement.

Early Engagements: Montenero and Pisa

On 1 July 1822, Hunt reunited with Byron in Italy at the Villa Dupuy, Byron's summer home just outside of Pisa in the neighboring hillside at Montenero. Hunt wrote to his sister-in-law, Elizabeth Kent, the next evening with a mixture of delight and bemusement. "When I landed,"

Hunt wrote, "I rode in one of the country carriages to Lord Byron's, who received me with the most marked cordiality, and then told me that I had come . . . at an eventful period" (*CLH* 1:186). Several years later in *Lord Byron and Some of His Contemporaries* (hereafter *LBSC*), when Hunt described his first meeting with Byron in Italy, he said nothing of Byron's "marked cordiality," stating instead that he hardly recognized his old friend, who had "grown so fat" that he appeared to be of "a very different aspect from the compact, energetic, and curly-headed person, whom I had known in England" (9). But in July of 1822, Hunt was more sanguine about the reunion, telling Kent that the "eventful period" was nothing more than a bit of "Italian nonsense" (*CLH* 1:186). According to Hunt, a domestic altercation between "Conte Pietro [Gamba]," Teresa Guiccioli's brother, and "a rascally footman" of Byron's had just occurred. After wounding the young Count, the servant threatened further violence but eventually broke down "weeping and wailing, and asking pardon for his offence." Hunt claimed that Byron made "light of the matter" (*LBSC* 10–1) but excused the servant from the household once tensions had cooled. Hunt's letter to Kent clearly suggests that he relished the privilege of being an eyewitness to the drama at the Villa Dupuy. Hunt appears to have stayed with Byron for the better part of the day, returning to Leghorn that evening where he met Shelley's friend Edward Williams (but apparently not Shelley) and wrote to his sister-in-law. The value of Hunt's letter to Kent, apart from providing interesting details of the reunion with Byron, emerges in what it reveals about Hunt's state of mind at the beginning of July. From his perspective, the reunion with Byron had been an exceedingly happy one: "Everything is going on *promisingly*" (*CLH* 1:187).

After reuniting with Shelley that same week, Hunt continued in this ebullient mood, spending a day sightseeing in Pisa with Shelley (an experience that would serve as the basis for the first of Hunt's "Letters from Abroad" series in *The Liberal*) and writing another long letter to his sister-in-law on 8 July. In this second letter, Hunt also provided additional details about his literary engagements with Byron, referring to their miscellany as "our new work" and stating that Byron "enters into it with great ardour." The "title," Hunt added, "will be the *Hesperides*. . . . You may announce the title at once, for I think it certain. It is Lord Byron's own" (*CLH* 1:189). This title was soon abandoned and another, *The Liberal*, adopted instead, but clearly both authors had been eager to engage in conversation about their collaborative work. In fact, Hunt managed to capture, with vivid immediacy, the communal energy circulating in the Casa Lanfranchi elsewhere in his 8 July letter to Kent: "I hear Lord B. coming to see me, but shall continue to write on." Hunt explained that Byron "has been, and taken some books out of my bookcase, and gone again, after discovering two or three theories in almost as many minutes" (*CLH* 1:189). Incidentally, at some point that same day, Byron wrote to John Murray to declare that, after two years, he had "obtained a permission from my Dictatress [Teresa Guiccioli] to continue [*Don Juan*]" (*BLJ* 9:182). While it would be difficult to prove that Byron's renewed interest in *Don Juan* had been accelerated by Hunt's presence in Italy, there is firm evidence to show that Hunt's "book-case" contained materials that Byron made immediate and creative use of for the new cantos of his satire. Indeed, at some point between July and September, Byron borrowed Hunt's personal copy of Charles Cotton's translation of Montaigne's essays, from which Byron took hints for the playful philosophical "doubting" that appears in Canto IX of *Don Juan*: "So little do we know what we're about in / This world, I doubt if doubt itself be doubting" (lines 135–6). Hunt later published an unflattering article in the *New Monthly Magazine* about Byron's private reading habits, using the copy of Montaigne that Byron had borrowed and marked as the basis for the discussion.[10] Although the article, as Hunt intended it, was to serve readers as a preview of the personality that would appear in much greater quantities in *LBSC*, the piece on Byron and Montaigne also provides us with strong additional evidence of the creative engagements between Byron and Hunt at the Casa Lanfranchi during the first week of their reunion in Italy.

The activities at the Casa Lanfranchi, however, came to a shocking halt when news arrived on or around 19 July that the drowned bodies of Shelley and Williams had been located on the coastline between Leghorn and Viareggio.[11] Byron, Hunt, Mary Shelley, and Edward John Trelawny, a supporter and friend of Byron and the Shelleys in Italy, soon learned the truth about the disappearance of Shelley and the crew of his schooner, the *Don Juan*, which had been missing since it departed Leghorn on 8 July. Trelawny would lead the recovery efforts and attend to the cremations: Williams's took place nearly a month later on 15 August and Shelley's the following day.[12] When Byron and Hunt returned to Pisa after these grim ceremonies, Byron was ill from swimming in the sun-scorched waters off the coast of Viareggio, and Hunt, who had remained in the carriage for the duration of Shelley's cremation, returned broken and bilious, fighting with Mary Shelley over the charred remains of Shelley's heart.[13] Against this bleak Tuscan background, preparations for the first number of *The Liberal* somehow managed to move ahead, and when the printed volume arrived in Italy in late October, the sight of it provided much needed relief and encouragement: "We were very much pleased to see the Liberal," Hunt told his nephew, Henry Hunt, adding "It is nicely printed & got up, & the outside look is both neat & rich. We only think that it has the air of being somewhat spun out, or not thick enough; & should wish in future that the number of pages should always *exceed* 200" (*LHLL* 119). Working under great personal duress, Byron and Hunt, with the diligent assistance of John Hunt and his son Henry, had put their creative resources to work in a remarkably short period, producing a handsome literary magazine that could only improve, as Hunt said, with a greater quantity of material in the next number. In its all-important first stage, the collaboration on *The Liberal*, from Hunt's perspective, continued to hold great promise.

The First Number of *The Liberal*: "The Florentine Lovers"

The first number of *The Liberal. Verse and Prose from the South* was published by John Hunt on 15 October 1822.[14] Early advertising had generated rumors of the collaboration between the radical Hunt brothers, Shelley, and Byron. Yet the alarm in the conservative press must have only increased the high sales figures and the large number of reviews, unforgiving as they were. Few reviewers ventured to look beyond the liberal politics and radical philosophies of the collaborators and responded, as we might expect, in severe terms of disapproval. Other rumors, however, would also begin to circulate, including one that linked the conservative John Murray to the radical miscellany itself, and copies of *The Liberal* were soon withdrawn from the shelves of Murray's Edinburgh booksellers, thus limiting circulation in at least one major urban center of distribution.[15]

Nevertheless, Byron and Hunt believed that the miscellany had great merit as a document of taste and an expression of liberal opinion.[16] For Byron, the miscellany also had practical and material value, for it presented an opportunity to publish controversial works, already written, that Murray had refused to handle. Chief among these was "The Vision of Judgment," which may have been given to Hunt as a welcome "present" (*LHLL* 116) the day he moved into the Casa Lanfranchi. A parody of Robert Southey's tribute to George III, *A Vision of Judgment* (1821), Byron's "The Vision of Judgment" has long been celebrated as a comic masterpiece. As Carl Woodring writes, "Few poems of equal compactness can boast so many levels of parody, satire, comedy, church-window symbolism, factual history dissolved in comic myth, and moral argument."[17] For Byron and Hunt, however, the poem was no cause for celebration after it made its public debut. Published without its intended preface, which had outlined the poem's parodic elements and intentions, "The Vision of Judgment" was deemed libelous and John Hunt was held to account for its appearance.[18] Byron and Hunt had published all of the materials in *The Liberal* anonymously (a tactic that led to much erroneous speculation in the reviews), but most critics correctly identified "The Vision of Judgment" as Byron's work.

Hunt's major contributions to the first number of *The Liberal* consisted of new material he produced in Pisa during July, August, and September of 1822. These included: "The Florentine Lovers," a work of prose fiction with an Italian theme; "Rhyme and Reason," a work of literary criticism with a satirical bent; "A German Apologue," a fanciful story with a clas-sical theme; the first installment of Hunt's "Letters from Abroad" series; and a verse translation of "Ariosto's Episode of Cloridan, Medoro, and Angelica" from the *Orlando Furioso*. The offerings were fully in line with the programmatic statement Hunt had issued in *The Liberal*'s preface:

> We wish the title of our work to be taken in its largest acceptation, old as well as new,—but always in the same spirit of admiring and assisting, rather than of professing. We just as much disclaim any assumption in it before the wise, as we disclaim any false modesty before all classes. All that we mean is, that we are advocates of every species of liberal knowledge, and that, by a natural consequence in these times, we go the full length in matters of opinion with large bodies of men who are called LIBERALS.
>
> (1:viii–ix)[19]

The emphasis on "we" is important here. Hunt emphatically announces *The Liberal* to be a social text given to "assisting" rather than "pro-fessing," while declaring that the contents are to be read as communal expressions of liberal solidarity rather than individual expressions of creativity. The miscellany's intended appeal to "all classes," moreover, gave it a formidable and revolutionary aspect. In fact, it has been sug-gested by more than one scholar that Byron and Hunt gave the term "Liberal" its modern political connotations when they appropriated it as the title and guiding theme for the miscellany. Indeed, according to Daisy Hay, "Liberalism," for Hunt, was a dynamic, politically charged concept that involved the "conviction to attack one's enemies," as well as a commitment to "speaking out against repressive policies, defending the freedom of the press and the causes of oppressed people."[20] Byron and Hunt both knew the word "Liberal" carried controversial political meaning, and by employing it as their guiding ethos in *The Liberal*, they willingly accepted the reality that they would be going, as Hunt put it, the "full length" in "every species of liberal knowledge."

Those lengths are readily apparent in the first number of the mis-cellany. Byron's "Vision of Judgment," as noted, earned libel charges soon after it appeared. Byron's other contribution to the first number, his "Letter to the Editor of 'My Grandmother's Review,'" though it did not contain libelous material, was a defense of the controversial first two cantos of *Don Juan*. Hunt's contributions to the first number of *The Lib-eral* were no less controversial in the themes and subject matter they ex-plored. "The Florentine Lovers," for instance, is positioned immediately after "The Vision of Judgment" and "Letter to the Editor," making it the third article in the first number of *The Liberal* and the first of Hunt's offerings therein. Its positioning thus gives it distinction within the vol-ume and Hunt's decision to reprint the story many years later in *The*

Seer (1840–41) confirms his high estimation of the work. The facts upon which the story is based, as Marshall notes, are to be found in Marco Lastri's *L'Osservatore Fiorentino*, a historical work that Mary Shelley probably first brought to Hunt's attention in Italy.[21] In "The Florentine Lovers," Hunt's benign statement that the "groundwork of this story is in a late Italian publication called the Florentine Observer, descriptive of the old buildings and other circumstances of local interest in the capital of Tuscany" (1:51) offers no suggestion of the socially and politically subversive message he was to weave from his source material.[22]

The story from Lastri that Hunt chose to retell in *The Liberal* revisited a theme to which he and Byron had always been particularly drawn: the awakening of the human passions within a socially, politically, and culturally conservative context. Set in fourteenth-century Florence when the Tuscan capital was "divided into the two fierce parties of Guelfs and Ghibelines" (1:51), Hunt's "Florentine Lovers" follows Lastri's version closely in its basic outline. The story is one of love and forgiveness, at the center of which are two young Florentines born into families on opposite sides of a politically contentious Florentine society: Dianora d'Amerigo, a Bardi, and Ippolito, a Buondelmonte. The events, both in Lastri's original and in Hunt's retelling, begin on the "great day of Pardon" (1:53), a symbolic occasion, being the start of the Lenten season in the Orthodox Christian and Catholic traditions, that foreshadows the story's comic ending. In both accounts, the Werther-like Ippolito suffers from unrequited passionate feelings for Dianora. In Lastri's account, however, Dianora has no prior knowledge of Ippolito's secret obsession. To lend dramatic interest and establish a basis for the attraction that develops between the two characters, Hunt creates a new backstory, just as he had for Dante's Paolo and Francesca in *The Story of Rimini*. In Hunt's retelling of Lastri, the initial encounter between Dianora and Ippolito is, in fact, highly reminiscent of the event that leads to the fatal kiss exchanged between Paulo and Francesca in *Rimini*: a shared act of reading. Hunt's "Florentine Lovers" become acquainted in church when Dianora observes that Ippolito has forgotten his prayer book and offers to share hers. Ippolito, having "felt almost suffocated with his sensations" (1:59), accepts the offer, and the "sensations" are soon shared by Dianora. Hunt places great stress on this event, prefacing the scene with a telling allusion to Aristophanes's speech in Plato's *Symposium* and a series of comments on "earthly" love. As Hunt explains, "In the South the church has ever been the place where people fall in love," adding that "There the voluptuous that cannot fix their thoughts upon heaven find congenial objects, more earthly, to win their attention." Highlighting the physicality of these "congenial objects" that surround Dianora and Ippolito, Hunt concludes approvingly that

all have a tendency to confuse the boundaries of this world and the next, and to set the heart floating in that delicious mixture of elevation and humility, which is ready to sympathize with whatever can preserve to it something like its sensations, and save it from the hardness and definite folly of ordinary life.

(1:52)

Hunt's commentary has striking implications, reinforcing the liberal values that he and Byron both wished to promote with their miscellany. Indeed, in "The Florentine Lovers," social, political, and spiritual boundaries break down in the context of a Catholic mass, privileging community and passionate feeling over social division and the "hardness" of "ordinary life." For Hunt, as for Ippolito and Dianora, the "earthly" takes on a spiritual significance of its own. Hunt, moreover, provides support for his decision to explore the human passions within the context of a sacred space, knowingly, by looking to literary history for his authority and reminding his (largely Anglican) readership that "It was in a church that Boccaccio . . . first saw the beautiful face of his Fiammetta. In a church, Petrarch felt the sweet shadow fall on him that darkened his life for twenty years after" (1:52–3).

After this initial passionate exchange between Ippolito and Dianora, Hunt follows Lastri's version of the events closely. Ippolito's mother, learning of her son's obsession with Dianora, visits a certain Contessa with connections to Dianora's family, from whom she procures a formal invitation and thus a second meeting between the two young Florentines. Hunt's retelling similarly contrives such a meeting when Ippolito's mother visits a distant relation to both the Bardi and Buondelmonte families. In the privacy of the domestic space at the Casa Bardi, Ippolito and Dianora reenact the scene from the previous Sunday: "Ippolito then, for the pleasure of revenging himself of the pangs he suffered when Dianora knelt with him before, took up the mass-book and held it before her, as she had held it before him . . . and Dianora took and held it with him as before, trembling as then, but with a perfect pleasure" (1:70). The controversial scene, which *Blackwood's* would single out for criticism, is given political weight and interest by Hunt, who prefaces the scene by informing readers that "There was a practice in those times, generated, like other involuntary struggles against wrong, by the absurdities in authority, of resorting to marriages, or rather plightings of troth, made in secret" (1:69).[23] Hunt would have known of such "secret" marriages from his reading in Shakespeare and other Elizabethan dramatists, but he also knew from the fourteenth-century "history of Ines de Castro" that the custom was "liable to great abuse" and that the "harm of it, as usual, fell chiefly on the poor, or where the condition of the parties was unequal."[24] The latter scenario, of course, is that in which Dianora and Ippolito find themselves because of the politics that divide their families and prevent the open acknowledgment of their shared passion.

The conclusion to "The Florentine Lovers" brings into sharp focus an important social dimension of the overarching message that Byron and Hunt wished to promote in *The Liberal*. As the passion between Dianora and Ippolito intensifies, they begin to meet each other surreptitiously at night. During one attempted assignation, however, Ippolito is caught, questioned, and eventually found guilty of trespassing and sentenced to death. On the day of his execution, he asks for and is granted permission to be led past the Casa Bardi. Dianora, as Ippolito anticipates, witnesses the grim procession and emerges to address the crowd that has gathered by giving a rousing plea for unity and reconciliation: "'People! Dear God! Countrymen! I am a Bardi; he is a Buondelmonte; he loved me; and that is the whole crime!'" At this, the "populace now broke through all restraint," and "sent for the heads of the two houses; they made them swear a treaty of peace, amity, and unity; and in half an hour after the lover had been on the road to his death, he set out upon it again, the acknowledged bridegroom of the beautiful creature by his side" (1:79). The conclusion, of course, is quite different from the tragic end that Paulo and Francesca meet in *Rimini*. Yet it is important to see Hunt's comic ending to "The Florentine Lovers" not simply as an idealization of a moment in Florentine history (according to Lastri, the events were indeed part of the historical record), but instead as a political story with relevance to a culturally regressive post-Napoleonic world. Indeed, the political message of "The Florentine Lovers" would seem to be that liberal progress is the responsibility of the "populace," the great agent of social change. As Susan Wolfson points out, in Shelley's *Defence of Poetry*, which Hunt may have read in Italy during the same period he composed "The Florentine Lovers," the author of *Queen Mab* had argued that the "social sympathies, or those laws from which . . . society results, begin to develop themselves from the moment that two human beings coexist," and this sympathetic coexistence, for Shelley, ultimately creates the "will of a social being . . . determined to action."[25]

If Hunt's decision to stage the awakening of the passions—both human and social—in "The Florentine Lovers" within the sacred space of a Catholic church was an attempt to shock readers into liberal awareness, then Byron would have readily approved of Hunt's daring methods. Byron had explored religious themes, with controversial results, in his powerful drama *Cain* (1821) and another poem on a biblical theme, *Heaven and Earth*, which would be published in the second number of *The Liberal*. Byron had also set an entire scene of *The Deformed Transformed* (1824), a drama that he prepared for publication during the period of his collaboration with Hunt in Italy, within the interior spaces of a Catholic church (St. Peter's Basilica) to explore the flesh and blood realities of human affairs.[26] In this late unfinished drama, Byron's primary interest was not the awakened power of the human passions, but rather the terrifying consequences of military conflict. Nevertheless, the use of religious settings in *The Deformed Transformed* and "The Florentine Lovers" is suggestive, for it shows that Byron and Hunt did not count themselves among the orthodox in their liberal explorations of religion and society.

"Ariosto's Episode of Cloridan, Medoro, and Angelica"

Hunt's major poetical contribution to the first number of *The Liberal*, a verse translation of "Ariosto's Episode of Cloridan, Medoro, and Angelica," was most likely another expression of liberal solidarity with Byron. Prior to Hunt's arrival in Italy, Byron told Thomas Medwin that he wished to translate Ariosto for *The Liberal*, and in December of 1822, Medwin apparently sent Byron his own "Translation from Ariosto" for the "next Liberal," but Byron, perhaps in consultation with Hunt, must have rejected the piece for publication, for Medwin's translation never appeared.[27] The fact that Hunt's translation of Ariosto appeared in the first number, however, should come as no surprise. Although Byron made a translation of Dante's Paolo and Francesca episode in 1820 that surely would have appealed to Hunt, he made few substantial efforts in Italian translation prior to completing the first canto of Luigi Pulci's *Morgante Maggiore*, which would appear in the fourth number of *The Liberal* in 1823.[28] Hunt's translation of Tasso's *Amyntas* (1820) had already earned the translator critical approval because of the work's fidelity to Tasso's original.[29] The demands of translation had indeed forced the author of *Rimini* to restrain from indulging in his otherwise loose style of versification. Byron may have learned of the *Amyntas* when Hunt arrived in Italy, but he was certainly aware of Hunt's translations from Greek and Latin in *Foliage* and perhaps an earlier translation of Anacreon that was published in *The Examiner* in 1816.[30] Hunt had also made a careful study of the major English translations of Ariosto and Tasso by Fairfax, Harrington, and Hoole. In fact, Hunt's published statements on Hoole show that the author of *Rimini* saw Ariosto's popular English translator as a weak imitator of Pope: "It was lucky . . . for this gentleman, that he had the period he wrote in almost all to himself. . . . nobody knew any thing about poetry, except that it had to repeat 'ingenious' common-places, to rhyme upon heart, impart, love, prove, &c., and to pause, as Pope did, upon the fourth and fifth syllables."[31] For Hunt, Hoole's translation of the *Orlando Furioso* was an obvious illustration of imitative verse written on the Popeian model—a "bundle of common-places" that lacked the "deep and varied intonation" of Ariosto's original.[32] Hunt's decision to translate Ariosto in 1822 for *The Liberal* was, then, on the one hand, a continuation of a long-standing critical assault on Ariosto's English translator. On the other hand, as we shall see, the "Episode of Cloridan, Medoro, and Angelica" may have acquired deep personal meaning for Hunt in the wake of Shelley's death.

Ariosto's "Episode of Cloridan, Medoro, and Angelica" actually comprises two related but separate episodes that bridge Cantos XVIII and XIX of the *Orlando Furioso*. The first and longest section of Hunt's translation is that which focuses on the story of Medoro and Cloridan from Canto XVIII. Ariosto's tale of two "Moorish youths" (1:142, line 9) engaged in battle against Christian forces during the time of Charlemagne is a rewriting of Virgil's story of Nisus and Euryalus from Book IX of the *Aeneid*. Byron, as we saw in the first chapter, had translated Virgil's episode in its entirety for *Hours of Idleness* in the spring of 1807. Hunt, of course, knew this, recalling on more than one occasion the unique experience he and Byron shared as juvenile authors. Drawing on the story of Achilles and Patroclus from the *Iliad,* Virgil had updated Homer's story with the Nisus and Euryalus episode in the *Aeneid*, and Ariosto, in turn, produced his own version of the story with Cloridan and Medoro. Evidence that Hunt may have translated the "Episode of Cloridan, Medoro, and Angelica" with Byron in mind in July or August of 1822 is also apparent in the thematic content of the material that he chose to translate. Ariosto, as Hunt points out in the preface to his translation, "has contrived to write the story of Angelica with that of Medoro in a manner singularly new and beautiful, and to reward the youth's virtue with life and love, without depriving the episode of its pathos" (1:141). The "singularly new and beautiful way" in which Ariosto had updated Virgil's Nisus and Euryalus story was to provide a comic ending, thus mitigating an otherwise tragic episode. Ariosto also provided a new motive for the two young soldiers to venture into hostile territory. In the *Aeneid*, Nisus and Euryalus are ambushed and die together after they cross into enemy lines, attempting to deliver military intelligence to their absent leader Aeneas. In Ariosto's retelling, Cloridan and Medoro are killed in a similar manner, but at the moment they meet their tragic end, Angelica, the heroine of Ariosto's epic, suddenly appears and falls in love with the beautiful young Medoro, restoring him to life. The lifeless body of the unfortunate Cloridan, meanwhile, is given a dignified burial by Medoro and Angelica before they depart.

Significantly, the motive that Ariosto contrived for the dangerous mission that Cloridan and Medoro undertake in the *Orlando Furioso* has striking resonance with the motive that led Byron and Hunt to the shores of Viareggio in August of 1822. In Hunt's translation, Medoro explains the motive thus:

> O Cloridan,
> I cannot tell thee how it swells my blood
> To think our lord [Dardinel] lies left upon the plain
> To wolves and crows; alas, too, noble food!
> When I reflect how pleasant and humane
> He always was to me, I feel I could
> Let out this life that he might be so,
> And yet not pay him half the debt I owe.
>
> (1:143, lines 33–40)

Medoro then concludes: "I will go forth,—I will,—and seek him yet, / That he may want not a grave's covering" (1:143, lines 41–2). After hearing his friend's impassioned speech, Cloridan is moved to join Medoro in the task of recovering Dardinel's body, declaring "My road then shall be thine:— / I too will join in such a work of love" (1:143–4, lines 58–9). Just as Medoro and Cloridan were bound by "a work of love" to recover Dardinel's body and provide their fallen commander with a proper burial, so too did Hunt and Byron readily accept the sad task of recovering Shelley's drowned body in the late summer of 1822. The resonance between the fiction and the reality could not have been lost on any reader of the first number of *The Liberal* who had any awareness of the tragic circumstances. Hunt and Byron had, in fact, discussed the inclusion of a tribute to Shelley in the first number of the miscellany.[33] The article, and perhaps the idea, originated with Trelawny, who supplied a draft to which Hunt, in consultation with Byron, made several additions and corrections. The article was abandoned in the end, with Hunt apparently finding Trelawny's grimly factual account of Shelley's burial too coarse and therefore inappropriate for publication. The abandonment of this intended tribute perhaps raises the possibility that Hunt's translation of Ariosto for the first number of *The Liberal* may have been composed, in part, as an alternative memorial for Shelley, a more artful tribute for his lost friend than Trelawny's submission, but in the absence of more conclusive evidence the idea must remain conjecture. Be that as it may, Hunt's Ariosto translation might be read as a poignant and complex statement of Hunt's mood in the late summer of 1822, doubtless capturing, on the one hand, his thoughts on Shelley and, on the other hand, his sympathies with Byron.

Hunt's translation of Ariosto, of course, should also be seen as something more than a versified record of a shared experience with his *Liberal* collaborator. The various layers of meaning in the text and the literary traditions from which it derives clearly suggest that Hunt wished to engage Byron creatively, reaffirming a mutual interest in both Italian literature and the classical tradition and its idealization of male friendship. As Webb observes, Hunt made another attempt to appeal to Byron's classical sensibilities in late October with a more playful act of translation—a lyric from Catullus that utilized the tradition of the *flagitatio*.[34] In this case, Hunt's translation, included in a letter Hunt sent to Byron on 29 October 1822, was intended as an attack on John Murray for deliberately withholding, as Byron and Hunt believed, the preface to "The Vision of Judgment"; the absence of the preface from the first number of *The Liberal*, as noted, had led to legal troubles and eventually a libel conviction for John Hunt. Byron's response to Hunt's minor work of Catullan translation, if Byron provided one, is not forthcoming, and Hunt's poem itself, in the end, did not appear in *The Liberal*. The "Episode of Cloridan, Medoro, and Angelica," however, was a more serious work of translation that was written in a higher register and thus probably would have had greater appeal for Byron. In fact, the choices that Hunt had to make in his translation of Ariosto reveal the serious, potentially damaging public consequences of his endeavor. Indeed, as we shall see, the textual evidence, which illuminates Hunt's complex handling of the episode's homoerotic subtext, the passionate relationship of Cloridan and Medoro, shows that Hunt was aware of this subtext in Ariosto's original.

Published texts that dealt with themes of same-sex desire could have serious consequences in Romantic England. According to Louis Crompton, the Society for the Suppression of Vice, founded in 1801 under George III, had "pursued a vigorous course," carrying out an increasing number of executions against individuals convicted of conduct the Society deemed illicit. The suppression of "obscene publications" was also one of the Society's "publicly declared aims," and material that celebrated or even brought attention to same-sex desire could not be treated lightly.[35] Byron likely knew this, having many years earlier attempted to offset the passionate sensibility in his translation of the Nisus and Euryalus episode with facetious notes and other cynical elements in *Hours of Idleness*. In his translation from Ariosto for *The Liberal*, Hunt exhibits a similar level of self-consciousness that was owing, in part, to Ariosto's more suggestive presentation of the relationship between Cloridan and Medoro. Whereas Virgil ultimately downplayed the attraction between Nisus and Euryalus by subordinating their shared passion to a higher form of love and duty toward Rome, Ariosto celebrated the flesh and blood passion that Cloridan and Medoro openly express. Indeed, for Ariosto, the story of the two young "Moorish" soldiers is one of "*vero amore*," where "true love," according to Patricia Palmer, "is understood to flow in overlapping circuits of desire. 'Amore,' unqualified, diffuse and without hierarchy of orientation, is the motive to action."[36]

Hunt's willingness to "go the full length," and thus advance *The Liberal*'s express social and political aims in exploring the human passions in the "Episode of Cloridan, Medoro, and Angelica," is confirmed when the 1822 translation is compared to Hunt's later published versions of the translation from 1855 and 1857. In these Victorian reworkings, Hunt transformed the original "perfect love" (1:142, line 12) between Medoro and Cloridan into a "tried affection" in what appears to be an attempt to mask the story's homoerotic subtext. Hunt also reworked lines that emphasized the deeply personal nature of the Cloridan-Medoro friendship: "Struck with amaze was Cloridan to see / Such heart, such love, such nobleness in a youth" (1:143, lines 49–50).[37] In the later versions, Hunt replaced "nobleness" with "duty," thus firmly introducing the sense of Virgil's story of Nisus and Euryalus, where the private love between the soldiers is inextricably tied to the public "service so noble" that the pair has agreed to undertake for Aeneas and Rome.[38] Hunt's revisions to his original translation of the "Episode of Cloridan, Medoro, and Angelica" were characteristic of his later editorial and revisionary practices regarding material that dealt with gender and sexuality.[39] Nevertheless, when Hunt's translation of Ariosto in *The Liberal* is read alongside its Victorian reworkings, it seems clear that in 1822 Hunt had a deliberately provocative statement to make about same-sex desire and the human passions.

The Second Number of *The Liberal*: "The Dogs" and *Don Juan* Canto XI

In September of 1822, Hunt, Byron, and Mary Shelley, along with Teresa Guiccioli and the Gambas, moved fifty miles north to Genoa. The Tuscan government had ordered the Gambas out of the region after a series of controversial episodes involving the local authorities, including the violent Masi Affair that had occurred earlier that year.[40] By the end of September, Byron, duty bound to Teresa and her family, thus chose to follow, while Mary Shelley and the Hunts separately made their way north.

There were other unsettling matters coming to light at this time. At the beginning of October, Hunt wrote to Elizabeth Kent from his new lodgings at Albaro, a spacious hillside house just outside of Genoa that the Hunts shared with Mary Shelley, providing his sister-in-law with news about the state of *The Liberal* and the collaboration. Hunt said that "Lord B. lives close to us, with the Gambas, in a palace," adding, "Since I wrote last, he is again for the Magazine plan, and I have written to my brother accordingly" (*CLH* 1:192). Hunt clarified the reason for Byron's new and perhaps surprising position with respect to *The Liberal* on 10 October 1822 in a letter to his brother thus: "People here do not approve of the new works being thrown into the Examiner, & Lord Byron, who is kind enough to say that my advantage is his great object, is still perfectly willing that the magazine should be proceeded with, provided you think it would be best. What <u>do</u> you think best, for really I cannot determine?" (*LHOL*). Hunt was understandably anxious about the state of the "magazine" since it was intended to serve as his primary source of income in Italy. The "people" to whom he refers his brother were Moore, who had been voicing his opposition to the collaboration in strong terms to Byron since January, and Hobhouse, who had visited the Casa Lanfranchi in the middle of September with the Hunts in residence.[41] As Hunt later reflected, "One of the arguments used" against the collaboration was "that the connexion was not 'gentlemanly'" (*LBSC* 48). But this, Hunt must have realized, was to state the matter in polite terms, for he reproduced a lengthy section from one of Hazlitt's *Plain Speaker* essays in *LBSC* in order to provide a more incisive account of the attempts being made by Moore and Hobhouse to put an end to the collaboration: "who would have supposed that Mr. Thomas Moore and Mr. Hobhouse, those staunch friends and partisans of the people, should also be thrown into almost hysterical agonies of well-bred horror at the coalition between their noble and ignoble acquaintance—between the patrician and 'the newspaper-man?'" (*LBSC* 54). And yet, despite the objections coming from his friends, Byron remained committed to Hunt and the miscellany, and plans for the second number moved ahead.

For the second number, the collaborators began to look outside of their immediate circle for contributors. Charles Armitage Brown, the close friend of Keats, had been in Italy since August. He had learned of *The Liberal* after visiting Hunt at the Casa Lanfranchi, where he was apprehensive about being introduced to Byron. But Byron "somehow . . . got the better of [Brown's] prejudice" and welcomed his contribution on "Les Charmettes and Rousseau," which appeared in the second number of the miscellany.[42] Hazlitt, meanwhile, had been approached by John Hunt to contribute, while Hunt asked his brother to contact Charles Lamb and said that he would write to Shelley's old Oxford companion Thomas Jefferson Hogg.[43] Mary Shelley, who did not contribute to the first number of *The Liberal*, offered *"an Italian story"* for the second number called "A Tale of the Passions," which Hunt thought "a very good one" (*LHLL* 122). The group of writers thus being assembled for the second number of *The Liberal* bore a resemblance to the mixed group of Cockneys and non-Cockneys that Hunt had gathered together and celebrated in *Foliage* in 1818 much to Byron's discontent. Byron, however, gave no signs of disapproval with this new arrangement, later advising Hunt to let his "home friends pull a little" (*BLJ* 10:83) more on the production side.

Hunt's creative intimacy with Byron also seemed to be gaining strength during the assembly of the second number. A jointly written letter by Byron and Hunt (a tactic that would be repeated) to Hunt's nephew Henry Hunt vividly captures the collaborators at work. In this early November letter, we learn from Hunt that Byron had been so impressed with the first number of *The Liberal* that he "thinks we may have six numbers a year instead of four." Buoyed by Byron's optimism, Hunt also showed great confidence in a new poem he had just finished—"The Dogs," a biting satire on the Duke of Wellington that was written, according to Hunt, "in the Don Juan style" and was "both political & 'facetious'" (*LHLL* 121–2). Hunt probably began composing "The Dogs" soon after writing to his brother on 26 October, for on 4 November Hunt sent a brief note to Byron, stating that he was at that moment "busy with my Dukes & Dogs," and on 9 November, Marianne Hunt recorded in her diary that Hunt had finished the satire on that day.[44] The poem was in Byron's hands for review sometime before 21 November, the day he returned Hunt's manuscript with a warning for his collaborator: "I would recommend you to think twice upon ['The Dogs'] before you publish them at the present moment" (*BLJ* 10:39). The advice had doubtless been offered with John Hunt's impending libel trial for "The Vision of Judgment" in mind. However, perhaps wanting to prove to his collaborator that he was willing to attack political enemies in the same fearless manner of his early *Examiner* days, Hunt ignored Byron's advice and proceeded with his satire for the second number of *The Liberal*.

Hunt's immediate inspiration for "The Dogs" was an "anecdote" printed in the *Journal of a Soldier of the Seventy-First* (1819):

> I at this time got a post, being for fatigue, with four others. We were sent to break biscuit, and make a mess for Lord Wellington's Hounds. I was very hungry, and thought it a good job at the time, as we got our own fill, while we broke the biscuit,—a thing I had not got for some days. When thus engaged, the Prodigal Son was never once out of my mind; and I sighed, as I fed the dogs, over my humble situation and my ruined hopes.
>
> (*CPW* 5:738)

Hunt used this anecdote as the epigraph for "The Dogs" and Byron, demonstrating his political solidarity with Hunt, used the same quotation in a note in *Don Juan* Canto IX. According to Neil Ramsey, the *Journal of a Soldier of the Seventy-First* was "one of the first and most popular private soldier's memoirs written in Britain after the French Revolutionary and Napoleonic Wars." Neither a sentimental memoir nor a statement of patriotic duty, the journal, with its emphasis on the mental and physical suffering of soldiers, Ramsey argues, offered "a corrective reading of war's destructive and terrifying nature."[45] With this context in mind, we can understand why Hunt and Byron were both drawn to the memoir as a powerful record of anti-war sentiment. Its popularity, moreover, may have suggested to Hunt a way to appeal to a wider group of readers, thereby extending *The Liberal*'s reach. Readers of the first number had already had a taste of more commercially oriented material in the first installment of Hunt's "Letters from Abroad" series.

The popular authority that the *Journal of a Soldier of the Seventy-First* provided may have also served as a way to justify the anti-war sentiment that pervades "The Dogs." But if there were any hesitation on Hunt's part about publishing the satire, Hunt knew that it contained nothing more or less controversial than what he had found in Byron's *Don Juan*. In a 26 October letter to his brother, Hunt revealed that he had prepared an article for *The Examiner*, "announcing the formidable arrival of <u>Don Juan</u> in Shooter's Hill, Lord B. having brought his hero into England" (*LHOL*). This article, as Webb explains, confirms that Hunt had read Canto XI of *Don Juan* (in manuscript) by the end of October. The later cantos of *Don Juan* were becoming increasingly political in focus, and politics would have certainly been a point of shared interest between the two *Liberal* collaborators. Before composing "The Dogs," for instance, Hunt may have already learned of Byron's decision to attack Wellington in *Don Juan* Canto IX, perhaps at some point during the first two weeks in July, for it was then that Byron wrote to Moore, asking for a copy of verses on Wellington that Byron had composed three years earlier.[46] These verses would serve as the opening apostrophe in Canto IX: "OH, Wellington! (or 'Vilainton'—for Fame / Sounds the heroic syllables both ways" (lines 1–2). The opening stanzas would have indeed provided Hunt with the confidence he needed to attack Wellington in *The Liberal* had he required it. In the preface to *The Liberal*, Hunt had already mocked Wellington for being "not so gentlemanly a man" but rather "a good hunting captain,—a sort of human setter" (1:x–xi), adding in the same sarcastic vein: "We allow him all his praise in that respect, and only wish he had not confounded the rights of nations with those of a manor" (1:xi). In *Don Juan* Canto IX, Byron had similarly criticized Wellington for his "great pensions" (line 6) and "half a million for [his] Sabine farm" (line 55). In fact, Byron had heightened the rhetoric with the shocking accusation, "You are 'the best of cut-throats,'" justifying the statement by reminding readers that "The phrase is Shakespeare's, and not misapplied" (lines 25–6). Aligning himself firmly with Hunt, Byron ended the opening apostrophe to Wellington in *Don Juan* Canto IX by sarcastically imploring the British general to "send the sentinel before your gate / A slice or two from your luxurious meals: / He fought, but has not fed so well of late" (lines 43–5). To this stanza, Byron added the note with the quotation from the *Journal of a Soldier of the Seventy-First* that Hunt had used as his epigraph for "The Dogs," thus ensuring a coordinated two-pronged assault on Wellington's character.

"The Dogs" was a satirical poem with a serious purpose as Hunt confirmed in the poem's introduction: "It is not the wish of the Liberal to write satire and personal politics; but if you insist upon our earning a right to be heard with the sword, it must be so. . . . we fight, like the Greeks and Spaniards, to obtain the right and the tranquility of speech, and not to trample on every body in turn" (1:245). The parallel that Hunt makes between the Greek and Spanish wars for independence and *The Liberal*'s fight for free speech would have reinforced the synchronicity between poetry and politics that Byron and Hunt both fully endorsed. Indeed, in the conclusion to Canto XI of *Don Juan*, which Hunt had recently encountered, the Byronic narrator made the following assertion of poetic strength: "I may stand alone, / But would not change my free thoughts for a throne" (lines 719–20). Expressing agreement with Byron on this score, Hunt's narrator in Stanzas 24 and 25 of "The Dogs" also refuses to remain a "mute" bystander in the "commonwealth's great cause":

> I'll be as free: there's not a stick at court
> Shall beat me in a thing I have to say;
> Tailors sha'nt cut me out, nor tongues cut short,
> Envying my very independent way;

Croker himself shall cry out "That's your sort,"
And loads of "lofty Scotchmen" cry, Huzza!
At least if they do not, 'twill only shew
How far one's rivals' jealousy can go.

(1:254)

In a lengthy note, Hunt clarified his attack on the "lofty Scotchmen" by specifically drawing attention to the writers for *Blackwood's* and concluding thus: "I have met with otherwise amiable Scotchmen, and with intelligent and eminent Scotchmen; but I never met with one, who was not more or less filthy in his talk;—I do not mean merely indecent, much less voluptuous, but absolutely filthy, in the style of Swift. It is most probably owing to certain modes of life; but it is high time for them to get rid of it, if they would not render a publication like Blackwood's as injurious to their character by its praises, as it is by [its] abuses of others" (1:266). As we saw in the previous chapter, Byron had strongly defended Hunt's character from *Blackwood's* attacks in "The Cockney School" articles and he would have sympathized with Hunt's remarks on the *Blackwood's* group in "The Dogs." Yet Byron, at this moment, may not have been fully aware of the extent to which Hunt may have intended to explore the acceptable limits of English "talk" in "The Dogs," for Hunt seems to have originally had the thought to do so through an act of close intertextual engagement with *Don Juan* Canto XI.

In an important series of uncanceled stanzas in "The Pack of Hounds," an unpublished early draft of "The Dogs" that Byron may have read, Hunt composed a lengthy *Don Juan*-like digression on the limits of polite discourse in English society, illustrating those limits through a discussion of the word "Bitch." While some of the content found in these unincorporated stanzas, it appears, served as the basis for the prose note to received Stanza 25 of "The Dogs" on *Blackwood's*, Hunt's stanzaic numbering in the draft suggests that the digression would have followed Stanza 28 in the published poem. In the first unincorporated stanza of this digression in "The Pack of Hounds," Hunt's speaker declares, "I hate extremely / Words that might please the gross sea-faring Dutch / . . . Such as Swift loves for instance, & the Scotch," but concludes facetiously: "Yet decently as I may talk, or primly, / I never, for the life of me, could see / How the word Bitch can hurt one's purity."[47] Several heavily revised stanzas follow, completing Hunt's digression, with the last stanza in the unincorporated sequence using the authority of Samuel Johnson to notable effect:

The greatest of the great men have had
An instinct like my own: there's Doctor Johnson,
Who certainly would use no phrases bad,
More than a [?chaste] dame before her own son.

And yet he said once, half in jest, half sad,
(I think I ~~see~~ hear him putting his best tones on)
"Sir, with respect to what is said of witches,
Nought proves the <u>non</u>-existence of the bitches."[48]

Although Hunt may have intended the digression to form part of an extended attack on Wellington, the theme of the unincorporated section is, more generally, that of linguistic decorum. Hunt's aborted section thus has importance primarily because it appears to show another revealing "conjunction," to recall Webb's phrase, with *Don Juan*—a creative intimacy that extends beyond the formal use of Byron's *ottava rima* and chatty narration in *Don Juan* to a close engagement with specific themes and subjects found in Byron's satire.

In Canto XI of *Don Juan*, for instance, Byron had doubtless rhymed "b[itche]s" with "riches" (lines 327–8) for shock effect, and a few stanzas later began a digression on the word "Damme" (line 337) and British and "Continental oaths" (line 338) more generally. The phrase "God damn!" (line 90) is one of the few native expressions Juan knows when he arrives in England, and Byron accordingly finds opportunity to pursue the theme of language in all of its comic, social, and political dimensions intermittently throughout the canto until the digression on "Damme" begins at Stanza 42. There, the narrator observes that "phrases of refinement" (such as "empressment") used in England have been "borrow[ed]" from France, "our next neighbour's land" (lines 329–31). For Byron, England's less refined island talkers are, by contrast, "downright and thorough," "as if the sea / . . . made even the tongue more free" (lines 334–6). The patriotic thrust of this concluding couplet, in fact, prompts the narrator to assert with evident pride in the next stanza that "the British 'Damme's' rather Attic" (line 337) and "quite ethereal" (line 343). However, the Byronic narrator also realizes, with more than a hint of irony, that native words like "Damme" are still "too daring" (line 343) to use in polite society. Byron would revisit the oath theme again in *The Island*, where it provides comic relief amidst one of the graver scenes in that late romance.[49] But *Don Juan* Canto XI remains a *tour de force* as an exploration of English *politesse* within the context of London high society as Byron once knew it. As such, Hunt's decision to withhold his thematically similar exploration of language from "The Dogs" suggests that there were, in fact, limits to his willingness to follow Byron's freedom-loving muse into print. Hunt, of course, may have realized that his digression on "Bitch" in "The Pack of Hounds," which has less of the comic subtlety and spirit found in Byron's parallel digression on "Damme," would have been unpalatable to a large section of readers he wished to reach with *The Liberal*. Hunt probably also knew that he was treading too close to the material in his Byronic model. In any event, "The Pack of Hounds" is a highly revealing text with important relevance to an understanding of Hunt's poetic art as well as his close literary engagements with Byron's *Don Juan* in the fall of 1822.

And yet for all of the formal characteristics and thematic concerns that "The Dogs" shares with *Don Juan*, Hunt's satire did not appeal to Byron. Although Byron would have sympathized with Hunt's political message, having already expressed similar attitudes toward Wellington in the opening stanzas of Canto IX, as we have seen, Byron found reason to quarrel with "The Dogs" in "a literary point of view":

> I shall only suggest two things to yr. judgement—in the *Dogs*—the first is to alter the motto—which is neither very good—nor true—for it is not a common phrase—at least to my knowledge—and I have heard the objurgations of many different communities—from the Dandy's to the Dragoman's. In ye. 2d. place—there are a few of the rhymes especially in the latter part which ought to be altered (Calendar / Purveyor for example[)].
>
> (*BLJ* 10:39)[50]

Byron here returns to the two standard objections he often expressed to Hunt: an objection to writers who take up subjects for which they lack requisite experiential "knowledge" and an objection to Hunt's imperfect and unconventional rhymes. Clearly, their old poetical differences, openly acknowledged during the course of Byron's reading and annotating of *Rimini* in 1815 and 1816, were still relevant. The timing of Byron's lukewarm reception of "The Dogs," however, could not have been worse. In early October, Byron, unbeknownst to Hunt, had written to Mary Shelley describing Hunt's children as "dirtier and more mischievous than Yahoos," adding "what they can[']t destroy with their filth they will with their fingers" (*BLJ* 10:11). Byron, it turns out, had discovered that Hunt's children had defaced some of the interiors of the Casa Lanfranchi. Byron had also shared his irritation with Murray in early October: "I have done all I can for Leigh Hunt—since he came here—but it is almost useless—his wife is ill—his six children not very tractable and [i]n the affairs of this world he himself is a child" (*BLJ* 10:13). A month later, Henry Hunt informed his uncle that Byron's letter had been making the rounds within the Murray circle and that the gossip had spread beyond Murray's bookshop. Inevitably, Byron's letter to Murray would alter the dynamics of the friendship and the public face of the literary relationship.

November 1822

While Hunt had made a concerted effort to appeal to Byron on personal, political, and literary grounds during the first three months of their collaboration on *The Liberal*, Byron had, since at least early October, been having reservations about the miscellany and his living arrangements with Hunt. After receiving the news about the Byron-Murray gossip from his nephew, Hunt promptly wrote to his collaborator, confirming his knowledge of the 9 October letter to Murray. Hunt's reply, a copy of which survives in Mary Shelley's hand, shows that he had taken the matter in stride but felt a profound sense of disappointment:

> The whole of this business is very clear. Murray is very much enraged; the Tories are equally so at your having taken so decided a part against them; and you, suffer me to say, did not do one of the best or wisest things in the world in making, at the same time, or at any other time, so much & so little of that egregious knave. As to myself, I mitigated your epistolary carbonadoes ~~against~~ of him, it seems, to pretty purpose; & certainly have to regret that you condescended to defend your connexion with us to such a fellow.

Hunt was convinced that Byron's rank stood firmly in the way of their friendship and the literary collaboration, for he added: "I confess myself inclined on this occasion, as I have been on some others, to wish that you were only a fine writer & a poet, & not a Lord besides: not because I am none, but because your Lordship & your Bardship sometimes get mightily at variance, & do not know well how to get out of it" (*LHOL* [11 November 1822]). Byron answered Hunt the same day, ignoring his comments about rank and questioning the rumors about the Murray letter, claiming only "I do *not* believe that I used [offensive] expressions . . . but it is not impossible that I may—and if it were so—*that* does not justify Murray's circulation . . . of a private Correspondence." Byron admitted that the comments on Marianne Hunt and the Hunt children were "very true," but he firmly denied that he had issued personal insults against Hunt, refusing to believe it "till I see [them]" (*BLJ* 10:32). Byron did, however, reveal his reservations about *The Liberal*, saying he always "doubted" its success, but was "willing to make the experiment (rather than see [Hunt] disappointed)—against the remonstrances of all parties" (*BLJ* 10:32–3). The thrust of this epistolary exchange is clear, bringing into focus the low state to which the Byron-Hunt friendship and literary collaboration had descended in mid-November of 1822.

There were hints all along of Byron's uneasiness with Hunt and the arrangements in Italy. One hint was apparently contained in a stanza Byron had intended for *Don Juan*. Hunt recorded the following anecdote in *LBSC*:

> [Byron] had the modesty one day to bring me a stanza, intended for "Don Juan," in which he had sneered at them all, adding, with respect to one of them, that nobody but myself thought highly of him. He fancied I should put up with this, for the sake of being mentioned

in the poem, let the mention be what it might; an absurdity, which nothing but his own vanity had suggested. I told him, that I should be unable to consider the introduction of such a stanza as any thing but an affront, and that he had better not put it in. He said he would not, and kept his word.

(77–8)

No stanza in *Don Juan* mentions Hunt by name; and, if Byron had drafted such a stanza, it has not been recovered. Hunt's description of the intended stanza, however, points to the section in Canto XI, in which Byron famously mocked Keats, "who was killed off by one critique" (line 473). In this same section of Canto XI, Byron wrote that "Wordsworth has supporters, two or three" (line 470), a remark that doubtless included Hunt silently among Wordsworth's few "supporters."

If Byron did keep his word and not explicitly name Hunt in *Don Juan*, Byron was still willing to attack Hunt's circle of friends in his satire just as he already had in his prose writings on Pope and the Cockney School. In fact, Byron's attitude toward the character of the Cockney had been given comic expression in Canto VIII, which had been completed by the beginning of August 1822 in Pisa and thus during the same period that he was collaborating with Hunt on the first number of *The Liberal*.[51] There is no evidence that Hunt saw the draft of Canto VIII, but therein for the first time in *Don Juan*, Byron used the derisive rhetoric that *Blackwood's* had earlier used against Hunt and his circle. As the draft of Canto VIII reveals, Byron had originally written the concluding two lines of Stanza 125 (received Stanza 126) thus: "You Citizens of London! — and of Paris! — / Just ponder what a pious pastime war is"; but he then canceled "Citizens" and inserted "Cockneys," which appeared in the published version.[52] Byron's satire here suggests that the experience of war, or even the experience of traversing a site of carnage like the recently ravaged Waterloo, was beyond the reach and comprehension of the untraveled London Cockney. In Canto X, Stanza 80, Byron continued his satire on the "Cockney spirit" (line 638), associating such "spirit," appropriately, with the urban environs of London as Juan arrives at "Shooter's Hill" (line 640). Yet besides this brief notice, Byron seems to have left the Cockney theme undeveloped in Canto X, a transitional canto which covers both Juan's departure from the Russian Court of Empress Catherine II and his arrival in England. The draft of Canto XI, however, shows that Byron returned to the Cockney theme as Juan makes his way to London. In Stanza 28, the narrator paints this cynical picture of a city newly outfitted with gas lighting and a "spreading" cohort of Cockneys as the manuscript draft reveals:

But London's so well lit, that if Diogenes
    Could recommence to hunt his *honest man*,
And found him not amidst the various progenies

Of this enormous city's spreading spawn,
'Twere not for want of lamps to aid his dodging his
    Yet undiscovered treasure.

(lines 217–22)

In the draft of line 219, Byron originally wrote: "He would not find him in the Cockneys' progeny's."[53] By substituting "various" for "Cockneys," Byron muted the satire on the Cockney character, making the reference less specific. After drafting the lines, Byron may have realized that the intended contrast between Diogenes's *"honest man"* and the London Cockney may have been too pointed a remark for Hunt when he came to read the draft of Canto XI in manuscript, perhaps in the fair copy made by Mary Shelley, who referred to Canto XI, incidentally, as Byron's "<u>savage</u> Canto."[54]

    In fact, with the state of the Byron-Hunt friendship in serious doubt in the middle of November of 1822, Mary Shelley took a decisive step and wrote to Byron on Hunt's behalf. She admitted that her letter was a "painful thing" to "put forward" given the circumstances, but it nevertheless shows the strength of her personal commitment to Hunt despite the various unresolved private issues relating to Shelley that still existed between them. In this 16 November letter, she informed Byron that Hunt "thinks much of this & takes it much to heart," adding that he feels humiliated at the idea that "his poverty & not your will consents" you to go on with *The Liberal*. Mary Shelley then boldly suggested that Byron write to Murray with "a few words . . . in explanation or excuse" because such an act was "due" to the "literary companionship with [Hunt]." She concluded that "It would be a goodnatured thing" and "a prudent thing—since you would stop effectually the impertinence of Murray."[55] Byron replied immediately, reiterating his regard for Hunt's well-being as well as his motives for supporting *The Liberal*, but categorically denied having disrespected "Hunt's poverty." Revealingly, he also explained that his "friendship" with Hunt was not what it might have seemed on the outside and that in such matters he was "very limited." Byron admitted that his friendship with Lord Clare (a Harrow School classmate) had been the only friendship for which he ever felt "deserve[d] the name" or came close to the idealized friendship that Hunt had sought. All of his other relationships with men, Byron said, were "men-of-the world friendships" (*BLJ* 10:34). Despite her best efforts to reconcile the wren and the eagle, Mary Shelley, in the end, found the Byron-Hunt drama exasperating, recording in her journal a few days later: "I shall be glad to be more alone again. One ought to see no one or many—& confined to one society I shall loose [sic] all energy except that which I possess from my own resources, & I must be alone for these to be . . . put in activity."[56]

    Yet Mary Shelley's letter to Byron may have had its intended effect. Perhaps feeling some remorse for his role in the drama, Byron wrote to his London agent, Douglas Kinnaird, two days after the exchange with Mary Shelley: "between M. & the Hunts—I am in a dilemma—as a Man always is—who wishes to do a good action" (*BLJ* 10:35). That same day he also wrote to Murray, strongly criticizing the publisher for disclosing the contents of the letter of 9 October about the Hunts: "I shall not abandon a man like H[unt] because he is unfortunate." In fact, it was in this letter that Byron issued Murray a striking ultimatum: "I shall withdraw from you as a publisher—on every account even on your own—and I wish you good luck elsewhere—but if you can make out that you treated H. fairly—you may reckon me in other respects—as yrs. very truly" (*BLJ* 10:36). Hunt had by this time terminated his practice of showing Byron the letters bound for England to his brother and nephew concerning work on *The Liberal*. Consequently, Hunt could now speak more candidly of his relationship with Byron and the state of the collaboration in his correspondence with his family in London. Indeed, in the very next letter he sent to Henry Hunt after the mid-November rupture with Byron, Hunt made this telling remark about their friendship: "Mrs. Shelley tells me [Byron] says nothing of me to her but the handsomest things; & I can only say, that from *first to last* it is he that has courted my society, not I his." Nevertheless, Hunt remained firm in his commitment to the partnership with Byron as a matter of business: "He does not quarrel at all with me, though I have been obliged to act as you may guess. *All goes well, & will do so*" (*LHLL* 125).

Several weeks later, Byron's letter to Murray of 25 December nevertheless captured the hollowness of the personal situation in Albaro in the late months of 1822: "Mrs. Sh[elle]y is residing with the Hunts at some distance from me—I see them very seldom——and generally on account of their business." In this same letter, Byron added: "As to any community of feeling—thought—or opinion between L[eigh] H[unt] & me—there is little or none—we meet rarely—hardly ever—but I think him a good principled & able man—& must do as I would be done by.—I do not know what world he has lived in—but I have lived in three or four—and none of them like his Keats and Kangaroo terra incognita" (*BLJ* 10:69). Although Hunt had made the near thousand-mile voyage from London to Italy, he apparently remained, like Keats, an untraveled Cockney with a matching set of circumscribed values and tastes. At the end of the year, after working through the Shelley tragedy and producing two successful numbers of *The Liberal*, Byron and Hunt were living only a mile away from each other but were otherwise "three or four" worlds apart.

The Third Number of *The Liberal* and *The Age of Bronze*

The new year, however, brought unexpected changes in Byron's attitude toward *The Liberal*. In December, apparently unbeknownst to Hunt,

Byron had made his first effort to write new material for the miscellany, sending *The Age of Bronze* to Mary Shelley to copy and for Hunt to read and review on 10 January 1823.[57] The next day, Byron began composing *The Island* with publication in *The Liberal* again firmly in mind. By 20 January, Byron had completed a first draft of *The Island*, which he again sent over for Mary to copy and for Hunt to review. That same day, he sent Hunt yet another poem for the third number of the miscellany, an epigram "on Mr. Coke's Philo-genitiveness" (*BLJ* 10:88). Earlier in the month, Hunt had written to his brother with news of the "horrible long wind . . . from over the snowy Alps" (*LHLL* 133) that had brought surprisingly colder temperatures to Genoa that year, but Byron's renewed and emphatic interest in *The Liberal* may have been the more surprising news coming out of Italy in January of 1823.

More surprises were forthcoming. Byron may have been unprepared to hear from Hunt a week later that at least one of the two new poems (*The Island*) he had offered for *The Liberal* had been strongly criticized by his collaborator. At the same time, with the first of these two poems, *The Age of Bronze*, Byron may have failed to make a strong case for its inclusion in the third number of the miscellany. Indeed, when Byron sent *The Age of Bronze* to Mary Shelley and Hunt, he included the following introduction:

> I have sent to Mrs. S[helley] for the benefit of being copied—a poem of about seven hundred and fifty lines hight—the Age of Bronze—or Carmen Seculare et Annus mirabilis. . . . it is calculated for the reading part of the Million—being all on politics &c. &c. &c. and a review of the day in general—in my early English Bards style—but a little more stilted and somewhat too full of "epithets of war" and classical & historical allusions[;] if notes are necessary they can be added.—If it will do for "the Liberal" it and the Pulci will form (in size that is) a *good* half number.—But of this you can judge.—It is in the heroic couplet measure—which is "an old friend with a new face["].
>
> (*BLJ* 10:81)

On one level, Byron's deliberate return to his "English Bards style" may have been an attempt to please Hunt. The author of the *English Bards*-inspired *Feast of the Poets*, we recall, was also the proud owner of Byron's annotated copy of the fourth edition. Yet Byron also surely knew that Hunt would bristle at his announcement of a return to the "heroic couplet." And yet perhaps the most telling moment in Byron's 10 January letter to Hunt is Byron's instruction that his *Liberal* collaborator, after Mary Shelley has finished copying *The Age of Bronze*, read it and "judge" its merits for himself.

Jerome McGann observes that the "immediate occasion" for *The Age of Bronze* was the "Congress of Verona (October—December 1822)

where the principal European powers met to complete the settlement of
European political affairs after the defeat of Napoleon" (*CPW* 7:120).
As Peter W. Graham further explains, the congress had turned the revolutionary tide of the Romantic age, "restoring European monarchs to
the thrones from which Napoleon had toppled them." And although Napoleon, who had died in 1821, still serves as a focal point in *The Age of
Bronze*, his own "selfish temptation to supplant . . . the tyranny of kings"
has, for Byron, made him a broken symbol of heroic possibility in a new
reactionary age.[58] In the satire's lengthy opening sections on Napoleon,
Byron nevertheless retraces the former French emperor's career, providing a "mature evaluation," as Frederick L. Beaty says, of his former alter
ego. As it turns out, Byron's new evaluation still consisted of many of his
old arguments from *The Ode to Napoleon Buonaparte* as well as the Napoleonic lyrics Hunt had published in *The Examiner* in 1815 and 1816.[59]
Hunt, as we have seen, had firmly rejected Byron's earliest assessments
of Napoleon's character, when Byron had despaired over Napoleon's failure to end his life in battle or by suicide. Hunt was also unimpressed by
Byron's two Napoleonic lyrics: the first, which had lamented Napoleon's
defeat at Waterloo ("Napoleon's Farewell"), and the second, which had
urged a rekindling of revolutionary spirit in France ("On the Star of 'The
Legion of Honour'"). In *The Age of Bronze*, Byron's old feelings about
Napoleon, however, have once again been altered. Though a "time may
come" (line 129) when Napoleon's example inspires liberty, the speaker
realizes that the prospects are dim. In Napoleon's place stands the "blest
Alliance" (line 395) of Prussia, Russia, and Austria, "A pious unity! in
purpose one— / To melt three fools to a Napoleon" (lines 398–9), as well
as a new group of "reactionary ministers gathered at Verona."[60] The Byronic narrator thus realizes the futility of thinking a return to an earlier
Napoleonic period is still possible:

> The king of kings, and yet of slaves the slave,
> Who burst the chains of millions to renew
> The very fetters which his arm broke through,
> And crushed the rights of Europe and his own
> To flit between a dungeon and a throne?
>
> (lines 255–9)

Byron is under no illusion about Napoleon, who had "crushed" his own
"rights" when he descended from sublime heights to live out his days as
a domestic prisoner on the isle of St. Helena: "Behold the grand result
in yon lone isle, / . . . Sigh to behold the eagle's lofty rage / Reduced to
nibble at his narrow cage" (lines 53, 55–6).

Hunt would have readily agreed with Byron's assessment of the Congress
of Verona, and all such reactionary congresses of the post-Napoleonic
era. Yet Byron's decision to retrace Napoleon's career with many

of the same arguments he had used during the period of his Napoleonic conversations with Hunt in *The Examiner* between 1814 and 1816 may have been ill-timed. Byron must have known that such arguments would fail to find a sympathetic admirer in his *Liberal* collaborator. Moreover, Byron's satire on Marie-Louise, included in the penultimate section of *The Age of Bronze*, would have only served to recall for Hunt the full scope of their political disagreements from the first phase of their friendship. Whereas Hunt had been willing to suspend his judgment of Marie-Louise's "abandonment" of Napoleon in 1814, in 1823, as Byron saw it, the "imperial bride, / . . . The mother of the hero's hope" (lines 729, 731) had not only abandoned Napoleon in a desperate hour but was now consorting with Wellington and carrying on a "petty reign" (line 741) as Duchess of Parma, Europe's "pastoral realm of cheese" (line 748). "Petty" is an important word in *The Age of Bronze*, suggestive of the conditions into which Napoleon, Marie-Louise, Continental Europe, and England have all fallen. Yet "petty" seen in a different light—that of domestic life and the flesh and blood realm of sociability—becomes the foundation for moral, physical, and philosophical well-being that Hunt endorses. In his argument with Byron over Napoleon's character, we recall, Hunt had humanized the fallen emperor in order to teach Byron that Napoleon, by having been reduced to a "narrow cage" and confronted with "petty quarrels upon petty things" (line 61), stood only to benefit from such a humbling position. In *The Age of Bronze*, however, it would have been clear to Hunt that Byron had refused to relinquish his long-held view of Napoleon as a sublime figure.

Hunt, in the end, may not have revealed his thoughts on *The Age of Bronze* to Byron even though he had expressly called for Hunt's critical judgment upon it. In a letter to Elizabeth Kent on 22 May 1823, however, Hunt openly criticized Byron's latest satire on stylistic grounds.[61] In another, earlier letter to Kent on 7 April 1823, Hunt also revealed that Byron had "recalled [*The Age of Bronze*], upon the ground of it's being of temporary interest & necessary to appear without <u>delay</u>" (*LHOL*). Byron's letter to Douglas Kinnaird of 1 February confirms Hunt's statement: "By the way—[*The Age of Bronze*] was intended for a third number of H[unt]'s publication—but as that will not be published—and this is a *temporary* hit at Congress &c.—(as you will have seen by the poem if you have received it) perhaps it had better be published *now alone.*" (*BLJ* 10:94). Notably, this is the first time that Byron had indicated his desire to publish *The Age of Bronze* "*alone.*" With this letter in mind, Peter Cochran argues that Byron's motive for withdrawing his satire, and indeed for suggesting that *The Liberal* had folded, was a deliberate attempt to put an end to the miscellany and therefore his involvement with Hunt. Byron's letter to Hunt of 25 January, which Cochran does not mention, may lend support to the theory. At the same time, however, the 25 January letter, as we shall see, also reveals that there were other literary disagreements between Byron and Hunt at this time that suggest Byron's reason for withdrawing his latest material from *The Liberal* was much more complex than he made it out to be in his letter to Kinnaird.[62]

Hunt's Reading of *The Island*

Byron's January letters to Hunt confirmed that he had fully recommitted himself to *The Liberal*. Byron's decision to begin *The Island* the day after he announced *The Age of Bronze* reinforced this commitment. *The Island*, however, needs to be analyzed within the context of the Byron-Hunt collaboration, for the detailed exchange that the two collaborators had about the poem provides important details about its textual history and may also reveal overlooked ideas with direct relevance to Byron's shifting attitude toward *The Liberal* at the end of the month.

McGann identifies the dates of *The Island*'s composition from the manuscript, upon which Byron recorded 11 January (on the first page), 14 January (at the end of Canto I), and 10 February (at the end of Canto IV, the poem's concluding canto). Importantly, McGann also notes that "several passages in the MS.," the only surviving manuscript, "were added after [Byron] had completed a first version of the tale" (*CPW* 7:130–1). Nothing further seems to be known of this "first version of the tale," which has probably not survived. Yet Byron's letter to Hunt of 25 January may provide useful information about McGann's "first version" or perhaps another early, unidentified version of *The Island*. Byron's letter makes it clear that he had sent an early version of *The Island* to Hunt (and presumably Mary Shelley for copying) sometime before 25 January but after 14 January:

> As I did not look over the transcription till yesterday I did not perceive yr. *penciled* remarks on the thing which I am about at present.—— You are kind in one point—and right in the other.—But I have two things to avoid—the first that of running foul of my own "Corsair" and style—so as to produce repetition and monotony—and the other *not* to run counter to the reigning stupidity altogether— otherwise they will say that I am eulogizing *Mutiny*.—This must produce tameness in some degree—but recollect I am merely trying to write a poem a little above the usual run of periodical poesy—and I hope that it will at least be that.
>
> (*BLJ* 10:89–90)

Byron here confirms that Hunt had read a "transcription" of *The Island* and that he had also seen Hunt's "*penciled* remarks" on the manuscript. This is a significant detail, for Hunt's annotations on *The Island* would constitute the only known example of Hunt's marginalia in one of Byron's working manuscripts. Byron's letter also makes it clear that Hunt did not give *The Island*, in this "first" or early version, a favorable review. Hunt appears to have criticized the poem's "style" (heroic couplets) as well as its politics—its mutiny theme. Such criticisms from Hunt would not have been surprising to Byron, but the fact that Hunt made them at a moment when tensions between the two friends were elevated may have been alarming. Significantly, Hunt may have unwittingly terminated the creative momentum that Byron had been channeling toward *The Liberal* throughout January. Indeed, the evidence suggests that Hunt may have presented Byron with the opportunity to exit the collaboration earlier than he had even intended. Less than a week after receiving and reflecting upon Hunt's disapproving marginalia in *The Island*, Byron informed Kinnaird of his desire to publish *The Age of Bronze* on its own. That same week, Byron had probably also made up his mind to pursue the same course with *The Island*.

In *The Island,* Byron drew upon historical sources to construct a poetical romance set in the South Seas. The events in the poem focus on the famous story of Captain William Bligh and his mutinous crew aboard the HMS *Bounty*. In his poetical retelling, Byron weaves two interconnected stories out of his source material. The first is that of the mutinous crew led by Fletcher Christian, who, in Byron's poem, ultimately chooses to cast himself from a cliff when British expeditionary forces attempt to capture him and bring his fellow mutineers to account for their transgression. The second story, which provides the poem's comic ending, is the romance that develops between Neuha, a Toobonai Islander, and Torquil, a displaced British sailor. Because of the emphasis Byron places on the romance between Neuha and Torquil, critics have often seen *The Island* as something of an anomaly, a poem that clearly shares certain features with Byron's Turkish Tales but is otherwise unique in its positive acknowledgment of the redeeming powers of nature and love as well as law and order.[63]

Hunt, it seems, had criticized *The Island* for being politically "tame," a criticism that anticipated Carl Woodring's remark that *The Island* "pays tribute repeatedly . . . to loyalty, discipline, authority, and 'whatever Duty bade.'"[64] The last stand made by Fletcher Christian and his comrades provides an illustration of these qualities in the poem:

> They stood, the three, as the three hundred stood
> Who dyed Thermopylae with holy blood.
> But, ah! how different! 'tis the *cause* makes all,
> Degrades or hallows courage in its fall.
> O'er them no fame, eternal and intense,
> Blazed through the clouds of death and beckoned hence;
> No grateful country, smiling through her tears,

Begun the praises of a thousand years;
No nation's eyes would on their tomb be bent,
No heroes envy them their monument;
However boldly their warm blood was spilt,
Their life was shame, their epitaph was guilt.

(Canto IV, lines 259–70)

Byron told Hunt that he would not "eulogiz[e] *Mutiny*" in *The Island*, and we can see here that Byron kept his word. Still, it must be noted that Fletcher Christian, like other Byronic heroes, defiantly counts himself among the "fearless and the free" (Canto III, line 164). And yet he also acknowledges the harmful consequences of his mutinous actions for those around him. In fact, as Woodring suggests, the "generosity of his remorse either indicates a maturer Byron or demands that we grant a degree of altruism in the mixture of guilt and defiance."[65] In the end, however, the Neuha-Torquil romance story takes priority over the Christian Fletcher mutiny narrative, giving *The Island* its comic ending.

It is perhaps surprising that Hunt seems not to have carefully considered the Neuha-Torquil story for there are clear parallels to his own romance poems and prose fictions, including those published in the first number of *The Liberal*: the story of Dianora and Ippolito in "The Florentine Lovers" and all three characters in "Ariosto's Episode of Cloridan, Medoro, and Angelica." In Hunt's stories, strong female protagonists, driven by both passionate feeling and liberal understanding, rescue or save male protagonists from tragic ends. That Byron had deliberately taken this same scenario into consideration when he composed *The Island* can be seen, as McGann points out, in his decision to rework his historical source material, completely reversing the roles played by Neuha and Torquil in the sources.[66]

As Byron saw it, moreover, the poetic style he used in *The Island* was appropriate for the romance portion of the story. Byron felt that the "periodical" audience for whom he was writing would have had no objections on this score, telling Hunt, "You think higher of readers than I do—but I will bet you a flask of Falernum that the most *stilted* parts of the political 'Age of Bronze'—and the most *pamby* portions of the <South Sea> Toobonai Islanders—will be the most agreeable to the enlightened Public;—though I shall sprinkle some *uncommon* place here and there nevertheless" (*BLJ* 10:90). Byron's stated intention to add some "*uncommon* place" to the poem was probably a direct response to specific criticisms that Hunt included in his marginalia. Since the period when his translation of "Atys" and the first version of *The Feast of the Poets* appeared in *The Reflector*, Hunt had been developing his poetic "System" to counter Pope's "commonplace" style. As such, Byron's response to Hunt's criticism may be a facetious inversion of Hunt's own critical terminology. Also telling is Byron's statement about the "*pamby* portions" relating

to the "Toobonai Islanders." In his *Life of Johnson*, James Boswell had
also used the phrase in a derogatory way, suggesting that "*namby-pamby*
rhymes" were written "to please" women readers.[67] In his 1818 review
of Hunt's *Foliage*, John Taylor Coleridge thought that Hunt's loose style,
radical politics, and lax morals were a reflection of a "namby-pamby disposition" (*RR* C2:759). And in an early review of Wordsworth's *Poems*
(1807), Byron followed Francis Jeffrey's lead, in suggesting that the Lake
Poet's attempt to dignify poetry with "namby-pamby" that once "soothed
our cries in the cradle" (*CMP* 9) was a clear challenge to the accepted
standards of poetic decorum. Andrew Nicholson, meanwhile, traces the
origins of the expression to Henry Carey's "Namby-Pamby. A Panegyric
on the New Versification, Address'd to A[mbrose] P[hilips] Esq." (1725),
in which it signified "[m]awkishness" or "puerility" (*CMP* 270).

Byron's own critical terms thus elucidate the stylistic point he wished to
make when he referred Hunt to the "*pamby* portions" of *The Island*. The
specific "portions" would seemingly constitute not only those involving
the Toobonai, but also those involving Neuha, a Toobonai Islander, and
Torquil. In fact, in the earliest description of the pair, we learn that they
are "children of the isles" (Canto II, line 274), who are "Lov'd to the
last whatever intervenes / Between us and our childhood's sympathy"
(Canto II, lines 277–8). What becomes clear in this opening description
of Neuha and Torquil is that their love, their innocence, and their shared
sympathy all point back to a state of childlike innocence. And the language that Byron uses to describe the physical characteristics of Neuha
and Torquil, as Byron had suggested to Hunt, reinforces the innocence
that defines their romance in *The Island*. In the climactic fourth canto,
for instance, when the lovers dive into the ocean and make for Neuha's
hidden sea-cave, Byron heightens the description with classically infused
"*pamby*" that seems it would have been appealing to Hunt had he encountered this section of the text: "And where was he, the Pilgrim of the
Deep, / Following the Nereid?" (Canto IV, lines 95–6) and "Did Neuha
with the Mermaids comb her hair / Flowing o'er ocean as it streamed
in air?" (Canto IV, lines 101–2). Hunt's tableaux of "Nymphs" in his
poem of the same name in *Foliage* is also lightly painted, with Nymphs
"slumbering through the air" (Part II, line 60), one "lifting her arms
to tie / Her locks into a flowing knot" (Part II, lines 73–4). *The Island*
makes other strong gestures at such stylings, with Torquil, who "Pursued [Neuha's] liquid steps" (Canto IV, line 114) to her underwater cave,

> Whose only portal was the keyless wave
> (A hollow archway by the sun unseen,
> Save through the billows' glassy veil of green,
> In some transparent ocean holiday,
> When all the finny people are at play).
>
> (Canto IV, lines 122–6)

Although we can find similar examples of what Byron refers to as *"pamby"* stylings elsewhere in his poetry, in *The Island* they take on new meaning. In the Donna Julia and Haidée episodes in *Don Juan*, for instance, the style that Byron adopted for these famously "sweet" romance scenes stands in sharp contrast to that offered by Byron's relentlessly intrusive narrator in Canto I (Stanzas 123–7) and Canto II (Stanzas 199–216) respectively. In *The Island*, however, the Neuha-Torquil romance, though closely resembling the Juan-Haidée story, is notably developed without the sarcasm that intrudes upon the romance vignettes in *Don Juan*. Byron's flippant treatment of love, patriotism, and religion in his satire, of course, had been decried by conservative readers and reviewers. And Byron seems to have had these readers in mind when he told Hunt that the *"pamby"* romance scenes in *The Island* were those that would "be the most agreeable to the enlightened Public."

Byron's defense of *The Island*, however, made little difference. By the end of January, he had already decided to withdraw the poem along with *The Age of Bronze* from *The Liberal*. Hunt sensed that his critical remarks on *The Island* may have influenced Byron's decision, writing in a letter to his sister-in-law, "Lord Byron has never written any thing for the Liberal, but a poem called the Island, which will after all be published by my brother by itself. I believe this is partly because he perceived I thought little of a great deal of it, which is written in a very <u>rhymy</u> & conventional way; but he says (which is true) that it is too long of it's kind, & moreover he wishes to see how the public still like him <u>out</u> of the Liberal" (*LHOL* [7 April 1823]). Hunt refused to look beyond the "conventional" couplets and the "tame" politics of Byron's *Island*. Hunt later defended his position in similar terms in *LBSC*: "Lord Byron would have put his 'Island' in [*The Liberal*], and I believe another poem [*The Age of Bronze*], if I had thought it of use." Hunt added that such would have been unnecessary, with both poems being "so much dead weight" (62). What Hunt did not admit publicly in 1828, however, was that his reaction to *The Island* and *The Age of Bronze* may have also been a factor in accelerating Byron's departure from the collaboration and the termination of *The Liberal*. In 1850, in the *Autobiography*, Hunt was only then willing to admit his role in the demise of the miscellany: "I must confess, that I did not mend the matter by my own inability to fall in cordially with his ways, and by a certain jealousy of my position, which prevented me, neither very wisely nor justly, from manifesting the admiration due to his genius, and reading the manuscripts he showed me with a becoming amount of thanks and good words" (3:59).

The Late Numbers of *The Liberal*: "The Choice" and "The Book of Beginnings"

By the beginning of February 1823, Byron had unofficially excused himself from *The Liberal*. Having had *The Island* (and *The Age of Bronze*) rejected by Hunt, Byron was now willing to embrace the advice that had just arrived from Thomas Moore:

> I am most anxious to know that you mean to emerge out of the Liberal. It grieves me to urge any thing so much against Hunt's interest; but I should not hesitate to use the same language to himself, were I near him. I would, if I were you, serve him in every possible way but this—I would give him (if he would accept of it) the profits of the same works, published separately—but I would *not* mix myself up in this way with others. I would *not* become a partner in this sort of miscellaneous "*pot au feu*," where the bad flavour of one ingredient is sure to taint all the rest. I would be, if I were *you*, alone, single-handed, and, as such, invincible.[68]

Byron reassured his friend, "Of Hunt I see little—once a month or so, and then on his own business, generally" (*BLJ* 10:105). It was becoming clear that the radical kinship that Shelley had envisioned with Byron and Hunt in Italy was no longer sustainable. For Byron and Hunt, the idealistic literary experiment and political collaboration on *The Liberal* had become a mere matter of "business."

Unlike the material that Hunt had produced for the first and second issues of *The Liberal*, the material he produced for the third and fourth numbers shows less creative sympathy with Byron's literary tastes and interests. The thematic concerns of Hunt's last two significant poetical contributions to the miscellany make this clear. For instance, "The Choice," Hunt's reworking of John Pomfret's poem of the same name, may have been written as an act of creative engagement not with Byron but with Mary Shelley, who produced her own version of "The Choice" sometime in the first half of 1823, perhaps at or near the same time as Hunt wrote his version.[69] Both poems are autobiographical meditations that look back to happier periods while wrestling with the sad realities of lost lives and friendships in the present. For Hunt and Mary Shelley, the poetical exercise may have even served a therapeutic function. Planned creative engagements, such as Hunt's famous poetry contests, had, of course, been staged with Shelley and Keats in England. But with Keats and Shelley both gone, Hunt could do little more than dream of "one happy house" outfitted with friends, books, and music:

> I'd have two friends live near me, perhaps three:
> Time was, when in one happy house——But he
> Has gone to his great home, over the dreadful sea.
> Oh Nature, we both loved thee!
>
> > (2:273, lines 235–8)

Written after Hunt's break with Byron, "The Choice" takes on complex meaning in the context of their personal relations. A meditation on art, friendship, and politics, the poem addresses Byron only through his absence, for the author of the brooding *Childe Harold* is nowhere to be found within the social or artistic landscape that Hunt sketches in "The Choice."[70] Although the poem does not privilege despair, in the end Hunt imagines his own death and final resting place, finding himself having to choose between two "vistas" at his "travail's end" (2:273, line 412): "One, in a gentle village, my old home; / The other, by the softened walls of Rome" (2:273, lines 414–5). The indeterminacy of the poem's final couplet gains its strength from forcing the reader to weigh "home" and "Rome" equally: the bucolic pastures of Hampstead are held in check by the beckoning walls, "softened" by the presence of two young poets, of Rome.

Hunt's decision to withdraw from literary engagement with Byron in the spring of 1823 is evident in another major poem written at this time and published in the third issue of *The Liberal*: "The Book of Beginnings." The poem is written in the same digressive style of "The Dogs," and thus in the style of *Don Juan*, but has none of the political satire of that earlier piece. "The Book of Beginnings" instead showcases the depth of Hunt's reading in literary history, focusing, as the title suggests, on the formal ways in which poems and stories have traditionally commenced. Yet the poem's playful surface belies the serious critical concerns that Hunt raises in the notes to the poem. Indeed, in the accompanying notes, Hunt attacks Pope's poetry and character with renewed interest and vigor. As such, it becomes evident that "The Book of Beginnings" was not written to appeal to Byron's poetical sensibilities in the same way that "The Dogs," "The Florentine Lovers," "Ariosto's Episode of Cloridan, Medoro, and Angelica," and perhaps other works produced for the first two numbers of *The Liberal* had been. Rather, "The Book of Beginnings," written at a time when the friendship had been irreparably severed, may have been Hunt's attempt to assert his own creative independence from the author of *The Age of Bronze* and *The Island*.

In Stanza 20 of "The Book of Beginnings," Hunt contrasts Pope with Dryden, praising "Dryden's Religio Laici" as having an exordium which "put to shame / All the monotonous lines we hold so dear, / Time-beaters for dull heads."[71] Hunt, of course, has Pope and his imitators in mind when he speaks of "monotonous lines," but he attempts to soften the blow: "Think not I blame / Nevertheless the glorious Rape o' the Lock, / The airiest wit that ever rais'd a joke." Hunt's qualification is half-hearted at best for in the notes to these lines, he takes the opportunity to criticize Pope's character. Indeed, Hunt contrasts Dryden and Pope with masculine bravado, declaring that the latter's "lady-like versification" lacks Dryden's "vigorous touch," which "rescues" the reader "from monotony." Hunt's renewed critical attack against Pope, the first explicit attack in the context of *The Liberal*, continues thus: "Of Pope, I have no scruple to repeat, especially as the public are now used to the repetition from others, that he had a poor ear for the music of his art, as well as for all other music" (2:121). Hunt adds, "what is called his system of versification, was made up of nothing but their unvaried repetition" (2:122). Hunt then criticizes the multitude of readers and writers who admire Pope's style for the ease of reading and imitating it. We might note that Byron had a very different notion of the work that the Popeian couplet demanded. Because of its highly compressed structure, Byron thought it was especially difficult to achieve the balance, rhythmically and substantively, that the couplet form required.[72] For Hunt, however, Pope's measure not only fails because of its "dull," repetitive quality but also because the "greatest poets" before Pope (Hunt may have Spenser and Milton in mind) were not content to use it.

In another lengthy note on Pope in "The Book of Beginnings," Hunt develops his critique of the author of *The Rape of the Lock* in a more personal way. Although Bowles, in his preface to his 1806 edition of Pope, had attacked the poet's personality—specifically, his moral character— Hunt claims that his reason for subjecting Pope's personality to critical scrutiny was to illustrate a literary quality, as suggested by a bust of Pope's head he once saw in the "British Institution." The "nose" of this bust, Hunt recalls, "seemed the very 'tip of taste'; as if it were snuffing up the odour of his Banstead mutton, or the flowers he had gathered for Miss Blount. And when I recollected the fine dark eye in his painted portrait, the simile was complete." Attempting to justify the writing of personalities, Hunt further explains that the "physical conformation of a writer becomes a just ground of criticism and illustration, when there can be no suspicion of malignity" (2:127). But the discussion of Pope's physical constitution, in Hunt's final analysis, seems calculated to offer little more than a provocation to his *Liberal* collaborator: "it is unnecessary to inform the reader, that [Pope] had a person equally small and infirm, and that he could not even dress without assistance. I cannot help thinking that there is the same difference between Pope and Dryden in their verses, as in their persons" (2:128). Although Hunt concludes his comparison by praising the genius of both poets, it becomes clear that he has executed his critique of Pope's character in "The Book of Beginnings" with an inordinate amount of personality. In the third number of *The Liberal*, Hunt may have thus been gesturing toward the *ad hominem* arguments that he would use against former friends and acquaintances in *Lord Byron and Some of His Contemporaries* in 1828. Indeed, given the context in which he composed "The Book of Beginnings"—his personal break with Byron over the Murray gossip and his creative disagreements with Byron over *The Age of Bronze* and *The Island*—we can surmise that Hunt's extended attack on Pope was, by design, no attempt to appeal to Byron's literary sensibilities or to work toward a reconciliation with his *Liberal* collaborator.

In July of 1823, Byron left Hunt, *The Liberal*, and Italy behind when he sailed for Greece. Hunt had informed Elizabeth Kent as early as 22 May of Byron's plans: "Lord B. does talk of going to Greece, & has reasons which I dare say may really induce him to do so; though I equally dare say, he will stick to the Greeks when he gets there, as little as he does to any thing else."[73] Hunt's cynical remark on Byron's fitness for commitment was perhaps another preview of the bitter assessment of Byron's character that would become public record in *Lord Byron and Some of His Contemporaries*. It is not surprising that Thornton Hunt, Hunt's eldest son, excised this sentence from Hunt's letter to Kent (and did the same to many similar letters relating to his father's friendship with Byron) when he collected, edited, and published Hunt's correspondence not long after his death. But Byron's departure for Greece, Hunt knew, also meant the end of *The Liberal*. "This you will doubt," he told Kent, but "it is certainly a doubtful matter whether he has more helped or hurt the Liberal. But at all events it will be better to set up another work with another title." Hunt was no longer living under the powerful illusion of a personal and creative fellowship with Byron in Italy—an illusion that had, nevertheless, propelled much of the creative work Hunt produced for the first two numbers of *The Liberal* between July and November of 1822. When Hunt reflected on his time with Byron in Italy five years later, he confessed that the radical experiment in collaboration had been a "mistake":

> As it was, there was something not unsocial nor even unenjoying in our intercourse, nor was there any appearance of constraint; but, upon the whole, it was not pleasant: it was not cordial. There was a sense of mistake on both sides. However, this came by degrees. At first there was hope, which I tried hard to indulge; and there was always some joking going forward; some melancholy mirth, which a spectator might have taken for pleasure.
>
> (*LBSC* 37)

By the spring of 1823, Hunt was now just as eager as Byron was to move on from the "black place" (*LBSC* 18) that Italy had become.

Notes

1　Percy Bysshe Shelley, *The Letters of Percy Bysshe Shelley*, ed. Frederick L. Jones, 2 vols. (Oxford: Oxford University Press, 1964), 1:557.
2　William H. Marshall, *Byron, Shelley, Hunt, and "The Liberal"* (Philadelphia: University of Pennsylvania Press, 1960), 1.
3　Percy Bysshe Shelley, *The Letters*, 2:344.

4 Jeffrey N. Cox, *Poetry and Politics in the Cockney School: Keats, Shelley, Hunt, and Their Circle* (Cambridge: Cambridge University Press, 1998), 188–9.

5 Countess of Blessington, Marguerite, *Lady Blessington's Conversations of Lord Byron*, ed. Ernest J. Lovell, Jr. (Princeton, NJ: Princeton University Press, 1969), 48.

6 Nicholas Roe, "Leigh Hunt, Charles Lamb, and Virginia Wolf," in *Romantic Presences in the Twentieth Century*, ed. Mark Sandy (Farnham: Ashgate Publishing, 2012), 17.

7 Byron himself spoke of *The Liberal* as a "failure." See his letter to John Hunt from 2 April 1823 in *'What Comes Uppermost': Byron's Letters and Journals*, ed. Leslie A. Marchand (Newark, DE: University of Delaware Press, 1994), 71.

8 Jane Stabler, "Religious Liberty in the 'Liberal,'" in *Branch: Britain, Representation and Nineteenth-Century History*, ed., Dino Franco Felluga. Extension of *Romanticism and Victorianism on the Net*. Web: 2. See also Daisy Hay, "Liberals, *Liberales* and *The Liberal*: A Reassessment," *European Romantic Review* 19, no. 4 (2008): 307–20.

9 Timothy Webb, "Arrival of Don Juan at Shooter's Hill: The Politics of Romance," in *Lord Byron 'Correspondence(s)'* ed., Christiane Vigouroux (Paris: François-Xavier de Guibert, 2008), 201, 206.

10 Leigh Hunt, "Passages Marked in Montaigne's Essays by Lord Byron," in the *New Monthly Magazine* for 1 January 1827, 27. Hunt confirmed that the copy of Montaigne "was lent [Byron] by myself while residing under the same roof with him; and he read the whole three volumes through with an interest, which he expressed in strong terms, and which, indeed, is very obvious."

11 James Bieri, *Percy Bysshe Shelley: A Biography*. repr. (Baltimore, MD: Johns Hopkins University Press, 2008), 651–2.

12 Bieri, *Percy Bysshe Shelley*, 654.

13 Bieri, *Percy Bysshe Shelley*, 655.

14 Marshall, *Byron, Shelley, Hunt*, 81; for Marshall's estimate of sales figures, see 162; for a list of reviews and notices, see Appendix IV, 240–5.

15 Peter Isaac, "John Murray II and Oliver & Boyd, His Edinburgh Agents, 1819–1835," in *Printing Places: Locations of Book Production & Distribution since 1500*, eds. John Hinks and Catherine Armstrong (New Castle and London: Oak Knoll Press & the British Library, 2005), 139.

16 Of the third number of *The Liberal*, Mary Shelley reported that "LB. is better pleased with it than any other." *The Letters of Mary Wollstonecraft Shelley*, ed. Betty T. Bennett, 3 vols. (Baltimore, MD: Johns Hopkins University Press, 1980–88), 1:338.

17 Carl Woodring, *Politics in English Romantic Poetry* (Cambridge, MA: Harvard University Press, 1970), 193.

18 Marshall, *Byron, Shelley, Hunt*, 126–34.

19 The text is taken from Leigh Hunt and Lord Byron, *The Liberal. Verse and Prose from the South*. 2 vols. (London: John Hunt, 1822–3). All references hereafter are taken from this edition and cited parenthetically by page number and line number (if applicable).

20 Hay, "Liberals, *Liberales*," 311.

21 Marshall, *Byron, Shelley, Hunt*, 76.

22 The source of Hunt's "Florentine Lovers" is in Marco Lastri, *L'Osservatore Fiorentino. Sugli Edifizi Della Sua Patria. Terza Edizione*. 8 vols. (Firenze: Presso Gaspero Ricci, 1821), 8:27–33.

23 See *BEM* 12, December 1822, 775–6.

24 See *A* 3:258. Hunt explored the story of the Prince of Navarre in an original drama he had called *The Secret Marriage*.

25 Qtd. in Susan J. Wolfson, *Romantic Interactions: Social Being & the Turns of Literary Action* (Baltimore, MD: Johns Hopkins University Press, 2010), 4.

26 See *CPW* 6:562–70. *The Deformed Transformed* was drafted early in 1822 but sent to Mary Shelley for copying in November of 1822 not long after Hunt must have written "The Florentine Lovers."

27 Thomas Medwin, *Medwin's Conversations of Lord Byron*, ed. Ernest J. Lovell Jr. (Princeton, NJ: Princeton University Press, 1966), 254. See also Lovell, *Captain Medwin: Friend of Byron and Shelley* (Austin: University of Texas Press, 1962), 133.

28 Byron seems to have started learning Italian in 1810 in Greece. See Leslie A. Marchand, *Byron: A Biography*, 3 vols. (New York: Alfred A. Knopf, 1957), 1:255.

29 See, for instance, the review in the *Monthly Magazine*: "We, therefore, think this translation superior to any thing of Mr. Hunt's which we have seen: it has more of what is good in his manner, and abounds in fewer of his faults" (*RR* C2:664).

30 In the Keats-Shelley House in Rome is an inscribed copy of the *Anacreonteius, Poeta Lyricus* (Cantabrigiæ: Recentioribus Typis Academicis, 1705) that Hunt apparently presented to Byron in April of 1816: because the "copy was not among the books sold at Byron's April 1816 auction," it "is apparent from the catalogue" that Byron "seems to have kept Hunt's gift and taken it with him to Continental Europe." See: www.keats-shelley-house. org/en/news/two-major-new-acquisitions-for-the-keats-shelley-memorial-association. The book also contains seven of Hunt's "autograph translations" of Anacreon's poetry. Had Byron indeed been in possession of the book, he thus would have presumably seen these translations. Hunt had published a translation of Anacreon in *The Examiner* on 31 March 1816 and included several more translations in *Foliage* in 1818. For more bibliographical details of this interesting relic of the Byron-Hunt friendship, see *The Library of the Late Edith Rockefeller McCormick* (New York: American Art Association Anderson Galleries, Inc., 1934), 10–1.

31 "Hoole's and Fairfax's Tasso" in *The Indicator*, March 29, 1820, 193–4.

32 See Hunt's introduction to "Ariosto's Episode of Cloridan, Medoro, and Angelica," in *The Liberal*, 1:139–40.

33 This article has been transcribed by Webb. See Timothy Webb, "Religion of the Heart: Leigh Hunt's Tribute to Shelley," *The Keats-Shelley Review* 7 (1992): 1–61.

34 Timothy Webb, "Catullus and the Missing Papers: Leigh Hunt, Byron, and John Murray," *The Byron Journal* 42, no. 2 (2014): 114. See also Susanna Morton Braund, "*Libertas* or *Licentia*?" in *Free Speech in Classical Antiquity*, eds. Ineke Slutter and Ralph M. Rosen (Leiden: Brill, 2004), 416.

35 Louis Crompton, *Byron and Greek Love: Homophobia in 19th-Century England* (Berkeley: University of California Press, 1985), 61–2.

36 Patricia Palmer, *The Severed Head and the Grafted Tongue* (Cambridge: Cambridge University Press, 2013), 57.

37 See H. S. Milford's highly useful collations for lines 12 and 50, respectively, in his edition of "Medoro and Cloridano" in *The Poetical Works of Leigh Hunt* (Oxford: Oxford University Press, 1923), 731.

38 Virgil, *Virgil*, trans. H. Rushton Fairclough, 2 vols. (Cambridge, MA: Harvard University Press, 1986), 2:130–1.

39 In 1839, for example, Mary Shelley questioned Hunt for censoring parts of Shelley's translation of the *Symposium*, which she was then preparing

for Edward Moxon's edition of Shelley's works. For the details of this relevant episode, see Michael O'Neill, "'Trying to Make It as Good as I Can': Mary Shelley's Editing of P. B. Shelley's Poetry and Prose," in *Mary Shelley and Her Times*, eds. Betty T. Bennett and Stuart Curran (Baltimore, MD: Johns Hopkins University Press, 2000), 191–4.

40 Bieri, *Percy Bysshe Shelley*, 616–9.

41 See Thomas Moore, *The Letters of Thomas Moore*, ed. Wilfred S. Dowden, 2 vols. (Oxford: Oxford University Press, 1964), 2:502.

42 See Brown's 5 September 1822 letter to Joseph Severn in *The Letters of Charles Armitage Brown*, ed. Jack Stillinger (Cambridge, MA: Harvard University Press, 1966), 103.

43 *LHLL* 126.

44 For Hunt's letter, see NLS MS. 43449. For Marianne Hunt's diary entry, see R. Brimley Johnson, *Shelley-Leigh Hunt: How Friendship Made History* (London: Ingpen and Grant, 1929), 337.

45 Neil Ramsey, *The Military Memoir and Romantic Literary Culture, 1780–1835* (Farnham: Ashgate Publishing, 2009), 109, 112.

46 *The Manuscripts of the Younger Romantics. Volume XIII: The Prisoner of Chillon and "Don Juan" Canto IX*, ed. Peter Cochran (New York: Garland Publishing Inc., 1995), 75–6.

47 The text is reproduced from BL Add. MS. 31808, f. 219.

48 BL Add. MS. 31808, f. 221.

49 In Canto III of *The Island*, one of Fletcher Christian's fellow mutineers of the "lower order," after being wounded, "Exclaimed 'G---d damn!' Those syllables intense,— / Nucleus of England's native eloquence" (*CPW* 7:57, lines 125–6).

50 The "motto" that Byron alludes to can be found in Hunt's draft ("The Pack of Hounds"), where it appears as "Eh! Ye pack of hounds!" and is followed by the attribution "Common-place Phrase," which has been canceled by Hunt in the manuscript and replaced with "Old play." Neither the attribution nor the motto appeared in the published version in *The Liberal*, thus suggesting that Hunt did, in fact, follow Byron's advice. See BL Add. MS. 31808, f. 204.

51 *The Manuscripts of the Younger Romantics. Lord Byron. Volume XI: "Ode to Napoleon Buonaparte" and "Don Juan" Canto VIII and Stanzas from III and IX*, ed. Cheryl Giuliano (New York: Garland Publishing Inc., 1997), 73–5.

52 *The Manuscripts of the Younger Romantics. Lord Byron. Volume XI*, 164–5.

53 *The Manuscripts of the Younger Romantics. Lord Byron. Volume IX: "Don Juan," Cantos X, XI, XII, XVI*, ed. Andrew Nicholson (New York: Garland Publishing Inc., 1993), 76–7.

54 Mary Wollstonecraft Shelley, *The Letters*, 1:284.

55 Mary Wollstonecraft Shelley, *The Letters*, 1:288.

56 Mary Wollstonecraft Shelley, *The Journals of Mary Shelley*, eds. Paula R. Feldman and Diana Scott Kilvert (Baltimore, MD: Johns Hopkins University Press, 1995), 443.

57 See *BLJ* 10:81.

58 Peter W. Graham, *Lord Byron* (New York: Twayne Publishers, 1998), 74–6.

59 Frederick L. Beaty, *Byron the Satirist* (Dekalb: Northern Illinois University Press, 1985), 174.

60 Beaty, *Byron the Satirist*, 175.

61 See MS. Pforz. LH 0094.

62 Peter Cochran, "Byron's 'Divided Loyalties,'" in *The Burning of Byron's Memoirs* (Newcastle upon Tyne: Cambridge Scholars Publishing, 2014), 33.

63 See Timothy H. Flake, "Byronic Heroism in the Island," *The Byron Journal* 25 (1997): 44–59.
64 Carl Woodring, *Politics in English Romantic Poetry* (Cambridge, MA: Harvard University Press, 1970), 222.
65 Woodring, *Politics*, 223.
66 See *CPW* 7:132.
67 James Boswell, *Life of Johnson*. repr. (Oxford: Oxford University Press, 1966), 129–30.
68 Moore, *The Letters*, 2:514.
69 Mary Wollstonecraft Shelley, *The Journals*, 490–4. The manuscript of Mary Shelley's "Choice" is dated July 1823 though it may have been started earlier in the year; Emily W. Sunstein suggests that she "composed" the poem specifically "for Hunt." See Emily W. Sunstein, *Mary Shelley: Romance and Reality* (Boston, MA: Little, Brown and Company, 1989), 239.
70 For a recent discussion of Hunt's "Choice," see Michael Edson, "Leigh Hunt, John Pomfret, and the Politics of Retirement," *European Romantic Review* 25, no. 4 (2014): 423–42.
71 The text is taken from *The Liberal*, 2:103 (97–135). Hereafter all quotations are cited parenthetically by page number.
72 Blessington, *Lady Blessington's Conversations*, 152.
73 MS. Pforz. LH 0094.

Conclusion
"A Painful Retrospect"

In the marginal space at the bottom of the last page of text in a copy of Hunt's *Lord Byron and Some of His Contemporaries* (hereafter *LBSC*), an early reader left the following manuscript note: "There is no book that hath not some corresponding good!—My bad memory above is it enabled me to read this <u>twaddle</u> again Christmas 1864 for the last time! certainly! Xmas day. 'Alone! but not lonely'!—May I never have worse company." On the same page "above" the note, the reader recorded the following details: "Finished November 14—1854" and "again June 21—1861." The reader, it turns out, had finished the book on two other occasions. On the title page, the following two notes appear in faded script: "read Decb. 1849" and "read again <u>1852</u>."[1] Despite making poor "company," Hunt's "<u>twaddle</u>" about Byron and his contemporaries clearly had more than ordinary appeal for this mid-nineteenth century reader. The reader's reaction to *LBSC*, however, was not unique. Many readers of Hunt's "Byron Book," as it has come to be known, have found it to be a volume that elicits strong, often hostile comment.[2]

Hunt admitted that he experienced "involuntary" feelings of "spleen and indignation" as he composed the lengthy Byron portion of *LBSC*.[3] For Hunt, to return to Byron even in imagination was, as he described the experience, "a painful retrospect" (*LBSC* v). Published in the winter of 1828, *LBSC* is a collection of loosely connected "Contemporary Memoirs" of Hunt's friends and literary acquaintances.[4] The two longest sections of the book, the opening chapter on Byron and a concluding autobiographical section, both dwell extensively on Hunt's "black" (*LBSC* 18) period in Italy. There, among other private distresses, Hunt lived through the death of Shelley, the failure of *The Liberal*, and the dissolution of his friendship with Byron. Yet these painful personal experiences, which may have moved some readers, jarringly coexist in *LBSC* with a strong and uncharacteristic tendency to use sarcasm and personality for derisive ends—namely, to discredit Byron's genius and literary celebrity. Moreover, Hunt chose to preface the book by disclosing his commercial motivations for producing it. The volume, as Hunt explained it, was a form of repayment to his publisher, Henry Colburn, who had financed the Hunts' return journey to

England in the fall of 1825. After failing to produce a projected work on an entirely different plan ("a selection" from Hunt's own writings "preceded by a biographical sketch" (*LBSC* iii)), Hunt said that he "finally made up [his] mind to enlarge and enrich [the work] with an account of Lord Byron" (*LBSC* iv). Such details, among other remarks relating to Hunt's struggle to produce the work for Colburn, were not reassuring advertisements for a book that was perceived to be controversial before it even appeared. Hunt did claim, however, that he had other purposes for producing his bitter portrait of Byron in *LBSC*, one being that "an exposition of the real feelings and opinions of any body superior to the ordinary run of mankind, would serve to strike out new lights for the conduct and improvement of the human race, even, perhaps, from what were considered his errors" (103). Few readers have found Hunt's reasoning on this score to be sufficient justification for the book's publication.

John Gibson Lockhart, for one, was violently offended by *LBSC*, writing in the *Quarterly Review* for April 1828:

> Mr. Hunt lays it down as an axiom, that it is impossible to have too much information about truly great men; and this principle has governed him throughout the composition of his autobiography. Whether Rousseau, or Montaigne, (from whom he takes his motto,) or Colley Cibber's apology, formed, to his fancy, the chief and best model, we know not; but on the whole, it is our opinion that the present work will remind ordinary readers of Brasbridge's Memoirs more frequently than of any others, except perhaps those of P. P.[5]

Lockhart's attempt to discern in *LBSC* a "chief and best model" inevitably leads him away from highly regarded examples of autobiography (Rousseau and Montaigne) to the worst illustrations of the genre: Joseph Brasbridge's *The Fruits of Experience* (1824) and the satirical "Memoirs of P. P. Clerk." The former volume, near contemporary with *LBSC*, was described retrospectively by a Victorian reader as being "full of pleasant gossip about the tavern-clubs, card-parties, and minor gaieties, of St. Brides."[6] For Lockhart, however, Brasbridge's memoirs, trivial as he believed they were, threatened social and literary decorum, reflecting the low state of English letters that was becoming even more apparent with the gossip-filled memoirs being produced about Byron after his death.[7] Lockhart, as we have seen, had a history of abusing Hunt in the pages of *Blackwood's Edinburgh Magazine* and his review of *LBSC*, as we might expect, was written in a savage manner. Yet, in the midst of the vitriol, Lockhart also managed to offer Hunt some sensible advice: even if all that Hunt had written about Byron were true, Lockhart suggested, Hunt could have remained "silent."[8] For the creator of the "Cockney School" series, such advice surprisingly shows a narrow understanding of Hunt's public character: silence had never been the practice of the former editor of *The Examiner*. And as Hunt stated in *LBSC*, "I merely state the truth, because others have mis-stated it, and because I begin to be sick of maintaining a silence, which does no good to others, and is only turned against one's self" (16). Hunt's preface to *LBSC* repeatedly emphasizes this need to speak the "truth" about Byron. Such self-assured pronouncements, of course, invite scrutiny. In fact, for Annette Cafarelli, the genre of biography itself, which the Romantics inherited, in large part, from Samuel Johnson, had long been regarded with suspicion. Cafarelli argues that "Johnsonian biography implicitly questioned the attainability of accuracy" and that the "*Lives [of the Poets]* revealed the instability of meaning in every verbal text."[9] Wordsworth, perhaps surprisingly among the Romantics, became highly suspicious of biography, believing the genre to be a detriment to the cultivation and maintenance of artistic genius. For Wordsworth, biography was "an *art*" of the most undesirable kind because its "laws," as he believed, were "determined by the imperfections of our nature, and the constitution of society." In other words, there was no "Truth" in biography "as in the sciences, and in natural philosophy, to be sought without scruple."[10]

The Byron portion of *LBSC*, which focused on "imperfections" and what Hunt called "disagreeable truths" (vii), would seem to confirm Wordsworth's reservations about the dangers of Romantic biography couched in the rhetoric of "Truth." Indeed, recent commentators have shown that Hunt's portrait of Byron in *LBSC* is a darkly subjective one: for Cafarelli, Hunt's Byron character in *LBSC* suffers from physical as well as mental "disorder and malaise," while his biographer remains vibrant and healthy.[11] For Julian North, Hunt's Byron character is a "failure" for his inability "to establish close relationships with friends and even with lovers," while his biographer remains a model of private virtue and domestic fulfillment.[12] There is no doubt that Hunt's "spleen and indignation," as he said, had directed his thoughts as he relived his relationship with Byron in *LBSC*. Nevertheless, Hunt's "Byron Book" is a more complex volume than its published contents alone suggest. Though little discussed, *LBSC*'s textual history, for instance, shows that Hunt was, as he claimed in the book's preface, a highly reluctant biographer of Byron. In the preface, which was probably written after the contents of *LBSC* had been assembled, Hunt expressed little confidence in his powers as a biographer, confessing that he "could not so well manage" (v) the Byron chapter; that he "became tired" of the autobiographical section; and that, in general, he "dreaded" the work, having developed a "dislike of . . . personal histories." As to the finished product, he managed only this one-line acknowledgment of the volume's merits: "Not that I have not written it conscientiously, and that it is not in every respect fit to appear" (iv). The negatives do little to reassure the reader of Hunt's claim.

Hunt's reluctance as a biographer becomes strikingly apparent when we compare his comments about *LBSC* to those made by other biographers of Byron. Thomas Moore's *Letters and Journals of Lord Byron, with Notices of His Life* (1830), which Jeffery Vail describes as "perhaps the most influential life of Byron ever written," may serve as a useful illustration.[13] Moore's authoritative two-volume biography, published partly in response to biographers like Hunt, set a high standard for biographers of Byron to follow, and Moore himself had been "well convinced" of the importance of his book and the soundness of his biographical methods:

> IN presenting these volumes to the public I should have felt, I own, considerable diffidence, from a sincere distrust in my own powers of doing justice to such a task, were I not well convinced that there is in the subject itself, and in the rich variety of materials here brought to illustrate it, a degree of attraction and interest which it would be difficult, even for hands the most unskilful, to extinguish.[14]

Notably, Moore's preface is just over one page in length, while Hunt's preface spans a full six pages. Hunt had intended to publish an additional six pages he titled "An Attempt of the Author to Estimate His Own Character," which would have presumably also been used as front matter in *LBSC*.[15] In *Letters and Journals of Lord Byron*, by contrast, Moore makes it apparent that his voice, the voice of the biographer, is inconsequential, for Byron's character speaks directly through the "rich variety of materials . . . brought to illustrate it"—the original letters, memoranda, journals, and poetry that Moore collected, assembled, and transcribed throughout his biography of Byron. Moore's methodology, unlike Hunt's less clearly defined approach, with its mixing of biographical and autobiographical elements, is organized and presented in a Boswellian manner. Like James Boswell, in his *Life of Samuel Johnson*, Moore, in his *Letters and Journals of Lord Byron*, presents himself as a compiler of facts relating to his subject's life and willingly recedes into the background of the text, allowing Byron to fill the foreground and dominate the biography. The approach had its intended effect on Mary Shelley, who found Moore's volume "elegant and forcible" and compiled with "judicious arrangement." Above all, she found it to be a mirror of reality: "the Lord Byron I find there is our Lord Byron . . . I live with him again in these pages."[16]

Mary Shelley's comments on Hunt's *LBSC* were also incisive. Although she said nothing of Hunt's portrait of Byron, she criticized Hunt's chapter on Shelley for "slurring over the real truth." More broadly, she knew that Hunt's "truth" or the "[real] truth—any part of it—[was] hardly for the rude cold world to handle."[17] Like many contemporary readers of *LBSC*, Mary Shelley probably also sensed that Hunt's self-conscious appeals to truthfulness and sincerity would do little to convince politically motivated critics like Lockhart of *LBSC*'s merits, or alter the perspective of a large population of readers who had been deeply attracted to Byron's poetry and celebrity. Hunt placed a great deal of emphasis on his truth-telling and it may be easy to dismiss this emphasis as affectation, a calculated attempt to gain the trust and sympathy of readers. Yet apprehension, reluctance, and self-doubt exist at the same time behind the self-consciously defiant and truth-telling biographical persona Hunt presented in the published volume. Crucially, the textual history of *LBSC*, which has its conceptual origins and ends in Hunt's autobiographical writing, also shows that Hunt's "painful retrospect" of Byron was not his last public statement on their ten-year friendship and literary relationship.

The Making of *Lord Byron and Some of His Contemporaries*

When he returned to England in 1825, Hunt had been out of the public eye for several years, having left his long-standing post as editor of *The Examiner* when he sailed to Italy in 1822. With the exception of *The Liberal*, the new works Hunt issued from Italy were either short-lived efforts like *The Literary Examiner* (1823) or critically neglected offerings like *Ultra-Crepidarius; A Satire on William Gifford* (1823).[18] Hunt's only other separately published volume during his time away from England was a translation of Francesco Redi called *Bacchus in Tuscany, A Dithyrambic Poem* (1825) that Hunt nevertheless believed "fell dead born from the press" (*A* 3:116). With *LBSC*, then, Hunt was essentially reintroducing himself to British readers and reentering a literary culture that had undergone significant changes in the relatively short period of time between his departure and his return. Keats, Shelley, and Byron were no longer living, and Walter Scott, Jane Austen, and Maria Edgeworth had set authors and readers on a new course, anticipating the great novelists of the Victorian age. The Romantic magazine had also become a fixture of the literary marketplace. In the newspapers and the magazines, "living writers," as H. J. Jackson explains, were increasingly "vulnerable" to the "intrusive curiosity" of these publications.[19] There was a vogue for personalities, memoirs, and biographies, and Byron's life attracted the most attention, with notable offerings from Thomas Medwin, R. C. Dallas, and Lady Blessington. The latest trends, however, also brought uncertainties about the quality of the writing being produced and the books being published. Jon Klancher describes the cultural moment in bleak terms: authors in the 1820s like Hunt were writing for a "debased modern middle-class world," upon which publishers such as Colburn capitalized, using the magazine format, in particular, to transform sordid entertainments like public executions or violent recreations like boxing into "national events" of great importance.[20] To produce a second *Rimini* or assemble another *Foliage* in such a cultural milieu was out of the question. Hunt, reluctantly, produced *LBSC* instead.

Timothy Webb has shown that the materials Hunt used in the assembly of *LBSC* have diverse origins. Some of the autobiographical material, for example, had been previously published in *The Examiner*. Hunt's lengthy chapter on Shelley was also constructed from materials that had been prepared earlier, including the biographical tribute that Hunt wrote soon after the Shelley's death in 1822.[21] The Shelley material, however, had not been published prior to its appearance in *LBSC*. Hunt, we recall, had rejected Edward Trelawny's factual account of Shelley's cremation ceremony for inclusion in *The Liberal*, believing its grim details unsuitable for a public audience. And even though Hunt attempted to enlarge the piece, joining his own prepared material on Shelley to Trelawny's account, the article was ultimately abandoned in late 1822.[22] At some point after this, Hunt had the idea of producing a more elaborate, volume-length tribute to Shelley that would have combined biography with poetry, including selections from "some of the best poetry [Hunt had] ever written." Hunt shared his plan with Elizabeth Kent, to whom he nevertheless admitted that the undertaking was "tearing" his "heart" and "imagination to pieces," thus forcing him to "compose it by small dribbles" (*LHLL* 152–3). Nothing more is known about this projected tribute to Shelley's memory, but there were other opportunities available for Hunt to commemorate his friend's life. Indeed, not long after Mary Shelley returned to England in 1823, she approached John Hunt with the idea of publishing a collected edition of Shelley's poetry. From the beginning, Mary Shelley wanted Hunt to write a biographical sketch for the collection. On 18 September she wrote to Hunt, requesting his assistance with the project:

> I spoke to your brother when I saw him concerning the publication of such MSS as I had of our S—and he agreed to it. . . . [Bryan Waller] Proctor asked me if I would write a biographical notice.—This, just at this moment would I think better come from you. I know you have prepared an article. This you might alter and enlarge, and without making a regular biography—write what we (you & I) would wish to be written.[23]

Over the course of the next several months, as she collected and assembled materials for the volume that would become *Posthumous Poems*, Mary Shelley made several more inquiries about the "biographical notice," but Hunt, finding it difficult to move forward with his own projected volume about Shelley, ignored his correspondent's requests.[24]

When *Posthumous Poems* appeared in 1824, however, Hunt found the courage he needed to write at length about Shelley after reading Hazlitt's caustic remarks on the volume in the *Edinburgh Review*. Hunt responded to Hazlitt by writing his own review of *Posthumous Poems*, but Hunt's review was rejected for publication in the end. Yet the rejection came at a moment when another, more financially promising opportunity to join Henry Colburn's pool of talented journalists arrived. On 1 September 1824, Hunt informed his sister-in-law that he had received "a fourth offer from Colburn to write for the *New Monthly Magazine*, which by the way looks well for my present standing with the public" (*CLH* 1:232). Charles Armitage Brown, who had been contributing to the *New Monthly Magazine* and had grown close to the Hunts when they moved from Albaro to Florence in August of 1823, may have served as the immediate link between Colburn and Hunt, but John Hunt, who had been in contact with the publisher at this time, also may have been involved in securing work for Hunt. In any case, Hunt had apparently refused earlier offers from Colburn, but eventually settled with the publisher on a long-term plan: "Colburn, after repeatedly invit[ing] me to write in his Magazine, has agreed with me . . . that I shall do so for a year certain & for £150 the first year, at the rate of 16 guineas a sheet; which he says is the largest pay given" (*LHOL* [4 November 1824]). Then, at some point in the first half of 1825, Colburn must have approached Hunt again for work on an even larger scale to be conducted in England, for on 30 August, Hunt informed Elizabeth Kent of the publisher's latest scheme:

> I received this morning £200 from Colburn. . . . It is of the greatest importance that we should return. It is the best thing to be done in a pecuniary point of view, striking while the iron is hot, for Colburn is very glad to have me, & already proposes plans of his own. He wants me to set up a newspaper! This I tell you, as a specimen [of] how much he is inclined to do.
>
> (*LHOL*)

There is no further mention of the Colburn-Hunt "newspaper" project after this and it may have fallen through soon after the Hunts returned to England. Hunt's acceptance of Colburn's "£200" for the return home, however, meant that he would need to work to compensate the publisher for the generous advance. Failing to do so in a reasonable period, Hunt explained in his preface to *LBSC* that his own delay contributed to Colburn's insistence that he put together the "Byron Book." By February 1827, Hunt seems to have committed himself to writing the memoirs that would be assembled for *LBSC*. Brown, who provides us with evidence of Hunt's projected volume at this time, had also provided his friend with some prudent advice about the undertaking:

> Respecting your Memoirs,—know I had heard of them long before you told me. They will be very interesting as far as Shelley, Keats, and Ld Byron are concerned. I can't promise so much for the

remainder, where you speak of the living. There every reader will, and with justice, suppose you guilty of partiality. You will describe people as they have behaved to you, not their general character. If you do otherwise, you will be different from all men else.[25]

In the end, Hunt did not follow Brown's directive. When *LBSC* appeared a year later, a "living" memoir, Hunt's autobiographical portion, constituted the longest section of the book. With the Byron section, moreover, Hunt seemed intent on setting himself apart from "all men else," exposing details of Byron's private life and drawing the poet's character in such a manner that even John Gibson Lockhart, the architect of the "Cockney School" series, found alarming.

Henry Colburn and *Lord Byron and Some of His Contemporaries*

Most of the correspondence exchanged between Hunt and Henry Colburn during the period *LBSC* was assembled has not survived. One revealing letter (undated) from Colburn, however, offers insight into his publishing relations with Hunt. At some point presumably during the second half of 1827, Colburn wrote to Hunt thus: "I am so extremely anxious that you should make all possible <u>additions</u> & corrections to the Byron Book." Colburn's statement makes it clear that Hunt had already delivered *LBSC*, in some form, to his publisher. We also learn from Colburn's letter something of Hunt's financial dealings; Colburn had apparently just sent Hunt money for his "<u>past exertions</u> to fulfill [the publisher's] wishes." Clearly, Colburn was, as Hunt had suggested in the preface to *LBSC*, providing direction during the assembly of *LBSC*, a fact Colburn underscored by warning Hunt that he should "for the present discard the thoughts of the novel" (*LHOL*). The reference here is to Hunt's first major attempt to produce a novel, *Sir Ralph Esher: or, Adventures of a Gentleman of the Court of Charles II*, which Colburn eventually brought out in three volumes in 1832. In late 1827, however, the publisher had other plans for his author, warning Hunt to resist indulging in novelistic pursuits and instead to stay focused on more readily saleable material like the "Byron Book."

Among Hunt's few surviving letters to Colburn from the period most relevant to the assembly of *LBSC* is one (in the Brewer Collection) dated 28 July 1827 and another (in the Berg Collection) dated 15 January 1828. In the former, Hunt made brief mention of a "letter" of Byron's that he wished to show Colburn. At the end of the Byron section of *LBSC*, Hunt published several private letters he had received from Byron during the early years of their friendship. The "letter" that Hunt wished to show Colburn may have been one he felt hesitant about printing and wanted a second opinion from the publisher before it appeared. Hunt's 15 January letter to Colburn is more revealing: its contents suggest that it had served as the basis for published comments Hunt had included in the appendix that was added to the second published edition of *LBSC*.[26] The appendix, it turns out, presented Hunt with an opportunity to express his disapproval with his publisher's handling of *LBSC*, especially the advertising tactics that Colburn had used before the book appeared in the winter of 1828.[27] Colburn, it seems, did not consult Hunt before he published lengthy extracts from *LBSC* in the *New Monthly Magazine*.[28] Klancher observes that "Colburn was the most notorious nineteenth-century practitioner of 'puffing,' having the books he published promoted and well-reviewed by his periodical."[29] For Hunt, Colburn's tactics were especially troubling. Hunt objected to both the quantity and the content of the extracts, which were drawn primarily from the Byron chapter. Hunt feared that readers would draw conclusions about *LBSC* (and its author) without ever picking up the book to examine *all* of the evidence presented therein. Lee Erickson points out that Hunt "was the last of the one-man journalists" of the Romantic age, struggling with the pressures of such work but exercising authorial control nonetheless over late ventures such as *The Companion* (1828), *The Tatler* (1830–32), and *Leigh Hunt's London Journal* (1834–35).[30] That Hunt may have expected to be involved in every stage of *LBSC*'s production, including its advertising, is therefore not surprising. At the same time, his strong objections to Colburn's advertising methods would seem to suggest that Hunt had surprisingly little awareness of Colburn's tactics even though he had been working with the publisher for a number of years.

There is additional evidence that shows Hunt's misgivings about *LBSC* at a late stage in its production. In late 1827 or early 1828, Hunt decided to withdraw a prepared chapter on William Hazlitt, his long-time friend and old "Round Table" collaborator, after the chapter had already been set up in proof by Colburn.[31] According to a note that appeared in the preface to *LBSC*, Hunt decided to withhold the Hazlitt chapter because "readers might have mistaken the object of it" (vii). Hunt's anger at Hazlitt had been mounting for several years and can be traced to private disagreements the two friends had had about Shelley. In fact, the Hazlitt chapter intended for *LBSC* has its beginnings in a sketch of Hazlitt that Hunt produced in Italy but never published.[32] The Hazlitt memoir that Hunt prepared for *LBSC* probably reused some of the material from this earlier character sketch. In any case, had the Hazlitt chapter appeared in *LBSC*, it may have helped to take some of the focus off of the bitter portrait of Byron, for in his memoir of Hazlitt, Hunt had used personality in similar ways, attacking Hazlitt's character for having publicly abused Shelley. Hazlitt, of course, was still living in 1828 and ostensibly on friendly terms with Hunt. As such, Hunt must have felt especially apprehensive about publishing the intended attack on Hazlitt and decided to withdraw the memoir just before *LBSC* appeared.

Despite Hunt's clear apprehensions about several different aspects of *LBSC*, the first edition (published in quarto) must have sold well and sold quickly, for by 25 March 1828 Colburn was calling for a second edition to be printed in two volumes octavo. Hunt wrote to Colburn's partner Richard Bentley with directions for the placement of new material to be included in the preface.[33] In addition to enlarging the preface, Hunt issued an *apologia* for *LBSC* in the appendix. Included were summaries of letters that Hunt had published in the *Morning Chronicle*, in which he fully explained his objections to the extracts that Colburn had published as advertisements for the book. Hunt also responded to private letters and notices from readers of the first edition, including a charge from "a kinsman," who claimed that Hunt had accused Byron of cowardice. Another charge issued from a reader of the first edition of *LBSC* was that Hunt had suggested Horace Smith had sympathies with Shelley's unorthodox religious principles. Hunt also printed a letter from "Mr. [Charles Valentine] Le Grice," a Christ's Hospital classmate of Lamb and Coleridge, who was outraged by Hunt's claim that his brother (Samuel Le Grice) had died "a rake," a claim for which Hunt duly apologized.[34] Crucially, all of these additions make it clear that Hunt had changed his mind about his "Byron Book" and was using the second edition of *LBSC*, in large part, to apologize to his readers: "as far as the sincerity in [*LBSC*] has taken a splenetic turn, which was a thing unnecessary, I wish it had never been written."[35]

Byron and the *Autobiography*

Hunt returned to *LBSC* many years later to gather material for his *Autobiography* (1850). Timothy Webb's investigations into Hunt's autobiographical writings and his close study of Hunt's "revisionary practices" confirm the extent to which Hunt essentially rewrote his relationship with Byron for the first incarnation of the *Autobiography*, drawing heavily from sections of *LBSC* but removing the emotional, anger-driven content.[36] Because Hunt wished the statements he published in the *Autobiography* to stand as his last and final comment on his friendship and literary relationship with Byron, a discussion of Hunt's autobiographical writing will serve as an appropriate conclusion to the present study.

Although Byron is mentioned throughout Hunt's *Autobiography*, Chapters XIX and XX of the third volume are specifically devoted to Hunt's friendship with Byron during its most intense period: the period in which they collaborated on *The Liberal* in Italy in 1822 and 1823. In the *Autobiography*, Hunt reintroduces his friendship with Byron with a telling illustration: the story of Luigi Alamanni, a sixteenth-century Italian poet who, Hunt says, had "in his younger days bitterly satirized the house of Austria" only to find himself "awkwardly situated" later in life in the role of "embassy to the court of Charles the Fifth" (*A* 3:1). When Charles the Fifth called the mature Alamanni to account for his youthful satire, Alamanni's response, according to Hunt, was: "'when I wrote that passage, I spoke as a poet, to whom it is permitted to use fictions; but now I speak as an ambassador, who is bound to utter truth'" (*A* 3:2). In 1850, as a mature author like Alamanni the "ambassador," Hunt clearly wanted to present himself to his Victorian readers as a biographer willing to present a different kind of "truth" about his relationship with Byron from that which he had provided in *LBSC*. At several points in Chapters XIX and XX of the *Autobiography*, Hunt reiterates the idea that he has matured as an author and is willing to revisit his relationship with Byron in a less hostile manner: "I was agitated by grief and anger, and . . . I am now free from anger." Hunt added: "I was far more alive to other people's defects than to my own, and that I am now sufficiently sensible of my own to show to others the charity which I need myself." Hunt also seems to have come to a new understanding about writing personalities that emphasized imperfections and infirmities: "I do not think it right to exhibit what is amiss, or may be thought amiss, in the character of a fellow-creature, out of any feeling but unmistakable sorrow, or the wish to lessen evils which society itself may have caused" (*A* 3:3). Instead of a "painful retrospect," the *Autobiography* thus promised to be something different: a work of reconciliation conditioned by the private strength and peace of mind that Hunt had discovered over the course of several decades. Hunt's acknowledgment of this change would have been an important admission for readers who had been unsettled by *LBSC*, for Hunt makes it clear that his retelling of his relationship with Byron will not be guided by the "splenetic feeling" that had dominated the portrait of the poet in *LBSC*.

Nevertheless, Hunt's disapproval of certain aspects of Byron's life and character is still very much a part of the Byron sections of the *Autobiography*. Hunt seems to realize this, but he attempts to justify his criticisms of Byron in 1850 by emphasizing the role "society" had played in conditioning Byron's personality. Indeed, Byron was still "the victim of a bad bringing up" but he had been unfortunately placed in "a series of false positions in society" by the "evils arising from the mistakes of society itself" (*A* 3:3). Even so, Hunt seems uneasy about having to make such statements about Byron, for his greatest urge in the *Autobiography*, as Webb has shown, is to seek reconciliation and apologize for his earlier opinions, not to justify them: "I am sorry I ever wrote a syllable respecting Lord Byron which might have been spared" (*A* 3:5).[37] Hunt also confesses that there had been inconsistencies in the presentation of his own character in *LBSC*: "I had prided myself—I should pride myself now, if I had not been thus rebuked—on not being one of those who talk against others. I went counter to this feeling in a book." And "to crown the absurdity of the contradiction," Hunt says, "I was foolish enough to suppose, that the very fact of my so doing would show that I had done it in no other instance! that having been thus public in the error, credit would be given me for never having been privately so! Such are the delusions inflicted on us by self-love" (*A* 3:5–6).

Although Hunt's rhetoric of forgiveness is expressed with great sincerity of purpose in the *Autobiography*, it might be argued that such rhetoric loses something of the vigor and the energy, ill-used as it had been, that had made *LBSC* a darkly compelling work. Yet Hunt apparently found an opportunity in the *Autobiography* to recall some of the complex emotion of *LBSC* when he revisited one experience in particular—that of walking the grounds of Byron's Casa Saluzzi at Albaro, listening to Byron's "very pleasant" (*A* 3:64) imitations of Samuel Johnson and matching them with his own imitations from Peter Pindar's *Bozzy and Piozzy: A Town Eclogue*. This memory, in fact, is one of the few potentially light-hearted moments in *LBSC*. Indeed, in that earlier text, Hunt had been willing to admit that it was "a jest between us, that the only book that was unequivocally a favourite on both sides, was Boswell's 'Life of Johnson'" (*LBSC* 65). In *LBSC*, Hunt nevertheless spoiled what might have been a charming anecdote with a cynical aside about Moore and a snide remark about Byron's "uneas[y]" laughter at the satirical imitations from Pindar, which were aimed at individuals in "high life" (*LBSC* 66). In the *Autobiography*, Hunt retained this anecdote but he excised the sneer at Moore and lessened the force of his remark about Byron. The most revealing part of Hunt's return to the Johnson-Pindar anecdote in the *Autobiography*, however, is the paragraph that immediately follows—a paragraph that is not found in *LBSC*:

> Ah! how I should have loved him, had he treated me with thorough candour himself, and set me that example of heartiness which it was my business to wait for rather than to originate, seeing that I was of the inferior rank, and in a condition to be obliged. It would have done, I think, a world of good on both sides; and what would it not have saved? Still, I ought to have discovered some mode, nevertheless, of exciting it; and I should have done so, had I known what was right and proper as well as I do now.
>
> (3:65)

This deeply confessional moment in the *Autobiography* is an unusual instance of the emotive Hunt making his reappearance in an otherwise deliberately controlled section of the text. The result is revealing, for Hunt's reaction is much more complex and searching than the carefully worded reflections and apologies found elsewhere in the same section. Indeed, Hunt seems to present the reader with a genuine reaction to a powerful memory, one that elicits an uneasy and perhaps irreconcilable mixture of sensibility, nostalgia, fellowship, and regret. Hunt acknowledges that as much as he may have desired a sympathetic friendship with Byron, there were inhibiting factors, some self-created and others imposed from without. Although Hunt admitted his own unwillingness to engage Byron in a "mode" suited to the poet's social position and temperament, Byron's rank appears to have been an especially powerful factor and ultimately a barrier to the friendship.

Hunt's self-consciousness about Byron's rank inevitably returns us to the dedication to Byron in *The Story of Rimini* that Hunt wrote and published in 1816. At that time, Hunt's public statement of friendship and creative solidarity with Byron had been transformed into a public embarrassment by politically conservative and unforgiving critics like John Wilson Croker of the *Quarterly Review* and John Gibson Lockhart of *Blackwood's Edinburgh Magazine*. The extent to which the criticism actually affected Hunt personally or creatively is difficult to say with any certainty. Yet the basic message these critics had sent about class and social standing remained a powerful force, doubtless shaping Hunt's memories of his friendship with Byron as they were reconstructed for the *Autobiography*. In fact, Eleanor M. Gates has suggested that the severe judgments of Hunt's earliest critics have persisted well into the twentieth century and perhaps beyond. "Biography and criticism," as Gates puts it, "can be more than a little right-royal," and a "good deal of this feeling can be said to characterize the earlier critics of Hunt's *LBSC* and more than enough of it remains among twentieth-century students of Byron to foster a very one-sided view of Hunt."[38] The present study of the Byron-Hunt friendship and literary relationship has made an attempt to address what Gates sees as this "one-sided view of Hunt" with respect to Byron by suggesting that there were meaningful and complex tensions at work in the Byron-Hunt relationship. Their disagreements about figures as diverse as Pope, Wordsworth, Keats, Napoleon, and the Cockneys were a spur to creative engagement and critical debate during the most productive periods in their lives. At the same time, there were many points of literary sympathy dating back to their precocious early years as juvenile authors and young satirists. Hunt's political prose in *The Examiner* and his poetical "Italianism" were, moreover, of exceeding and unquestionable interest to Byron. Hunt, meanwhile, was among the first to promote Byron's political career in the House of Lords. The editor of *The Examiner* even welcomed the opportunity to print (and argue with) Byron's controversial views on Napoleon during the years leading up to the French emperor's defeat at the Battle of Waterloo. Hunt also routinely supported Byron and his poetry in *The Examiner* and was among the first critics to celebrate and defend *Don Juan*. It thus becomes clear that despite their personal and artistic differences, the "two thunderbolts" of British Romanticism, the wren and the eagle of Shelley's imagination, managed to transform their literary sympathies and their critical disagreements time and time again into a creative and meaningful dialogue.[39]

Notes

1 Leigh Hunt, *Lord Byron and Some of His Contemporaries* (London: Henry Colburn, 1828), 513. Private collection.
2 Henry Colburn, the publisher of *LBSC*, referred to the volume as Hunt's "Byron Book" in an undated letter from late 1827. See *LHOL*. Other contemporary readers reacted in the margins of their copies of *LBSC* with a similar level of intensity. See, for instance, Teresa Guiccioli's copy of *LBSC* in the Pforzheimer Collection: Pforz BT (Guiccioli, T.) 06 v. 1–2.
3 James Boswell expressed similar feelings when he came to write about the late Sir John Hawkins. Boswell explained: "I have suppressed several of my remarks upon his work. But though I would not 'war with the dead' *offensively*, I think it necessary to be strenuous in *defence* of my illustrious friend, which I cannot be without strong animadversions upon a writer who has greatly injured him." See *The Life of Johnson*. repr. (Oxford: Oxford University Press, 1966), 20.
4 *LBSC* 165.
5 John Gibson Lockhart, "Review of Leigh Hunt's *Lord Byron and Some of His Contemporaries*," *Quarterly Review* 37, no. 74 (March 1828): 406.
6 John Timbs, *Walks and Talks about London* (London: Lockwood & Co., 1865), 203.
7 James Treadwell, *Autobiographical Writing and British Literature, 1783–1834* (Oxford: Oxford University Press, 2005), 78.
8 Lockhart, "Review of Leigh Hunt's *Lord Byron and Some of His Contemporaries*," 414.
9 Annette Wheeler Cafarelli, *Prose in the Age of Poets: Romanticism and Biographical Narrative from Johnson to De Quincey* (Philadelphia: University of Pennsylvania Press, 1990), 20–1.
10 *Letter to a Friend of Robert Burns* in *The Prose Works of William Wordsworth*, eds. W. J. B. Owen and Jane Worthington Smyser, 3 vols. (Oxford: Oxford University Press, 1974), 3:121.
11 Cafarelli, *Prose*, 149.
12 Julian North, *The Domestication of Genius: Biography and the Romantic Poet* (Oxford: Oxford University Press, 2009), 87.
13 Jeffery W. Vail, *The Literary Relationship of Lord Byron & Thomas Moore* (Baltimore, MD: Johns Hopkins University Press, 2001), 164.
14 Thomas Moore, *Letters and Journals of Lord Byron, with Notices of His Life*. 2 vols. (London: John Murray, 1830), 1:vii.
15 A proof set is in the Houghton Library at Harvard University. See MS. Eng 1668.
16 Mary Wollstonecraft Shelley, *The Letters of Mary Wollstonecraft Shelley*, ed. Betty T. Bennett, 3 vols. (Baltimore, MD: Johns Hopkins University Press, 1980–88), 2:101.
17 Mary Wollstonecraft Shelley, *The Letters*, 2:94.
18 In fact, in the Murray circle, it was suggested that Byron was the author of *Ultra-Crepidarius*—a rumor that he strongly denied. See *BLJ* 11:117, 123.
19 H. J. Jackson, *Those Who Write for Immortality: Romantic Reputations and the Dream of Lasting Fame* (New Haven, CT: Yale University Press, 2015), 35.
20 Jon Klancher, *The Making of English Reading Audiences, 1790–1832* (Madison: University of Wisconsin Press, 1987), 62–3.
21 Timothy Webb, "Correcting the Irritability of His Temper: The Evolution of Leigh Hunt's *Autobiography*," in *Romantic Revisions*, eds. Robert Brinkley and Keith Hanley (Cambridge: Cambridge University Press, 1992), 269–71.

22 Hunt's article has been transcribed by Timothy Webb in "Religion of the Heart: Leigh Hunt's Unpublished Tribute to Shelley," *The Keats-Shelley Review* 7 (1992): 43–55.
23 Mary Wollstonecraft Shelley, *The Letters*, 1:384.
24 Mary Wollstonecraft Shelley, *The Letters*, 1:412.
25 Charles Armitage Brown, *The Letters of Charles Armitage Brown*, ed. Jack Stillinger (Cambridge, MA: Harvard University Press, 1966), 268.
26 The holograph draft is in the Berg Collection at the New York Public Library. See Berg Coll MSS. Hunt.
27 Leigh Hunt, *Lord Byron and Some of His Contemporaries*. 2 vols. (London: Henry Colburn, 1828), 2:410, 417–8.
28 Michael Eberle-Sinatra, *Leigh Hunt and the London Literary Scene: A Reception History of His Major Works, 1805–1828* (New York: Routledge, 2005), 118.
29 Klancher, *Making of English*, 62.
30 Lee Erickson, *The Economy of Literary Form: English Literature and the Industrialization of Publishing, 1800–1850* (Baltimore, MD: Johns Hopkins University Press, 1996), 87.
31 The near-complete proof set is in the Houghton Library. See MS. Eng 1668 (2).
32 *LBSC* 202–9.
33 *LHLL* 187.
34 Hunt, *LBSC* (2), 2:419, 423–4.
35 Hunt, *LBSC* (2), 1:xvi.
36 Webb, "Correcting the Irritability," 272.
37 Webb, "Correcting the Irritability," 279.
38 Eleanor M. Gates, "Leigh Hunt, Lord Byron, and Mary Shelley: The Long Goodbye," *Keats-Shelley Journal* 35 (1986): 153.
39 Percy Bysshe Shelley, *The Letters of Percy Bysshe Shelley*, ed. Frederick L. Jones. 2 vols. (Oxford: Oxford University Press, 1964), 2:442.

Bibliography

Manuscript Collections and Sources

Seymour Adelman Letters and Documents Collection, Bryn Mawr College Library

Ashley Collection, The British Library

Beinecke Rare Book and Manuscript Library, Yale University

Henry W. and Albert A. Berg Collection, New York Public Library

Luther A. Brewer Collection, University of Iowa Libraries

Byron Society Collection, Drew University Library

David R. Cheney Papers, Ward M. Canaday Center at the University of Toledo

James T. Fields Collection, The Rauner Library at Dartmouth College

John Forster Collection, The National Art Library at the Victoria & Albert Museum

Houghton Library, Harvard University

John Murray Archive, The National Library of Scotland

Carl H. Pforzheimer Collection, The New York Public Library

Western Manuscripts, The British Library

Primary Sources

Anderson, Robert, ed. *A Complete Edition of the Poets of Great Britain.* 13 vols. London: John & Arthur Arch, 1792–95.

Anonymous. "The Life of Lord Byron." In *The Complete Works of Lord Byron*, ix–xxiii. Brussels: Librairie Lechalier, 1830.

———. Advertisement for Leigh Hunt's *Story of Rimini. Morning Post.* February 5, 1816.

———. Advertisements for Lord Byron's *Siege of Corinth* and *Parisina*; Leigh Hunt's *Story of Rimini. Morning Post.* February 14, 1816.

———. "Infantine Theatricals." *Morning Post.* December 5, 1805.

———. "The Young Roscius." *Bury and Norwich Post.* December 5, 1804.

———. "*March* 12, 1802." *The Chester Chronicle.* March 12, 1802.

———. Notice of Leigh Hunt's *Juvenilia. The Monthly Mirror.* July 1801, 59.

Blessington, Marguerite, Countess of. *Lady Blessington's Conversations of Lord Byron.* Edited by Ernest J. Lovell, Jr. Princeton, NJ: Princeton University Press, 1969.

Boswell, James. *Life of Johnson.* repr. Oxford: Oxford University Press, 1966.

Brown, Charles Armitage. *The Letters of Charles Armitage Brown.* Edited by Jack Stillinger. Cambridge, MA: Harvard University Press, 1966.

Byron, George Gordon, Lord. *The Manuscripts of the Younger Romantics. Lord Byron. Volume XI: "Ode to Napoleon Buonaparte" and "Don Juan" Canto VIII and Stanzas from III and IX.* Edited by Cheryl Fallon Giuliano. New York: Garland Publishing Inc., 1997.

———. *The Manuscripts of the Younger Romantics. Volume XIII: "The Prisoner of Chillon" and "Don Juan" Canto IX.* Edited by Peter Cochran. New York: Garland Publishing Inc., 1995.

———. *'What Comes Uppermost': Byron's Letters and Journals.* Edited by Leslie A. Marchand. Newark, DE: University of Delaware Press, 1994.

———. *The Manuscripts of the Younger Romantics. Lord Byron. Volume IX: "Don Juan," Cantos X, XI, XII, XVI.* Edited by Andrew Nicholson. New York: Garland Publishing Inc., 1993.

———. *Lord Byron: The Complete Poetical Works.* Edited by Jerome J. McGann. 7 vols. Oxford: Oxford University Press, 1980–93.

———. *Lord Byron: The Complete Miscellaneous Prose.* Edited by Andrew Nicholson. Oxford: Oxford University Press, 1991.

———. *The Manuscripts of the Younger Romantics. Lord Byron. Volume IV: Miscellaneous Poems.* Edited by Alice Levine and Jerome J. McGann. New York: Garland Publishing Inc., 1988.

———. *Byron's Letters and Journals.* Edited by Leslie A. Marchand. 12 vols. Cambridge, MA: Harvard University Press, 1973–82.

———. *The Works of Lord Byron: Letters and Journals.* Edited by Rowland E. Prothero. 6 vols. London: John Murray, 1898.

Chalmers. Alexander, ed. *The Works of the English Poets, from Chaucer to Cowper.* 21 vols. London: J. Johnson; J. Nichols and Son, 1810.

Coleridge, Samuel Taylor. *Biographia Literaria.* Edited by James Engell and W. Jackson Bate. The Collected Works of Samuel Taylor Coleridge. 2 vols. Princeton, NJ: Princeton University Press, 1983.

Croker, John Wilson. *The Croker Papers. The Correspondence and Diaries of the Late Right Honourable John Wilson Croker.* Edited by Louis J. Jennings. 3 vols. London: John Murray, 1885.

Dacre, Charlotte. *Hours of Solitude.* Romantic Context: Poetry. Edited by Donald H. Reiman. New York: Garland Publishing, 1978.

Dallas, Alexander Robert Charles. *Correspondence of Lord Byron.* 3 vols. Paris: Galignani, 1825.

Dallas, Robert Charles. *Recollections of the Life of Lord Byron.* London: Charles Knight, 1824.

Dante [Alighieri.] *The Divine Comedy: Inferno.* Translated by Charles S. Singleton. 2 vols. Princeton, NJ: Princeton University Press, 1970.

Fellowes, Robert. "Some Account of Thomas Chatterton." *The Monthly Mirror.* July 1799, 143–6.

Gray, Thomas. *The Complete Poems of Thomas Gray,* Edited by H. W. Starr and J. R. Hendrickson. Oxford: Oxford University Press, 1966.

Hazlitt, William. *New Writings of William Hazlitt.* Edited by Duncan Wu. 2 vols. Oxford: Oxford University Press, 2007.

———. *The Letters of William Hazlitt.* Edited by Herschel Moreland Sikes et al. New York: New York University Press, 1978.

———. *The Complete Works of William Hazlitt.* Edited by P. P. Howe. 21 vols. London: J. M. Dent & Sons, Ltd., 1930–34.

———. *The Round Table.* 2 vols. Edinburgh: Archibald Constable, 1817.

Hobhouse, John Cam. *The Diary of John Cam Hobhouse*. Edited by Peter Cochran. 2009. https://petercochran.wordpress.com.

———. *Byron's Bulldog: The Letters of John Cam Hobhouse to Lord Byron*. Edited by Peter W. Graham. Columbus: Ohio State University Press, 1984.

Hunt, Leigh. *Leigh Hunt Online: The Letters*. The University of Iowa Libraries. http://digital.lib.uiowa.edu/leighhunt

———. *The Selected Writings of Leigh Hunt*. Edited by Robert Morrison and Michael Eberle-Sinatra. 6 vols. London: Pickering & Chatto, 2003.

———. *Leigh Hunt: A Life in Letters*. Edited by Eleanor M. Gates. Essex, CT: Falls River Publications, 1998.

———. *Leigh Hunt's Autobiography: The Earliest Sketches*. Edited by Stephen F. Fogle. Gainesville: University of Florida Press, 1959.

———. *The Poetical Works of Leigh Hunt*. Edited by H. S. Milford. Oxford: Oxford University Press, 1923.

———. *The Correspondence of Leigh Hunt*. Edited by Thornton Hunt. 2 vols. London: Smith, Elder, & Co., 1862.

———. *Wit and Humor*. London: Smith, Elder, and Co., 1856.

———. *The Autobiography of Leigh Hunt*. 3 vols. London: Smith, Elder, and Co., 1850.

———. *Stories from the Italian Poets*. 2 vols. London: Edward Moxon, 1846.

———. *The Poetical Works of Leigh Hunt*. London: Edward Moxon, 1832.

———. *The Companion*. London: Hunt and Clarke, 1828.

———. *Lord Byron and Some of His Contemporaries*, 2nd ed. 2 vols. London: Henry Colburn, 1828.

———. *Lord Byron and Some of His Contemporaries*. London: Henry Colburn, 1828.

———. "Passages Marked in Montaigne's Essays by Lord Byron." *New Monthly Magazine*, January 1, 1827, 26–32.

———. *The Indicator*. London: Joseph Appleyard, 1820–21.

———. *Foliage; or Poems Original and Translated*. London: C. and J. Ollier, 1818.

———. *The Descent of Liberty, A Mask*. London: Gale, Curtis, and Fenner, 1815.

———. *The Feast of the Poets,* 2nd ed. London: Gale and Fenner, 1815.

———. *The Reflector: A Quarterly Magazine, on Subjects of Philosophy, Politics, and the Liberal Arts*. 2 vols. London: John Hunt, 1811.

———. "Memoir of Mr. James Henry Leigh Hunt. Written by Himself." *The Monthly Mirror*, April 1810, 243–8.

———. [ed.] *The Examiner*. London: John Hunt, 1808–21.

———. *Classic Tales, Serious and Lively. With Critical Essays on the Merits and Reputations of the Authors*. 5 vols. London: John Hunt, 1806–7.

———. *Juvenilia; or, A Collection of Poems*, 3rd ed. London: J. Whiting, 1802.

Hunt, Leigh and Lord Byron. *The Liberal. Verse and Prose from the South*. 2 vols. London: John Hunt, 1822–23.

Johnson, Reginald Brimley. *Shelley-Leigh Hunt: How Friendship Made History*. London: Ingpen and Grant, 1929.

Johnson, Samuel. *The Lives of the Poets. A Selection*. Edited by Roger Lonsdale. Oxford: Oxford University Press, 2009.

Juvenal. *The Satires of Decimus Junius Juvenalis*. Translated by William Gifford. London: W. Bulmer and Co., 1802.

Keats, John. *The Poems of John Keats.* Edited by Jack Stillinger. Cambridge, MA: Harvard University Press, 1978.

———. *The Letters of John Keats.* Edited by Hyder Edward Rollins. 2 vols. Cambridge, MA: Harvard University Press, 1958.

Lamb, Charles. *The Letters of Charles and Mary Anne Lamb.* Edited by Edwin W. Marrs, Jr. 3 vols. Ithaca, NY: Cornell University Press, 1975–78.

Lastri, Marco. *L'Osservatore Fiorentino. Sugli Edifizi Della Sua Patria. Terza Edizione.* 8 vols. Firenze: Presso Gaspero Ricci, 1821.

Lau, Beth. *Keats's Paradise Lost.* Gainesville: University Press of Florida, 1998.

Lockhart, John Gibson. "Review of Leigh Hunt's *Lord Byron and Some of His Contemporaries.*" *Quarterly Review* 37, no. 74 (March 1828): 402–26.

———. [William Wastle, Esquire., pseud.] "The Mad Banker of Amsterdam; or the Fate of the Brauns." *Blackwood's Edinburgh Magazine* 3, no. 17 (August 1818): 530–3.

———. [Z., pseud.] "On the Cockney School of Poetry. No. 3." *Blackwood's Edinburgh Magazine* 3, no. 16 (July 1818): 453–6

———. [PRESBYTER ANGLICANUS., pseud.] "Note to the Editor, *Enclosing a Letter to the Author of Beppo.*" *Blackwood's Edinburgh Magazine* 3, no. 15 (June 1818): 323–9.

———. [Z., pseud.] "On the Cockney School of Poetry. No. 2." *Blackwood's Edinburgh Magazine* 2, no. 8 (November 1817): 194–201.

———. [Z., pseud.] "On the Cockney School of Poetry. No. 1." *Blackwood's Edinburgh Magazine* 2, no. 7 (October 1817): 38–41.

Medwin, Thomas. *Medwin's Conversations of Lord Byron.* Edited by Ernest J. Lovell Jr. Princeton, NJ: Princeton University Press, 1966.

Moore, Thomas. *The Letters of Thomas Moore.* Edited by Wilfred S. Dowden. 2 vols. Oxford: Oxford University Press, 1964.

———. *Memoirs, Journal and Correspondence of Thomas Moore.* Edited by Lord John Russell. 8 vols. London: Longman, Brown, Green, and Longmans, 1853–56.

———. *Letters and Journals of Lord Byron, with Notices of His Life.* 2 vols. London: John Murray, 1830.

Murray, John. *The Letters of John Murray to Lord Byron.* Edited by Andrew Nicholson. Liverpool: Liverpool University Press, 2007.

Nathan, Isaac and Lord Byron. *A Selection of Hebrew Melodies, Ancient and Modern by Isaac Nathan and Lord Byron.* Edited by Frederick Berwick and Paul Douglass. Tuscaloosa: University of Alabama Press, 1988.

Percy, Thomas. *Reliques of Ancient English Poetry.* 3 vols. London: John Nichols, 1794.

Reiman, Donald H., ed. *The Romantics Reviewed: Contemporary Reviews of British Romantic Writers.* Part A, *The Lake Poets.* Part B, *Byron and Regency Society Poets.* Part C, *Shelley, Keats, and London Radical Writers.* 9 vols. New York: Garland Publishing, 1972.

Schwartz, Lewis M. *Keats Reviewed by His Contemporaries: A Collection of Notices for the Years 1816–1821.* Metuchen, NJ: The Scarecrow Press, Inc., 1973.

Shelley, Mary Wollstonecraft. *The Journals of Mary Shelley.* Edited by Paula R. Feldman and Diana Scott Kilvert. Baltimore, MD: Johns Hopkins University Press, 1995.

———. *The Letters of Mary Wollstonecraft Shelley.* Edited by Betty T. Bennett. 3 vols. Baltimore, MD: Johns Hopkins University Press, 1980–88.

Shelley, Percy Bysshe. *The Manuscripts of the Younger Romantics. Vol. II: The Mask of Anarchy.* Edited by Donald H. Reiman. New York: Garland Publishing Inc., 1985.

———. *The Letters of Percy Bysshe Shelley.* Edited by Frederick L. Jones. 2 vols. Oxford: Oxford University Press, 1964.

Southey, Robert. *Robert Southey: Later Poetical Works, 1811–1838.* Edited by Lynda Pratt et al. 4 vols. London: Pickering & Chatto, 2012.

Spenser, Edmund. *The Yale Edition of the Shorter Poems of Edmund Spenser.* Edited by William A. Oram et al. New Haven, CT: Yale University Press, 1989.

Spevack, Marvin, ed. *Isaac D'Israeli on Books: Pre-Victorian Essays on the History of Literature.* London: British Library and Oak Knoll Press, 2004.

Suckling, Sir John. *The Works of Sir John Suckling: The Non-Dramatic Works.* Edited by Thomas Clayton. 2 vols. Oxford: Oxford University Press, 1971.

Timbs, John. *Walks and Talks about London.* London: Lockwood & Co., 1865.

Virgil. *Virgil.* Translated by H. Rushton Fairclough. 2 vols. Cambridge, MA: Harvard University Press, 1986.

———. *Virgil.* Translated by Francis Wrangham et al. 2 vols. London: Henry Colburn and Richard Bentley, 1830.

Webb, Timothy. "After Horsemonger Lane: Leigh Hunt's London Letters to Byron (1815–1816)." *Romanticism* 16, no. 3 (2010): 233–66.

———. "Leigh Hunt to Lord Byron: Eight Letters from Horsemonger Lane Gaol." *The Byron Journal* 36, no. 2 (2008): 131–42.

White, Henry Kirke. *The Remains of Henry Kirke White.* Edited by Robert Southey. 2 vols. London: Vernor, Hood, and Sharpe, 1808.

———. *Clifton Grove, a Sketch in Verse with Other Poems.* London: Vernor and Hood, 1803.

Wordsworth, William. *The Letters of William and Mary Wordsworth: VIII. A Supplement of New Letters.* Edited by Alan G. Hill. Oxford: Oxford University Press, 1993.

———. *The Prose Works of William Wordsworth.* Edited by W. J. B. Owen and Jane Worthington Smyser. 3 vols. Oxford: Oxford University Press, 1974.

Secondary Sources

Altick, Richard D. *The English Common Reader: A Social History of the Mass Reading Public, 1800–1900.* Chicago, IL: University of Chicago Press, 1957.

Amarasinghe, Upali. *Dryden and Pope in the Early Nineteenth Century.* Cambridge: Cambridge University Press, 1962.

Anonymous. *The Library of the Late Edith Rockefeller McCormick.* New York: American Art Association and Anderson Galleries, Inc., 1934.

Bainbridge, Simon. *Napoleon and English Romanticism.* Cambridge: Cambridge University Press, 1995.

Bate, Walter Jackson. *The Stylistic Development of Keats.* London: Routledge & Kegan Paul, 1958.

Beatty, Bernard. "'Accomplished Verse' and 'Awakened Hearts': Byron's 'Thyrza Poems.'" *The Byron Journal* 33, no. 2 (2005): 79–96.

Beaty, Frederick L. *Byron the Satirist*. DeKalb: Northern Illinois University Press, 1985.

———. "Byron and the Story of Francesca da Rimini." *PMLA* 75, no. 4 (1960): 395–401.

Bieri, James. *Percy Bysshe Shelley: A Biography*. repr. Baltimore, MD: Johns Hopkins University Press, 2008.

Blainey, Ann. *Immortal Boy: A Portrait of Leigh Hunt*. New York: St. Martin's Publishers, 1985.

Blunden, Edmund. *Leigh Hunt's "Examiner" Examined*. repr. Hampden, CT: Archon Books, 1967.

Bowers, Will. "Hunt, Byron, and *The Story of Rimini*—A Literary Challenge to 'the Public Mind.'" *Romanticism and Victorianism on the Net* 59–60 (April–October 2011). www.erudit.org/en/journals/ravon.

Brand, C. P. *Italy and the English Romantics*. Cambridge: Cambridge University Press, 1957.

Braund, Susanna Morton. "*Libertas* or *Licentia*?" In *Free Speech in Classical Antiquity*, edited by Ineke Slutter and Ralph M. Rosen, 409–28. Leiden: Brill, 2004.

Burnett, T. A. J., ed. *The British Library Catalogue of the Ashley Manuscripts*. 2 vols. London: The British Library, 1999.

Cafarelli, Annette Wheeler. *Prose in the Age of Poets: Romanticism and Biographical Narrative from Johnson to De Quincey*. Philadelphia: University of Pennsylvania Press, 1990.

Cameron, Kenneth Neil, Donald H. Reiman, and Doucet Devin Fischer, eds. *Shelley and His Circle*. 10 vols. Cambridge, MA: Harvard University Press, 1961–2002.

Cantarella, Eva. *Bisexuality in the Ancient World*. Translated by Cormac Ó Cuilleanáin. New Haven, CT: Yale University Press, 2002.

Christie, William. *The Edinburgh Review in the Literary Culture of Romantic Britain: Mammoth and Megalonyx*. London: Pickering & Chatto, 2009.

Clark, Roy Benjamin. *William Gifford: Tory Satirist, Critic, and Editor*. New York: Columbia University Press, 1930.

Clubbe, John. "Between Emperor and Exile. Byron and Napoleon, 1814–1816." *Napoleonic Scholarship* 1 (1997): 70–84.

Cochran, Peter. *Byron, Napoleon, J. C. Hobhouse, and the Hundred Days*. Newcastle upon Tyne: Cambridge Scholars Publishing, 2015.

———. *The Burning of Byron's Memoirs*. Newcastle upon Tyne: Cambridge Scholars Publishing, 2014.

———. *Byron's Romantic Politics: The Problem of Metahistory*. Newcastle upon Tyne: Cambridge Scholars Publishing, 2011.

———. *Byron and Bob: Lord Byron's Relationship with Robert Southey*. Newcastle upon Tyne: Cambridge Scholars Publishing, 2010.

———. "*Romanticism*"—*and Byron*. Newcastle upon Tyne: Cambridge Scholars Publishing, 2009.

———. "Byron Tests the Freedom of Southwell." In *Liberty and Poetic License: New Essays on Byron*, edited by Bernard Beatty, Tony Howe, and Charles E. Robinson, 10–19. Liverpool: Liverpool University Press, 2008.

Cook, Daniel. *Thomas Chatterton and Neglected Genius, 1760–1830*. New York: Palgrave Macmillan, 2013.

Cox, Jeffrey N. *Romanticism in the Shadow of War: Literary Culture in the Napoleonic War Years.* Cambridge: Cambridge University Press, 2014.

———. "Re-Visioning Rimini: Dante in the Cockney School." In *Dante and Italy in British Romanticism*, edited by Frederick Burwick and Paul Douglass, 183–203. New York: Palgrave Macmillan, 2011.

———. "Leigh Hunt's *Foliage*: A Cockney Manifesto." In *Leigh Hunt: Life, Poetics, Politics*, edited by Nicholas Roe, 58–77. New York: Routledge, 2003.

———. *Poetry and Politics in the Cockney School: Keats, Shelley, Hunt and their Circle.* Cambridge: Cambridge University Press, 1998.

Crompton, Louis. *Byron and Greek Love: Homophobia in 19th-Century England.* Berkeley: University of California Press, 1985.

Cronin, Richard. *The Politics of Romantic Poetry: in Search of the Pure Commonwealth.* London: Macmillan Press, Ltd., 2000.

Cutmore, Johnathan. *Contributors to the "Quarterly Review."* London: Pickering & Chatto, 2007.

Dart, Gregory. *Metropolitan Art and Literature, 1810–1840.* Cambridge: Cambridge University Press, 2012.

David, Saul. *Prince of Pleasure: The Prince of Wales and the Making of the Regency.* New York: Atlantic Monthly Press, 1998.

Dawson, P. M. S., "Byron, Shelley, and the 'New School.'" In *Shelley Revalued: Essays from the Gregynog Conference*, edited by Kelvin Everest, 89–108. Leicester: Leicester University Press, 1983.

Duff, David. "The Casket of My Unknown Mind: The 1813 Volume of Minor Poems." In *The Unfamiliar Shelley*, edited by Alan M. Weinberg and Timothy Webb, 41–68. Farnham: Ashgate Publishing, 2009.

Dyer, Gary. *British Satire and the Politics of Style, 1789–1832.* Cambridge: Cambridge University Press, 1997.

Eberle-Sinatra, Michael. *Leigh Hunt and the London Literary Scene: A Reception History of His Major Works, 1805–1828.* New York: Routledge, 2005.

Edgecombe, Rodney Stenning. *Leigh Hunt and the Poetry of Fancy.* Madison, NJ: Fairleigh Dickinson University Press, 1994.

Edson, Michael. "Leigh Hunt, John Pomfret, and the Politics of Retirement." *European Romantic Review* 25, no. 4 (2014): 423–42.

Elledge, Paul. *Lord Byron at Harrow School: Speaking Out, Talking Back, Acting Up, Bowing Out.* Baltimore, MD: Johns Hopkins University Press, 2000.

Elwin, Malcolm. *Lord Byron's Wife.* New York: Harcourt, Brace & World, Inc., 1962.

Erdman, David V. "Lord Byron and the Genteel Reformers." *PMLA* 56, no. 4 (1941): 1065–4.

Erickson, Lee. *The Economy of Literary Form: English Literature and the Industrialization of Publishing, 1800–1850.* Baltimore, MD: Johns Hopkins University Press, 1996.

Flake, Timothy H. "Byronic Heroism in the Island." *The Byron Journal* 25 (1997): 44–59.

Franklin, Caroline. *Byron: A Literary Life.* New York: Palgrave Macmillan, 2000.

Fuess, Claude M. *Lord Byron as a Satirist in Verse.* New York: Columbia University Press, 1912.

Fulford, Tim. *Romantic Poetry and Literary Coteries: The Dialect of the Tribe.* New York: Palgrave Macmillan, 2015.

Gates, Eleanor M. "Leigh Hunt, Lord Byron, and Mary Shelley: The Long Goodbye." *Keats-Shelley Journal* 35 (1986): 149–67.

Gates, Payson G. *William Hazlitt and Leigh Hunt: The Continuing Dialogue.* Essex, CT: Falls River Publications, 2000.

Graham, Peter W. *Lord Byron.* New York: Twayne Publishers, 1998.

———. *"Don Juan" and Regency England.* Charlottesville: University of Virginia Press, 1990.

Griffin, Robert J. *Wordsworth's Pope: A Study in Literary Historiography.* Cambridge: Cambridge University Press, 1995.

Hay, Daisy. "Liberals, *Liberales* and *The Liberal*: A Reassessment." *European Romantic Review* 19, no. 4 (2008): 307–20.

Hayden, John O. *The Romantic Reviewers.* London: Routledge & Kegan Paul, 1969.

Higgins, David. *Romantic Genius and the Literary Magazine: Biography, Celebrity, Politics.* New York: Routledge, 2005.

Hill, B. W. *British Parliamentary Parties, 1742–1832.* London: George Allen & Unwin, 1985.

Holden, Anthony. *The Wit in the Dungeon: The Remarkable Life of Leigh Hunt. Poet, Revolutionary, and the Last of the Romantics.* Boston, MA: Little, Brown and Company, 2005.

Houck, James A. "Byron and William Hazlitt." In *Lord Byron and His Contemporaries*, edited by Charles E. Robinson, 66–84. Newark, DE: University of Delaware Press, 1982.

Isaac, Peter. "John Murray II and Oliver & Boyd, His Edinburgh Agents, 1819–1835." In *Printing Places: Locations of Book Production & Distribution since 1500*, edited by John Hinks and Catherine Armstrong, 131–46. New Castle and London: Oak Knoll Press & The British Library, 2005.

Jackson, H. J. *Those Who Write for Immortality: Romantic Reputations and the Dream of Lasting Fame.* New Haven, CT: Yale University Press, 2015.

———. *Marginalia: Readers Writing in Books.* New Haven, CT: Yale University Press, 2001.

Keach, William. *Arbitrary Power: Romanticism, Language, Politics.* Princeton, NJ: Princeton University Press, 2004.

Kelsall, Malcolm. "Byron's Politics." In *The Cambridge Companion to Byron*, edited by Drummond Bone, 44–55. Cambridge: Cambridge University Press, 2004.

———. *Byron's Politics.* Sussex: The Harvester Press, 1987.

Kendall, Kenneth E. *Leigh Hunt's Reflector.* The Hague: Mouton & Co., 1971.

Klancher, Jon. *The Making of English Reading Audiences, 1790–1832.* Madison: University of Wisconsin Press, 1987.

Krawczyk, Scott. *Romantic Literary Families.* New York: Palgrave Macmillan, 2009.

Kucich, Greg. "Leigh Hunt and Romantic Spenserianism." *Keats-Shelley Journal* 37 (1988): 110–35.

Landré, Louis. *Leigh Hunt: Contribution a L'histoire du Romantisme Anglais.* 2 vols. Paris: Sociétié D'Édition, 1936.

Langbauer, Laurie. *The Juvenile Tradition: Young Writers and Prolepsis, 1750–1835.* Oxford: Oxford University Press, 2016.

Levy, Michelle. *Family Authorship and Romantic Print Culture*. New York: Palgrave Macmillan, 2008.

Luzzi, Joseph. *Romantic Europe and the Ghost of Italy*. New Haven, CT: Yale University Press, 2008.

Marchand, Leslie A. *Byron: A Biography*. 3 vols. New York: Alfred A. Knopf, 1957.

Marshall, William H. *Byron, Shelley, Hunt, and "The Liberal."* Philadelphia: University of Pennsylvania Press, 1960.

Mason, Nicholas. *Literary Advertising and the Shaping of British Romanticism*. Baltimore, MD: Johns Hopkins University Press, 2013.

McDayter, Ghislaine. *Byromania and the Birth of Celebrity Culture*. Albany: The State University of New York Press, 2009.

McGann, Jerome J. "'My Brain is Feminine': Byron and the Poetry of Deception." In *Byron and Romanticism*, edited by James Soderholm, 53–76. Cambridge: Cambridge University Press, 2002.

———. *Fiery Dust: Byron's Poetic Development*. Chicago, IL: University of Chicago Press, 1968.

McGhee, Richard D. *Henry Kirke White*. New York: Twayne Publishers, 1981.

Miller, Barnette. *Leigh Hunt's Relations with Byron, Shelley and Keats*. New York: Columbia University Press, 1910.

Mizukoshi, Ayumi. *Keats, Hunt and the Aesthetics of Pleasure*. New York: Palgrave Macmillan, 2001.

Mole, Tom. "*Blackwood's* 'Personalities.'" In *Romanticism and Blackwood's Magazine*, edited by Robert Morrison and Daniel S. Roberts, 89–99. New York: Palgrave Macmillan, 2013.

———. *Byron's Romantic Celebrity: Industrial Culture and the Hermeneutic of Intimacy*. New York: Palgrave Macmillan, 2007.

Moore, Doris Langley. *Lord Byron: Accounts Rendered*. New York: Harper & Row, 1974.

———. *The Late Lord Byron*. New York: Harper & Row, 1961.

Morrison, Robert. "*Blackwood's* Byron: The Lakers, the Cockneys, and the 'Throne of Poetical Supremacy.'" *Romanticism* 23, no 3 (2017): 272–81.

Morrison, Robert and Daniel S. Roberts, eds. *Romanticism and Blackwood's Magazine*. New York: Palgrave Macmillan, 2013.

Nicholson, Andrew. "Napoleon's 'Last Act' and Byron's Ode." *Romanticism* 9, no. 1 (2003): 68–81.

North, Julian. *The Domestication of Genius: Biography and the Romantic Poet*. Oxford: Oxford University Press, 2009.

O'Connell, Mary. *Byron and John Murray: A Poet and His Publisher*. Liverpool: Liverpool University Press, 2014.

Oliensis, Ellen. "Sons and Lovers: Sexuality and Gender in Virgil's Poetry." In *The Cambridge Companion to Virgil*, edited by Charles Martindale, 294–311. Cambridge: Cambridge University Press, 1997.

O'Neill, Michael. "'Trying to Make It as Good as I Can': Mary Shelley's Editing of P. B. Shelley's Poetry and Prose." In *Mary Shelley and Her Times*, edited by Betty T. Bennett and Stuart Curran, 185–97. Baltimore, MD: Johns Hopkins University Press, 2000.

Pal-Lapinski, Piya. "From Risorgimento to Fascism: The Politics of *Parisina*." In *Byron: The Poetry of Politics and the Politics of Poetry*, edited by Roderick Beaton and Christine Kenyon Jones, 213–25. New York: Routledge, 2017.

Palmer, Patricia. *The Severed Head and the Grafted Tongue*. Cambridge: Cambridge University Press, 2013.

Parker, Mark. *Literary Magazines and British Romanticism*. Cambridge: Cambridge University Press, 2004.

Pite, Ralph. *The Circle of Our Vision: Dante's Presence in English Romantic Poetry*. Oxford: Oxford University Press, 1994.

Pratt, Willis W. *Byron at Southwell: The Making of a Poet*. Austin: University of Texas, 1948.

Ramsey, Neil. *The Military Memoir and Romantic Literary Culture, 1780–1835*. Farnham: Ashgate Publishing, 2009.

Reiman, Donald H. "Shelley as Agrarian Reactionary." In *Romantic Texts and Contexts*, 260–74. Columbia: University of Missouri Press, 1987.

Richardson, Thomas. "John Gibson Lockhart and *Blackwood's*: Shaping the Romantic Periodical Press." In *Romanticism and Blackwood's Magazine*, edited by Robert Morrison and Daniel S. Roberts, 35–45. New York: Palgrave Macmillan, 2013.

Ricks, Christopher. "Dryden's Triplets." In *The Cambridge Companion to John Dryden*, edited by Steven N. Zwicker, 92–110. Cambridge: Cambridge University Press, 2004.

Roberts, Michael. *The Whig Party, 1807–1812*. repr. London: Frank Cass & Co. Ltd., 1965.

Robinson, Charles E. *Shelley and Byron: The Snake and the Eagle Wreathed in Fight*. Baltimore, MD: Johns Hopkins University Press, 1976.

Robinson, Jeffrey C. "Hunt and the Poetics and Politics of Fancy." In *Leigh Hunt: Life, Poetics, Politics*, edited by Nicholas Roe, 156–79. New York: Routledge, 2003.

Roe, Nicholas. "Leigh Hunt, Charles Lamb, and Virginia Wolf." In *Romantic Presences in the Twentieth Century*, edited by Mark Sandy, 13–26. Farnham: Ashgate Publishing, 2012.

———. *Fiery Heart: The First Life of Leigh Hunt*. London: Pimlico, 2005.

Roper, Derek. *Reviewing Before the Edinburgh: 1788–1802*. Newark, DE: University of Delaware Press, 1978.

Saglia, Diego. "Matrimonial Politics: Two References to Marie Louise of Austria in Byron's Poetry." *The Byron Journal* 26 (1998): 112–5.

Shaw, Philip. "Leigh Hunt and the Aesthetics of Post-War Liberalism." In *Romantic Wars: Studies in Culture and Conflict, 1793–1822*, edited by Philip Shaw, 185–207. Aldershot: Ashgate Publishing, 2000.

Shemek, Deanna. "That Elusive Object of Desire: Angelica in the 'Orlando Furioso.'" *Annali d'Italianistica* 7 (1989): 116–41.

Short, Clarice. "The Composition of Hunt's *The Story of Rimini*." *Keats-Shelley Journal* 21 (1972): 207–18.

St Clair, William. *The Reading Nation in the Romantic Period*. Cambridge: Cambridge University Press, 2004.

Stabler, Jane. "Religious Liberty in the 'Liberal, 1822–23.'" *Branch: Britain, Representation and Nineteenth-Century History* (January 2015): 1–13. www.branchcollective.org/?ps_articles=jane-stabler-religious-liberty-in-the-liberal.

———. "Second-generation Romantic Poetry I: Hunt, Byron, Moore." In *The Cambridge History of English Poetry*, edited by Michael O'Neill, 487–505. Cambridge: Cambridge University Press, 2010.

———. "Leigh Hunt's Aesthetics of Intimacy." In *Leigh Hunt: Life, Poetics, Politics*, edited by Nicholas Roe, 95–117. New York: Routledge, 2003.

Stauffer, Andrew. "Byron's Lyrics and the Politics of Publication." In *Byron: The Poetry of Politics and the Politics of Poetry*, edited by Roderick Beaton and Christine Kenyon Jones, 24–31. New York: Routledge, 2017.

Stead, Henry. *A Cockney Catullus*. Oxford: Oxford University Press, 2016.

Steier, Michael P. "Lord Byron and the Empress Marie-Louise: A New Letter to Leigh Hunt." *The Byron Journal* 45, no. 2 (2017): 135–40.

Stewart, David, *Romantic Magazines and Metropolitan Literary Culture*. New York: Palgrave Macmillan, 2011.

Sunstein, Emily W. *Mary Shelley: Romance and Reality*. Boston, MA: Little, Brown and Company, 1989.

Thorpe, Clarence DeWitt. "Leigh Hunt as Man of Letters." In *Leigh Hunt's Literary Criticism*, edited by Lawrence Huston Houtchens and Carolyn Washburn Houtchens, 3–73. repr. New York: Octagon Books, 1976.

Throsby, Corin. "Byron, Commonplacing, and Early Fan Culture." In *Romanticism and Celebrity Culture, 1750–1850*, edited by Tom Mole, 227–44. Cambridge: Cambridge University Press, 2009.

Treadwell, James. *Autobiographical Writing and British Literature, 1783–1834*. Oxford: Oxford University Press, 2005.

Tuite, Clara. *Lord Byron and Scandalous Celebrity*. Cambridge: Cambridge University Press, 2014.

Turley, Richard Marggraf. *The Politics of Language in Romantic Literature*. New York: Palgrave Macmillan, 2002.

Vail, Jeffery W. *The Literary Relationship of Lord Byron & Thomas Moore*. Baltimore, MD: Johns Hopkins University Press, 2001.

Watkins, Daniel P. *Social Relations in Byron's Eastern Tales*. Madison, NJ: Farleigh Dickinson University Press, 1987.

Watson, Alex. *Romantic Marginality: Nation and Empire on the Borders of the Page*. New York: Routledge, 2012.

Webb, Timothy. "Catullus and the Missing Papers: Leigh Hunt, Byron, and John Murray." *The Byron Journal* 42, no. 2 (2014): 111–22.

———. "Stories of Rimini: Leigh Hunt, Byron and the Fate of Francesca." In *Dante in the Nineteenth Century: Reception, Canonicity, Popularization*, edited by Nick Havely, 32–53. Oxford: Peter Lang, 2011.

———. "'Unshadowing the Rialto': Byron and the Patterns of Life." *The Byron Journal* 39, no. 1 (2011): 19–33.

———. "Leigh Hunt's Letters to Byron from Horsemonger Lane Gaol: A Commentary" *The Byron Journal* 37, no. 1 (2009): 21–32.

———. "Arrival of Don Juan at Shooter's Hill: The Politics of Romance." In *Lord Byron 'Correspondence(s),'* edited by Christiane Vigouroux, 176–217. Paris: François-Xavier de Guibert, 2008.

———. "Correcting the Irritability of His Temper: The Evolution of Leigh Hunt's *Autobiography*." In *Romantic Revisions*, edited by Robert Brinkley and Keith Hanley, 268–90. Cambridge: Cambridge University Press, 1992.

———. "Religion of the Heart: Leigh Hunt's Tribute to Shelley." *The Keats-Shelley Review* 7 (1992): 1–61.

Wheatley, Kim. "Conceiving Disgust: Leigh Hunt, William Gifford, and the *Quarterly Review*." In *Leigh Hunt: Life, Poetics, Politics*, edited by Nicholas Roe, 180–97. New York: Routledge, 2003.

Wolfson, Susan J. *Romantic Interactions: Social Being & the Turns of Literary Action*. Baltimore, MD: Johns Hopkins University Press, 2010.

Woodring, Carl. *Politics in English Romantic Poetry*. Cambridge, MA: Harvard University Press, 1970.

———. "Leigh Hunt as Political Essayist." In *Leigh Hunt's Political and Occasional Essays*, edited by Lawrence Huston Houtchens and Carolyn Washburn Houtchens, 3–71. New York: Columbia University Press, 1962.

Index

For Product Safety Concerns and Information please contact our EU
representative GPSR@taylorandfrancis.com
Taylor & Francis Verlag GmbH, Kaufingerstraße 24, 80331 München, Germany

www.ingramcontent.com/pod-product-compliance
Lightning Source LLC
Chambersburg PA
CBHW071513110726
47908CB00003B/825